The Great Disaster

GENOCIDE OF THE KAZAKHS

Valeriy Mikhailov

Translated by Katharine Judelson

STACEY
INTERNATIONAL

The Great Disaster: Genocide of the Kazakhs

STACEY PUBLISHING LTD
19 Catherine Place
London SW1E 6DX
Tel: +44 (0)20 7221 7166; Fax: +44 (0)20 7792 9288
Email: info@stacey-international.co.uk
www.stacey-international.co.uk

The publishers would like to acknowledge the generous support of
Shyngys Kulzhanov in the translation and production of this book.

ISBN: 978-1-909022-26-3

1 3 5 7 9 0 8 6 4 2

CIP Data: A catalogue record for this book is available from the British Library.

Printed and bound in Turkey.

Contents

Foreword   5

I.   The Eyes of Hunger   9

II.   Filipp Goloshchekin   17

III.   The Execution of Tsar Nicholas II and his Family   37

IV.   The Sovietization of Turkestan   70

V.   The Tsar-Slaying Bolshevik in Kazakhstan   100

VI.   The Green Light from Stalin for Class War   115

VII.   Tragedy of a Nation   141

VIII.   Rout of the Kazakh Intelligentsia   164

IX.   The Beginning of Universal Collectivization   196

X.   Anti-religious Repression   215

XI.   The 'Great Breakthrough'   234

XII.   Peasant Uprisings   269

XIII.   The Second Wave of Coercive Collectivization   288

XIV.   Disaster Throughout the Steppes   305

XV.   'Hammer and Sickle' Brings Death and Starvation   340

XVI.   Requisitioning – Hunger as a Weapon of Terrorism   355

XVII.   The Demon Flew Inside the Hurricane   378

Glossary   382

Notes   385

According to popular Kazakh belief
there is a demon flying in every hurricane.
That is why when people see
a black whirlwind they drive it off
with a curse, calling out: 'Fly away to
the House of the Devil!'

Foreword

The Soviet Union still existed when, in 1990, the first Russian edition of *The Great Disaster* was published in Alma-Ata. Its print run of 50,000 copies sold out immediately and sparked enormous public interest in Kazakhstan and beyond.[1] The stories told in the book had been concealed for decades. It was only in the course of 'glasnost' and 'perestroika' when 'tens of millions of Soviet citizens became passionately involved in studying their country's past'[2] that people began to discover not only the horrors of the 'Great Terror' and other Stalinist crimes, but were able for the first time to read about the Kazakh famine of the early 1930s. This catastrophe had always belonged to the 'blank spots' of Soviet history. Now, the general public became aware of this almost forgotten tragedy. News about the unimaginable death rates during the famine, the uprooting of the mostly nomadic Kazakhs and the devastating economic losses brought lasting discredit to Soviet power. And, most importantly, survivors started to speak about their traumatic experiences. In 1987, poet and journalist Valeriy Mikhailov began to collect their reminiscences. In the following years, his extraordinary commitment resulted in several extended Russian and Kazakh editions of his eminent work, which is now available to the English-speaking public in Katharine Judelson's translation.

Born in 1946 as a descendant of 'special settlers' who had been deported to Kazakhstan during the years of collectivization, Mikhailov always had a genuine interest in the history of Stalinist repression and its victims. This interest caused him not only serious personal problems – for example, when he used the then strictly forbidden term 'special settlers' in a poem in 1980 – but ultimately guided him to a story still more heartbreaking than the history of the deportees. In an interview published in 2008, he remembered how it all began:

Everything began with the history of my family's tragedy. Afterwards, when I was a student at the faculty of Geology, I had to travel around a lot in the republic [i.e. Kazakhstan, R.K.], to the most remote of places. In the auls, I talked to the old Kazakhs.

Not all of them spoke openly with me, but fortunately, some did not hide the truth. Step by step I understood the dimension of this catastrophe, but at that time I did not realize that this was a great national tragedy.[3]

The Kazakh famine, which reached its climax in the years 1932–33, was not an isolated catastrophe, but one of the worst episodes of a famine that hit the whole Soviet Union to some degree. Some regions were struck particularly badly, such as the Ukraine, the Northern Caucasus and the Volga region. The collectivization of the countryside, dispossession of the Kulaks and, in the Kazakh case, the sedentarization of the nomads caused this famine of unprecedented proportions. Numbers differ, but most historians tend to agree that between 1.2 and two million Kazakhs lost their lives and hundreds of thousands became refugees. The backbone of the Kazakh nomadic economy was almost completely annihilated. More than 90 percent of the region's livestock was lost during these years. It took years for the economy to recover, while repercussions of the demographic losses are noticeable still today in the population statistics.

The book's most gripping chapters deal with the experiences of people trapped in an ever-tightening vice of state demands, hunger, and impending death from which it was virtually impossible to escape. Mikhailov does not spare his readers any of the horrible aspects of famine: violence and theft among the hungry, cannibalism, child abandonment and the gruesome sights of dead bodies piled high in the steppe. Hunger destroyed Kazakh society and culture. When the famine came to an end, nomadism had practically ceased to exist and almost one third of the Kazakh population had died. Furthermore, Mikhailov assures readers that Bolshevik authorities in Kazakhstan, led by the First Secretary of the Kazakh Party organization, Filipp Goloshchekin, showed no signs of compassion or solidarity with the starving population. Instead of helping the pauperized, they rather thought about new strategies of subjugation and annihilation. This is why Mikhailov calls the famine genocidal.

The Great Disaster is part of a slowly but constantly growing body of scholarly literature on the Kazakh famine, its origins and outcomes. While Mikhailov emphasizes the role of Goloshchekin as the main culprit and argues that his thirst for 'blood' (p. 109) played a decisive role for the assault on the Kazakh nomads, other authors offer slightly different interpretations. Based on documents in Kazakh and Russian archives that were largely not available to Valeriy Mikhailov (who nevertheless comes to many similar conclusions), the French scholar Isabelle Ohayon and her Italian colleague Niccoló Pianciola accentuate the part played by the leading Bolsheviks' goal to modernize the Soviet economy, the ruthless requisitions of cattle and grain, the forced collectivization and the failed sedentarization campaign as important preconditions for the famine.[4] While generally agreeing with this position, other historians argue that tensions between European peasant settlers and the indigenous Kazakh population as well as the merciless struggles among the hungry for scarce resources worsened the situation. In a certain way, according to this argument one could almost say that the state had delegated the question of death and survival to the very people involved. This approach has led to a gradual reappraisal of the role of the population in the famine-stricken regions. They are no longer only considered as passive victims of an almighty state, but they are also conceptualized as individuals with their own interests, agendas and – albeit often limited – options. In the long run, the famine did not only drastically affect the demographic composition of Kazakh society, but it also changed its social and cultural structures. Detailed studies of the famine 'from below' underlined its enormous significance for the definite enforcement of Soviet power in the Kazakh steppe.[5]

In Kazakhstan, interest in the famine has considerably decreased since the mid-1990s. The political and economic difficulties of transition absorbed people's attention and left only small room for problems of the past. Besides this, the famine of 1932–33 became the subject of heated political debates between the Ukraine and Russia. Many Ukrainian historians and politicians called the 'Holodomor' genocide. In Kazakhstan, elites and historians chose another option; they tried to remain silent about the famine in public, assigning the topic to the narrow circles of historical research. Only occasionally did Kazakh politicians mention the famine in the most general terms. They conceptualized the years of hunger as an external 'tragedy' that had come from outside. This situation has changed in part over the last years, reaching its tentative climax in 2012, when Kazakh President Nursultan Nazarbayev opened a major memorial to the famine victims in Astana. But memorials – as impressive and important as they might be – are only symbolic representations of the past. They are designed as sites of mourning and commemoration and therefore communicate only vague ideas of what the famine meant to those who underwent it. The most powerful testimonials are the voices of the people who witnessed and survived the great disaster. In this book, some of them tell their stories.

Robert Kindler, Berlin

❧

I. The Eyes of Hunger

'The first thing I remember is the moon. It was autumn and cold; we were on the road. I was wrapped up warmly, jolting up and down in a cart. All of a sudden we stopped and I saw an enormous moon up in the black sky. It was a full round moon, shining brightly. I was lying on my back and looked up at it for a long time – I couldn't take my eyes off it.

'Then I turned over and could clearly see what looked like tree stumps on the ground with hooked branches stretched out like arms. There were many of them on both sides of the road. They were people, frozen stiff and lying silent on the ground.

'I guessed what was there; I did not need to ask questions. The grown-ups would not have answered anyway but I knew there was some terrible mystery hovering over those frozen people. When I grew up I asked about them, and then I was told everything. They were corpses. My grandmother was astonished that I could remember, as I had been no more than two. But I did remember – the moon, the journey, the corpses. That had been in 1931 and we had been on our way from our deserted *aul* [settlement of nomad herders] to Turgai.'

The poet Gafu Kairbekov was telling his story in his usual rather muffled voice – gently, as if he too was surprised: 'My second memory is bound up with Turgai. It is a small town, a district capital, and it stands on a hill. Below it there is a little river and all the streets slope steeply down to it. We children used to run to the river barefoot. In my memory there are people out in the streets – many grown-ups. They can't walk; they're crawling on all fours so feeble they can hardly move along; they have no strength left. When they can't go any further they start scratching at the earth with their nails; they lie on the earth like logs. We step over them as we go. On our way down to the river we have to step over several of them. Down there, on the riverbank, an animal is being killed. It is towards that slaughter that the hungry people are crawling. Those who manage to get there will drink the blood of the animal.'

'Then comes my third memory. We were living in the yard of the district distribution office, where our uncle – Mama's elder brother – worked. The yard was wide with a fence all around it: there was a heavy gate in the wall which was always locked. We kept livestock there – not many animals, but they had to be carefully guarded, otherwise there would be nothing left for all those who ate in the canteen. They used to dish out gruel there: it was anybody's guess what went into it.

'My brother – he was ten years older than me and died in the war later on – used to drag in the large buckets of swill. After you ate some of it, your stomach didn't feel quite so empty. We little ones were strictly forbidden to leave the yard at that time. We would look through the cracks in the gate to see what was going on outside. Opposite the yard was a low earthen wall with people standing nearby. They were waiting. The animals in the yard were so desperately thin they could hardly stand up; the cows were giving birth to dead calves and the ewes to dead lambs. Their carcasses and the animals that couldn't stand up any more were dragged out of the gate. People would hurl themselves at the still-warm bodies. They would start eating the meat straight away, tearing at it with their hands.'

Kairbekov sat with his head bent slightly forward, drawing on his cigarette. He fell silent and looked out of the window.

'Those are my very first childhood memories. We only survived because my father – who could read and write – and my uncle worked in the distribution office. Then I grew up a bit. I can remember 1934 quite clearly. We were still living in Turgai. Life was getting easier for people: those who had managed to survive the worst years were issued with food aid, but in general life was still hard. Deportees started turning up in Turgai; some forty-odd from various ethnic groups arrived, all implicated in the assassination plot against the Bolshevik leader Kirov. They were hungry and frightening; they could get no work and used to roam the streets, the whole bunch of them. We children, of course, would run up to look at them. I went with the others once, forgetting Grandmother's ban, and they started chasing me – two or three enormous men. They frightened me to death. I still don't know how I escaped. They caught up with me right by the gate, but Granny and Uncle drove them away. They rescued me.

'One time before the war, when I was around ten, we were out in a cart gathering fuel. Brushwood, rushes, dry grass – they would all go into the stove. We had hardly left the town when the wooden wheels began to creak, as they lurched over something. The ground seemed even, just sand, but we were making heavy weather of it. The creaking sound was strange and sinister; it made you feel uneasy. I jumped down from the cart. In the sand all round me there were bones. Who had scattered them there? As we gathered grass and dry branches, we saw bones, bones everywhere. They were lying on the surface or slightly covered over with sand. Then skulls began to appear, human ones. "Those were once people," I thought to myself. "How many of them perished here?" Back home I told people about it, and the grown-ups explained that starving people had been trying to reach the town, but had perished on the way. There was nobody to bury them and that was why dead bodies were strewn about.

'Our family was always going outside the town – to cut grass, to collect firewood, to play on nearby mounds. We small boys weren't going to rest till we had explored all the houses round and about. Whether you can believe it or not, the whole of Turgai was ringed about with human bones. Those people with no strength left must have crawled together to the district centre, hoping to get hold of something edible and save themselves from starvation.

'We never went back to our *aul* though. There was nothing to go back to.'

We started smoking and my companion's face still looked calm, as if he was relating ordinary things. Only his remote stare gave him away.

'Sometimes when I think back to those days, I remember a conversation I once had with Gabit Musrepov in 1958 when we first got to know each other. He may be considered a classic Kazakh today, but then he was accused of various ideological transgressions and was hardly ever in print – he was even denied Party membership for some time. At that time I was a young editor working in a publishing house.

'One day Musrepov asked me round to his home. "Where are you from, my young *dzhigit* [a word used by the mountain peoples of the Caucasus and in Central Asia for a bold young horseman]?"

'"From Turgai."

'"That's all to the good. If you come along with me, you'll learn something about your Turgai."

'He was in a good mood and joking despite all his troubles. Now when I think back, I realize that he had a fighting spirit and would not let his critics get the better of him. It was probably to keep up his spirits that day that he told me a funny story:

"'It was in the summer of 1934—'". As he spoke there was a sparkle in his eye and he was smiling, but then a sudden gloom came over him and he went on in a sad voice: "There was hunger all around us, people were worn out. There weren't enough food handouts being issued. Farming was falling apart. The Area Party Committee sent me to Aktyubinsk. When I got there everyone in the Regional Committee was terrified. I asked them what the matter was. It turned out that Kirov was on his way there."

"'Well, and what are you afraid of?' I asked."

"'What on earth can we show him?' they gasped, their eyes popping out of their heads. 'He'll see what things are like here and we'll get it in the neck!'"

"'Ask for help, the people here are desperate,' I said."

"'What do you mean ask for help? We're scared to even look him in the eye!'"

'Musrepov laughed as he told me that they had then persuaded him to go and meet Kirov, while they hid away as best they could.

"'So I met their visitor, we introduced ourselves and then set off – at his insistence – to Turgai. I told him about Kazakh history, Kazakh customs, as we drove to the very edge of your Turgai."

'At this point Musrepov dissolved into merry laughter and then went on.

"'As we approached, out there in front of us we could just make out what appeared to be a black lump. What was it? Perhaps just a mirage in the heat haze – it was impossible to tell. From the distance it looked like a square stone with a large bird sitting on it. A rather strange bird at that – larger than an eagle or a bustard. Several times it disappeared somewhere, before settling back down on the black stone. As we drew nearer, the bird vanished altogether, as if it had evaporated in the hot air."

"'We trundled over still closer to it and at last were able to make it out. It was a car out in the steppe! The people from your town were coming out to meet us – the district chiefs of Turgai! They were hurrying, as fast as they could, but didn't make it: the water in the radiator had boiled away. The young men in our car cottoned on to what had happened and started laughing. 'A resourceful lot, your people in Turgai! At the slightest hitch they're taking it in turns to climb up on to the bonnet. And we had thought it was a bird!'"

"'At first Kirov had had no inkling of what was going on."

"''Well, fellows,' he asked, 'what made you keep climbing up on to the car?'"

"'The Turgai chiefs blushed and lowered their gaze. Kirov fell silent in bewilderment and then burst into helpless laughter. He clutched at his stomach and almost fell over."

"'That was your people from Turgai!" concluded Musrepov in a strangely quiet sad voice. He fell silent for quite a time. Then he looked straight at me and said with a mournful look in his eyes: "One day I'll tell you another story, also about your Turgai."

'It was from then that we came to know each other well and our friendship lasted almost thirty years. I do not remember exactly when it was, but later on Musrepov was to keep his promise. Although years have passed since then, I can remember what he told me word for word.'

Gafu Kairbekov's voice became quieter and more pensive than ever.

'In 1932 Kazakhstan was in the grip of terrible hunger. Musrepov with four of his comrades wrote a letter to the Party's Area Committee, about the extremes of the collectivization drive. As a result they were all accused of nationalism. Musrepov said that they thought their end was near, that their lives meant nothing to that executioner brandishing a bloodstained sword. He referred to Filipp Goloshchekin, Stalin's Party chief in Kazakhstan.

'Winter had started early that year: it was October and Alma-Ata [now Almaty] was already deep in snow. Then, all of a sudden, Musrepov was summoned to the Area Committee.

"'Well now, off you go to Turgai, if you're so worried about your people," Goloshchekin said to him, with a sneer of a smile. "You can see with your own eyes out there that nobody's going hungry."

'Musrepov set off. By way of a companion, for some reason, he was given an official from the Area Committee. With great difficulty they managed to get as far as Kustanai, where winter conditions were at their harshest. They went to the Executive Committee's office; the chairman was someone who found himself in Kazakhstan not through choice.

"'So you're a deportee just like me," he said. "What on earth brought you out here? The road's deserted, snowstorms are raging and you're 500 *versts* from Batpakkara. You'll freeze to death or be eaten."

'He said all that in a calm voice and was clearly not joking.

"'What's more, there's no means of getting there," he added. "All the horses were eaten at the time of the famine. There are two horses for the

Executive Committee, which are used to take me around. Since you insist I'll let you have them, but I can't let you go without an armed guard. You're risking your lives."

'They made the rest of the journey on a sleigh accompanied by two armed men; the sleigh-driver also had a rifle.

'A snowstorm began out in the steppe after the *aul* of Aulie-Kol. Clouds of fine snow soon hid the sun and they could no longer make out the road. They kept coming adrift from it, which made the horses stop. Suddenly Musrepov noticed that there was something sticking out of the snowdrifts like the gnarled branches of a saxaul tree. He jumped down from the sleigh and walked over to it: there were human corpses under the snow, piled randomly on top of each other. He walked on and caught sight of more corpses which had been collected up and laid out in heaps. Musrepov told me: "They were like torches lighting our way; it was thanks to them that we could keep to the road, since the corpses stuck out along both sides of it. I've never seen anything so terrible."

'After a deep sigh Musrepov went on: "Thanks be to Allah, we did not meet anyone on the way, otherwise there would have been nothing left of either the horses or us. We were quite sure about that. Once more we thought back gratefully to the chairman from the Executive Committee who had supplied us with food and given us oats for the horses – otherwise we should have perished. I always think kindly of his spirit and hope that he has long since found a resting place in a better world."

'They managed to extricate themselves from the snowdrifts and make their way along that road of the dead. They passed through completely empty *auls*. The local man sent along with them told them the numbers of the settlements: the only things that told them apart were those numbers, for there was not a soul remaining there. They then approached a small town of *yurts*, an unusual sight for Kazakhs. Many towns like that one had sprung up in the steppe when the collectivization drive began. The *yurts* had been arranged in rows and there was a number hanging from each of them, as if they were urban houses in an urban street. There were large covered wagons as well – new ones covered with white felt matting. The driver explained that they had only recently been confiscated from local landowners. He added that there had been plenty of people living in the area a mere two or three months ago. Now it was all a deathly silence. There was not a sound to be heard, only the rustle of the wind blowing the snow along. A dead town of white *yurts* set in the white snow.

'They went into one *yurt* and then another: all the belongings were in place, just people were missing. It was as if life had come to a sudden halt and the people had simply disappeared.

What really struck Musrepov was a large and prosperous-looking covered wagon. Inside it had brightly coloured silk blanket covers, satin cushions and delicately patterned carpets with thick pile. The belongings lay collected together in a heap in the middle, as if the owners had gone out of their home just seconds earlier and were about to come back again. That was only his first impression though: the felts and carpets on the wagon floor were all frozen stiff and snow was coming in through the open *tundik* – the hole at the top of the roof.

'They took a closer look and the enormous heap of clothes seemed to resemble a small hut. There was a small hole in the middle of it, like a dark window into some strange world. Suddenly all four of the men, even the two who were armed, took fright at exactly the same moment. A shiver of fear ran through them and they began to back towards the door – they could not take any more and went outside. Musrepov was the last to leave the wagon. He lingered on the threshold, as if he felt that there really was someone inside the little hut made of piled clothes.

'They did not go into any of the other *yurts* or wagons, as if there was something to be frightened of inside. They went back to the edge of the silent town piled high with snow and stood there with their heads lowered. It was time to return to the sleigh. As they made their way back, doubts began to creep into Musrepov's mind: was there really no one out here? Where were the bodies of the dead in that case? He put these questions to the man from the Area Committee, who never left his side. The fellow replied that in Turgai there were many such *yurt* "towns" and that at the beginning of autumn people had crept out of them to make their way elsewhere. They had set off for Kustanai, Chelkar, for the Urals, in the direction of Alatau or for the Syr-Darya River. Almost all of them died on the way. The piled corpses we had been passing were theirs. Both the guards from Kustanai accompanying us nodded in agreement. Musrepov asked the Party official from the Area Committee how he knew that and the only answer he was given was a sad smile.

'It was hard work dragging their feet out of the snowdrifts as they went back to the sleigh. Suddenly Musrepov, who was unable to shake off his sense of foreboding, went back to the wagon with a white felt roof, which they had entered. His companions went with him.

'"Heavens, there are someone's footsteps here!" one of them called out. 'They clustered together near the strange prints in the snow. They were absolutely fresh ones.

'"What was it? A fox?"

'"No, nothing like a fox! It's more like ... but it can't be ...!"

'The men followed the prints, which led straight to the wagon. They pushed open the door. All of sudden a high piercing sound rang out inside the empty dwelling. It made everyone's blood run cold. Was it the whine of a dog, the desperate yowl of a cat? It was accompanied by a gurgling sound.

'From a tiny hole in the little "hut" a small living creature leapt out and threw itself at the group of men. It was covered in blood. Its long hair was frozen in bloody icicles sticking out to each side; its legs were thin and black like those of a raven. It had wild eyes and a face caked with dried blood, smeared with drops of fresh blood. It bared its teeth and red foam came out of its mouth.

'All four of the men recoiled and rushed away, unable to think in their terror. When they looked back, the creature was no longer anywhere to be seen.

'"What was it?" asked Gabit in a hoarse whisper, as he looked at his companions. They said nothing, unable to stop themselves shivering with fear. Nobody said a word. Only later, back in Kustanai did one of Musrepov's companions say to him: "You probably think it was a *jinn* – it wasn't. I took a look at it, a long clear look. It was human. It was a child. A little Kazakh girl of seven or eight."

'"No, no!" shouted Musrepov, as unspeakable anger surged within him, anger that was unstoppable – but powerless.

'"It was Hunger! The eyes of Hunger! The very curse of Hunger."

Gafu Kairbekov had come to the end of his story. Someone knocked at the door which had been locked, so that we would not be interrupted.

'Lower down in the pile there had probably been her parents as well – her father and mother,' he said. After that he went to unlock the door.

II. Filipp Goloshchekin

At the end of October 1932, the twelfth anniversary of Kazakhstan was being celebrated with due pomp and ceremony in Alma-Ata. This was around the same time as Musrepov's journey through blizzards in the snowswept Turgai steppe, looking in horror at the deserted *auls* and the desperate feral little girl – the last inhabitant left behind in the empty 'town' of white *yurts*.

On the eve of the anniversary a celebratory meeting of the city Soviet was being held, as befitted the occasion: Party and Soviet organizations were duly represented, as were other public bodies. The texts of telegrams sent by the presidium to Comrade Stalin and Comrade Goloshchekin were read out. The next day, 22 October, *Kazakhstanskaya Pravda* published the telegrams so that those who had not been fortunate enough to be present for the celebrations should still feel involved in the memorable occasion.

'Dear Comrade Stalin!' began the first telegram. 'Kazakhstan has now reached the age of twelve. Soon we shall be able to celebrate fifteen years of the October Revolution.' There followed a report on how the decision taken by the Central Committee of the All-Union Communist Party (Bolsheviks) [CCACP(B)] on 17 September 1932 relating to animal husbandry in Kazakhstan was 'dealing a crushing blow at class enemies, opportunists, chauvinists and nationalists.'

At the end there were greetings and toasts for those who had reached well-deserved heights of achievement: 'The Party activists send you their militant Bolshevik greetings! Long live the Leninist Central Committee! Long live the leader of our Party and the international proletariat – Comrade Stalin!' Although it was peacetime the greetings were militant, as the class struggle was intensifying with each passing day.

While the leader of the Party and the international proletariat was referred to as 'Comrade Stalin', the figure in charge of Kazakhstan's Party

17

organization, Goloshchekin, was referred to in a less formal way, by his name and patronymic – Filipp Isaevich. Without a doubt this set Comrade Stalin apart from the rest: at the unassailable height from which he managed everything, an ordinary form of address would have been out of the question. Yet the missive sent to the local leader somewhat further down from those giddy heights was warmer and more relaxed, so that he should not feel in any way hard done by.

Dear Filipp Isaevich!

On the occasion of Kazakhstan's twelfth anniversary the celebratory meeting of the Alma-Ata City Soviet sends ardent greetings to you, an experienced Leninist, under whose leadership Kazakhstan has advanced to its twelfth anniversary with great victories. In the struggle on two fronts against opportunism, in the struggle on two fronts with regard to the nationalities question, you are leading the Kazakhstan Party organization from victory to victory on the basis of Lenin's nationalities policy and overcoming the difficulties on the way.

Under your leadership new Bolshevik cadres have been trained among Kazakhs and representatives of eastern national minorities.

Under your leadership Kazakhstan has joined the foremost ranks of the great Union: it has been transformed from an extremely backward region into an agrarian-industrial one.

Long live the victorious construction of socialism!

Long live the experienced Leninist, Comrade Goloshchekin!

Presidium of the Celebratory Meeting

The man who had been addressed with such feeling by the Presidium was sitting there as one of its members. He was a heavily built man of fifty-six, wearing a field-jacket buttoned up to the top; he had wavy dark hair, which was starting to turn grey, a neatly trimmed moustache and beard. The expression in his brown, prominent eyes was majestic and stern. He knew how to bring pressure to bear on his subordinates through his solid appearance and air of importance, through his indisputable authority as an old-guard Bolshevik and the harsh judgements delivered in his reports and speeches, which lasted many hours. He could be bluntly ironic in discussions, when everything would be decided by his rather arrogant cut

18

and thrust, and finally he was known for the merciless fury and cruelty, which he meted out to those who opposed him. For the most part his local comrades-in-arms would adapt to the overpowering force of his will: they were constantly praising his achievements enthusiastically and in the loftiest of tones, loudly proclaiming toasts in his honour and organizing ovations.

Two weeks after that there were celebrations for the fifteenth anniversary of the October Revolution. The second secretary of the Area Party Committee, I. Kuramysov, wrote the following words about his immediate superior in a jubilee edition of *Kazakhstanskaya Pravda*, 7 November, 1932:

> It would be inadmissible not to single out the role played by one of the finest Bolsheviks in the history of the development of Soviet Kazakhstan – one of Lenin's prominent comrades-in-arms, who has devoted over seven years of his life and work to the struggle for socialism in Kazakhstan – the role played by the experienced leader of the Kazakhstan Party organization, Filipp Goloshchekin. With every justification he is respected, loved and trusted by all the working masses of Kazakhstan. There is no more reliable theoretician and practical leader in Kazakhstan than Filipp Isaevich Goloshchekin, as time has shown us again and again. His work, his speeches, reports and articles we regard as models of a truly Bolshevik combination of revolutionary theory and revolutionary practice. He is an example for the Bolshevik struggle for the organization and building of socialism.[1]

Only ten weeks later this matchless hero of both theory and practice – if we are to believe Kuramysov – was removed from the post he held and recalled to Moscow. Everything that had needed to be done by the Bolsheviks in Kazakhstan he had already completed.

Yet when it comes to the sincerity and truthfulness of his subordinates, it is difficult not to have doubts. All the more so given that Goloshchekin, when taking leave of his friends and comrades in the Party organization, told them straight to their faces that there was not a single honest communist in Kazakhstan. True to his habit of making systematic observations before drawing conclusions, he had divided the Bolsheviks of Kazakhstan into three categories: those who did not respond to their education and training, chameleons who kept changing colour and, finally, those who used to blame all miscalculations and shortcomings on him, Goloshchekin.

Let us turn, however, to evidence of a more objective nature regarding the activities and character of F.I. Goloshchekin, who devoted over seven years to the 'struggle for socialism in Kazakhstan'.

The entry on him in the *Soviet Encyclopaedic Dictionary* is extremely brief:

> Goloshchekin, Filipp Isaevich (1876–1941) Soviet state and Party worker. Member of the Communist Party of the Soviet Union since 1903. Elected to the Central Committee of the Russian Social-Democratic Workers' Party in 1912. During the October Revolution he was a member of the Petrograd Military-Revolutionary Committee and took part in the struggle for Soviet power in the Urals and Siberia. After 1925 he was secretary of the Kazakhstan Area Committee of the All-Union Communist Party (Bolsheviks). In 1933 he was made Chief State Arbitrator with the Council of People's Commissars of the USSR. He was a member of the Central Committee of the All-Union Communist Party (Bolsheviks) from 1927–34 (he had been a candidate-member of the Central Committee since 1924), member of the All-Union Central Executive Committee and the Central Executive Committee of the USSR.[2]

Another encyclopaedia on the Civil War provides more detail:

> From a contractor's family. Graduated as a dentist in 1903. In December 1917 he became a member of the Yekaterinburg Committee of the Russian Social-Democratic Workers' Party (Bolsheviks) and was appointed as the military commissar for the local Soviet. In February 1918 he was made military commissar for the Urals region and a member of the Regional Party Committee and of the regional Soviet. In May of that year he was made military commissar for the Urals Military District and at the same time (from September 1918 to January 1919) he was the chief political commissar for the Third Army (in charge of party-political work in military units and among the civilian

population in the district where the Third Army was stationed). From December 1918 he was a member of the Siberian Bureau of the Central Committee of the Russian Communist Party (Bolsheviks) [RCP (B)] and military commissar for the Urals Military District. He was a delegate to the VII and VIII Congresses of the Russian Communist Party (Bolsheviks) – at the VIII Congress he associated himself with the 'military opposition'. In April–June 1919 he was a member of the Revolutionary Military Committee of Turkestan on the Eastern Front. From August he chaired the Chelyabinsk Provincial Revolutionary Committee. Between October 1919 and May 1920 he was a member of the Turkestan Commission of the All-Union Central Executive Committee and the Council of People's Commissars of the Russian Socialist Federal Soviet Republic. From 1921 he engaged in economic work and work for Soviet and Party organizations.[3]

In the *Greater Soviet Encyclopaedia* more new details emerge. First and foremost, the precise dates of his birth and death are provided: 'Born 26 February (9 March in the Western calendar), 1876 in Nevel, died 18 October, 1941.' Later on we are told:

A dentist by profession. In 1906 he joined the St Petersburg Committee of the Russian Social-Democratic Workers' Party and its Executive Committee. Took part in the conference of the enlarged editorial board of the *Proletarian* (Paris, 1909); later he worked in the Moscow Committee of the Russian Social-Democratic Workers' Party. He engaged in Party work in Moscow, Petrograd and the Urals. Subjected to repression. During the October armed uprising in 1917 he was a member of the Petrograd Military-Revolutionary Committee (in charge of its department for external and internal communications). After the October Revolution he was secretary of the Perm and Yekaterinburg Provincial Party Committees and the Urals Regional Party Committee. In 1921 he was chairman of the Chief Mining Department in Moscow. In 1922–25 he was chairman of the Provincial Executive Committees of the Soviets and a member of the Russian Communist Party (Bolsheviks) in Kostroma and Samara and then secretary of the Area Committee for the Communist Party (Bolsheviks) in Kazakhstan. From 1933 he was the Chief State Arbitrator with the Council of People's Commissars of the USSR. A delegate to the XI–XVII Party Congresses.[4]

Some key details of Goloshchekin's pre-revolutionary activity are specified in the *Historical Encyclopaedia*:

> He carried out Party work in St Petersburg, Kronstadt, Sestroretsk, Moscow and other towns. After the First State Duma was dissolved he was arrested and sentenced to two years' imprisonment. A year later he was released but then rearrested on 1 May 1907. After being arrested in 1909 he was banished to the Narym region, from which he escaped in 1910. After the Prague Conference, he resumed party work in Moscow but was soon arrested again and banished to the Tobolsk Province. After escaping from there, he worked in Petrograd (1913) and later in the Urals, where he was arrested again and deported to the Turukhansk Area where he remained until the February Revolution.[5]

In the same publication there was a detail not to be found in any other of the reference volumes: 'Subjected to illegal repression in the period of Stalin's cult of personality. Posthumous rehabilitation.'

Yet the most detailed account of Goloshchekin's life is to be found in an old newspaper not easily obtainable for the general reader. His biography appeared on 18 September 1925 in the Kazakhstan Party newspaper *Soviet Steppes* (the predecessor of *Kazakhstanskaya Pravda*). It is of interest because it is a record of Goloshchekin's own words: some of his favourite turns of phrase appear in it. By all accounts this is the only biography published in his lifetime, lending it particular value.

LIFE IN THE PARTY

New Secretary of the Kazakhstan Area Committee of the RCP (Bolsheviks) FILIPP ISAEVICH GOLOSHCHEKIN (on the occasion of his arrival in Kazakhstan)

Filipp Isaevich Goloshchekin was born in 1876 in the small town of Nevel in the Vitebsk Province. His parents were from the petty bourgeoisie and engaged in small-scale building contracts.

Goloshchekin was initially educated in a four-class urban school and later, after home tutoring, took the entrance exams for the local technical school and gymnasium. He passed the exams but was not able to attend because only a limited number of Jewish pupils could be accepted. For all intents and purposes Filipp Isaevich covered the six-year gymnasium programme and then between 1901 and 1903 studied at dental school, where he successfully completed his course. Between 1896 and 1900 he worked as a shop assistant in a stationery shop.

Since his childhood Filipp Isaevich had been an avid reader, but in a rather haphazard and non-systematic way in all manner of fields. Initially he was fascinated by philosophy and later by social sciences. He began to read illegal publications in 1900 but on a very limited scale.

In 1903 in St Petersburg, where he passed the entrance exams for the dentistry department of the Medical Academy, he met comrades who worked within the Party organization and introduced him to their political circle. Soon afterwards, however, he was banished from the capital and lived in Vyatka till 1905, where he had a dental surgery and organized political studies for a circle of pupils from secondary-education institutions.

By the beginning of autumn 1905 Filipp Isaevich had sold his dental surgery and moved back to St Petersburg where he engaged in full-time Party work. Initially he entered the Bolsheviks' military organization, working with a group of soldiers from the Peter and Paul Fortress.

He was sent to the St Petersburg District organization, where he began by carrying out propaganda work at the Izhorsk Factory and in Sestroretsk. Later he was made Party organizer in the same Area and was elected to represent it in the St Petersburg

Party Committee. He attended a number of conferences of the St Petersburg Party organization.

He was arrested three times at mass meetings of workers from the Izhorsk Factory: on the first two occasions he was released immediately after the names of those arrested had duly been noted, but on the third occasion he remained in police custody for several weeks. A case of 129 counts was drawn up against him in the Tsarskoye Selo gendarmerie.

In the summer of 1906 Goloshchekin was arrested with the whole of the St Petersburg Committee and tried in the Trial of the Nineteen, at which he was given a total sentence of three and a half years in the Peter and Paul Fortress. The case was quashed and Goloshchekin was released on bail. When he came out of prison he was sent by the St Petersburg Committee to the Nevskii District of the city, where he replaced Comrade Zinoviev before the London Congress. In the Nevskii District, Goloshchekin was elected to the St Petersburg Party Committee and was also made a member of its Executive Committee.

On the eve of May Day 1908 he was again arrested and was incarcerated in Kresty Prison in the capital until June 1909. After his release he was sent by the St Petersburg Committee to Paris as a delegate to the Bolshevik Conference, where the matter of the break with the 'Recallists' was finally settled. From Paris, Goloshchekin travelled to Leipzig where he was supplied with literature which he took to Vilnius. From there he went to St Petersburg, where he took part in the struggle against the 'Recallists' and the 'Liquidators'. Soon after that, on instructions from the Central Committee, he was sent to Moscow to replace Comrade Tomskii who had been appointed a Central Committee agent.

Goloshchekin worked in Moscow till the winter of 1910, when he was arrested together with the Moscow Committee and Y.M. Sverdlov in the flat of the engineer Timkov. He was sentenced to five (as far as he can remember) months in prison and then banished to Narym. After a few months of this internal exile Goloshchekin was arrested along with other comrades (including Kozyrev and Kuibyshev) for organizing a Marxist circle and then had to spend several months imprisoned in Tomsk. The case was dropped and he was escorted back to internal exile in Narym. In the summer of 1911 he escaped from Narym and made his way back to St Petersburg where he devoted himself once more to Party work. He was then sent by the Central Committee to Moscow, where the Party organization under Comrade Breslav had collapsed, to reinstate it and to prepare for the election of delegates to the Prague Conference.

Comrades Zinoviev, Malinovskii and Filipp Isaevich were elected as conference delegates from the Moscow Party organization. It was at that conference that Goloshchekin was elected as a member of the Central Committee.

After the Prague Conference he was arrested on his return to Moscow and after a short period in custody there, in Taganka Prison, he was banished to Tobolsk. He soon afterwards escaped from Tobolsk and arrived back in St Petersburg. During the work of the Third Duma he worked in the St Petersburg Committee as the Central Committee representative. After Sverdlov had been arrested in the flat of Comrade Petrovskii, the house containing Malinovskii's flat (where Goloshchekin happened to be) was surrounded. He managed to get away and was then issued with a Central Committee directive to leave for the Urals. He worked for a few weeks there but, when returning from the Motovilikha plant to Yekaterinburg where his flat was at the time, Goloshchekin was arrested. As it turned out later, on orders from Malinovskii. When he first arrived in the Urals, the secret police had already known about him, but for several weeks they had not been able to catch him. After spending some time in Yekaterinburg prison, Goloshchekin was banished to the Turukhansk Area, where he remained until the February Revolution.

After the February Revolution Goloshchekin arrived in St Petersburg in early March and worked there till the April

Conference. After that he was sent to the Urals. He was secretary of the Perm Provincial Party Committee and then secretary of the Urals Regional Committee and the Yekaterinburg Provincial Committee.

In the interval until the surrender of Perm (December 1918) he held various Party and important Soviet posts (member of the Urals regional Soviet, commissar for the Military District, Chief Political Commissar for the Third Army and so on). After the III Congress he was a member of the Central Committee's Siberian Bureau until Kurgan was taken. From August 1919 until June 1920 he was a member of the Turkestan Central Committee and the All-Russian Central Executive Committee. From July 1920 till July 1921 he was chairman of the Chief Mining Department and was then sent by the Central Committee to Bashkiria to organize congresses there. From March 1921 to January 1923 he was chairman of the Kostroma Provincial Executive Committee and a member of the Provincial Party Committee. Between May 1922 and July 1923 he was secretary of the Central Committee's Urals Bureau and from September of that year he held the office of chairman of the Samara Provincial Party Committee and was a member of the Revolutionary Military Soviet of the Volga Military District.

During his time in the revolutionary underground Goloshchekin went by a number of aliases: Filipp, Boris Ivanovich, Georges and Fran in his secret correspondence with N.K. Krupskaya. At the present time F.I. Goloshchekin is a candidate-member of the Central Committee and secretary of the Kazakh Area Committee of the Russian Communist Party (Bolsheviks).

He arrived in Kzyl-Orda [now Kyzylorda] on 12 September.

Goloshchekin's career path took him from shop assistant in a stationer's at the age of twenty, to Party member and dental technician at the age of twenty-seven, to professional revolutionary by the age of twenty-nine. This meant that Goloshchekin allied himself to the Bolsheviks at a fairly mature age. Taking his fiery nature and thirst for activity into consideration, it can be assumed that his choice of career was carefully thought through: before joining the ranks of the Russian Social-Democratic Workers' Party this energetic man, who had engaged in 'haphazard and non-systematic' reading 'in all manner of fields' and who had been 'fascinated by philosophy and later by social sciences', would have considered more than one trend in political and social ideas.

After becoming a Bolshevik, Goloshchekin threw himself into Party work. The mere list of places where he engaged in propaganda activities, not to mention the way he kept popping up in various places after the Revolution, shows that by nature he was a man for special assignments, one who made sure instructions were carried out: he was as people would say nowadays – a troubleshooter. He was not in his element when it came to theoretical research or profound intellectual activity: he needed to be involved in direct action – underground work prior to the October Revolution or the procurement of food supplies in the Kostroma region in the hungry year of 1921.

The reminiscences of his contemporaries – particularly those which touch on the pre-revolutionary period of Goloshchekin's life – give us some idea of the man's character and ideas.

Vladimir Lenin's wife, Nadezhda Konstantinovna Krupskaya, wrote about the events of 1912 linked with the Prague Conference:

> Vladimir Ilyich has already gone to Prague. Filipp [Goloshchekin] arrived with Brendinskii on their way to the Party conference. I had only known Brendinskii, who worked in transport, by name. He lived in Dvinsk and his main function was to convey the literature he received to Party organizations, mainly those in Moscow. Filipp was having doubts about Brendinskii. Before setting off abroad, Filipp had visited his father. Brendinskii had rented a room from Filipp's sister. Filipp's old father warned him that he should not trust Brendinskii who was behaving rather strangely, living beyond his means and throwing money around. Two weeks before the conference Brendinskii was arrested but then released a few days later. While he had been in prison, he had been visited by several people who were then arrested, but who precisely had been arrested was not clarified. What had also made Filipp suspicious was the plan for them to cross the border together. Filipp came to our flat together with Brendinskii and

I was pleased to see them, but then Filipp gave me a signal of a handshake combined with a meaningful look and I realized that he wanted to tell me something about Brendinskii. Later on, out in the corridor, he spoke to me about his doubts. We agreed that he would leave and that he and I would meet up later after I had had a talk with Brendinskii to sound him out and then decide how to proceed.

My conversation with Brendinskii turned out to be a very strange one. We had received information from 'Friday' that the literature had been sent off successfully and brought to Moscow, but the Muscovites were complaining that they had not received a single thing. I began asking Brendinskii about the address or the people to whom he was due to bring the literature, but he was ill at ease by this time and said that he used to pass it on to his workers. I began to ask him what their surnames were and he started obviously picking names out of the blue and saying he did not remember their addresses. It was plain that he was lying. I started inventing things, saying that the conference would be in Brittany and that Lenin and Zinoviev had already set off there. Later I arranged with Filipp that he and Grigorii would leave that night for Prague and he would leave a note for Brendinskii to the effect that he was leaving for Brittany. That was what we did.

I was very proud to have spared the conference an agent provocateur.[6]

It was not the first time that Nadezhda Konstantinovna had seen Goloshchekin: in the summer of 1909 he had come to Paris and met Lenin on several occasions. On 25 July 1909 he wrote a letter from Paris saying that after 'acquainting himself with the literature and talking to Lenin, he was now convinced that the political course adopted by the Proletarian was the theoretical position taken by revolutionary Social-Democrats and that only by following that path would we be in a position to consolidate the Party and to organize the masses round it.'[7]

Nadezhda Krupskaya carried on secret Party correspondence and Goloshchekin was one of her permanent correspondents. Two extracts from Krupskaya's letters provide insight into the progress of organizational and propaganda work. At the beginning of the twentieth century she noted with irritation: 'There is so much confusion here in Russia! The main problem is that people attach too much importance to local patriotism. When you read people's letters it makes you sad.'[8] Patriotism had always been a problem for the advocates of 'permanent revolution': in order to fan a worldwide conflagration, firewood first had to be chopped locally, in Russia's own backyard.

Later, in 1913, Krupskaya wrote: 'We recently received a letter from the Urals saying that work had been going splendidly there during the summer. In Yekaterinburg there are around two hundred organized Party members, a hundred in Motovilikha and fifty in Perm. There are Social-Democratic organizations in all the factories. They are all Party people and *Pravda* readers.'[9] She noted that Central Committee member Goloshchekin, who had arrived in Yekaterinburg in February, was helping people in the Urals to carry out 'splendid work'. A few weeks before his arrest he had set up new Party cells in the factories there.

On 3 March 1913 Goloshchekin returned from Perm. In Yekaterinburg station he was recognized by secret agents and arrested. When under arrest he identified himself as a newspaper correspondent and presented the authorities with a passport in the name of Samuil Kotisse. He felt sure that the secret police had been informed of his movements by Malinovskii.

Goloshchekin was banished to the village of Selivanikha in the Turukhansk Area, where he found himself in close proximity to two key figures in the Bolshevik movement. Yakov Sverdlov, destined to become leader of the Russian Soviet Federative Socialist Republic, was being held in that same settlement, where he 'was known to be under surveillance'. Goloshchekin had known Sverdlov well back in Moscow and from their shared banishment in Narym. Joseph Stalin was also nearby, living in the village of Kureika.

On 3 September 1913 Sverdlov wrote to his Lithuanian comrade V.S. Mitskevich-Kapsukas: 'Another two groups arrived here after us and we're expecting a third. There are three people in each group. An old friend of mine has also turned up with whom, a few years ago, I travelled to Siberia after being tried for one and the same offence. Naturally I was glad to see him. He shares my quarters.'[10] The reference is to Goloshchekin. On 7 September 1913 the local police inspector wrote in one of his reports: 'The political deportees assigned here – Yakov Sverdlov, Nikolai Orlov, Shaya

Goloshchekin made off to Monastyr [the village of Monastyrskoye, the centre of the Turukhansk Area], creeping through the woods.'[11] (Shaya was Goloshchekin's real name – he had been born Shaya Itskovich.)

Soon Sverdlov was transferred to Kureika where Stalin was living. Later he wrote to his friends in St Petersburg: 'There are two of us. There's a Georgian here with me, Dzhugashvili, an old acquaintance whom I met in another place of exile. He's a good fellow but too much of an individualist when it comes to everyday life.' Because they were both suspected – with good reason – of wanting to escape, they were separated, and Sverdlov was sent back to Selivanikha with Goloshchekin. In his book about Sverdlov, K. Lisovskii quotes the report submitted by the Turukhansk police superintendent to the Yenisei governor: 'The deportee Yakov Sverdlov entrusted to my supervision arrived on 22 July of this year (1913) at Monastyrskoye and was quartered in the small village of Selivanikha near Turukhansk.'[12] Goloshchekin's name is not mentioned in that book, nor indeed in any title published before his rehabilitation.

Sverdlov and Goloshchekin shared lodgings in Selivanikha and lived there for nearly a year. During that time he wrote many personal letters and often referred to his 'friend Georges' (as he referred to Goloshchekin). He sketched a vivid portrait of Goloshchekin in these letters. In one dated 3 March 1914, sent to Paris to his old comrade V.A. Dilevskii, banished to Narym with him, Sverdlov wrote:

> Our hunger for something new, for variety, is so strong that it's hard to put into words. My friend is always changing the timetable for his various activities. We have been here, the two of us, since the end of the summer. We're still just the two of us. We haven't got on each other's nerves yet, we don't quarrel or [illegible word] each other. Yet we both miss other people. We just want to be part of a crowd. I've never written to you about it before, but I and my friend are different in many respects. That, of course, is a good thing. At least arguments start up sometimes. Our arguments start up for a variety of reasons. We hardly ever argue about politics, in that respect we see eye to eye. What we want is a fuller life.[13]

From this letter it is evident that, at this point, surveillance was not strict when it came to correspondence.

The life led by the two banished friends in Selivanikha seems to have been a very free one. They were definitely not deprived of all human pleasures – they even went fishing and hunting. On 22 March 1914 Sverdlov wrote to his friend K.A. Egon-Besser:

I find myself in hunters' country. Out here you can bag foxes, arctic foxes and wolverines. For hunting no special knowledge is required. I and my friend have set a few traps. Every other day we have to go 9–10 *versts* on skis sheathed in leather. The weather is wonderful, the countryside magnificent and the air is splendid.[14]

Sverdlov's letters to his wife Klavdiya Novgorodtseva are more forthcoming. On 27–29 June 1914 Sverdlov wrote to her about his friend Georges in particular detail – usually he would devote just a few lines to him. He was seriously worried:

I have been spending a few days with Georges. Things are going badly with him. He has become a real neurotic and is turning into a misanthrope. While viewing people in general or in the abstract positively, he is extremely critical when it comes to specific individuals with whom he has to be in contact. As a result he's at odds with everyone. Apart from me, of course, because I understand what a good fellow he is, that his heart is in the right place. I've come to realize that it is definitely impossible for him to remain for a long time somewhere far from life seething with activity. He'll go to pieces and create conditions for himself that will make his existence intolerable.

It's bad that he has hardly any personal friendships, even fewer than I do. He is oppressed by friends having forgotten him, although he never talks about that. Up until now hardly anyone has sent him anything at all out here. When his sister was in St Petersburg, things were better, it has to be said. He needs to be moved to a better place. But how can that be done? Even if it was another remote hole like this one, it would need to be one where he would have to exert himself simply to 'fight to survive'. If only there could be some outlet for his energy. For the time being I want to ask you to write to him. His good relations with me carry over to you and the children as well. A friendly letter in the conditions out here means so much. If you can, send him one or two books of literature. Poetry would be good. Apart from me he has nobody to talk to, let alone to have a heart-to-heart with. At the same time he is full of good cheer and optimism when it comes to social issues! I was there when he received your letter and he was extremely happy.[15]

Sverdlov, curiously, adds that 'The only person who writes to me often is Berta' – a reference to Goloshchekin's wife Berta Josifovna Perelman. She had been a member of the Bolsheviks' Moscow Soviet in 1903 and had been arrested together with Goloshchekin and Sverdlov, and then banished to the Narym District. After the Revolution she worked in Samara and Sverdlovsk. She had been Goloshchekin's wife, whom he had abandoned with their small son in 1911. Sverdlov mentioned her often in letters to his wife. On 19 January 1914 he wrote that Berta had: 'embarked on a dressmaking course and in two or three months' time would be able to start earning. She had at one time been a seamstress, but had not worked for about ten years and had forgotten everything she used to know.'

In September 1914 Sverdlov was transferred once more to Selivanikha. He and Goloshchekin were lodged with a fisherman and hunter by the name of Samoilov. On 2 October he wrote to his wife:

It would appear that I shall be living here, together with Georges, for about two months and after that I shall perhaps be going back to Kureika. For the time being we're talking and arguing a little as well. We shall go to Monastyrskoye often to fetch telegrams and often we learn about the most important news from people we happen to meet on the way.[16]

In Western Europe a cruel war was raging and Russian soldiers were dying at the front. In Selivanikha, however, life seemed oppressively dull, giving rise to its own problems. On 27 October Sverdlov wrote to his wife:

I'm still living here with Georges. At least once a week Georges or I go to Monastyrskoye. Georges is full of energy and in that respect he's somehow younger, less tired than I am.

Driving about on a dog-drawn sledge is rather tiring. We have two dogs of our own for this purpose. With large dogs like these we can go to fetch food, water and firewood. This year we're not buying firewood. We go out and chop it in the forest and then bring it home. I've set up a fishing line by the river, but so far I've only caught one fish – a *taimen* weighing just over 16 kilos. I've been out to pick red currants on several occasions. They're frozen over now but they taste rather like our cranberries, only finer and more delicate. That's how we pass the time till the evening, then we sit down with a book till it's time to sleep. We have absolutely no friends or sources of intelligent conversation except each other. There is little to envy us for, my dear ...[17]

On 16 November, he wrote again:

My brain seems to have gone to sleep for good. During the first month of life out here with Georges it was a rare event when a thought took shape.

Life with him has helped a good deal to wake up my ideas. He is quite a lively character. He always has plenty of questions which he tries to resolve through conversation. When it comes to theory, I am definitely more experienced and many of the questions which he has just come up against no longer attract my attention. This does not mean that we are contented out here with just the two of us, don't think that we have a lively comradely atmosphere here.

Our conversations are mainly centred on the war. This enormous European war is bound to draw a clear line between what went before it and what comes after.[18]

Later, on 12 January 1915, in another letter to his wife:

This is my second day in living quarters of my own. You mustn't think it is after some quarrel with Georges. Nothing of the kind. We're still in the same building but having rooms of our own is better all the same. We used to have shared quarters consisting of two tiny rooms. We used to read and work in one of them, because the second – the kitchen – was very uncomfortable.

Our habits were rather different. Georges would always go to bed
regularly at 12. Sometimes I'd go to bed earlier, but usually two
hours later than he did. That would prevent him from sleeping
and I would go out into the kitchen. Even that would disturb
him. Often we would talk away for several hours. As before we
have our dinner and supper together and we share all expenses.[19]

Soon no more letters were required: Klavdiya came out to be with her
husband and they settled in Monastyrskoye, where family life resumed.
She later recalled: 'His health was gradually improving here in Selivanikha,
although life there was no picnic. Food was incredibly expensive and the
wretched allowance he was getting was barely enough for a half-starved
existence: bread, cereals, the deportees had virtually no vegetables. There
was no meat other than venison, no eggs or flour. Butter, potatoes and
milk were rare luxuries. It was difficult to get hold of sugar, salt, matches
or tobacco.'[20]

Soon the situation was sorted out with regard to milk and butter, for
the Sverdlovs acquired a cow:

Our constant visitors included Yakov Yefimovich Bograd, Boris
Ivanov, Georges Goloshchekin, who followed Yakov from
Selivanikha to Monastyrskoye, and other deportees. Often after
serious conversations or lectures we would go out into the *taiga*
[forest], a whole crowd of us ... In the frozen silence Russian
songs of freedom would flow forth or militant hymns of the
Russian proletariat of that period would ring out: my special
favourites were 'Warsaw March' and 'Red Banner'.[21]

By this time there were some twenty deportees in Monastyrskoye and the
Sverdlovs' rooms had become their focal point for political studies. One
of them, Boris Ivanov, would remember:

We – Dolbeshkin, Bulatov, Goloshchekin, Bograd, the Sverdlovs,
Valentina Sergusheva, Ivan Petukhov, myself and others saw in
the New Year, 1916. Yakov Mikhailovich took on the role of
chief cook. Three hundred *pelmeni* [dumplings] stuffed with deer
meat stood ready to be boiled out in his porch. The two tables
in his room had been covered over with newspapers and on these

glistening frozen *omul* fish and venison had been laid out looking most inviting. There were two kettles ready for brewing brick tea.

The New Year celebrations were ushered in by Yakov Yefimovich Bograd. Not only was he the oldest person there, but he was a doctor of philosophy and mathematical sciences.

The word 'Comrades!' rang out in his bass voice: 'Tsar Nicholas and his pack of executioners wanted to freeze us to death in the snows of Turukhansk, but we are alive and seeing in this bloodstained fighting year full of good cheer and hopes for a brighter future …

How eloquent Yakov Yefimovich was! However, though he was a man of venerable years and philosophical credentials, his words here are perhaps overly dramatic. He could not truly have thought that the monarch desired to freeze to death the dozen or so deportees out in the snows of Turukhansk, whose very existence he was unlikely to have known about. As for the 'pack of executioners', they definitely did not justify such a description since they allowed their 'victims' to feast undisturbed to celebrate the New Year. As time was to show, Siberian cold was not to be the death of any of them. If we take a sober view of it all, what reasons did they have for losing heart? Others were freezing in the trenches under fire from enemy bullets and yet here they were sitting in a warm hut washing down a hearty meal with tea.

In fact, Tsar Nicholas did not decide the question of life and death for them: the opposite was to be the case. Three and a half years later, two of those seated at that table on New Year's Eve would decide the fate of the former Tsar of Russia and his family.

Another fourteen years after that, when the 'brighter future' they had been dreaming of had long since dawned, hardly anyone was still alive when New Year's Eve came round in 1932. In one of the many collective farms bearing the name of Sverdlov, seven kilometres from the town of Aulie-Ata [now Taraz] in the land of Kazakhstan, Goloshchekin was ruling as unchallenged sovereign. People there had certainly perished of hunger and cold.

In the neighbouring *aul* the last inhabitant was dying: a young Kazakh who had been eating human flesh for several days. Rendered insane by his hunger he had knifed a woman to death; he confessed this to a visiting commission. This plague had swept away tens of thousands of people in the land of the Kazakhs and in many parts of Russia, the Ukraine, Central Asia and Siberia. Yet the victims of that famine were not criminals. Nor were they people banished thousands of *versts* from their homes or those who lived in the subarctic *taiga*: they were people living in their own homelands.

Did Goloshchekin perhaps recall, as information flooded in about the famine and cannibalism, how he had been preparing venison dumplings for New Year's Eve in 1916 in the distant Siberian village of Monastyrskoye?

❖

III. The Execution of Tsar Nicholas II and his Family

An official article written by V.N. Alexandrov and Y.N. Amiantov to mark the ninetieth anniversary of Goloshchekin's birth opens as follows:

> At the end of September 1919 a joyful meeting took place in House No. 7 on Moscow's Mokhovaya Street, where the secretariat of the Central Committee of the Russian Communist Party (Bolsheviks) stood. The veteran communist F.I. Goloshchekin was reunited with his adolescent son. Since the beginning of 1918 F.I. Goloshchekin had been carrying out crucial Party work in the Urals and he had lost touch with his wife and son, who had turned to the Central Committee of the Party with a request for help to find their husband and father. Staff from the Central Committee secretariat found Goloshchekin and organized this meeting with his son. Filipp Isaevich was not able to spend much time with the boy since a new important Party assignment awaited him and so, once again, they were separated. F.I. Goloshchekin's life did not belong to him or his family – it was dedicated entirely to the Party of the Bolsheviks.[1]

We might wonder why Berta Josifovna Perelman had not turned earlier to Sverdlov – her old comrade from the revolutionary underground and banishment in Narym – to whom she had once written fond letters. The chairman of the All-Russian Central Executive Committee knew full well where his close friend Georges had been after early 1918, having maintained regular telegraphic links with him and received him in his Moscow flat. Of course, there may have been specific reasons why contact

37

was being sought with the husband and father at this point. A short time later, Berta Perelman took her own life; Goloshchekin wrote in a Urals newspaper that she had had the strength to 'abandon this life with dignity'.

The brevity of the reunion in that house on Mokhovaya Street is hardly surprising. What could Goloshchekin have said to his son, whom he had hardly ever seen? He would hardly have told him how, just over a year earlier, he had taken from Yekaterinburg – in one of three heavy crates with similar contents – the head of a boy, of roughly the same age as his son, preserved in spirit.

Historians O.A. Vaskovskii and E.I. Moiseyev regretfully comment that: 'So far very little is known about the life of Filipp Isaevich Goloshchekin, a prominent figure from the Communist Party, who played an important role in the Party's military and political work and was a staunch Leninist.'[2] One of the most significant chapters in Goloshchekin's life is linked with that village in the Urals, yet historians skirt round it in complete silence. The same can be said of Alexandrov and Amiantov and indeed of all the other researchers in our country, right up until the very recent past.

Before we turn to that episode, however, let us look back once more to the period before the Revolution. In the book mentioned earlier which Sverdlov's wife, Klavdiya Timofeyevna, had written, one of the photos bears the following caption: 'Sverdlov with a group of comrades returning from internal exile.' Striking figures, looking well fed and warmly dressed in fur hats and coats, look at the camera with anticipation. Goloshchekin is dressed even more conspicuously than the rest: he wears a round fur hat and a rough winter coat like those worn by the Ostyak people of Siberia. The day before the photograph was taken he and Sverdlov had had to undertake a long journey. Klavdiya Sverdlova wrote at the time:

At the very beginning of March 1917 thrilling news reached Monastyrskoye: the tsarist autocracy was over.

The departure had had to be a hurried affair. They had to cover over 3,000 *versts* with horse-drawn sleighs to reach Krasnoyarsk. The only route open to them was via the River Yenisei and the ice might have started breaking any day.

Yakov did not delay for a moment. He and Georges Goloshchekin packed their things immediately and then left straight after they received the telegram.

There was a fierce Turukhansk snowstorm swirling round them, but almost the whole of Monastyrskoye's population came down to the bank of the river. They shook hands with Sverdlov and Goloshchekin, who was leaving with him, wishing them a safe journey.

They travelled hard, scarcely ever leaving their sleighs, so keen were they not to waste a single minute. They stopped in various villages and settlements on the way only to change horses and to have a look at fresh newspapers. They got through in time, although towards the end of their journey they had to skirt round numerous holes in the ice where it was thawing. Risking their lives in the process, they reached Yeniseisk without mishap, although they could have fallen through the ice at any moment. Then the route to Krasnoyarsk and Russia lay open ahead of them![3]

On 15 March the travellers reached Antsiferovo, where they ran out of money. They went to see District Commissar Korf and showed him the identification document issued to them by the authorities in Yeniseisk which opened with the words: 'To all the authorities and to the population of free Russia …' In response, Korf gave them ten roubles, which meant that Sverdlov and Goloshchekin were able to continue their journey.

On 20 and 21 March they took part in a meeting of the Krasnoyarsk Soviet and the day after they left for Petrograd. Klavdiya Timofeyevna continued her account as follows:

They arrived on 29 March and went straight from the station to the home of Yakov's sister Sara. She told me later on how her brother Yakov had turned up out of the blue.

Before she had had time to answer even a tenth of their questions, Sara remembered that she needed to offer her brother something to eat after his journey. Suddenly Sverdlov clutched his head in horror.

'Georges, oh Georges!' he groaned.

'Why Georges, which Georges?'

'It's Goloshchekin. I left him down at the front door, out in the street. But half an hour's passed since then. You'd better go down to him, or otherwise he'll kill me, without fail. He's easy to recognize: he's tall and thin with a small beard and a moustache and wearing a black hat. A regular Don Quixote.'

Sara quickly went outside and recognized Goloshchekin straightaway. He was shifting from one foot to the other looking miserable. She came back in with him, made tea for both men and then led them to the Tavrichesky Palace. It was at that very time that the first conference for representatives of the Soviets from the largest towns in Russia was taking place.[4]

Soon after the October Revolution Sverdlov was made chairman of the All-Russia Central Executive Committee and Goloshchekin was sent to Perm in the Urals, where he headed the Provincial Party Committee. Such an appointment would have been unlikely without Sverdlov's involvement, who – as Lenin himself was to write – took upon himself a mountain of organizational work. It was probably important to him to have a completely reliable man of proven worth in the Urals, in view of the fact that the former Tsar Nicholas II and his family had been in Tobolsk under house arrest ever since August 1917.

It was Alexander Kerensky, the head of the Russian Provisional Government, who had the Tsar sent to Tobolsk. Why there in particular? Kerensky's own explanations, both at the time and subsequently, were extremely unclear. He maintained that Siberia was safer and that the Governor's house there was a good comfortable one. The most probable answer was probably the one suggested by N.A. Sokolov, the perceptive lawyer who conducted the inquiry into the killing of the Tsar's family: 'There was only one motive for bringing the Tsar's family out to Tobolsk, different from all the others indicated by Prince Lvov and Kerensky: distant cold Siberia was the region to which others had been banished in the past.'[5]

The 'others', of course, were the Decembrists and other revolutionaries, who had been banished to Siberia by the ancestors of Nicholas II. It is well known that there had been a fair number of freemasons among the deportees. Kerensky, himself a high-ranking mason, and his government, which included numerous freemasons, clearly had old scores to settle.

The Decembrists, back in their day, had considered what to do with the Tsar and his family after his overthrow. Opinion had been divided: some had recommended that the Tsar and his immediate relatives should be executed, others that he should be sent into exile abroad. The Leninists, when they came to power, were uncertain about the issue. By this time those in control had to take the 'masses' into account, wondering whether openly disposing of the Tsar might incense the populace. What if the uneducated devout people should venture to defend the Lord's Anointed or seek revenge for his death? For tactical reasons it was necessary to lie, to create an illusion of legality and justice. There ensued a number of announcements: 'We shall let the people try their crowned executioner' and so on. Leon Trotsky was appointed chief prosecutor for the undertaking – the son of a millionaire was to prosecute the Tsar in the name of the people. Yet no such trial was organized – why not? There were two possible reasons: either the Bolsheviks feared a high-profile public trial would harm their cause, or they were seeking to divert attention from what they were actually planning.

Until the spring of 1918 the Romanovs lived relatively freely in the Governor's house. In the meantime (if we are to believe Sverdlov's biographers, E. Gorodetskii and Y. Sharapov) monarchists were starting to gather in Tobolsk: 'the small town was being flooded with Black Hundreds' literature, appeals from Purishkevich, Bishop Germogen, and monarchist leaflets.'[6] With hindsight, but nevertheless with true revolutionary vigilance, the authors write of the danger that the Tsar's family might have been able to escape. It is not clear, however, why the 'counterrevolutionary officer class' delayed its arrival, if forces which were anxious to set the Tsar free had already assembled in Tobolsk.

T. Melnik-Botkina, daughter of the Tsar's physician, recalled in 1921 that soldiers from one of the platoons guarding the Tsar had said that they would let the imperial family leave in safety. Those soldiers would appear also to have been growing soft.

In his book *The Tragic Fate of Nicholas II and his Family*, Pierre Gilliard, the tutor of Tsarevich Alexei, quotes the following extract from his diary for 17 March 1918:

Their Majesties, despite the desperate sense of alarm that was growing from day to day, continued to hope that among the people still loyal to them some might emerge who would try to set them free. The conditions in which they were being held had never been so conducive to their escape before, since in Tobolsk there was not yet any representative of the Bolshevik government. It would have been easy with support from Colonel Kobylinskii [commander of the guard in both Tsarskoye Selo and Tobolsk], already predisposed in our favour to deceive the insolent and at times careless supervision by our custodians. All that was needed were some sufficiently energetic men, who would have implemented an appropriate plan on the outside with the necessary resolve.[7]

Men of resolve did not, however, come forward. Gilliard went on to point out:

We insisted in the Tsar's presence, on more than one occasion, that he should remain ready for any kind of opportunity. He set two conditions which made the undertaking far more complicated: He would not agree to family members being separated or to leaving the territory of the Russian Empire.[8]

That was the kind of man the Russian Tsar was. Realizing that it would be impossible to meet those conditions and how dire the consequences of his decision would be, he was determined not to leave his homeland. The same applied to the Tsarina who stated to Gilliard: 'Not for anything in the world do I wish to leave Russia.'

The Bolshevik usurpers on the other hand reacted in a very different way when their own backs had been against the wall: as Anton Denikin was closing in on Moscow, Lenin and his cronies were already preparing to bolt and go abroad, their cases packed with plundered gold and diamonds – the 'Party cashbox'.

Let us return, however, to Sverdlov's biographers. 'As early as the Smolny era [while Lenin's headquarters were in the Smolny Institute] Sverdlov was receiving alarming news from Tobolsk.'

Gorodetskii and Sharapov write:

In the second half of March, Military Commissar F.I. Goloshchekin, a representative of the Urals Regional Soviet, came to Moscow to inform Sverdlov about the situation in Tobolsk and he told him of the decision taken by the Urals Soviet to request the government to transfer Nikolai Romanov to Yekaterinburg. That would put paid to the plans of the counter-revolutionaries and place the Romanovs under the reliable surveillance of the working men of the Urals.

THE EXECUTION OF TSAR NICHOLAS II AND HIS FAMILY

Sverdlov agreed with the proposal from the Urals Soviet. The presidium of the All-Russia Central Executive Committee gave its approval for the transfer of Nikolai Romanov to Yekaterinburg on condition that the regional Soviet and Goloshchekin in person would assume full responsibility for the implementation of this plan and for guarding Nikolai Romanov right up until the time when his trial would be organized.[9]

Even from the above small extract it is clear that the authors contradict themselves, presenting the facts back to front.

No one can doubt that Sverdlov was paying close attention to events connected with the Tsar and was in control of the action taken by Regional Military Commissar Goloshchekin. It is most likely that he summoned his friend 'Georges' to Moscow in order to receive a detailed account from him and to issue further instructions. There is proof for this interpretation of events. At the beginning of May 1918 the All-Russia Central Executive Committee decided to transfer the Romanov family to Yekaterinburg and entrusted this task to V.V. Yakovlev. In Yekaterinburg Yakovlev began to be suspected of treachery; in response, Sverdlov telegraphed Beloborodov (head of the Executive Committee of the local Soviet) and Goloshchekin as follows:

Everything that Yakovlev is doing is the direct implementation of the order I gave. I shall inform you of the details by special courier. Do not issue any instructions regarding Yakovlev: he is acting in accordance with the directions received from me at 4 o'clock this morning. Do not embark on anything without our agreement. We trust Yakovlev completely. Once more I stress – no intervention. Sverdlov.[10]

This demonstrates that the local authorities did not know all the details regarding the transfer of the Tsar's family to Yekaterinburg showing, yet again, who was ultimately in charge. The three repetitions of the order (issued at 4 o'clock in the morning!) clearly reflect irritation at too much initiative being shown.

On 17 April 1918 Nicholas II noted in his diary:

> We arrived in Yekaterinburg. We were delayed for four hours at one particular station. There were hefty altercations between the local commissars and those travelling with us. In the end the local ones got the upper hand. The train then moved to another goods station. Yakovlev handed us over to the local Regional Commissar and then the three of us got into an automobile and travelled through empty streets to the Ipatiev House which had been prepared for us.[11]

Investigator Nikolai Sokolov wrote in his book *The Murder of the Tsar's Family* as follows:

> In the spring of 1918 there was a special detachment of railway police, which carried out executions within the confines of the railways – when firing squads were required. It was headed by a peasant, Parfyonii Samokhvalov, who also served as a driver in the Soviet's road-transport depot. It was he who was given the task of bringing the Tsar and Maria Nikolaevna from the station to the Ipatiev House.

At the subsequent investigation Samokhvalov testified as follows: 'I do not remember the actual date, but I remember that in April I was summoned to the building of the Yekaterinburg District Court by Commissar Goloshchekin, who told me to make sure that everything was in order with the vehicles at the depot.' A few days later Samokhvalov was told to bring a car round to the Ipatiev House:

> Commissar Goloshchekin, Commissar Avdeyev and some other people ... came out of the house and got into the cars and we then went to the station Yekaterinburg-1. When we arrived at the Yekaterinburg-1 station, I heard from the people there that the Tsar had been brought to Yekaterinburg. On arrival we drove in the cars to the place where a first-class coach was standing, which was surrounded by soldiers. The Emperor and the Empress came out of the coach and one of their daughters. They then got into my automobile. Once again we drove to that same house with a

44

fence round it, which I mentioned earlier. Goloshchekin was in charge of the whole operation. When we had driven up to the house, Goloshchekin said to the Tsar: 'Citizen Romanov, you may go inside'. The Tsar went through into the house. Goloshchekin then ushered the Tsarina and one of the Grand Duchesses and a few servants into the house. When the Tsar had been brought to the house, people started collecting around it. I remember that Goloshchekin shouted: 'Cheka [secret police] men, you should be doing something about this!' The onlookers were dispersed.[12]

Sokolov drew the following conclusion: 'Goloshchekin, Yurovskii [the Cheka leader] and Zaslavskii [representing the local Soviet] were the people with power over the Tsar's family from the first moment they arrived in Yekaterinburg.'[13] As early as 13 April 1918 Zaslavskii had arrived in Tobolsk leading a detachment of Red Army soldiers in order to guard the Tsar and his family, after securing the right to replace the 'unreliable' Red Army detachment from Omsk. He did not succeed in doing so.[14]

In the archives of the Sverdlov Regional History Museum there is a picture entitled *Handover of the Romanovs to the Urals Soviet*. V.N. Pcholin, the artist commissioned to paint this canvas in Sverdlovsk to mark the tenth anniversary of the October Revolution, noted the following details in his sketchbook:

Natural landscape ... forest in the distance. Two huts on a sandy square with grass round it ... a departing train with steam coming out of its engine.

Those present: Commissar Yakovlev and his assistant handed over the Romanovs surrounded by forty Red Army soldiers.

Comrade Beloborodov, Comrade Goloshchekin and Comrade Didkovskii (members of the Urals Soviet) took over responsibility for them ...[15]

Pcholin completed the commission with true socialist-realist enthusiasm. He depicted two small groups of people looking tensely at each other in front of a chain of soldiers and a train swathed in smoke in the background. In the faces of Nicholas II, the Tsarina and Grand Duchess Maria there is dismay and alarm, while Yakovlev stands in front of the others, eyes ablaze, with his right hand stretched towards the people who have come to meet them as if to say: 'Duly delivered, here you are!' On the other side stand Beloborodov in a black leather jacket, Goloshchekin in a great coat and a tall fur hat, Didkovskii and a Red Army soldier – all coldly confident and restrained.

Goloshchekin has been recorded for posterity shown in half-profile, with a Mephistophelean pointed beard, holding himself in a strikingly proud way. He is in the foreground, yet at the same time to one side of the scene, observing.

Beloborodov's telegram to Moscow reporting the event read as follows: 'To Sverdlov heading the All-Russia Executive Committee, and to Lenin, Chairman of the Council of People's Commissars: Commissar Yakovlev handed over to me the former Tsar Nikolai Romanov, the former Tsarina Alexandra and their daughter Maria STOP They have all been transferred to a house under guard STOP.' The significance of this is that while previously all information sent to Moscow had been addressed to Sverdlov, now another recipient had appeared – Lenin. From now on the house began to be referred to by the Bolsheviks as the 'House for a Special Purpose'. The very name suggests a premeditated crime.

Sokolov was to write:

The arrival of the Emperor in Yekaterinburg brought Goloshchekin into the limelight as the 'man in charge'. It was not only that! The open use of the term 'man in charge' also made it clear why Sverdlov had sent his old comrade 'Georges' to be for all intents and purposes the governor of the Urals immediately after the October Revolution. As soon as the Bolsheviks came to power, this was tantamount to signing the Russian Tsar's death sentence. It was also immediately clear who would be implementing the sentence. This is why 'Don Quixote' did not trust anyone else to take his victim to the specially prepared trap.

In addition to his wife, Alexandra Fyodorovna, the Tsar's whole family was imprisoned with him: his daughters – Olga (twenty-two), Tatyana (twenty), Maria (eighteen), Anastasia (sixteen) and his incurably ill son, Alexei (fourteen).

Nicholas II continued to make entries in his diary, as he had been accustomed to do over many years (this is now kept in the Central State Archive for the October Revolution).

'It is a good clean house. In order to go to the bathroom we have to go past the sentry at the door of the guards' room. There is a high fence of wooden planks all round the house just over four metres from the windows. There are five sentries in the small garden as well.

2 May: Steps to make the house more like a prison continued. This morning an old painter whitewashed over all the glass in the windows of all the rooms. It is as if mist is looking in through the windows. There is always one of the commissars in the garden keeping watch on the garden, on us and the sentries.'[16]

Nobody complained about the conditions they were being held in, but the emotional strain grew daily.

Later on one of the guards, Yakimov, testified as follows:

Sometimes they used to sing. I used to hear religious chanting. They sang the 'Cherubim's Song' ... Meanwhile the guards would be drinking and making a noise. The guards, who had been attracted to this task by the prospects of good money and easy work watching these royal prisoners, used to annoy and harass them: they would accompany the Grand Duchesses to the lavatory, lean back against the door while the lavatory was being used, write 'various indecent words' on the walls, draw obscene pictures and bawl out revolutionary songs such as 'You fell as a sacrifice in the fatal struggle', 'Let us renounce the old world' or 'Comrades, let us march in step'.

Later Nicholas II made the following entry in his diary: '6 May: Have reached the age of fifty, seems strange even to me ...' Every day the Tsar and his daughters would go out into the garden. Alexei had to be carried out, because he had a bad leg. On 16 July the family took its last walk in that garden; did they know that the end was coming?

On 14 July the priest Storozhev celebrated mass for the last time in the Ipatiev House. The service was conducted under the watchful eye of Commandant Yurovskii. Storozhev was later to recall:

At a specific point in the mass the prayer 'Rest in peace with the Saints' is read. For some reason, on this occasion the deacon sang this prayer instead of reciting it and I too began to sing, but we had only just begun, when I heard the members of the Romanov family standing behind me kneel down.[17]

In the early hours of 17 July Nicholas II and his family were shot. Goloshchekin, in his capacity as Regional Military Commissar, was directly responsible for organizing and supervising the murder without any trial or investigation. Very little has been written in the former Soviet Union about this and, as a rule, what has been recorded was done so only reluctantly, with no mention of any details connected with the shooting, obscuring the role of the organizers of this deed.

In their book about Sverdlov, Gorodetskii and Sharapov describe what happened in the following words:

The Front was very near and Yekaterinburg could only hold out for a matter of days.

During the night of 16–17 July the Urals Regional Executive Committee assembled. The oldest Bolshevik there and an experienced revolutionary, Commissar for Urals Finance, F. Syromolotov, pointed out that in this complex situation there was only one way out – executing the Tsar immediately [nothing was said in relation to the wife and children] and then informing the Soviet government of this.

The proposal from Fyodor Syromolotov supported by Voikov, Andreyev, Bykov and other members of the Urals Regional Soviet, was adopted unanimously.[18]

In their book there is no word about the actual execution of the Tsar and his family, yet the authors intimate that they possess some special information, opening the chapter entitled 'The Last Conspiracy of the Romanovs' with the following passage:

48

Yakov Sverdlov liked reciting lines from Pushkin's poem 'Liberty':

O autocrat on high!
You and your throne I despise.
I'll watch you fall, your children die
With cruel, exultant eyes.[19]

Neither in Sverdlov's wife's memoirs, nor in the published volume of his letters is there a single word to the effect that Sverdlov especially enjoyed those particular lines. Perhaps, however, the authors have some information not in the public domain. Whatever the case, they make no mention of Goloshchekin, Beloborodov or Yurovskii – the main instigators of the execution.

Another writer from Sverdlovsk, Yakov Lazarevich Reznik, writes even more briefly on the subject in his book about the Cheka officer Y.M. Yurovskii, published in Sverdlovsk in 1968: 'On the night of 16–17 July Yakov Yurovskii, Grigorii Nikulin, Pavel Medvedev and Pyotr Yermakov put the sentence into effect.' For Yurovskii this was his hour 'centre stage'. It was after this that his career in the secret police took off. Once again there is no mention of Goloshchekin.

M.K. Kasvinov in his voluminous book *Twenty-three Steps Down*, published in Moscow in 1978, devotes a single line to the execution: 'On the night of 16–17 July everything came to an end.'

G.Z. Joffe, in his monograph *The Great October Revolution and the Epilogue of Tsarism*, published in Moscow in 1987, does not mention the moment of the execution. What was it that these official Soviet historians of the Party and the Revolution kept silent about for decades, in compliance with private instructions from 'above'?

The bloody massacre had taken place in one of the downstairs cellars: behind it there was just a storeroom with no windows. The only window in the cellar opened into Voznesenskii Lane and it had iron bars on the outside and was sunk well below the ground surface. Sokolov was to conclude: 'The very selection of that room speaks for itself: the murder had been rigorously planned. The room was the perfect torture chamber. The laws of that period termed murders of this kind "dastardly".'[20]

After Yekaterinburg had been taken by White forces, they had the opportunity to interrogate various people who had been involved in these events. A guard by the name of Proskuryakov testified as follows:

In the evening Yurovskii said to Medvedev that the Tsar's family was to be shot that night. He gave orders to warn the workers about that and to collect the sentries' revolvers. Pashka Medvedev carried out Yurovskii's order to the letter. At midnight Yurovskii began to wake up the Tsar's family, demanding that they dress and gather downstairs. According to Medvedev, Yurovskii explained the situation to the imperial family, saying that the night was going to be a dangerous one and that there could be shooting on the streets. They were standing in two rows. Yurovskii himself began to read out to them from some paper. The Tsar did not wait for him to finish and asked Yurovskii: 'What next?' According to what Pashka said, he raised his hand holding the revolver and replied to the Tsar: 'This is next!' When they had all been shot, Andrei Strekotkin, as he himself told me, stripped them of their valuables. Yurovskii immediately collected them together and took them upstairs.[21]

Another guard by the name of Yakimov was clearly shielding himself from possible trouble, when he testified with reference to what another had witnessed:

Yurovskii and Nikulin led the way. Behind them walked the Tsar, the Tsarina and their daughters: Olga, Tatyana, Maria and Anastasia and then came Botkin, Demidova, Trupp and the cook Kharitonov. The Tsar himself was carrying his heir. Behind them came Medvedev and the Latvians, i.e. the ten people who had been living in the downstairs rooms and who had been selected by Yurovskii from Cheka forces. Yurovskii spoke to the Tsar in these words: 'Nikolai Alexandrovich, your relatives tried to rescue you, but they did not succeed. We are obliged to shoot you ourselves.' Immediately some shots rang out. Revolvers were used exclusively. After the first shots 'female screaming' broke out. The shot victims began to fall over, one after the other. The Tsar was the first to fall and after him his Heir. Demidova seems to have been writhing about as she tried to shield herself with a cushion. She was then stabbed with bayonets. When they were all lying on the floor, the bodies were inspected and extra

50

shots and stabbings took place. From among the members of the Tsar's family only Anastasia was mentioned as being bayoneted. Someone must have then brought in some sheets from upstairs. People began to wrap the bodies in those sheets.[22]

Bolshevik Pavel Medvedev was the man among the guards empowered to act on Yurovskii's behalf. At 7 o'clock on the evening of 16 July he already knew that he would be killing the Romanovs that night. The Urals communists had not yet discussed it and they had not taken a unanimous decision to execute the Tsar, but Yurovskii had already said to the commander of the guard: 'Today, Medvedev, we shall shoot the family – all of them.' He instructed him to warn the guards around 10 o'clock so that they should not be alarmed if they heard gunshots.

During his questioning, Medvedev gave the following account:

> At around midnight Commandant Yurovskii began to wake the Tsar's family. Nicholas II himself and the whole family rose, dressed and washed; approximately one hour later all eleven of the prisoners came out of their rooms. After they had gone downstairs, they went into the room at the end of the main house. Twenty-two people assembled there: eleven persons due to be executed and eleven armed men [all of whom he mentioned by name]. When they had all been shot and were lying on the floor in various positions, there was a great deal of blood splashed about and moreover thick blood, lying clotted. All of them, except the Tsar's son Alexei, were dead by this time. Yurovskii fired two more shots at Alexei from his revolver and after that the boy stopped groaning. In my presence none of the members of the Tsar's family asked any questions or complained. There were no tears, no sobs.[23]

In his written statement the guard Strekotkin recalled:

> The prisoners were already lying on the floor dripping blood, while the Tsar's heir was still sitting on his chair. For some reason it took a long time before he fell from his chair and he was still alive. They began shooting him at close range in the head and chest and eventually he did fall off his chair. The little dog which

one of the daughters had brought with her was also shot. The corpses were taken out to the lorry that was waiting in the yard. The second person to be placed on a stretcher was one of the daughters of the Tsar, but she began to show signs of life: she began to cry out, but then covered her mouth with her hand. What was more, another of the daughters and a woman who had been in the service of the Tsar's family also turned out to be still alive. Nobody was able to shoot them at that point, because all the doors inside the building were open by this time. That was when Comrade Yermakov, seeing that I was holding a bayonet, suggested that I should finish the task. I refused and then he took the weapon out of my hands and began to bayonet them. That was the most terrible moment of their death. It took them a long time to die, they were calling out and groaning, writhing in pain. The death of the woman in the Tsar's service was particularly gruesome. Yermakov stabbed all over her chest with the weapon. The blows from the bayonet were so powerful that the blade went right through her into the floor every time.[24]

Igor Nepein, a writer from Chelyabinsk, was the first person to 'leaf through' the pages of books that had not been accessible to Soviet readers. Using material from books by N. Sokolov, P. Gilliard, R. Wilton and others, he published an article in the paper *Urals News* about the terrible crime. Yet the conclusions drawn by Nepein were relatively straightforward ones:

Arbitrary lawlessness was the order of the day in the Ipatiev House, without any control or accountability regarding the decision to kill the prisoners, including the children among them. They were executed in an unspecified place and without the purpose and the nature of their crimes having been established at the very dawn of Soviet power. Did this not serve as one of the preludes to the mass executions and repression of the thirties, forties and fifties under Stalin?[25].

Yet a decision as important as this could not have been taken arbitrarily. Those at the centre of power — as can be seen from the earlier part of this chapter — were paying careful attention to the transfer of the Romanovs and their fate. Any local initiative had been strictly prohibited and it goes without saying that a Party man as disciplined and conscientious as Goloshchekin would never have indulged in any improvisation of that kind. He would have made sure to wait for approval and would never have presented the government with a *fait accompli* – and he should have had no difficulty communicating with Moscow, since we know that telegraph links were functioning properly.

In her *Memories of Lenin*, Nadezhda Krupskaya writes about it dispassionately: 'The Czechoslovaks were beginning to draw near to Yekaterinburg, where Nicholas II was in prison. On 16 July he and his family were shot by us. The Czechoslovaks were unable to rescue him, they only took Yekaterinburg on 23 July.'

They would have had a whole week to spare (which they could naturally not have known about at the time). Was it that they did not want to take any risks? If they had really been keen to try Nicholas II, then they would have taken him out of the city in those days that remained to them – Military Commissar Goloshchekin and others were able to withdraw perfectly safely. Yet no attempts were made to evacuate the Tsar and his family. Nobody had been planning to move the Romanovs again: they had not been brought to Yekaterinburg with that in mind.

As early as 4 July Goloshchekin had left for Moscow to see Sverdlov and to obtain special instructions regarding Nicholas II and his family. He stayed in the Sverdlovs' flat where he was informed by Beloborodov about the events in Yekaterinburg. He knew that Yurovskii had been made the new commandant in the 'House for a Special Purpose' and that the guard consisting of local soldiers had been replaced by Cheka 'Internationalists', who were always referred to as Latvians. Goloshchekin returned from Moscow to Yekaterinburg on 14 July just as Yurovskii was preparing for the murder.

The meeting of the Yekaterinburg Soviet on the night of 16–17 July 1918, which allegedly decided the fate of the Romanovs, was no more than the usual Party stage-managing, designed to deceive the 'working masses'. Yurovskii recalls: 'On 16 July an encoded telegram was received from Perm containing the order to eliminate the Romanovs ... On the 16 July at 6 o'clock in the evening Filipp G–n [Goloshchekin] issued instructions for the order to be carried out. A vehicle was to arrive at 12 o'clock to take away the corpses.'[26]

Twenty-four hours later at dead of night, three sons of Grand Duke Konstantin Romanov were executed in Alapayevsk on orders from Beloborodov along with two other Romanovs – Grand Duke Sergei Mikhailovich and Grand Duchess Yelizaveta Fyodorovna (the Tsarina's sister). They were then thrown down a disused mine shaft.

According to an eyewitness, Yelizaveta Fyodorovna, a well-known advocate of compassion:

> Just crossed herself and prayed out loud: 'Lord, forgive them, for they know not what they do.' When the bodies were recovered from the shaft three months later, at the edge of the shaft next to Yelizaveta Fyodorovna, the body of one of the other victims was found with a bandaged hand. Battered and bruised and after serious blows to the head, the Grand Duchess had tried even here to lighten the sufferings of one of her fellow men.[27]

A few days earlier, on the night of 13 July, Nicholas II's brother Mikhail met his death in Perm: this 'unauthorized act' of 'proletarian revenge' was carried out by the chairman of the Motovilikha Soviet, Gavriil Myasnikov, with the help of men from the Cheka and the local militia. The avengers showed the Grand Duke false documents and then took him, along with his secretary, Johnson, out to the forest and shot him.

Was it by chance that all the Romanovs who had not left the country by then, happened to be in one area – the Urals? Or that they and their loved ones and retainers were annihilated? Was it by chance that the dynasty of the Romanovs, which had come to the throne in 1613 in the Ipatiev Monastery, should be eliminated in the Ipatiev House? All the evidence points to the fact that the execution had been planned and approved at the centre of government.

What kind of people were they who decided the fate of Nicholas II and the members of the House of Romanov?

Let us start with the 'ringleader', Vladimir Ilyich Lenin, who was always most reluctant to show himself before the masses. His wife Nadezhda Konstantinovna recalls an episode from his youth, for – as Sherlock Holmes might have said – a small detail can be as eloquent as a fly in a glass of milk. While out hunting in Shushenskoye one day, young Lenin had found himself stranded on a piece of dry ground overrun with frightened hares. Making nimble use of an oar, Vladimir had finished off so many of 'our smaller brothers' that the cargo afterwards almost made the bottom of his boat cave in. He complained to his happy wife that he could have brought home more but that there was nowhere to put them. It might have appeared that the banished Marxists – Lenin and Krupskaya – were going hungry in Shushenskoye and lived only from what they managed to hunt, but in fact that was ample sustenance. Each week the young Marxists used to slaughter a sheep and, when they grew tired of mutton, they would buy veal from the local peasants. This seemingly inconsequential story reveals much about Lenin's tenacious character.

Now let us turn to a similar, perhaps more brutal, detail from the young life of another revolutionary. While languishing in Yekaterinburg prison, young Yakov Sverdlov and his Social-Democrat friends used to pass the time by hanging rats or drowning them in slop buckets. As we can see, the inclinations of the future leaders of the proletariat were already well defined.

Further telling details can be found in the lives of other high-profile revolutionaries: Bolshevik Pyotr Yermakov had killed a police agent in 1907 and beheaded him. Bolshevik Gavriil Myasnikov subjected Archbishop Andronik of Perm to long torture and then buried him alive, for which he was interviewed by Felix Dzerzhinsky.

Another of Mikhail Romanov's executioners was the Bolshevik Markov, who had been convicted of murder even before the Revolution and who was up to his elbows in blood soon after Red October. He had the distinction of being awarded a special Soviet pension for services rendered and also, in his turn, recalled what had once been a taboo subject: 'While on an assignment in Moscow in 1918, I went to see Comrade Y.M. Sverdlov and he took me to see Lenin, who asked me about the elimination of Mikhail Romanov and I told him that everything had been above board. Then he said: "That's good, you acted properly."' This was despite the fact that Markov had stolen a silver watch from Mikhail Romanov's secretary, Johnson.

Now we come to Goloshchekin. Historian of the Revolution, V.L. Burtsev, told investigator Nikolai Sokolov about him:

I know Goloshchekin and I recognize him in the photograph you showed me. He was a typical Leninist. In the past he organized many Bolshevik study circles and he took part in all manner of expropriations. Bloodshed would not stop a man like that in his tracks. This character trait of his was particularly striking: a born 'executioner', cruel and with a degenerate streak as well.

To this Doctor Derevenko – who had been the Tsar's physician – added: 'Local Bolshevik Yurovskii would turn pale in the presence of Goloshchekin.'

Yakov Yurovskii was the son of a criminal who had been deported to Siberia. He had initially opened a watchmaker's shop and then a photography studio, where he used to take pictures of the richest citizens of Yekaterinburg. Later, he headed a branch of the Cheka that used to rob people whom his colleagues identified from photographs taken in advance. Stealthy, secretive and cruel, he was very much in Goloshchekin's mould. His brother Leib used to say that Yakov 'loved oppressing people' and Leib's wife, Ele-Leya, considered him 'a despot and exploiter'. After 1919, as a leading member of the Cheka, Yurovskii was living in a grand house in Yekaterinburg with his wife (one of the main party organizers there) and his daughter who had a prominent role in the local Komsomol (the youth division of the Communist Party). Clearly they were a close-knit family. Three more descriptions of him are pertinent: 'an inveterate criminal' (S. Mengulov), 'a cold-blooded executioner' (S. Gibs) and 'the most reliable of communists' (Lenin).

Under the leadership of Commandant Yurovskii, seven corrupt volunteer 'internationalists' from the I Kamyshlovskii Regiment went into action – Andreas Vergazi, Laslo Gorvat (who killed the Tsar's physician, Dr Botkin), Viktor Grinfeld, (who was to win renown later under the name Imre Nad), Emil Fekete, Anselm Fisher, Isidore Edelstein and three guards, who were local residents: Vaganov, Medvedev and Nikulin. Of them, historian S. Naumov wrote:

It is possible to form a picture of the morals of these 'knights of the Revolution' from the numerous factual reports of their drunkenness, thefts of the Tsar's belongings and also their robbing of corpses. By way of 'fee' for their part in the murder of the Romanovs, Medvedev acquired 'a pair of men's socks and a woman's petticoat'. In addition he stole sixty roubles, three silver rings and a number of handkerchiefs.[28]

The morning after the execution of the Imperial family, the looting

Yuròvskii's room was piled high with valuables. He and his comrades chortled away, wallowing in obscenities, having the time of their lives. After trying on the royal uniforms they picked up everything that was for grabs. Later, they set off to Moscow in three railway coaches filled with belongings of the Imperial family: mainly gold and diamonds. All this was shared out between the looters and the commissars' wives fought bitterly over the royal jewels. Some locals also had a look-in: the soldiers of the guard made off with hundreds of items between them. One of the Cheka men, Sakharov, was given a gold ring set with turquoises which had once belonged to Grand Duchess Anastasia by way of a souvenir. Another looter, Didkovskii, gave a pair of boots to a female acquaintance of his. Even Goloshchekin, on his way to Moscow, presented a young Bolshevik by the name of Golubeva, the Party treasurer's wife, with a pair of shoes and a pillow. Golubeva was very proud of this gift and used to refer to her pillow as 'historic'.

A telegram was dispatched to Moscow:

To the Chairman of the Council of People's Commissars, Comrade Lenin, and to the Chairman of the All-Russia Central Executive Committee, Comrade Sverdlov.

From the Presidium of the Regional Soviet of the Workers' and Peasants' Government in Yekaterinburg:

Given that the enemy was drawing closer to Yekaterinburg and the Cheka had discovered a major White Guards' conspiracy aimed at seizing the former Tsar and his family STOP We have the documents STOP In response to the resolution adopted by the Presidium of the Regional Soviet, Nikolai Romanov was shot dead on the night of 16 July STOP His family has been evacuated to a safe place STOP With regard to this we are issuing the following announcement given that counter-revolutionary bandits are now approaching the red capital of the Urals and the possibility that the crowned executioner might have escaped the People's Court BRACKET a conspiracy has been discovered led by White Guards planning to seize the Tsar himself and his family and the compromising documents will be published BRACKET the Presidium of the Regional Soviet implementing the will of the revolutionary people decided to shoot the former Tsar Nikolai Romanov COMMA guilty of countless bloody acts of violence against the Russian people COMMA on the night of 16 July 1918 the sentence was implemented STOP The Romanov family who had been kept under guard with him so as to uphold public order has been evacuated from the city of Yekaterinburg STOP We the Presidium of the Regional Soviet ask your permission to edit and publish this document and the documents concerning the conspiracy and are sending them by special courier to the Council of People's Commissars and the Central Executive Committee and waiting by this apparatus and ask for your urgent reply ...[29]

It may have been a coincidence, but in the text there is a mistake regarding the date. However, the members of the Urals regional Soviet lied when it came to the 'evacuation of the family' of the executed Tsar, deliberately deceiving the population.

The White Guards' so-called 'conspiracy' mentioned in the telegram, as was revealed later, had been concocted by the Cheka people themselves with the help of Pyotr Voikov, a member of the Executive Committee of the Urals Soviet, who had also composed the planted letters from the White Guards to Nicholas II.

On 18 July a meeting of the presidium of the All-Russia Central Executive Committee was held. In Protocol No. 1 it was noted: 'Members listened to information about the shooting of Nikolai Romanov [the telegram from Yekaterinburg]. It was decided after discussion to adopt the following resolution: the All-Russia Central Executive Committee, as represented by its presidium, acknowledges the decision of the Regional Committee as correct ...'[30]

On the same day – as we are told by Gorodetskii and Sharapov – during the meeting of the Council of People's Commissars, Sverdlov came rapidly into the room, bearing a different version of events: 'He took his usual place behind Lenin. When N.A. Semashko completed his exposition of the project for healthcare, Sverdlov leant forward to Lenin and said something to him. Lenin then turned to the assembled gathering with the words: "Comrades, Sverdlov requests your attention for a special announcement."'

Sverdlov began:

I have to tell you that we have just received information from Yekaterinburg. Czechoslovak mutineers and White Guards are on the outskirts of the town. In view of the danger now threatening the town, the former Tsar, Nikolai Romanov, has been shot. The presidium of the All-Russia Executive Committee has decided to approve the actions of the Yekaterinburg Soviet.

After Sverdlov had finished, for a brief minute those sitting in the small hall of the Council for People's Commissars focused their attention on the information he had given them. After listening to the announcement Lenin proposed: 'Let us now turn to the reading of the statutes – article by article – concerning the People's Commissariat for Education.'[31]

On 21 July the press office of the All-Russia Central Executive Committee sent a telegram from Moscow dated 19 July to the Yekaterinburg Regional Soviet:

At the first meeting of the Presidium of the Central Executive Committee of the Soviets held on 18 July, Chairman Sverdlov relayed the direct wire received from the Urals Regional Soviet about the shooting of former Tsar Nikolai Romanov STOP In recent days the red Urals capital Yekaterinburg was under serious threat as Czechoslovak bands drew near STOP At the same time a new counter-revolutionary conspiracy was uncovered aimed at seizing the crowned executioner from Soviet authorities STOP In view of these circumstances the Urals Regional Soviet resolved to shoot Nikolai Romanov and this was effected on 16 July STOP Nikolai's wife and son were sent to a safe place STOP Documents concerning the exposed conspiracy were sent to Moscow by special courier STOP After making the announcement Sverdlov recalled events regarding the transfer of Romanov from Tobolsk to Yekaterinburg when a similar plan of the White Guards aiming to arrange a Romanov escape was discovered STOP Recently there had been plans for trying the former Tsar for all his crimes against the people but events now unfolding prevented us from organizing such a trial STOP The presidium after discussing all the circumstances obliging the Urals Regional Soviet to decide to shoot Romanov resolved that the Central Executive Committee as represented by its presidium would acknowledge the decision of the Urals regional Soviet as correct STOP The chairman then announced that important material was now at the disposal of the Central Executive Committee namely documents of Nikolai Romanov – his diaries which he kept recently and diaries of his wife and children and Romanov's own correspondence STOP Among others are letters from Grigorii Rasputin to Romanov and his family STOP All these materials will be sorted and published in near future STOP Continuation to follow.[32]

Sokolov maintains that this telegram was found in the building of the Urals Regional Soviet. He has pointed out: 'As early as 17 July after 9 o'clock Sverdlov had received another telegram with different contents. It was removed from the Yekaterinburg telegraph office.' It read: 'Moscow, Kremlin: To the Secretary of the Council of People's Commissars Gorbunov with request for confirmed receipt. Tell Sverdlov that the whole family suffered the same fate as its head while officially the family perished while being evacuated. Beloborodov.'

G.Z. Joffe voices doubts as to whether this later telegram was genuine, but admits that it may have been:

'If it were to be admitted that the given telegram was genuine, the lie would have been deliberate,' wrote I. Nepein [as if the deliberate nature of the lie had not already been demonstrated by the first telegram sent to Moscow]. Why was that done? One could suggest one idea behind it. At that time, the time when socialist legality was being established, the shooting of children without a trial or investigation would not have served the interests of the central government. In people's minds there was no sin greater than the murder of innocent children.

This suggestion is a rational one, though it is expressed clumsily. Firstly, what could the children possibly have been tried for? Secondly, what became of the 'establishment of socialist legality' is common knowledge – by the end of 1918 tens of thousands of people had been executed without trial or investigation. Thirdly it was not the shooting of the Tsar's family that was disadvantageous for the central authorities but the specific, grisly circumstances of the shooting.

On 20 July Goloshchekin was the first to announce at the meeting of the Presidium of the Regional Soviet in Yekaterinburg that the Tsar had been shot. On 21 July leaflets about the event appeared in the town. Sokolov concludes: 'The main thing announced in both Moscow and Yekaterinburg was one and the same: the Tsar had been 'executed in accordance with the will of the people' while the lives of his family had been spared.

Sverdlov and Goloshchekin both told the same lie.'

Of these dealings, Pierre Gilliard – tutor to the former Tsar's children – was to write:

> It was the Russian people who had to be deceived, who had to have no knowledge of the events. Yet the murderers were anxious. The agents whom they kept behind in Yekaterinburg to cover up their tracks, kept them informed about the course of the investigation. They kept track of each step in its progress. When they at last realized that the truth would come out and that the whole world would soon learn what had happened, they took fright and tried to shift the responsibility for their wicked deeds onto other people. They then began to accuse the socialist revolutionaries, saying they were guilty of the crime and that they had sought to compromise the Bolsheviks in this way. In September 1919 twenty-eight people were arrested by the Bolsheviks in Perm and tried after being falsely accused of involvement in the murder of the Tsar's family. Five of them were sentenced to death and executed.
>
> This shameless farce testifies once more to the cynicism of those people who had no compunction about sending innocent citizens to death so as not to be held responsible for one of the greatest crimes in history.[33]

In the years that followed the Bolsheviks kept silent about the wickedness perpetrated in Yekaterinburg or tried to shield the central authorities from blame. There was only one occasion when this publicly failed: at a very advanced age Pyotr Yermakov blurted out at a meeting of Young Pioneers that the shooting of the Tsar was a personal directive from Lenin.[34]

However, other examples of authoritative testimony indicating the direct involvement of Lenin and Sverdlov in the executions do exist.

Trotsky recalled in his *Diary in Exile*:

> I arrived in Moscow from the front after the fall of Yekaterinburg. When talking to Sverdlov, I asked: 'Where is the Tsar now?' – 'Everything's over with him.' – 'And where's the family?' – 'The family suffered the same fate.' – 'All of them?' I asked in astonishment. – 'All of them,' replied Sverdlov. – 'Who took the decision?' – 'We took the decision here. Lenin felt that no live figurehead should remain, particularly in our difficult conditions.'[35]

Not that this dismayed Trotsky, who went on to write:

> In general the decision had been not only expedient but even essential. The execution of the Tsar's family was not simply in order to frighten and terrify the enemy and deprive him of hope. It was also to shake up our own ranks and make clear to them that in the future it would be a question of total victory or total collapse. It is possible that among Party members from the intelligentsia there probably were doubts and head-shaking, but the worker and peasant masses did not doubt for a minute: they would not have understood any other decision and would not have accepted one. Lenin sensed this clearly: the ability to think and feel for the masses and with the masses was well developed in his case, particularly at great turning points in history.[36]

Indeed, writing in 1920, Trotsky came to believe that: Leninism is genuine freedom from formal prejudices, from moralizing doctrinaire attitudes and in general from all types of conservative ideas aimed at holding back the will for revolutionary action.'[37]

Stalin's former secretary, Bazhanov, who fled abroad, was later to share what he knew about the execution:

> Perhaps the city of Yekaterinburg continues to bear the name Sverdlov, because it was in that city that the Tsar's family was killed in July 1918 and part of the responsibility for that murder lay with Yakov Sverdlov, the official leading representative of the Soviet government there, who – acting on instructions

from Lenin – shrewdly dissociated himself from any official responsibility and informed the local Bolshevik authorities in the Urals that he was leaving them to decide what the fate of the Tsar's family should be.[38]

Contemporaries adopted varying views on the shooting. Patriarch Tikhon of Moscow and All Russia said during one of his sermons:

> Yet we, to our great sadness and shame, lived to see the day when the violation of God's commandments was not only not regarded as a sin, but was justified as something lawful. In recent days a terrible act took place: our Sovereign, Nikolai Alexandrovich, was shot. Obeying the teaching of the word of God, we should condemn this act, otherwise the blood of the executed man will fall on us as well and not only on those who committed this act – even if we are called counter-revolutionaries for doing this or have to languish in prison or face the firing squad. We are ready to suffer all this, hoping that the words of Our Saviour might apply to us as well: 'Blessed are they that hear the word of God, and keep it.'[39]

Likewise, Nikolai Bukharin wrote in caustic tones in his 'Angry Notes' about the executed children of the Tsar: 'who in their day were shot up a little – they had outlived their usefulness.'[40]

After he had visited the cellar in the Ipatiev House, poet Vladimir Mayakovsky wrote the following lines (which were not printed until 1956):

> Ask and let a coin be tossed:
> Should a human life be lost?
> I don't intend to count the cost
> Straightaway let two be tossed.
> No executions! I vote 'No!'
> History's course we have now turned,
> The past has all been swept away.
> Mankind and communists have learned
> To thirst for blood is not the way.

Mayakovsky clearly felt the horror of the Tsar's fate.

It might have seemed that everything had turned out well for Goloshchekin and his accomplices. However, M.K. Diterichs describes the following scene:

> On 19 July, in the morning, Yermakov and friends were conducting the most open of conversations in the Communist Club. They did not need to hide anything from each other or be embarrassed by anyone. They went over the names of those who had been killed, noting that valuables had been sewn into the belts of their clothes and commented that 'appearance was of no concern to dead people'. Someone inquired: 'How were those killed dressed?' Partin replied: 'They all had underwear on.' Kostourov complained: 'We've had to deal with all that for two days in a row. Yesterday we buried them, today we reburied them'.[41]

It turned out that there would be still more work to do. Below there follows an extract from an article by Igor Nepein:

> Pyotr Yermakov, the Military Commissar from Verkhneisetsk, was summoned not for the shooting but to destroy the corpses. Only someone with detailed knowledge of the woods in the environs of the city could have done that. Yurovskii was not familiar with them, but Yermakov was and he suggested a place: not far from the village of Koptyaki, in the remote Four Brothers copse to the west of the road, there was an old disused mine with a single open shaft. Traffic was not allowed along the Koptyaki road from 17 to 19 July.
>
> On 17 July, an employee of the Commissariat for Supplies appeared in the chemist's shop 'Russian Company' in Yekaterinburg on behalf of Commissar Voikov and demanded from the shopkeeper 'without delay or excuses' that he provide him with forty litres of sulphuric acid. At the same time between 120 and 135 litres of petrol were also delivered to the mine, which had already been cordoned off.[42]

And so the bodies were destroyed.

It is time to turn attention to one more figure: Pyotr Lazarevich Voikov. He was one of those who had travelled with Lenin in a sealed train from Switzerland to Russia through the territory of Kaiser Wilhelm's Germany.

Later he worked as the Soviet ambassador in Warsaw for three years. He was killed in 1927 by a young Russian émigré, Boris Koverda. Voikov was a significant participant in the massacre, organizing the destruction of the corpses with sulphuric acid. Details about him are provided by a member of the Urals Executive Committee, a former Austrian prisoner of war, I.P. Meier:

> When we went in [to the cellar] Voikov was busy inspecting the shot bodies to check whether anyone was still alive. He turned each one of them over face upwards. He took the gold bracelets belonging to the Tsarina, which she had been wearing till the bitter end …

Was he a looter? Or did he collect the valuables together in the single pile of 'diamonds' (weighing about 8 kilos) which Yurovskii, as he writes, took to Moscow? The answer may never be known, however, in 1927 Voikov was accustomed to wear a ring with a shimmering ruby, which he himself acknowledged as having been taken from one of the victims.

Meanwhile, the investigation into the murders revealed that at the bottom of the shaft into which the bodies had been thrown, a dismembered finger had been found. Nepein continues his story as follows:

> Under cover of darkness on 17 July, the bodies of the persons who had been shot in the Ipatiev House were brought to Four Brothers' copse and thrown down an open mineshaft. That was all at the first instance.
>
> When Goloshchekin learnt about this on the morning of 17 July, he flew into a rage. He felt the task was unfinished. The corpses had only been buried, but not destroyed and they could easily be appropriated by the White Guards, who were already approaching the city. That was when people started rushing out for petrol, sulphuric acid and spirit.
>
> All that came in useful on 18 July when Goloshchekin gave orders for the bodies to be destroyed under his personal supervision, so that he could see what was going on. In the opinion of investigator Sokolov, General Diterichs and the British journalist Wilton, that was how the situation appeared. The bodies of the executed victims were dragged out of the

mineshaft and placed on a clayey area in front of it. This is where the petrol, sulphuric acid and spirit were brought. Goloshchekin gave orders for the members of the Tsar's family to be decapitated. The pieces of neck-bands and neck-chains found by the investigators bear traces of cuts which could easily have been the result of decapitation using a sharp or cutting tool. Finally, although teeth take longest of all to burn, not a single tooth was found in the clothes, on the ground or in the earth infill of the shaft. According to the investigation commission, the heads of the Tsar and the members of his family were stored in spirit, packed into wooden crates and taken by Goloshchekin to Moscow as undeniable proof of what had been done.

Then work started on the main task – the destruction of the corpses. They were cut into pieces with axes. (Burnt bones and valuables with traces of the cut and shattered precious stones were found in the course of the investigation). Petrol and sulphuric acid was poured over the remains and then they were burnt.

After that Goloshchekin left Yekaterinburg in a luxury railway coach late on the evening of 19 July and travelled straight to Moscow. He took three heavy crates with him.[43]

The crates were made of planks and tied round with rope. Goloshchekin told his curious fellow travellers that they contained models of shells for the Putilov factory. However, when they arrived in Moscow he took the crates straight to the Kremlin, to Sverdlov's flat.

Historians inside the Soviet Union, like those from abroad, focus on the nature of Nicholas II's murder. I.R. Shafarevich, for example, was to write:

This was not a question of claimants to the throne removing their predecessors as previously – in the case of the murder of Peter III or Paul I. Nicholas II was shot while Tsar: this ritual act drew a line under many centuries of Russian history, so that it can only be compared with the execution of Charles I in England or that of Louis XVI in France.[44]

In August 1981 at a Congress of Russian Orthodox youth in San Francisco, Bishop Nektary of Seattle considered the possible mystical implications of the murder:

> The Emperor is anointed of God. He is the sacramental image, the carrier of the special power of the grace of the Holy Spirit. This divine power, which acts through the anointing by God, restrained evil, the 'mystery of iniquity'.
>
> The Holy Apostle Paul, in the Second Epistle to [the] Thessalonians, writes: 'The mystery of iniquity is already in action but is not fulfilled up to today, until there will be taken away from the midst he who restraineth' (II Thes. 2:7).
>
> The devil already, it seems, had for a long time been trying to manifest antichrist but could not because of the divine grace fully active though the anointing by God: 'he who restraineth' did not give him such a possibility.
>
> In order for the 'mystery of iniquity' to receive freedom of action, it was necessary to take from the midst the 'restraining one', which precisely occurred by the allowance of God because of the sins of the Russian people.
>
> Thus occurred the frightful deed – regicide.
>
> The Emperor, the Anointed of God, the Protector of the Orthodox Church, the Head of the Orthodox Government was killed. 'He who restraineth' was killed. And from that moment the 'mystery of iniquity' received freedom; and we are all witnesses to the unrestrained reign and propagation of evil in the whole world.
>
> From what we have said above, it is absolutely clear that the evil deed was ritualistic, and not a political killing.

It was not until the middle of the 1920s that the Bolsheviks acknowledged that the whole of the Tsar's family had been killed with him.

There is no evidence that the executioners were plagued by their consciences. On the contrary, they boasted and took pride in their revolutionary exploit. In 1927 Yurovskii and his assistant Nikulin even attempted to organize a celebration to mark the tenth anniversary of the execution of the Romanovs. The murderers donated to the Museum of the Revolution the tools used for the execution of the former Tsar and his family. They also suggested that a collection of documents and reminiscences of those taking part in the shooting should be published. However, an oral reply from Stalin was conveyed to Goloshchekin via an official from OGPU (Joint State Political Directorate): 'Do not print anything. In general keep quiet.'[45] As we have seen, this wise advice kept Soviet historians of the Party from telling the truth for over sixty years.

The Soviet regime did everything possible to wipe from Russia's memory the image of the last Tsar – the holy martyr sacrificed for his people and his faith – until it itself disappeared, like an evil spirit.

In August 2000 the Bishops' Council of the Russian Orthodox Church glorified the Tsar and his family as martyrs in the host of Russian New Martyrs and Disciples: Emperor Nicholas II, Empress Alexandra, their son and heir Alexei and their daughters Grand Duchesses Olga, Tatyana, Maria and Anastasia.

In June 1930 when already in Alma-Ata, Goloshchekin delivered a report from the Area Committee at the VII All-Kazakhstan Conference. By that time the first wave of collectivization had already caused popular uprisings throughout Kazakhstan which the First Secretary condemned as 'anti-Soviet actions on a mass scale':

> Typically ... these were led exclusively by semi-feudal elements, *ishans* [leaders of Muslim communities] and the clergy. The provocative behaviour through which they influenced the rural population consisted in their announcing that Soviet power had been overthrown by the British, the Poles and the Chinese and that the state was now headed by the son of Nicholas II with two adjutants – Kerensky and Trotsky.

According to the shorthand report, laughter broke out in the hall. If there was anyone among those present it was Goloshchekin himself who knew what fate had been meted out to the Tsar and his family. Yet, did the delegates at the conference know that Goloshchekin had been one of the main organizers of the killing of the Tsar and his family?

Recently I put that question to Kazakh writer Galym Khakimovich Akhmedov, who had been present at that gathering.

'Of course we knew, how could we not have done?' he replied. 'People had known right from the moment when he appeared here in Kazakhstan.'

❖

IV. The Sovietization of Turkestan

Goloshchekin's arrival in Kazakhstan and his immediate appointment to the top position of power has never been fully explored by historians. *Essays on the History of the Communist Party of Kazakhstan* (1963), for example, devotes but a single sentence to the event: 'The Central Committee sent a group of leading Party workers and Soviet officials to Kazakhstan headed by the old-guard Bolshevik and well-known Party figure, F.I. Goloshchekin, who was elected as First Secretary by the Party's Area Committee.' This does not tell us where or when Goloshchekin was elected as First Secretary, when he was sent to Kazakhstan, or indeed who elected him.

A collection of articles entitled *Under the Banner of Lenin's Ideas* also devotes the briefest of passages to the subject: 'In the report from the Area Committee of the RCP (B) delivered by the old-guard Bolshevik, F.I. Goloshchekin, who had been sent by the Central Committee of the RCP (B) to work in Kazakhstan, attention was drawn.'

In fact nobody had elected Goloshchekin as First Secretary – certainly not the communists of Kazakhstan; as was common in those times, he had been assigned to the post. The Orgburo (Organizational Department) of the Central Committee of the RCP (B) had, as early as 1923: 'sent out more than 10,000 people to posts in the remote regions of the country of which around half were prominent ones. This meant that Party leaders started to gain experience not in the provinces or in the midst of major political events, but within the Party apparatus.'[1]

Stalin placed Lazar Kaganovich in charge of the Organizational Department – a man who a few years later would coordinate the collectivization of agriculture. This new 'forge for cadres' which – as was common knowledge – decided everything, now began to operate. Its fundamental principle, formulated by Stalin at the XII Congress of the RCP (B), was the following: 'Party workers should be selected in such a way as to ensure that people in post should be those capable of implementing directives, able to understand them and to accept them as something close to their heart and capable of putting them into practice.'

In two years Kaganovich's department made 8,761 appointments of which 1,222 were to Party organizations. V. Kostikov notes that: 'By 1927 Stalin already had his own loyal *nomenklatura*. Directives could now be sent out without any obstacles in their way. From start to finish they would be obediently executed.'[2] The man to lead this work in Kazakhstan would arrive in the autumn of 1925. Party democracy came into its own a little later – in December of that year, at the Fifth All-Kazakhstan Conference of the RCP (B), Goloshchekin was obediently elected by the local communists.

Had Goloshchekin ever set foot before in the land of the Kazakhs he had been sent to lead? There is no record of any previous visit. When appointing people to work in the outlying regions, the Bolsheviks did not attach much importance to knowledge of local conditions, language and so on. Far more important was the length of time the appointee had been in the Party, as well as his revolutionary experience and training: in these respects Goloshchekin's credentials were more than adequate. He had been just about everywhere; important missions for the Central Committee had taken him the length and breadth of the country, to the Urals, Bashkiria, the Volga region and even to Turkestan.

Of the situation in Turkestan, historian V.P. Nikolaeva writes:

> The October Revolution liberated the working people of Turkestan from ethnic and social oppression, opening up for them the great path of socialist construction. When it came to the liquidation of the system of ethnic-colonial oppression, however, the difficult consequences of the long years of the colonial policy of the tsarist regime and of the Russian imperialist bourgeoisie in Turkestan were not removed straightaway.[3]

The 'Great Path' was initially built over the bones of those who fell victim to the Civil War, economic collapse and hunger. Turkestan found itself cut off from Russia by the Urals, Aktyubinsk, Trans-Caspian, Fergana and Semirechensk fronts. In addition, during the decade before the First World War there was a marked increase in the cultivation of cotton plantations in areas which had been previously given over to grain – as a result the Republic of Turkestan was no longer able to feed itself. Worse was still to come: the year 1917, according to the Eastern Calendar, was the Year of the Snake – the harbinger of disaster – and the lands fell victim to drought. Grass burned and the harvest failed. There followed a long hard winter.

At a meeting of the Turkestan Central Executive Committee in November 1918, Turar Ryskulov, who had been appointed head of the Commission for Combating Hunger, pointed out:

> The result of this was that hunger reigned supreme, followed, without fail, by disease. Whole families were dying. According to data sent in from the provinces, the number of people dying of hunger and disease has reached as much as 25 or 50 per cent depending on the part of the country. Only a tenth of livestock has survived.[4]

Turkestan then incorporated the southern part of present-day Kazakhstan – the Semirechensk and Syr-Darya regions. The Kirgiz nomads who had formerly populated those areas suffered worst of all. In the town of Aulie-Ata and the nearby *kishlaks* (villages in the plains) human corpses had not been cleared away after emaciated poor peasants had wandered through the steppe looking for something to eat. Those that survived were sent back to their home district, where prosperous relatives were obliged to take in the hungry and feed them under strict supervision by the *aul* and district commissars. Food depots were set up but they were only able to feed a small proportion of those who needed help.

S. Khodzhaev, Turkestan's Commissar for Health, reported in October 1918:

> From the information I have at my disposal it is clear that almost half the Kirgiz population is going hungry and there is a comparatively small number of starving people among the settled population. The Kirgiz, especially in the districts a long way from the towns, were unable to sow their fields in the summer because they had no seedcorn, while those Kirgiz engaged solely in animal husbandry ate their livestock. In the steppe areas only very few Kirgiz families will be able to manage till the summer of next year without help with food.[5]

The catastrophe was growing. At the end of 1918 around a million people were starving. Money was necessary to avoid catastrophe, at least forty million roubles, as Ryskulov pointed out at the meeting of the Central Executive Committee of the Turkestan Republic on 13 December of that year.

On 30 December the Turkestan Central Executive Committee gave instructions to all Soviets of Deputies to undertake measures to combat hunger. The famine and disease resulting mainly from social upheaval and human action was referred to as a 'natural disaster'. The Turkestan CEC appealed to all organizations in the republic to put an end to this famine.

Nothing like this had ever happened in these fertile lands and the public had no idea of the scale of the problem. In this respect the argument between Ryskulov and a certain G. Agarevskii in Tashkent's *Our Newspaper* in 1918 is most revealing, shedding light on prevalent attitudes. The debate took place over a number of articles. In an article published in Issue No. 265 and addressed 'To the Kirgiz Intelligentsia' Agarevskii wrote:

From the history of economics it is well known that all so-called pastoral or nomadic peoples were poor and carefree. Indeed, it could not have been otherwise: people frequently on the move cannot take large numbers of possessions with them and if the saying 'Two moves are as bad as a fire' has any truth in it, we need to recall that the lives of nomads involve countless moves from place to place all the time, moves in which many things are damaged, broken or abandoned. This means that nomads simply do not have the chance to amass material wealth and we know that a people without economic power will not have a heritage of non-material culture either, no chance to create science and art. Nomads are never in a position to compete with settled populations and it can be said with a good deal of confidence that such people are bound to be living in a state of economic dependence or economic slavery in relation to the settled population and you know full well that economic dependence leads to political dependence. Recently it was noted in newspapers that there are more Kirgiz in the Syr-Darya region than all the other ethnic groups put together, but to whom does all the wealth belong? Without doubt to the settled population.

The nomads have ideas of their own which a settled person cannot possibly share: among them human life has little value – if the relatives of a murderer pay compensation to the family of the murder victim that will be an end to it. Stealing livestock or abducting girls is seen as daring and brave. Naturally what is acquired in this way is little valued – easy come, easy go: what can impoverish the victim does not make the thief's fortune. Naturally, given his simple requirements, the nomad will make do, except in the case of economic or political upheavals – as long as there is plenty of pastureland, wide open spaces all around him, light, sun, warmth and he only has to cope with short winters and extremely rare epidemics and so on. Last year and this one have shown what a nomad's love for carefree roaming can cost him: people are dying from hunger and disease, while his animals – his only source of wealth – are perishing from lack of food.

So I ask myself: what has the Kirgiz intelligentsia been doing up till now? Writing petitions, sending out and receiving official letters. Why did you not call upon the Kirgiz people to opt for a settled way of life or at least for a more rational way of keeping their animals? You cannot blame the tsarist regime, because its laws had encouraged nomads to adopt a settled way of life: it was enough for a nomad to start planting, sowing or building on any plot of unoccupied land and then that plot, in accordance with the law and the nomad's wishes, would become his. When nomads began to argue about whether they should continue to wander or settle down, when the voice of reason needed to be heard, where were you all? Were you in offices, actively interceding on their behalf? Finally, where were you last year, when the consequences of the carefree nomadic life were clear for all to see? Did your angry letters ring out in the newspapers? Did you write a single appeal to the public or to the government for help? It is only now that you are at last trying to do something and, evidently, only as regards limited forms of direct assistance for the hungry, such as opening canteens or procuring grain. You are, of course, better informed about the life of the nomads than I am, but allow me to ask you why, after the Turkestan Central Executive Committee has provided money and put arrangements in place, you are just sitting around doing nothing? If you were planning to wage a wide campaign, why have you not called in specialists in farming and economics, of both the practical and theoretical variety and worked out with them an agricultural plan?

It is time, Comrades, to come to grips with the situation and fast.

Your simple people, with its patriarchal way of life, deserves more attention than has been devoted to it in the past.

From newspaper reports I have learnt that Ryskulov has suggested that, in addition to seeking help from government funds, people should turn directly to members of the public for support. In response to this appeal I have donated, in all sincerity, 500 roubles from my own meagre funds to the people exhausted by hardship. I feel sure that the public will respond to your appeal, Comrade Ryskulov, and will provide this help in money or manpower, as best they can.[6]

A few days later, in Issue No. 276 of the same newspaper, Turar Ryskulov sent a reply to Agarevskii entitled 'On the Question of Famine':

Without writing at length I should like to say first and foremost that Citizen Agarevskii's letter has been written too late. An appeal like that should have been made two years ago, when some faint indications of hunger out in the steppes were first being observed, and not when this natural calamity has assumed an enormous scale.

If the author of that letter sees himself as entitled to accuse the Kirgiz intelligentsia and to point out their past mistakes, the fact that their angry letters did not 'ring out' in the newspapers and that they did not call upon the public and government for help, before replying to all of that, I would ask you, Citizen Agarevskii, where were you and all the 'leading members of the intelligentsia'? Why were you not writing angry letters to the newspapers and making no mention, even once, of the imminent disaster? You had witnessed the horrors of famine last year, but you kept your careful distance from the hungry, fearing infection.

Admittedly there were isolated instances in your account when some sympathy came to the fore, but this was superficial 'philanthropy' instead of a real rescue effort and it would have been more likely to send the stricken to their graves.

There are no grounds for accusing the Kirgiz intelligentsia, if only for the fact that it was tiny and therefore unable to influence the many millions of the general population, among whom that intelligentsia would have been termed 'semi-Muslim' and would not have been trusted at all. Admittedly attitudes towards that intelligentsia have changed but, at the same time, their fellow countrymen could have been galvanized into action not so much through words as through something else. There are also no grounds for accusing the Kirgiz intelligentsia of forgetting the needs of their people and doing the rounds of administrative offices, 'interceding on their behalf'. Surely you (the Russian intelligentsia) were behaving in a similar way in Turkestan? Why did you not try to raise the educational level of the native population throughout a whole half century? You had a sacred duty to draw attention to the poverty and oppression, which reigned throughout the Muslim world, instead of extolling the 'poetry of the East', where there was none.

In the letter from Citizen Agarevskii there are occasional instances of a complete failure to understand certain phenomena in the life of nomads: for instance, when justifying the former government and expressing astonishment as to why the Kirgiz did not adopt a settled mode of life he writes: 'You cannot blame the tsarist regime because its laws had encouraged nomads to adopt a settled way of life'. Surely Citizen Agarevskii is aware that those laws gave wide opportunities to various district elders and *bais* to oppress the Kirgiz poor and to favour the *bais*, who had no desire to 'stay put', to abandon their *kumys* [fermented mare's milk] and their summer pastures in the mountains. If that same old regime had defended the poor against the *bais*, given them good land wrested from the rich who had seized their lands and equipped them with weapons, we would have seen the Kirgiz duly settled long ago.

Another typical passage in the letter is where its author asks: 'Why, after the Turkestan Central Executive Committee has provided money and put arrangements in place, are you just sitting around doing nothing?'

That is what we are hearing from all those who have not devoted much thought to the famine and who, thanks to their lack of understanding of all the difficulties involved, conclude that the problem of hunger has gone away now that some bodies have been set up to bring help to the hungry. I would say, however, that they should remember and not shrink away from the hungry, regarding them as the lowest scum of society and then perhaps we might be able to banish hunger. We should not need to go begging to the prosperous. They themselves must help and indeed are morally obliged to do so.

While refraining from expression of any further criticism, but as the person leading the drive to combat hunger, I cannot help but welcome the sympathy for the hungry expressed by Citizen Agarevskii and his donation of 500 roubles along with his encouragement of the local intelligentsia for their involvement 'better late than never'. I hope that all those of a humane disposition will follow his example. This applies in particular to the prosperous section of the population in Turkestan, which has finally abandoned its criminal indifference to the suffering poor on the brink of death.[7]

The public has often been viewed as self-absorbed and blind – were the Party and Soviet leaders in the Republic of Turkestan just as bad? As Ryskulov had pointed out, the leading 'European' officials were still underestimating the role and importance of the local population during the Revolution:

> Comrade Tobolin, for instance, declared outright at one of the meetings of the Turkestan Central Executive Committee that the Kirgiz, for example, being economically weak from the Marxist point of view, were bound to die out whatever happened. For that reason, it was more important for the Revolution to spend funds on better support for those fighting in the Civil War rather than on combating hunger (that goal could not be achieved anyway).[8]

As we see, the local Marxists – 'deserving leaders of the October coup in Turkestan' – were not too concerned about the poorest masses, in whose name they had allegedly brought down the former regime before directing them towards 'the Great Path of socialist construction'.

In that same year of 1918, railway workers rose up in Ashkhabad rallying with slogans which read: 'For Soviet power, but against certain worthless commissars!', 'For Soviet power but without the Bolsheviks!'

That very same Tobolin, in the chair at the First Congress of Soviet Deputies from Turkestan, shouted: 'It is not a delegation but rather artillery that needs to be sent there, so that not a single hair from the head of a counter-revolutionary remains.'[9]

On 12 February 1919 *Our Newspaper* published more of Ryskulov's words in a column entitled 'About the Starving'; by this time the situation was critical and a million starving people had already been registered, while far more still remained unregistered: 'Comrade Ryskulov notes that there has been an unsympathetic response to the drive to combat hunger from local executive committees.' He had suggested that a decree be brought in to tax the prosperous classes, regardless of their ethnic origin, but that 'Comrade Kazakov had refused categorically to tax them … so as to avoid acquiring another enemy. The Supreme Revolutionary Council and the Central Executive Committee agreed with Kazakov.'[10]

In March 1919 Ryskulov delivered a speech at the VII Emergency Congress of the Soviets from the central commission for combating hunger in Turkestan. He reported that among the 970,000 registered hunger victims three quarters were Kirgiz nomads – only a quarter were from the settled population – and in total nearly two million were suffering from malnutrition. After all their livestock had been slaughtered:

> the wretched nomads had hurried to nearby centres of population hoping to find charity or the chance of some kind of work, so as to eke out an existence. Others had continued to lead their nomadic lives, eating anything they could lay their hands on – green leaves from bushes, tortoises, green grass, clover, bitter roots of plants and other substitutes for food, which were without doubt impossible to digest and dangerous for human consumption (such as crushed cotton seeds). The tragic situation of the nomadic poor sunk to its lowest depths after cases were reported of their having actually eaten human flesh and, in their desperation, fought over sacks full of human flesh. Cases of hungry parents selling their own small children as slaves to the *bais* became a horrific commonplace and was soon widespread.[11]

'Proletarian power' had granted the impoverished peasants five million roubles, although as early as the end of 1918 Ryskulov had asked for at least forty million. Five million was not enough. According to the data collected by the commission a third of the starving population actually died. Ryskulov accused the Area Food Directorate of being more concerned with supplying the army and those institutions who issued demands 'with clenched fists':

> If the starving proletariat had been able to turn to the same Central Executive Committee or the same Food Directorate and insist on their rights – also with clenched fists – the ensuing picture would be very different. The starving proletariat, however, in particular those born and bred in the region, were dying and unable to insist on their rights. The number of dead was on an enormous scale. It can be said that those who died saved the situation or that they even saved the Soviet regime, since, if those millions of the starving had also come along with their clenched fists and demanded their share, they would not have left a stone standing and would have overturned everything. Yet those elements were unaware of their own potential strength, because they were not organized. That is why we are obliged to admit that although we did not feed them, they saved the overall situation. The Area Food Directorate declared that they could not give them anything. Yet to build Soviet power on the bones of the local proletariat, as certain people would have us do, is wrong.[12]

In the meantime another blow was dealt to the local population through the introduction of the grain monopoly followed by the dictatorial banning of local bazaars and the requisitioning of agricultural produce, involving the seizure of grain down to the last handful.

In the spring of 1919 the Turkestan Central Executive Committee sent two specially authorized officials to the Fergana region to deal 'exclusively with Kirgiz matters'. In Andizhan they were met with the following sight: Party and Soviet officials were riding out in horse-drawn carriages, while peasants harnessed themselves instead of horses to plough their land. Telegraphs were sent from Dzhalal Abad, meanwhile, to say that the Kirgiz were giving them a happy welcome and thanking the Soviet regime for the attention finally being shown to them: 'They are complaining that the last three years in the history of the proletarian revolution have caused economic and spiritual devastation.'[13]

Sokolov, Chairman of Turkestan's Council of People's Commissars, also paid a visit to the Fergana region. He personally confirmed the shocking situation:

> The Muslims are being robbed of everything. They are not just being robbed but killed as well. Instead of protecting them, our soldiers are robbing and killing. In the *kishlaks* the people have been terrorized and are fleeing. Gangs of brigands are on the increase. Perhaps some people are insisting that it is not the Party but the Red Army which is responsible for all the violence. Yet it is the Party that calls the tune. The Muslim proletariat is asking Russians for help, but the latter reply that they don't trust the Muslims. The Muslims are being persecuted, even killed. The Muslim poor are having to look on, while our detachments destroy their property indiscriminately, killing their wives and children as they go. How can the Muslim nationalists ever feel friendly towards us, when all they see from us is outrage and insults? We are turning them into nationalists.[14]

In June 1919 the III Area Congress of the Turkestan Communist Party was held. One of the delegates, a Muslim peasant, addressed the meeting as follows: 'We, the Muslim poor, who were treated like animals under Nicholas the Bloody, are now treated as such by the new proletarian government. Or even worse, although we did not oppose Soviet power …'[15] A response echoing these sentiments came from Zhusupbek Aimautov in his book, *The Psychology of Choosing a Profession* (1935), which was published in the Kazakh language at the Moscow printing works of the Council of Nationalities: 'War, revolution, robbery, hunger, freedom for national minorities, autonomy – all these are things which the Kazakh and Kirgiz peoples could not even have dreamt of, but they have now cast them into the embrace of poverty and endless hardship.'[16]

How many victims were carried off by that famine, which Ryskulov believed was unprecedented? There are no precise figures. He stated in March 1919 that the number of dead was enormous, yet it was not until the end of that year that the disaster was brought under control. In the preface to his book *The Revolution and the Indigenous Population of Turkestan*, written several years later, Ryskulov notes that the organization of the emergency commissions for combating hunger, using dictatorial powers, 'saved hundreds and thousands of proletarians and the poor (according to statistical data almost 100,000 people).'[17] A million lives were saved but at least two million people had been starving, leaving a million dead. Mustafa Chokaev cites a broadly similar figure in his book *Turkestan under the Rule of the Soviets* (published in Paris, 1935). According to Soviet sources 1,114,000 people perished.

Ryskulov considered that hunger was one of the main reasons for the appearance of the *basmachi* (anti-Soviet movement) in Turkestan. The famine had not been the result of natural disasters but had stemmed from political and economic factors. Until the time of revolutionary unrest, there had been no *basmachi* movement in those parts. The punitive activities of the new regime, its heavy-handed and merciless atheism and economic plundering had inevitably given rise to opposition.

In view of the incessant looting and lawlessness brought about by the opposition, by 9 July 1918 the Fergana region had been placed under martial law. In 1922 according to K. Atabaev, chairman of Turkestan's Council of People's Commissars, not only *basmachi* opposition (for that read banditry) had occurred, but a 'definite popular uprising'. On 18 July 1922 when reporting to the fifth meeting of the Fourth Plenary Session of the Turkestan Central Executive Committee in Tashkent, Atabaev explained the emergence of the *basmachi* movement:

Railway workers brought Soviet power to Fergana and it took them a long time to form close ties with the local population. At the very time when Soviet power was being established in Fergana, a group from the Muslim intelligentsia together with *ulems* [theologians and lawmakers] convened a congress of Muslim warriors and peasants. At that congress a government for an autonomous Turkestan was elected. It declared an amnesty for all looters and thieves, appealing to them to join the ranks of a national army which was being organized in Fergana. Among others, Irgash was invited to this congress – a former thief and looter, who had been sentenced to hard labour by the tsarist government and who had returned to his homeland after the Revolution. He was appointed *kurbashi* – head of the defence of the city of Kokand.

A special detachment was dispatched by the Soviet authorities to Kokand to suppress this gang. It was led by Comrade Perfiliev, who proceeded to lay siege to the city. The autonomous government issued a declaration inviting all Muslims to join the ranks of the national army to defend the religion of Islam, national freedom and the autonomous government. People from the nearby *kishlaks* responded to the call and started arriving in Kokand with hoes, axes, hunting rifles and so on. Fighting went on for three days. During that time the autonomous government disappeared and Irgash likewise. By the time Kokand was taken the only people remaining in the city were those who had come in from the *kishlaks* to help and it was those people who suffered the most.

Our detachment consisted exclusively of *dashnaks* [members of the Armenian National Party known as 'Dashnaktsu-tyun'], who had quickly taken stock of the situation and decided to make money out of it. Most of the violence took place in the trading quarter. All the local traders were shot and their property was taken away to warehouses and railway carriages used for storage: what remained was burned. The population was subjected to violent reprisals and looting and the city was destroyed.

After seeing such cruel reprisals, the population of Fergana started believing what the supporters of autonomy had been telling them, namely that the Bolsheviks really were robbers and bandits, that they did not believe in anything and were against religion and against God.

Our slogan 'Away with the old world! Away with the bourgeoisie!' was put into practice in approximately the following way. 'Old world' was taken to mean all the mosques and madrasas, which were closed down; Muslim judges and *ulems* were arrested, while the struggle against religious prejudices found expression in the burning of the Muslims' holy book, the Koran, in the city of Margelan by representatives of the Soviet authorities. The Friday mosque in Andizhan was turned into a barracks for Muslim detachments.

Our detachments attacked mosques and threw bombs at praying *ishans* [Muslim community leaders] and *ulems*. As a result the whole class of *ulems* and *ishans* went over to the *basmachi*.

The local *bais* were viewed like the bourgeoisie in Europe: they were arrested and sent to prison and only released on payment of special contributions. Here it should be noted that the attempt on Lenin's life also led to repressive measures against the *bais* in Fergana. They were being arrested and taunted with shouts of 'You rogues even tried to kill Lenin!' That was how the class struggle was played out.

We also introduced a grain monopoly and requisitioning of food: the peasants working the land and craftsmen, in a word the whole population, rose up against the Soviet regime and Soviet practices and went over to the *basmachi*, which lent political significance to what had once been just a gang of bandits.

Over the course of four years we failed to eliminate that movement, regardless of the approaches we used. When the Soviet government found itself confronted by this uprising, which was constantly growing stronger, it consolidated its position in the towns and used these as their bases in the struggle against the *basmachi*.

Initially our Red Army units were not coordinated under a single line of command and each town acted independently against the *basmachi*. The Red Army detachments being used consisted mainly of *dashnaks*, who had no links with the local population and were hostile to it, because Armenians going about their ordinary lives used to compete as traders against the local population in their efforts to earn their livelihood. At one time we were planning to eliminate the *basmachi* with fire and the sword. To that end all sizeable *kishlaks* 'infected by *basmachi* ideas' were subjected to merciless destruction, which of course made the population more and more antagonistic to Soviet rule. Nor did the general occupation of the whole of the Fergana region improve relations.

This situation had a very bad influence on the mood of our Red Army soldiers and in anger born of despair they often massacred completely peaceful communities.

As a result of all this, both those in command and the ordinary soldiers of the Red Army started to believe that the whole population consisted of *basmachi*.

It was from this point of view that punitive policies were promoted. For a fairly long time hostage-taking became common practice. So many hostages were soon being taken that there was nowhere left in the whole of Fergana, where they could be held in isolation.[18]

It was in the midst of this situation that Goloshchekin arrived in Turkestan. He was sent by the Central Executive Committee as part of a commission to assess the situation in Turkestan; this was with Eliava (the chairman), Frunze, Kuibyshev, Bokii and Rudzutaks. Their arrival was made possible by the closing of the Orenburg Front, which took place in September 1919. The commission was subject to strict Party control and supervision in the name of the Central Committee of the RCP (B). It was called upon to correct the mistakes which had been made by the local leadership during implementation of the nationalities policy.

As we are assured by the historian V.P. Nikolaeva, the RCP (B) and the Soviet government 'approached the question as to the composition of this commission for Turkestan with the utmost care' including in it 'people of proven worth in responsible posts in the Party and the Soviets, seasoned Bolsheviks with considerable experience in organizational and political work and with a knowledge of Turkestan'.[19] The last assertion is highly suspect. A mere glance at an encyclopaedic dictionary reveals that neither Eliava, the chairman of the commission, nor its other members – Rudzutaks, Kuibyshev, Bokii and above all Goloshchekin – had been to Turkestan and could not possibly have had knowledge of it. Frunze had been there, though only in his distant youth, when he had studied in Vernyi and used to go on foot to visit his mother in Pishkek (modern Bishkek).

The Turkestan Commission arrived in Tashkent on 4 November 1919. Political meetings had been organized at various points along its route. On 2 November in Kazalinsk, one of the Muslim delegates of the All-Russian Conference of Communist Organizations of the Peoples of the East greeted the envoys from Moscow, representing the 'central authorities, which have not forgotten the proletariat of Turkestan and are responding to its needs'.[20] Indeed the central authorities were unlikely to forget the proletariat of Turkestan, given that so much had been staked on it for the shady venture they called 'World Revolution'.

After destroying the Kokand government's plan for an autonomous Turkestan in September 1917 at the II Muslim Congress, and creating the Cheka – important because as an institution it separated Church and

State, in turn ensuring that schools were secularized – the Council of People's Commissars of the RSFSR issued an appeal signed by Lenin 'To all Working Muslims in Russia and the East':

> Arrange your national life freely and without obstruction. You have the right to do so. Be mindful of how your rights, just as the rights of all peoples in Russia, are upheld by the whole might of the Revolution and its organizations – the Soviets of Workers', Soldiers' and Peasants' Deputies.

It was clear by this time that in the view of the Bolsheviks, working Muslims were only able to arrange their national life freely when threatened with the bayonets of the *dashnaks*, who had become Red Army soldiers so as to protect themselves from the predatory eye of the Cheka. They would only become aware of their newly won rights through the subsequent violation of their religious sensibilities.

Contemporary writer Y. Paporov (in the journal *Yunost*, Issue No. 1, 1990) writes that the appeal from the Council of People's Commissars of the RSFSR 'was passed on by word of mouth. It particularly inspired the local intelligentsia who had taken to their hearts the liberating policies of the October Revolution.' We might wonder how the author came up with this interpretation – does he simply ignore the fact that representatives of the Soviet regime had been burning the Koran and throwing bombs at priests while they prayed?

There is little sign of inspiration to be found in the writings of Aimautov (cited above) or Party leader Atabaev, who expresses only rapture in his report. If anyone was inspired after reading the appeal from the Council of People's Commissars, it would have been a delusion of the deceived, robbed of conscience or intelligence: as is written in the Bible, 'By their deeds shall ye know them.' By their deeds, not their words.

A few days after the arrival of the commission, a letter from Lenin was published in the Tashkent newspapers entitled: 'To our Communist Comrades in Turkestan'. Lenin turned to them 'not in his capacity as Chairman of the Council of People's Commissars and of the Council for Defence, but as a member of the Party' – coming down from the orator's tribune, so to speak. He went on:

The establishment of appropriate relations with the peoples of Turkestan is of tremendous importance for the Russian Socialist Federal Soviet Republic, we might even say of importance for world history.

For the whole of Asia and all the world's colonies, for thousands of millions of people, the relations between the Soviet Workers' and Peasants' Republic towards weak and formerly oppressed peoples will also be of practical significance.

Lenin urged the communists of Turkestan:

To establish comradely relations with the peoples of Turkestan, to demonstrate to them through their actions the sincerity of our wish to wipe out all traces of great-Russian chauvinism so as to take up the selfless struggle against worldwide imperialism … to have the most profound confidence in our Turkestan Commission.[21]

This meant that Soviet Turkestan was to become a model for the whole of the East in the 'world struggle against imperialism'. We have already seen the kind of model this was: millions falling victim to hunger and disease after a mere two years of the new regime; the destruction and burning of Kokand (its population in 1897 had been 120,000 and in 1926 it was only 69,300) and many *kishlaks* 'infected by *basmachi* insurrection'; the outrages of militant atheism; economic despotism and so on.

In a report delivered on 22 November 1919 to the II Congress of the Communist Organizations of the Peoples of the East, Lenin stated that 'the social revolution is gaining ground in Western Europe by the day, by the hour and the same is happening in America and England.'[22] After Russian Bolsheviks had breached the imperialism of old, 'a still greater task, a still newer task will be facing the representatives of the working masses of the East'.[23] And what great task might that be? He explained:

In the history of the advance of world revolution, which will – to judge by its beginnings – take many years and require much effort, you will be called upon to play an important role in the revolutionary struggle, in the revolutionary movement, and in that struggle to become part of our struggle against international imperialism as well.[24]

Further on Lenin described the task in even more precise terms:

Here you have a task before you, which was not one facing the communists of the whole world before: starting out from general communist theory and practice and adapting to specific local conditions not to be found in European countries, you need to be able to apply that theory and practice to local conditions, in which the main mass of the population is the peasantry and in which the struggle is against not capital but vestiges of medieval times. This is a difficult and unusual task, but one that is especially rewarding, because a mass of people is drawn into this struggle which had previously not taken part in one. On the other hand, thanks to the organization of communist cells in the East, you will have the opportunity of establishing the closest of links with the Third International. You must find special forms for this alliance between advanced workers from all over the world and the masses from the East often living in medieval conditions and still being exploited. *We shall implement in our country on a small scale, what you will be implementing on a large scale in large countries* [my italics] and this second task you will, I hope, accomplish successfully. Thanks to the communist organizations in the East, which you represent, you will be linked to the advanced revolutionary proletariat. It is up to you to embark upon this task and make sure in the future that communist propaganda be spread in each country in a language understood by its people.[25]

Not a single word about the million people who had starved to death in Turkestan, total oblivion when it came to the essential needs of the country, exhausted by civil war, economic collapse and hunger. Just an obsessive concern with the spectre of world revolution.

This may have been why later, in September 1921, Lenin gave the following instructions to A. Joffe, who was sent as deputy chairman of the Turkestan commission to Tashkent:

> For the whole of our *Weltpolitik* [world policy] it is terribly
> important to win the trust of the local population – three and
> four times over – to prove that we are not imperialists and that
> we shall not tolerate any deviation in that direction. We have
> to be extremely strict about this. This will have repercussions in
> India, in the East – it is no joking matter. Here we have to be
> careful 1,000 times over.[26]

This exhortation has been interpreted in a very vague and narrow fashion.
A. Azizkhanov, for instance, believes that Lenin was emphasizing here
the importance of the 'nationalities policy of the Soviet republics' for
the country's foreign policy.[27] Paporov stresses that the leader was calling
on Joffe and his comrades to act 'with a profound knowledge of their
objective, with tact and an appreciation of the local conditions'.[28] This
leads us to ask the question: what was Lenin's main idea and main aim?
It is quite clear that for Lenin caution, the trust of the native population
and intolerance of imperialist bias were important not in themselves,
but as a means for the seduction and conquest of the East and for the
ultimate victory of World Revolution.

Evidently Lenin was well acquainted with the tricks played by the
comrade communists of Turkestan, given that he requested them most
earnestly to establish comradely relations with the peoples living in that
region. It was not for nothing that the commission he sent there began
its work with a thorough purge of the leading Party workers in Turkestan.
Nikolaeva writes:

> The Turkestan Commission had been given the task of helping the
> working people in the area root out chauvinists and nationalists
> from Party and Soviet institutions and ensure the ideological
> principles of the local Party bodies. The greatest danger at that
> time was a leaning towards great-power chauvinism, against
> which the Turkestan Commission waged a merciless war.
> Certain workers were expelled from the Party and banished from
> Turkestan for serious violations in their implementation of the
> nationalities policy. These included a group of former leading
> Party workers – Kazakov, Sorokin, Timlyantsev, to whom it was
> recommended that they should leave Turkestan.

Legal trials were held of former tsarist officials, who had found their way into Soviet bodies and had been misusing their power. The Soviet authorities banished around one thousand such people from the region.[29]

Let us recall how Sorokin, mentioned above, a mere six months before his banishment had grown indignant at the outrages instigated by Red Army men against Muslims. Had he really been transformed into a chauvinist so rapidly? When the tsarist officials – now accused of infiltrating Soviet organizations – were in charge a few years earlier there had been no hunger, no killings, no robberies or sacrilege against religion.

The former chairman of the commission, Eliava, was to point out later, in 1928, the known difference between the ideas of the Communist Party, the ideas of the Soviet regime and the implementation of those directives: 'It was all a question of the *human material* [my italics] at work in the country concerned' and at that stage this 'material' was not implementing the directives correctly; this was the reason why various errors and exaggerations had occurred. As usual, all sins were blamed on those implementing the ideas, while the immunity of the ideas themselves and those in charge continued to be protected.

Goloshchekin who, together with Kuibyshev, was to lead the Party work, travelled with the new revolutionary committee of the Fergana region to the city of Kokand on 11 November 1919. At that time a regional congress took place there to discuss the economic situation along with the problem of the struggle against the *basmachi*. Members of the Revolutionary Committee and Goloshchekin convened an extra night-time session of the congress, which immediately decided to 'dismiss and disband itself' so that in the provinces work could begin under the leadership of the new Revolutionary Committee.

On 13 November, Goloshchekin arrived in Skobelev with the commander of the troops, Brigadze. Once there he completely changed the composition of the Fergana Revolutionary Council. The next day he gave a speech at a meeting of the Soviet in a packed hall and by 16 November he was already in the coal mines of Kyzyl-Kiya, where he addressed a rally and attended a Party meeting. There then followed a journey to Andizhan, Jalal Abad and Osh, which resulted in a total purge of all local Soviet and Party bodies, excluding from them any 'tsarist officials, traders and speculators'; a report dated 28 November 1919 led to a re-registration of the whole Party organization in the region.

This cavalry charge against local Party cadres was effected within a matter of days and by a man who had only arrived in Turkestan a week before. What sense was there in that onslaught? A mere six months later – in July 1920 – Party forces were once again redeployed after 'the Turkestan communists, infected by colonialist and nationalist attitudes, had been placed at the disposal of the Central Committee'[30]; this committee would decide what should become of them next. Over and over again the composition of the Turkestan Commission was changed and promises made to the hard-pressed people, assuring them that the 'paradise of the World Commune' would soon dawn amidst the violence, devastation and humiliation of the human spirit in their republic. The national 'bourgeoisie' of Turkestan was not given the chance to arrange its life 'freely and without obstruction'. Naturally we might assume that Turkestan's communists were enjoying incomparably greater freedom than other local citizens; this was not the case.

The comrades recently arrived from Moscow, from the Centre, were immediately concerned by the fact that there were multiple bodies – three Area Committees – acting independently of each other: those of the RCP (B), of foreign communists and of the Muslim communist organizations. As Nikolaeva writes: 'Using the separate existence of the Party organizations, the nationalists led by T. Ryskulov were gradually turning the Muslim Bureau into a centre uniting nationalist elements.'[31]

After informing Moscow that the Muslim Bureau had assumed some functions of government institutions, the Turkestan Commission was accordingly instructed to act and on 15 January 1920 it amalgamated the three communist organizations in the area.

Regarding the establishment of proper control of the situation, however, they had been beaten to it: 'A group of Party workers representing local nationalities, which had not had the necessary Party-political training and lacked a clear grasp of the theoretical heritage of Marxism-Leninism, proved unable to maintain a logical Marxist position and, viewed objectively, embarked on a nationalist path.'

This group was headed by Ryskulov and Khodzhaev, members of the Party's Area Committee. They endeavoured to subordinate class interests of the working people of Turkestan to 'general national interests' and thus to subordinate the mass of the Muslim population to the indigenous bourgeoisie. They maintained that the native population, from a class point of view, was homogenous and that the process of class differentiation was not to be observed in the peasant masses. In a memorandum sent to the Central Committee of the RCP (B), Ryskulov pointed out that in Turkestan there were, allegedly, two main groups: 'the oppressed exploited colonial natives and European capital'.[32]

Let us unpick the real issue here by translating this excerpt from Party language into something more human. The communist comrades of Turkestan from the Muslim Bureau had been promised by the Council of People's Commissars and Lenin that they were able freely and without obstruction to arrange their national life. Believing this, they set up their own Turkic Communist Party and later on their own Turkic Republic. Ryskulov referred to this in his address to the Fifth Area Conference in January 1920. Yet if they had moved towards autonomy, the Turkestan Bolsheviks would have moved too far from the all-embracing control of Bolshevism, which sought to entrench consistently Marxist positions (or World Revolution), at the expense of the general national interests of individual countries.

A commission of well-trained Bolsheviks was sent from the Centre to scrutinize those who had not had adequate training and to discover who might be distracted by the needs of their peoples and forget about the World Commune. This scrutiny appears not to have been sufficiently rigorous in the beginning: the Centre had not imagined that the natives would be so quick off the mark and it had not equipped its envoys with instructions prohibiting autonomy. As Nikolaeva explains:

> The complexity of the sociopolitical situation in the area, the concentration of the Turkestan commission's activity – first and foremost on the struggle against great-power chauvinism – led to a temporary lack of vigilance with regard to anti-Party propaganda spread by the nationalists. The members of the commission were initially disunited when it came to their assessment of the slogan calling for a 'Turkic Republic'. F.I. Goloshchekin, one of the members of the Turkestan commission, was hesitating [a clear sign that there had not been any instructions from the leadership]. For a time V.V. Kuibyshev was supporting Eliava's view.[33]

Within a month people were no longer hesitating: 'With the help of the Central Committee of the RCP (B)', as pointed out by Azizkhanov, mistakes were beginning to be corrected. On 23 February 1920 the Turkestan commission 'decisively rejected' the idea of a Turkic Republic and a Turkic Communist Party and two weeks later the Central Committee of the RCP (B) had overturned the decision of the Fifth Area Party Conference 'adopted under the influence of national-deviationists'. In a letter to the Central Committee dated 15 March, it was stated that in the territory of Turkestan there should be a single Communist Party and that it should form part of the RCP (B) with the rights of a regional organization.

The 'national-deviationists' did not agree with the Central Committee's decision. At the beginning of May they sent a delegation to Moscow headed by Ryskulov, who was still attempting to achieve complete independence for Turkestan. The detailed report which the delegation brought to the Central Committee had been signed by Ryskulov, Khodzhaev and Bek-Ivanov. In this document, as we are told by Nikolaeva:

> Behind the fine phrases about the great importance of the spread of revolution to the East, it was possible to sense the idea of the need patiently to wait until the peoples of the East, led by their own national bourgeoisie and after passing through the stage of national-liberation struggle, should be ready for Soviet power. Once again mention was made of the shared interests of the whole of the indigenous population. The delegation insisted that all power should be transferred to the Turkestan Central Executive Committee, that a separate Muslim army be created, subordinate to the Turkestan government, which would be entitled to defend its own internal order and that the Turkestan Commission be disbanded.'[34]

For six weeks these questions were discussed until Lenin announced his final decision: 'It is essential, in my view, to reject Comrade Ryskulov's project.'[35]

Soon afterwards, the Turkestan Area Party Committee, consisting mainly of Ryskulov's supporters and accused of impeding the implementation of Central Committee decisions, 'was disbanded at the insistent request of the communists of the republic'; Translated from Party-speak this meant 'on instructions from the Centre'.

Lenin's lessons regarding Turkestan were carefully noted by Goloshchekin, as can be seen from his behaviour throughout his

Kazakhstan period. This explains why the leader of the 'national-deviationists', Ryskulov, was to become a fervent opponent of Goloshchekin, against whom he struggled bitterly for many years.

The six-month mission to Turkestan, during no period of which had he been studying the local conditions and way of life, had made Goloshchekin in Moscow's eyes – and perhaps his own – a specialist in eastern matters. Stalin and Kaganovich appointed him as the Party's leading representative in Kazakhstan. In September 1925 Goloshchekin was to return to the former land of Turkestan, to the part of it which, after the subdivision of the territory, had become the Republic of Kazakhstan.

Goloshchekin would not have known that shortly before, on 21 January 1925 – the first anniversary of Lenin's death – the native population of the old town of Tashkent, duly liberated by the Revolution, had been made, on instructions from the local authorities, to kneel for several minutes: if he had, he would no doubt have approved.[36]

In 1918, 1,200,000 people were starving, a figure which rose to 2 million in 1922 – more than a million people perished from starvation and disease during this time and a thousand children were rendered homeless. By the time Goloshchekin arrived, Kazakhstan was just starting to recover from the disastrous consequences of the Civil War and the famine of 1921–22. The gross yield of grain in 1925 was 472,000 tonnes, approximately the same as before the Civil War. Livestock numbers were also recovering after the hard times and had risen to 26 million, almost twice the 1922 figure, though less than before the Civil War. In comparison with 1923, commodity circulation was now over four times greater. Kazakhstan by this time was trading actively with countries beyond its borders. The cooperative movement was gaining ground within agriculture and by 1 October 1925 there were 2,811 cooperatives of various types functioning in the country, employing over 320,000 people. More than a thousand of these were Kazakh cooperatives, which employed 62,546 people. In short, life in the steppes, which had suffered a great deal during the Civil War was gradually returning to normal. In 1925 the Area Party Committee noted: 'There is a fall to be observed in the absolute figures for poor peasant holdings and they account for a smaller percentage of the total than before, while there is an increase in middle-sized farms.'

On 1 December 1925 the Fifth All-Kazakhstan Conference opened in Kzyl-Orda's Commercial Club. The delegates were greeted by Comrade Peters of the Central Control Commission, who had arrived from Moscow for the occasion. He declared that 'the moment has virtually arrived', about which Lenin said: "Every cook in our country must learn to administer the state." It was not a joke.'[37] Goloshchekin then took the floor. It was the first long speech Goloshchekin had made in Kazakhstan, his 'inauguration speech' as it were. In it he described in broad terms the basis for subsequent policy and for this reason it merited special attention.

In the ten short weeks that had passed since his arrival in the land of the Kazakhs, Goloshchekin had established that 'there really is no Soviet power as yet in the *auls*, the *bais* and the clans predominate.'[38] The most interesting aspect of this discovery is that Goloshchekin had never actually left his office to visit an *aul*. Indeed, during his time as First Secretary, Goloshchekin never once visited an ordinary Kazakh *aul*.

In order to demonstrate the above-mentioned thesis, which was indisputable as far as he was concerned, Goloshchekin resorted to a reliable tactic. He read the conference delegates a letter, which had been addressed to the Bolsheviks of Kazakhstan by the Central Committee of the Party a year before:

> The Kirgiz organization ... found itself in conditions which made its work particularly difficult. The size of its territory, the small population, the lack of convenient means of communication, the backward nature of the peasant holdings, almost total illiteracy of the population and so on – all that created major problems in the drive towards socialist construction.
>
> Now that Kirgiz territories have been united in a single republic, the problems are on the increase. The Central Committee, taking into account that the Soviets in the Kirgiz Republic were in a particularly difficult position and that there were virtually no Soviets in the *auls*, considers it essential that all measures be adopted to set up Soviet power in the *auls* and *kishlaks* ...[39]

'A year has passed since then, how up-to-date is the letter?' asked the lecturer, turning to his audience.

'Up-to-date!' came the answer from somewhere in the hall.

That was enough: the force of an authoritative opinion had been sufficient. It was eight years since the October Revolution and it suddenly came to light that Soviet power had not yet reached the *auls*.

This was how Goloshchekin not only put a line through eight years of work by the communists of Kazakhstan, but also began to lay the theoretical foundation necessary to justify the need for extreme measures.

'Surely that doesn't mean we have to make a revolution all over again?' someone asked.

'Oh, yes it does,' was his opinion.

First of all Goloshchekin described the work of the Area Committee – and of course, first and foremost, his own work – in 'uniting the Kazakh lands' in dramatic terms, romantically elevating his own character, Goloshchekin spoke of the Revolution itself:

When I say: 'the capital is Kzyl-Orda,' I sense that a smile will start appearing on very many of your faces. If you had not come here at this time but a few months earlier, you would not just have smiled, but your smile would have been a bitter one – made bitter by sand and dust. If you look carefully, you will notice miscalculations and many shortcomings, but Comrades, who was *making the Revolution then* [my italics] in white gloves? Who and which class is able to make a revolution, without there being any casualties?

What kind of revolution was he talking about in this, the ninth year after October 1917? What casualties should a people be prepared to suffer, when it had only just been able to resume normal peacetime existence? No direct reference was made to these issues at this point. Hints were, however, already being dropped and the course of future action intimated.

It would be very good if we were to be offered a large, well-organized town with plenty of amenities. That would be splendid, but our miracle and our bold vision are such, that we have decided to create our capital and carry out our task precisely in Kzyl-Orda, in the heart of Kazakh lands.[40]

After holding up to shame 'the most ancient forms of nomadic migration' and the 'most backward forms of commodity exchange', Goloshchekin came out with a slogan calling for the 'Sovietization of the *auls*'. As he understood it, it was the 'one form of organization for the backward Kazakh nation': these words were recorded in the Area Committee report. In an article printed in the newspaper *Soviet Steppes* the slogan was interpreted in far more detail:

> To say that there is no Soviet power in Kazakhstan would be wrong. There is Soviet power here, but if a broader view is taken of the Sovietization of Kazakhstan, not simply as the organization of the masses, but as a question of the form in which that will take place – call it national self-determination, if you will – the form in which cultural and political advance will be possible, the form which will bring economic liberation in its wake, the form which will make it possible to shake off exploitation, then we have to admit that there are major shortcomings here.[41]

Goloshchekin did not go out of his way to substantiate his assertion regarding the domination of the *bais*. For him the opinion of 'one Kazakh in a responsible post and clearly well acquainted with the reality of the *auls*' was enough. The man in question had assured him that the Soviet apparatus at the lowest level had been distorted and transformed into a tool of clan-based oppression and exploitation, and that the same thing was happening in economic institutions.

At first glance this is a paradox: there was Soviet power in Kazakhstan but it was not properly established – this was why the republic needed to be 'Sovietized'. Goloshchekin, however, did not admit to anything contradictory in his conclusions. For him it was clear that the republic – which extended over enormous territory – had, strictly speaking, barely been touched by the October Revolution. Perhaps he felt himself to be the Messiah, the leader called upon to forge the Revolution here in Kazakhstan – another, lesser, Red October.

Soon his idea, picked up by local administrators, would swirl through the steppes like a whirlwind, gathering force and speed – a black, destructive whirlwind.

It did not take Goloshchekin long to deal with 'deviationists':

> Is there a nationalist deviation within our Party? Yes. The first was the most detrimental one – great-power chauvinism. I gather this

from reports sent in from certain provincial committees. Another deviation among Kazakhs is also of a nationalist kind, influenced by the Alash-Orda party which is very powerful too. It might seem that both sides are to blame, but an objective reply would be different. Guilty first of all were European communists, because lack of trust in them was an undeniable historical phenomenon and their task was to resolve that dilemma, to win trust.[42]

The speaker did not name the leaders of the most dangerous of deviations and neither did he name the leaders of the 'Kazakh nationalist deviation'. When it came to the latter, however, he did insinuate who they might be, immediately listing by name those who allegedly confined all their activities to the struggle between groupings. By a strange coincidence those at fault were all leading Kazakh communists: U. Zhandosov, N. Nurmakov, S. Sadvokasov, S. Khodzhanov, S. Mendeshev, T. Ryskulov and N. Tyurekulov. Once again no proof was required; again, one nameless witness was enough:

> It has reached the point that when I asked a comrade: 'Tell me, please, are the resolutions of the Central Committee and the Area Committee implemented in your province?' – he thought for a moment and then replied: 'You know, CC resolutions and Area Committee resolutions are general directives. What we implement is what one of the comrades writes down'
> For the struggle between groups they're ready to use the courts and the militia. If someone needs to be arrested in good time, they'll have him arrested. If necessary, a statement will be written and signed by ten witnesses and a case will be opened. That's what things have come to.[43]

Within a very short time almost all the 'leaders' of the groups had been accused by Goloshchekin of local nationalism. His true aim was clear from the start: to remove all dangerous rivals. For that no method was more effective than hanging political labels round the necks of influential 'nationalists'.

The haste with which Goloshchekin exposed his first enemies suggests that he had decided right from the start to make the most of powerful support he enjoyed in Moscow. He wanted to silence his opponents – that is, anyone who had an opinion of his own and the will to stand up for it, cutting short any attempt to disobey his dictates. He did not want to listen to anyone or take into consideration other opinions. All he needed were men who would carry out his instructions obediently, without question.

It was clear that Goloshchekin was also planning to neutralize those who might influence the hearts and minds of the people: the Kazakh intelligentsia. At first he was quite cautious in his assessments, did not mention any names and even tried to sound unbiased and objective in his judgements:

> Here we are up against two deviations. On the one hand this intelligentsia is being opposed on account of its nationalist deviations – infantile leftist ideas. If we were to speak against the Kazakh intelligentsia indiscriminately and keep reprimanding it for its past and present sins, without involving it in our socialist construction and failing to make it more accessible, then while opposing the Kazakh intelligentsia, we would at the same time be following the Russian intelligentsia: avoiding one extreme we would find ourselves up against another and be playing into the hands of great-Russian chauvinism. Complete rejection, complete denigration of the Kazakh intelligentsia is wrong, but the other deviation is not the solution either – the complete merging with this intelligentsia, when the borderline between communists and non-Party people is blurred and when the Alash-Orda party has more ideological influence than the communists.[44]

Most striking here is the call for the intelligentsia to be more acceptable – for it to be reduced to some common denominator and robbed of its individuality, special features and nuances. Despite the ridiculous desire to make one pattern fit all, it is still clear that the intellectual guillotining of the intelligentsia would be an operation designed to make the heads of the finest roll. Naturally this did not worry Goloshchekin in the slightest: on the contrary, all this would seem perfectly necessary to him. He continued in a similar vein: 'It [the Kazakh intelligentsia] needs to be involved in purposeful work, differences within in it need to be ironed out, but this would not rule out struggle against bourgeois-nationalist ideology.'[45]

Goloshchekin warned conference delegates that when it came to matters of ideological influence and leadership, it was best to keep at a clear distance from members of the Kazakh intelligentsia. This would ensure that they were kept well outside any even slightly significant cultural or social activity and confined to the fields of technology or economics. For the time being Goloshchekin was dealing in generalities, not yet pointing his finger at concrete enemies. That would come later.

After pointing out the signposts to be followed in the imminent struggle, Goloshchekin ended his speech with a rousing appeal: 'Let us unite around the Central Committee and accomplish the supreme task of liberating the working masses, in particular the working masses of the Kazakh people.'

(*Enthusiastic applause.*)

V. The Tsar-Slaying Bolshevik in Kazakhstan

The 'liberation' began immediately and continued on a steadily increasing scale, although the working masses were unlikely to have understood from whom or what they were being liberated and whether they needed that liberty.

The local newspapers had not yet forgotten how to make jokes and as well as insistent headlines such as 'The Ulcer of Hooliganism has to be Eradicated' and 'More Rigour, Less Mercy' they did allow themselves tiny capers aimed at exposing a nameless leadership:

A WORKING LIFE: LETTER FROM A HORSE
No rest for me by day or night –
they drive me here and drive me there.
Do you really think that's right?
No labour code for this old mare!
They goad me on and driver too,
as if we're two of a kind.
Worn out by trips the whole night through:
no overtime, but never mind!
I'm writing in now to complain
for his sake and for mine.
Please do not treat us with disdain.
Listen to a neigh like mine.

[Translated from Horse-speak into journalese by NIKOLA][1]

In Kzyl-Orda's State Theatre A.V. Lunacharsky's new play *Poison*, complete with a gypsy choir, was followed by a historical play by N. Lerner entitled *Ruler of Russia*, directed by V.A. Chernobler.

Newspaper readers were now treated to contributions from a whole army of workers' correspondents covering the rural areas and, apart from the offerings of Party Correspondent No. 14, articles were sent in by 'Cotter Pin', 'Hammer', 'Janus', 'Netrel', 'Red', 'No. 1093', 'Itch', 'Steam Engine', 'Dnestrovskii', 'Tractor' and 'Frowner'. 'Our Kazakh Women are still Slaves' was a typical front-page headline and all citizens were called upon to prepare for the campaign 'Day for the Abolition of Bride Money'. In the meantime, a certain comrade of one of the enslaved women of the East, who had since broken away from slavery, was composing topical rhymes for the newspapers:

Gods I threw away forever
And took up books instead.
For my little boy to be clever,
He'll go to school, I said.

Like a beetle in the spring
The clubhouse glows with light.
The priest in vain his hands shall wring,
I'll not give in to fright.

To the library I did go
To find the newsy paper.
To read about the *Kulak* foe,
His every crime and caper.

Come on then, you peasant poor
Take up your books and read.
The *kulaks* soon will march no more,
The Soviets they shall heed!

Judging by the pages of *Soviet Steppes* at that time, the town of Kzyl-Orda, and indeed the whole world, was caught up in dramatic events: the Russian-Asiatic canteen owned by the cooperative Tashkent was attracting customers with the offer of strong drink; the threat of locusts was hanging over Dzhetys; an elderly lady aimed her revolver at Mussolini and shot him in the nose; the Leningrad commercial association 'Hygiene' was advertising condoms in five different sizes; women oppressed by Sharia

Law were stirred by a slogan for International Women's Day – 'May Red Komsomol Scarves replace the Yashmak!'; one of the residents of Kazakhstan's capital declared, à la Tolstoy, 'I cannot remain silent!' before writing an article entitled 'Spring Howl', in which he angrily wrote that 'stray dogs are dying not in the specified place. Their corpses are lying about in the streets and not being cleared away.' A mere six or seven years later those same streets of Kzyl-Orda and the streets of other cities, including those of the new capital Alma-Ata, would be littered with corpses. By then there would be no space in the newspapers for them: people could, after all, remain silent.

Meanwhile a small hardly discernible swirling cloud of the finest dust was approaching the *auls*. On 20 January 1926 the republic's main newspaper printed a leading article with the headline: 'Help for the Kazakh Farmers Planning to Settle'. After criticizing the former policy for colonizing the steppe, which had robbed Kazakhs of almost all the hayfields in floodplains bordering on the rivers as well as the best winter and summer pastures, the author repeated the conclusion arrived at by the recent Party conference: namely that the Kazakh pastoral economy was in a state of catastrophic decline and that its critical situation was beyond repair. It was therefore suggested that the lands taken away from the nomads should be returned to them in order to improve the situation regarding animal husbandry; this had been affected far more seriously by War Communism and the Civil War than by Stolypin's reforms and was now recovering at a rapid pace. Danger was, according to the leadership, threatening from another quarter. Therefore 'the conference proposed that the process of settling the nomads should be embarked upon without delay!' People who had been nomads for hundreds of years were forced to change their way of life at the stroke of a pen.

In order to make tilling the land more palatable for these people, the Council of People's Commissars of the RSFSR exempted nomads and those leading a semi-nomadic existence from the universal agricultural tax for five years. The newspaper exclaimed: 'The whole of the steppes will find out about this legislative act tomorrow – every *kishlak* and every *aul*.'

On 19 April Ryskulov, in the same newspaper, wrote:

Who established and on what grounds that the Kazakh people must and will make the transition to a settled way of life? There will be a trend of development in that direction, but it will reach completion in the distant future. For the time being the natural conditions and opportunities for development are of a very different kind. To talk in general about the transition from animal husbandry (implying that all Kazakhs are engaged exclusively in animal husbandry) to land cultivation reflects complete ignorance of today's situation among the Kazakhs.

Officially Ryskulov was arguing with M. Brudnyi, who a week earlier had published an article about the Kazakh proletariat; in essence, however, he was responding to those supporting the theory of 'immediate settlement', well aware that this campaign, for which nobody had prepared the ground, was bound to end badly.

Brudnyi had been writing about the fact that economic development of Kazakhstan which undermined the region's *auls* would bring poverty to enormous numbers of people and inevitably cause enormous losses; yet, it was argued that disbanding the clan structure of the *auls* would be 'yeast for the nation', for its future – by creating a local proletariat.

It was suggested that without a proletariat of its own (which, in fact, already existed) the Kazakhs would be unable to emerge as a nation. Without responding to this strange theory, Ryskulov presented successes in animal husbandry and land cultivation as compatible and interlinked with Kazakh industry. For him the future of local industry meant expanding the extracting and processing sectors.

These ideas did not suit Goloshchekin as they did not match his picture of the future; he soon declared open war on the 'insubordinates' who had suggested them. By this time Ryskulov was working in Moscow as Deputy Chairman of the Council of People's Commissars of the RSFSR and another of Goloshchekin's major opponents, Khodzhanov, had had his reputation destroyed and was now regarded as a 'national-deviationist'. Goloshchekin's main attack was therefore directed at another man of similar views: Smagul Sadvokasov. At the Third Plenary Session of the Kazakhstan Area Committee held at the end of November 1926 Goloshchekin stressed: 'We disagree with Comrade Sadvokasov specifically with regard to the October Revolution. At the same time, when I assert that we need to introduce a small-scale October to our *auls*, you are against any kind of October Revolution. Yet surely the land reforms we are now introducing are our October Revolution?'

'What makes you think I am against land reform?' asked Sadvokasov, interrupting him.

Goloshchekin did not pay any attention to him; he was not in the habit of providing direct answers to questions and would not tolerate interruptions.

'The economic conditions obtaining in the *auls* need to be changed,' concluded Goloshchekin. 'Our point of view is that a veil should not be drawn over the class relations, which already exist, which are maturing and developing. The poor need to be supported in their class struggle against the *bais*. If this involves civil war, we would support that.'

It seems fair to assume that Goloshchekin relished war. Verbal battles were unnecessary for him: 'Comrade Mauser', as Goloshchekin was known, made the decisions. Soviet historians regarded him as a prominent Party figure in military situations and such a reputation was indeed deserved: in Yekaterinburg he had 'cobbled together workers' detachments' and sent them out to fight against the White detachments of Ataman Dutov, who was later to lead the partisan movement. However, Goloshchekin himself had never been directly involved in fighting, having been too busy with organizational activities. Aware of this gap in his career, in 1920 Goloshchekin wrote: 'I asked not to be given a responsible post but to be given the opportunity to go the front as an ordinary Red Army soldier.'[2] By that time, however, the Civil War was almost over and the forty-four-year-old was not given that opportunity. So, in the end, he was never actually called upon to fight.

Goloshchekin was evidently not against turning the class struggle against the *bais*–if necessary–into civil war. Goloshchekin told this to Sadvokasov, fanning the fierce exchange for all it was worth. Sadvokasov, for his part, declared at the Second Plenary Session of the Area Committee in May 1926 that, when it came to the question of the peasantry, 'the slogan should be not civil war but civil peace,' warning that 'without that we shall lead our economy to ruin'.

✤ ✤ ✤

So it was that at the Fifth Conference, Sadvokasov, People's Commissar for Education, was branded a national-deviationist and the main onslaught of Party criticism was subsequently directed at him. The term 'Sadvokasovism' was constantly appearing in the newspapers and did so for at least five years; this was well after Sadvokasov was made to leave Kazakhstan and had since died in Moscow. What exactly was his dangerous deviation?

Judging from *Essays on the History of the Communist Party of Kazakhstan*, the struggle against the 'national-deviationists' only really got underway when Goloshchekin arrived in the republic. Goloshchekin delivered his first report in Kazakhstan at the Fifth Conference:

> The conference resolutely condemned the struggle between groups set in motion by the national-deviationists, S. Khodzhanov, S. Sadvokasov and others. They undermined the Party charter and the standards of Party life by organizing meetings 'at home', behind the back of the Party bodies, using legal and investigatory bodies for the struggle between groups and brought alien elements into the Party's ranks. The delegates revealed the true facts, when the national-deviationists started involving Komsomol members and young people in that struggle.
>
> The communists of Kazakhstan dealt a fatal blow to the anti-Marxist theory of the nationalists regarding the predominance of the 'clan principle' and 'clan democratism' and their insistence that there is no class struggle in the *auls*.
>
> After resolutely criticizing the anti-Party activity of the national-deviationists and pointing out the danger, which the divisive behaviour of such groups represents for the consolidation of the Party organization, the conference called upon the Area Committee and the Control Commission to stop any attempts to encourage such groups and not to flinch at the use of special measures to bring pressure to bear on Party members encouraging anyone to engage in friction between groups, particularly when grass-roots organizations and the Komsomol are drawn into it. These decisions taken at the conference played an important role in the further consolidation of the Party organization at

Area level and in the ideological and organizational rout of the national-deviationists.[3]

A year later the Third Plenary Session of the Area Committee was held between 25 and 30 November 1926:

[It] exposed the class essence of the nationalist groupings inside the Kazakh Party organization, which had reflected the views and interests of the capitalist elements in the towns and of the *bais* in the *auls*. While pretending to defend the interests of the Kazakh people, the nationalist groups came out against socialist transformations and against the Leninist nationalities policy of the Communist Party. Over a long period they waged a struggle against the Party's Leninist line sometimes openly, sometimes furtively, using dastardly methods such as slander, in-fighting, defamation and seeking to undermine the authority of the bodies representing Soviet power. They sought to exploit the temporary difficulties experienced by the Party and the country and deliberately remained silent about the achievements of socialist construction in the republic.

One of these groupings was headed by S. Sadvokasov, who had occupied a number of important posts in the republic during the 1920s. His group, which presented the *bais* as peaceful toilers in the *auls*, came out against any restrictions or exclusions directed at them. They also opposed efforts to wipe out vestiges of pre-revolutionary socio-economic relations in the *auls* and to restructure them in keeping with socialist principles. Sadvokasov, while advocating 'civil peace' in the *auls*, declared outright that 'there was no need to expropriate the *bais*', maintaining that it was possible to steer the *auls* on to the track of socialist construction without disrupting the existing pre-revolutionary socio-economic relations. Sadvokasov and his associates also opposed the introduction of measures to improve the system of land tenure and they objected to plans for resettling Russian and Ukrainian peasants from other parts of the country in Kazakhstan. In all these endeavours they were drawing close to the bourgeois nationalists – men from the Alash-Orda party.[4]

More or less the same words were used in the collection of articles entitled *Under the Banner of Leninist Ideas*, published in 1973 by the Institute for the History of the Party affiliated to the Central Committee of the Communist Party of Kazakhstan – unsurprising, given that the author of the relevant contributions was the same: S.B. Baishev.

Nowadays, as real history is revealed before us in ever more detail instead of the version distorted by Soviet scholars, it is becoming increasingly clear which disasters resulted from the long years of civil war directed against the peasantry and unleashed by the state. Historical records show that it was not the military action in 1918–21 but the practices of War Communism in rural areas which devastated the economy and caused unprecedented famine in Kazakhstan. In June 1918 committees of poor peasants were set up, which helped to strip 50 million hectares of land from 'rich' peasants – approximately a third of the agricultural land at that time. More or less simultaneously, during the first collectivization instigated by Lenin (not that of the late 1920s and early 1930s), the material base for the *kulaks'* farms was destroyed and the *kulaks* as a class were eliminated. Regular military units were fighting at full strength to suppress peasant uprisings. The scale of peasant rebellion is illustrated by the fact that in the Tambov province almost a third of the adult population joined Antonov's army, forming eighteen well-armed regiments. It was with great difficulty that Tukhachevsky's forces succeeded in breaking down the resistance after a series of bloody battles.

French historian J. Ellenstein wrote in 1975 that 'Russia in 1922 was like Bangladesh in 1972'. In the winter of 1921–22, 25 million people were suffering from hunger. People were eating acorns, grass, bark and carrion and there were even cases of cannibalism. In the Land of the Soviets millions of desperate hungry citizens were roaming the streets. Between 5 and 8 million people died of hunger. Poverty and malnutrition gave rise to epidemics of typhus and cholera. Between 1917 and 1922 there were 22 million registered cases of typhus and 2 million people died from the disease. By way of comparison, during the First World War the number of Russians who died reached 2.5 million; during the Civil War a million Russians perished, while a further 3 million died from various epidemics.

The total (approximate) drop in Kazakhstan's population between 1918 and 1922 was over 15 million. If we subtract from that the 2 million who left Russia after the Revolution, then the remaining 13 million were victims of hunger, disease and bullets fired by their fellow countrymen (or perhaps by the hundreds of thousands of 'internationalists', enlisted to help the Bolsheviks dispense punishment in their country, which had been brought to its knees).

So, after all that, is it surprising that the 'national-deviationist' Sadvokasov came out in favour of 'civil peace' in the Kazakh *auls*? He knew all too well what the policy of War Communism had brought peasant Russia; he remembered what became of the Kazakhs in Turkestan and in the north and west of the republic, whose number of deaths totalled over a million. In the meantime, Goloshchekin maintained that nomads who had no experience of revolution and therefore could not appreciate the beneficial activity of the poor peasants' committees had no right to consider that the October Revolution had reached the *auls*.

As early as 1923, Sadvokasov stated at the Third Party Conference: 'At the present time the country [critic Uraz Isaev commented that for country here we should read '*aul*'] is not hoping for upheavals, but for creative, peaceful work: it is not new expropriations which will rescue the country but work and science.'

Then in 1926, after Goloshchekin's thunderous declarations at the Second Plenary Session of the Area Committee, Sadvokasov expressed his worries in the following words:

I am personally in contact with certain people and view our situation with alarm, because voices are starting to ring out in our midst to the effect that the October Revolution needs to be brought to the *auls* [Isaev points out once again that *auls* are mentioned here in place of *bais*], but I believe that this would not result in anything useful, only demagogy.[5]

Reading Isaev's comments alongside this passage, it is clear how Comrade Sadvokasov's ideas were being distorted: all he wanted was to warn his comrades-in-arms that they should avoid acting without thinking. Sadvokasov's words were being blatantly misrepresented. He saw that Kazakh *auls* consisted mainly of middle-sized farms and he was therefore concerned mainly for the middle peasants – in reality this was the majority of the Kazakh people. He would soon be proved right: a special commission set up by the Council of People's Commissars of the RSFSR calculated in 1925 that 64.7 per cent of the rural population consisted of middle peasants, 24 per cent of poor peasants and 6.9 per cent of prosperous peasants or *kulaks*.

At the Third Plenary Session of the Area Committee, where fierce arguments had broken out between Goloshchekin and Sadvokasov, another speaker – the Chairman of the Kazakhstan Council of People's Commissars, N. Nurmakov, who regarded the poor peasants and farm labourers as the main stratum of the *aul* population – expressed views broadly similar to those of Sadvokasov:

> Some comrades think that the situation in the *auls* is one that cannot be resolved or one which can only be resolved by expropriating the *bais*' farms. I am of the opinion, Comrades, that today, after ten years of Soviet power in Kazakhstan and when the commanding heights are all in the hands of the proletarian state, we are sufficiently strong to be able to bring influence to bear on the *bais* using different methods: we shall not need to resort to the same method that our Party used when power was being won in the early days of the October Revolution.[6]

Nurmakov suggested that the power of the *bais* should be weakened through taxation policy, the development of cooperatives and other means, but did not win any support for this proposal.

Musin, a delegate from Semipalatinsk, similarly proposed the 'crushing of the *bais* order'. Kaipnazarov repeated the ideas Goloshchekin had expressed a year before, maintaining that there was no Soviet power in the *auls*. Zhandosov insisted on immediate expropriation – this, however, aroused numerous objections. Delegates stated that such a hasty measure might give rise to anarchy and that in many provinces there were no 'feudal landowners' any more.

As Togzhanov points out:

> Zhandosov is mistaken in his opinion that the poor peasants in the *auls* all hate the *bais*. It is not true. If that were the real situation, it would not be so difficult for us to organize Party and Soviet organizations in the countryside.

Finally it has to be said that there is quite a widespread belief among our Kazakh comrades that the October Revolution has had no impact on the *auls* and that they have remained pre-revolutionary. As I see it, that is incorrect both in theory and in practice.

Goloshchekin adopted a position somewhere between the two sides and even reprimanded Zhandosov for being too far to the left. He indicated that the Party would not drop the idea of action against the *bais* and, if it proved necessary, then they would be taken to court. Finally, if there was no alternative, they would not shrink from shedding blood – that of the *bais*. Zhandosov had suggested 'taking the Revolution to the *auls*' (something which Goloshchekin himself had suggested not long before), but emphasized that 'the Revolution does not become more powerful just because the word is pronounced with a rolling of "Rs"'[7]. Similarly Goloshchekin warned against 'jumping over' stages of development without properly passing through them and suggested that first of all special bodies should be set up, which would change existing conditions – namely Party cells in the *auls*.

Goloshchekin realized that cohesion within the clans in the *auls* was so strong that it would not be possible to overpower it at one fell swoop; it would involve training a communist within each *aul*, on whom they could rely in the future when putting Party directives into practice. As early as the Second Plenary Session of the Area Committee, Goloshchekin had raised this 'most urgent question' about communists within the *auls*:

I looked into this question and the picture that emerged was far from encouraging. What might have led the *aul* communist to join the Party? In one cell the Comrades declared that they had heard people saying that all those who registered as Party members would receive seed loans for planting from the state.

In the Semipalatinsk province, when a commission arrived in one of the *auls* and asked if there were people who wanted to join the Party, they answered that the *bais* would probably release a few.

The actual motives mentioned for joining the Party were of a rather suspicious kind, nobody is paying any subscriptions and 90 per cent of the communists are illiterate. A whole range of documents shows that there is no understanding of what class struggle means and the interests of the Party are always seen as second to those of clan groups.[8]

These were the conclusions Goloshchekin felt obliged to draw. The delegates to the Third Plenary Session told similar stories about Bolsheviks in the rural areas. When an *aul* communist was asked what the Komintern was, he replied 'A big Commissar'. When asked what politics was, he answered: 'cunning'. When asked what the Central Executive Committee or the Council of People's Commissars was or who Kalinin and Munbaev were, he did not know. (In general the answers were to the point. The fact that they could not remember the names of the All-Union and local leaders was unsurprising – there were many.)

Goloshchekin listened attentively to the speakers, who grew increasingly emotional as they argued without understanding the crucial issue: in order to sweep like a whirlwind through the *auls* the differences between various groups had first to be brought to the fore – that is, their differences in income and attitudes. It was the only way to set a class struggle in motion, to unite the poor peasants and incite them against the wealthy ones.

This was what Goloshchekin stressed when he took the floor during that meeting:

> The third point which I wish to dwell on is the question brought up by Comrade Musin about the fact that we shall be unable to set up Party cells in the *auls*, before the main socio-economic and other conditions there change. That idea which would appear correct from the logical point of view, is not, however, a correct one. Under a dictatorship of the proletariat we start by building a special body, which will change the situation … We set up a Soviet of working people, we build a communist party which will be able to steer the *auls* of Kazakhstan on to a different track.[9]

Once again Goloshchekin gives himself away by making clear the aims he set himself upon coming to Kazakhstan: he had arrived to carry out a revolution. In this vast land, which had no proper communications linking it to the Centre and was so difficult to administer, he believed there was no echo of Russia's October Revolution. There had been a dictatorship of the proletariat for nine years in Russia, but out in Kazakhstan, as Goloshchekin saw it, there was no dictatorship and no proletariat. Everything had to start from scratch – the creation of the Soviets of the working people and the building of the Communist Party.

The Sovietization of the *auls* was, for all intents and purposes, the Sovietization of Kazakhstan. This was why Goloshchekin stressed at the Second Plenary Session that 'we cannot drive forward our work in all fields without organizing the poor farmers of Kazakhstan.'[10]

At the Fifth Conference in 1925 Goloshchekin made it clear that the Kazakhs had not yet even 'smelled the October Revolution'. At this stage he displayed a degree of sympathy for the people concerned, something he did not exhibit often. It would seem that Goloshchekin was proud of himself when he embarked upon the task which stood before him – the Sovietization of this backward republic with its enormous expanses of land and its illiterate nomads, with a group of nationalists still to be found inside the Party apparatus and in cultural institutions (the unabashed or secret supporters of Alash-Orda, for whom the key demand was that their people should be left in peace):

> We shall concentrate our efforts on the workers, the Kazakhs, the bulk of the Kazakh nation as such, the poor peasants, the farm labourers – *we have not yet approached the latter. We have not yet come close* to that source [my italics], the source of energy and popular wisdom, the source of healthy instincts. The very essence of the slogan 'Let us turn to the *auls* and the villages!' means that we should turn to this source and *start drinking* [my italics] from that source flowing from the people, rather than the water which has been stagnant for years and has even begun to smell brackish.[11]

Those were the concluding words of Goloshchekin's speech at the conference. His speech produced a strange impression on his audience. Despite the convoluted language and tautologies Goloshchekin usually employed in his lengthy demagogic addresses, it was rarely that he used imagery. Yet on this occasion – not just once or twice, but many times over – he used the word 'source', linking it directly with the people: they were a source of energy, a source of popular wisdom, a source of healthy instincts and finally he declared that he and his comrades should *start drinking from that source.*

What could possibly be drunk from a source provided by the Kazakh people, from those human beings?

One thing and one only – blood.

How Goloshchekin would proceed to utilize that source has only recently been made public: the only thing researchers are still unable to agree upon is the number of his victims. Did the number come to 1,200,000 dead as the result of starvation or was it closer to 1,700,000?

I remember an occasion when I was carefully leafing through the greyish-yellow pages of a dog-eared old newspaper. The file was from 1927 and suddenly I saw a portrait with a cross right through it. Goloshchekin had been photographed in profile, against the sun. There were streaks of grey in his wavy hair and beard, his gaze was compelling and cruel, his lower lip pressed tight, his nose long and prominent but not fleshy, with flared nostrils – there was a clean, energetic line to it. Had he posed for the photographer or had the latter just caught his typical expression? It was obviously not just any old photograph, because this particular one would be frequently reproduced in the newspapers in the future. It is easy to imagine that journalists were well-informed about the likes and dislikes of the First Secretary and knew that this particular photograph would be to his liking. Yet one reader of this particular file, or perhaps a reader of the newspaper before it had been stored away, had drawn a defiant cross right through the profile of the 'First Secretary of the Area Committee, Goloshchekin'. It must have happened a long time ago, because the purple ink was extremely faded. Beneath the wispy Mephistophelian beard there was a caption for the portrait written in large capital letters: 'MURDERER'. The newspaper in question was the issue of *Soviet Steppes* for 30 May 1927.

I came across one other photograph of Goloshchekin in an issue of the same paper for 7 November 1932. It too had a cross through it. The caption this time was 'LOUSE!'.

None of the photos of other comrades had crosses through them.

Those nameless critics of Goloshchekin knew quite well what kind of man had decided the fate of the people of Kazakhstan.

It therefore did not seem like a coincidence when I read Goloshchekin's concluding speech at that conference, his insistent relishing of the word 'source'. There was something smacking of a vampire's passion in that inappropriate combination of words.

Even skilled politicians are sometimes carried away by their emotions and this was not the first time Goloshchekin's megalomania had surfaced, revealing his urge to accomplish a whole revolution. Other related weaknesses were also evident: his sense of infallibility (sometimes masquerading as self-criticism), his intoxication with his own eloquence (resulting in speeches which lasted for whole days – sometimes the Party audience would be obliged to listen to him for two days in succession) and so on. With his words he was instigating his own small version of the October Revolution in Kazakhstan. Goloshchekin did not waver when ordered to inflict genocide on Kazakhstan. He was not afraid of blood. People had been warned.

VI. The Green Light from Stalin for Class War

The task of building a radiant future in Kazakh lands created practical challenges for Goloshchekin. Though the Kazakh Bolsheviks obediently followed his lead, they soon realized that he was not familiar with local conditions and had no wish to find out about them; they therefore began to form opinions of their own. Goloshchekin did not like objections and immediately embarked on a fight against the disobedient, using all possible means.

During the first years of his leadership in Kazakhstan he did not go so far as to physically remove his political opponents, this is not to say he did not wish to. At that stage Stalin was not yet giving Goloshchekin full rein.

Instead, the disobedient were brought to trial. It is worth noting that in the first three specially orchestrated trials – in Shakhtinsk in 1928, in the case against the so-called Working Peasants' Party (which took place behind closed doors in 1930) and in that against the Industrial Party in 1930 – there were no communists among the accused.

It was only in 1931 that Stalin demanded for the first time that a political opponent be shot. The figure involved was the now well-known Martemyan Ryutin. The Politburo, however, stopped its leader from unleashing terror – Ryutin was merely expelled from the Party.

Organizational obstacles of this kind were serious hindrances for Goloshchekin: instead of using a radical solution for a problem, he was obliged to wage a long parliamentary struggle. Yet he longed to have it over with the troublesome 'nationalists'. In one of his speeches he indirectly intimated his real objectives. This occurred at a meeting of key Party members in Kzyl-Orda, which was held on 16 October 1928. At the end of his long speech, Goloshchekin declared with excitement:

115

In general when I speak of groupings, I have in mind nationalists. When I mention activities of Sadvokasov's kind, I also have in mind those of Khodzhanov, Ryskulov and Mendeshev and of all those who associate with them. They are all cut from the same cloth.

The objective conditions making it possible for groups like this to operate have not yet been eliminated: the former leaders are alive and *they still walk the land* [my italics], although admittedly not that of the Kazakhs.[1]

Goloshchekin had previously been more conciliatory towards the nationalists. At the Second Plenary Session of the Kazakhstan District Committee in a discussion 'On Ideological Deviations', Goloshchekin noted that 'a growing national awareness is to be observed among the Kazakhs' and confidently singled out the *bais* as the 'leaders of this national awareness'. He went on to ask:

What is currently dangerous in our *auls*? If the poor farmers get poorer or the *bais* richer? There is no danger involved in supporting the poor farmers too much ... I repeat, Comrades, there is no point in spending time discussing that first alternative and it would be still worse to make a song and dance about that, but because people keep talking about it, we have to turn our attention to it ... If we start making a big noise about deviationists, that won't cut any ice. That's not the way to go about things. We need to take into account the special conditions facing Kazakh communists. Patience, forbearance, training, self-education and deep trust shown to those who deviate.[2]

Initially, we see, Goloshchekin presenting himself to the public as the patient, attentive educator.

Then the merciless fight began.

The Third Plenary Session of the Kazakhstan Area Committee of the All-Russia Communist Party (Bolsheviks) unanimously condemned all the groups [those of Sadvokasov, Khodzhanov and Ryskulov] and stopped their attempts to lead the Party organization in Kazakhstan away from the Leninist path.

The Plenary Session called upon Party organizations and all communists to wage a resolute struggle against ideological and organizational misinterpretations of the Party line and to intensify their ideological struggle against Alash-Orda and against the 'right' and 'left' deviations among Kazakh communists.[3]

Goloshchekin set himself the task of creating social divisions within the *auls*, fanning class struggle – something which was bound to meet with opposition. It was not the first attempt by Bolsheviks from outside the region to promote antagonism within the Kazakh *auls*. In January 1923 at the Third Kazakhstan Conference, in a report by Wainshtein, Chairman of the Kazakhstan Trade Union Council, a militant appeal had been made for comrades 'to remain implacable towards the oppressors, to intensify their onslaught against the exploiters – the *bais* and the *begs*.'[4]

At that stage – as later recalled by the writer Sabit Mukanov – Sadvokasov and those who shared his views could still 'speak out openly'.

They stated frankly that in the Kazakh *auls* there had never been oppressors and the oppressed and so there could not have been any kind of class struggle … On that occasion Sadvokasov had been able to make a long speech, which he ended with the words:

If you read the word *baza* [base] back to front you get '*azab*': '*azap*' in Kazakh means 'disaster', 'suffering', 'pain' – and the letter 'p' sounds almost like 'b' in conversation. The class struggle will not bring anything to the Kazakh *auls*, apart from disasters and suffering.[5]

In 1923, however, everything remained at the level of theoretical arguments. After Goloshchekin arrived, everything changed. The same Mukanov wrote when piecing together his memories of July 1926:

It was not without satisfaction that I learnt that the leaders of the 'right-wing nationalists' who had gathered in Orenburg were coming to the end of the road. Filipp Isaevich Goloshchekin, the First Secretary of the Kazakhstan Area Committee, turned out to be not just a man with a rare capacity for work, but also a far-sighted, if not to say rather cunning, politician. With the support of the Party organization in the Area, he demolished Khodzhanov's group and removed Khodzhanov from the leadership. Sadvokasov had a hard time as well. He became timid and cautious and stopped openly expressing his nationalist views, but at the same time was still pursuing his former policies. It did not, however, prove easy to deceive Goloshchekin, a communist of the old guard, who prior to the Revolution had gone through the school of the Bolshevik underground. Sadvokasov, however, by now was like a boat at sea in a storm. The wave that would overturn it was gathering momentum.[6]

The large-scale introduction of the class struggle into the Kazakh *auls* began in 1927. On 14 February *Soviet Steppes* printed an article entitled 'On the Question of the October Revolution in the *Aul*'. The author clearly had in mind the beneficial work carried out by the committees of poor peasants, when he wrote: 'The villages have experienced their own October Revolution but in the *auls* we have not yet resolved the question of the October Revolution, we have merely placed it on the agenda. We have a dictatorship of the proletariat in the Centre but the *bais* hold sway in the *auls*.'

The Area Committee sent journalist Gabbas Togzhanov on a three-month assignment to one of the *auls* in the Dzhetys Area and soon afterwards, on 4 July, his first article appeared, entitled 'The *Auls* as they are Today'. He produced a colourful illustration to represent the theoretical tenets outlined at the Plenary Session. As the author explained, all six of the communists in the settlement were accustomed to go to the mosque and pray to Allah. The secretary of the Party cell admitted that the *bais*, the prominent figures and the mullahs were in control of everything: 'In the minutes we write that the pre-election campaign went well, but that's all lies.' The sixty-year-old Party member explained in a simple way why he used to go to the mosque: 'I do not have many years left. At my time of life, how can I forget about God? If I'm expelled from the Party for that, I do not object.'

On 28 August Togzhanov's second article appeared – 'Sovietization is the Only Way'. He wrote that the Sovietization of the *auls* 'had not been put into practice at all'. One of the prominent locals – a trader who had four wives – used to resolve disputes among the local inhabitants. The *aul* meanwhile was headed by a real *aksakal* [elder]: a powerful *bai* who had 800 sheep, over a hundred horses, several camels and cows and three wives (originally there had been five):

> We had the 'good fortune' to talk to this Shaltabai-*aksakal* in person. For a long time he insisted that 'although he was a *bai*, he was a true Soviet man'. He always used to help poor peasants and continues to do so. He's 'for the communists', because 'I have been a communist since the times of Nicholas'. He also boasted that in his *Sat* clan, there were no disobedient people, that all the poor and middle farmers obeyed him.

A blow was dealt to the obedient that autumn during the elections to the Soviets, when dozens of experienced Party workers were sent out into the provinces. 'For the first time the Party ploughed the furrow of the class struggle in the *auls*,' wrote Goloshchekin on 1 November 1927 in *Soviet Steppes*, 'and helped the poor and middle peasants of the Kazakh steppes to understand what the Soviets were – not deliberately planted individuals or clan representatives, but bodies that would express their interests as workers.'

This prompted an army of people to take shape, who were later to make a sad name for themselves as 'false *belsende*' or 'false activists'. The poor peasant committees in Kazakhstan were no less zealous than their Russian models, when it came to interference and robbery.

In November 1927 the Sixth All-Kazakhstan Party Conference was held in Kzyl-Orda. On this occasion Goloshchekin unleashed decisive blows at the 'national-deviationists', who still dared to contradict him and used heavy artillery in his arguments with them for the first time. He began his address with the words: 'In order to introduce you more effectively to the course of the policy now being pursued by the Area Committee, I shall allow myself a somewhat immodest step.' At this point Goloshchekin reminded his audience how, after the Third Plenary Session, complaints had been made against him to the Central Committee. As a result, 'the idea came to me that we should ask the Central Committee, or at least its secretaries, to evaluate our work.'

From among all the secretaries, Goloshchekin had chosen the General Secretary, Stalin. He proceeded to read from his 'Five Questions to Comrade Stalin':

We have raised the question not about how to enliven existing Soviets, but about how to organize real Soviets. Nine-tenths of our organization support this approach and only a very small minority (Sadvokasov and his associates on the one hand) is shouting that this approach, and in particular raising the question of the class struggle and an 'October Revolution', is tantamount to civil war and incompatible with the resolutions adopted at the XIV Congress, and (Zhandosov, on the other hand) sees such measures as too weak and suggests that we should embark upon expropriation. It is in connection with this main policy of the Area Committee that we need an answer.

He went on to pose questions to Stalin concerning Party development, relations between nationalities, the indigenization of the Party apparatus and finally about the 'whole direction of policy in Kazakhstan'. 'I have already received a short answer to these questions,' he continued modestly and proceeded to read out a historic message: 'Comrade Goloshchekin! I think that the policy outlined in your note is in the main the only correct one. J. Stalin.'[7]

His hands were no longer tied; Goloshchekin no longer needed to stand on ceremony with the disobedient. He had, however, noted the need to assert his authority. He went on to inform the delegates that he 'had discovered by chance a mandate he possessed, which had been issued to me and other comrades by Vladimir Ilyich Lenin and written in his own hand.'

The document – relating to the creation of the Turkestan Commission and dating from 1919, which had nothing to do with the then current agenda – was read out in full. However, Goloshchekin knew the power attached to authority and the real power it enjoyed in a Soviet context. Now everyone at the conference knew that Lenin had sent him to the region and that he had Stalin's firm support.

Goloshchekin had never before spoken so brazenly to his comrades in the Party. He then presented the conference with his views of the opposition, condemning their arguments as 'scraps of gossip, a collection of slogans taken from various nationalist platforms'. An extract from the conference report printed in *Soviet Steppes* on 22 November 1927 reveals the picture he painted of the opposition during this speech:

Goloshchekin: It is not difficult for the opposition to collect gossip from within Kazakhstan. They probably heard it from Sadvokasov and Munbaev and it had probably been written by Toibo. Tumailov had written in from Turkmenistan.

Toibo: I have nothing to do with him.

Goloshchekin: He is your friend. Take him with you and go wherever you like, to Hindenburg, to join Abramovich's party, he's inviting you along too ... Now I should like to say something about the leadership here in Kazakhstan. You know how Zinoviev put it: 'Goloshchekin has been presented with Kazakhstan as his own personal domain' – those were Munbaev's words. (Laughter.) When and in which year did the mass-scale Kazakh organization enjoy such growth and momentum? They have never been the same as in those years again. Let the 'leaders' of any other groups try and speak out against the Area Committee. They would all be smashed inside a week. (Loud applause.)

Now I shall open wide the brackets I talked to you about in my opening address. I said that the Kazakhstan organization had matured over that period and thrown off the swaddling clothes which had been impeding its growth. As we all know, when swaddling clothes are thrown off, they are often not very clean and it is dirty swaddling clothes like that which the Kazakhstan organization has thrown off. (Laughter, applause.)

Toibo: You haven't understood!

Goloshchekin: Just smell them! (Laughter, applause.)

In the years that followed people went on laughing and clapping their hands, though outside the doors of such meetings there were people collapsing, swollen from malnutrition. Of course they were laughing – the man in charge was laughing.

Goloshchekin reigned supreme both on the platform and in the presidium. He threw out pithy rejoinders, interrupted other speakers, and relished his own heavy-handed wit. Then Uraz Zhandosov, a member of the opposition, took the floor: 'We are not blind nationalists ... and are well aware ...'

Goloshchekin interrupted: 'Not blind ones, but clear-sighted nationalists!'

Guffaws broke out in the hall once again and there was loud clapping. Goloshchekin ignored the interruption and went on to address what he termed 'Little October' – the redistribution of pastureland and ploughed fields in the *auls*:

> That is what Comrade Sadvokasov was shouting out against at the Second Plenary Session – precisely 'Little October'. We really did succeed and in practice brought about a clash of interests between the poor peasants and the *bais* concerning land: we obliged the poor peasants to take land away from the *bais*, helping them to do that ourselves. That is what I call class struggle!

His sense of achievement is easy to understand: for two years he had been trying to promote precisely this antagonism in order to create social divisions within the *auls*, employing the ancient principle of 'divide and rule'. In this Goloshchekin was no pioneer; he was merely following in the footsteps of his teachers. One of them – Yakov Sverdlov, Chairman of the Council of People's Commissars – had as early as 20 May 1918 formulated this key thrust of Bolshevik policy:

> Only if we are able to divide the rural population into two irreconcilable and hostile camps, if we can set the same civil war alight there which was being waged until recently in the towns, if we can succeed in driving a wedge between the poor peasants and the rural bourgeoisie – only then shall we be able to say that we shall accomplish in the villages what we have succeeded in doing in the towns![8]

Evidently the Bolsheviks sought to unleash civil war. Only if they were able to poison relations between different groups and force mutual destruction, would the occupiers consolidate their hold on power.

It seems that Goloshchekin was not in the least concerned with the farming economy of the people of the steppes, though it formed the very material of their lives. As more and more class struggle appeared, there were fewer and fewer sheep and horses to be seen. When the struggle reached its culmination, people began to die of hunger.

Back at the conference, Goloshchekin was congratulating himself for defending the idea of self-taxation in Moscow:

> We started out from the principle that what is important is not the quantity of money [economic advantage], but that poor peasants should be able to 'tax' the *bais* and that the poor peasants should be able to organize themselves on that basis. That is what we see as work based on class interests.

> In Moscow, in the Council of People's Commissars, not everyone understands what we are doing – some people are interpreting the law in too literal a sense. What we are engaged in is a social task. What did the chairman of the commission from the People's Commissariat for Finance propose? 'Why are you going about things in this way?' he asks. 'If you can still bring in revenue, let's raise taxes.' (Laughter.) That is what Sadvokasov has been suggesting for the last week to the Party bureau – that we should reduce self-taxation and raise agricultural taxes. As you see, any positive initiative can be distorted.[9]

Sadvokasov, the delegate from the Syr-Darya Province, retorted:

> In the Kazakh *auls* there has been no October Revolution, only a very small version involving the redistribution of ploughed lands and hayfields. We did not transfer tools of production to the poor peasants. For that we would need to have a more thorough picture of the activities of the *bais* in the *auls*. We need to decide whether to expropriate the expropriators in the Kazakh *auls*.

E. Ernazarov from the newspaper *All-Kazakh Aksakal* leapt to Goloshchekin's defence:

> Soviet power has been in existence for ten years. The Kazakh Republic only seven years, but we have only begun to see practical results from the work of our organization over the last two years, since the time when Goloshchekin began working

here and supervising these efforts. As a former inhabitant of an *aul* I support major changes in our *auls*.

Following this, there was a mass attack of Sadvokasov, with Toktabaev and others declaring: 'That's enough playing about with the Sadvokasovs. They don't help with the work of our Party, they simply hold it up.'

Particularly keen among the attackers was Izmukhan Kuramysov, who in the near future would become the Second Secretary of the Area Committee. He was a demagogic speaker, fond of mocking his opponents, who played the fool somewhat when addressing an audience:

Sadvokasov's come round to thinking that the *bais* and the *kulaks* will be at the head of the column advancing to socialism. (Laughter.)

Now he says that if you are determined to expropriate the *bais*, that will, of course, be painful for me – we shall expropriate both the *bais* and the *kulaks*. (Laughter.)

I had already pointed out that Sadvokasov, with the *kulak* and the *bai*, will advance to socialism as a threesome. Comrades, I think this idea is rotten to the core. It is not a proper Kazakh or Party approach to the question.

As regards the question of industrialization, Sadvokasov has not yet revealed his cards. In the old days he used to say that if we had leather there was no need to send it to Moscow, we should build a factory in Kazakhstan and process our own Kazakh (Laughter) national leather (Laughter). If Moscow and central factories were to grind to a halt, that was no concern of his.[10]

There was no end to the criticism heaped on Sadvokasov for his proposal that processing industries might be set up in Kazakhstan. When he argued in the journal *Bolshevik* that it would be easier to export cloth from Kazakhstan rather than to make two journeys – first to Moscow with the Kazakh wool and then back again with the 'Moscow' cloth made from the wool – there were immediate attacks against him in the newspapers, who painted him as a proponent of *bai* ideology. Uraz Isaev, for example, wrote a lengthy article in the Party newspaper attacking the 'well-known Don Quixote of National Democracy'. He supported his argument by quoting the Chairman of the Council of People's Commissars, Rykov, who at the IV All-Union Congress of the Soviets declared: 'As industrialization is introduced, the various parts of the Union will become increasingly dependent upon each other.'

Today it is clear where that path of economic development led us. Sixty-one years later that very same newspaper printed articles about the consequences of the 'interdependence' which had complicated everything in our country:

> It is no secret that our republic had long since been assigned the role of a source of raw materials for our country. What does this mean in practice? It means that over half the economic potential of Kazakhstan is subordinated to the Union's requirements. Every year the contribution from the enterprises concerned to our republic's budget represents only a tiny share of the profits they receive. Meanwhile, almost all the output from Kazakhstan consists of raw materials sent to other republics for processing. In conditions like these how can the local market supply people's everyday needs? Of course it cannot. That is why up to 70 per cent of our consumer goods have to be imported from outside Kazakhstan.
>
> What is the solution? Economic factors need to be the predominant consideration regarding the relations between the Centre and the republics, not administrative ones, and an all-Union market must become the basis for economic mechanisms. Only such a market can ensure proper accountability and self-financing, can ensure an exchange of equivalent values. Is there any reason to doubt that *perestroika* [restructuring], against such a background, would move forward at a far greater pace or that the view of Kazakhstan as a republic unable to satisfy all its own essential needs would simply vanish into thin air?[11]

Back in the 1920s the idea that *perestroika* – the notion of restructuring or rebuilding embraced by the Soviet Union in the 1980s – would be necessary as a result of the current economic path was not considered.

At this stage some things in Kazakhstan had not yet been destroyed. 'Petty-bourgeois proprietors' for example were starting to rise like dough from out of the kneading trough, though in the opinion of the Bolsheviks they were from the ranks of the politically ignorant peasantry and were attempting to grow rich. This instinct was against the founding principles of communism and had to be brought down fast, in truly Bolshevik fashion. However, on the day he died – 20 July 1926 – Felix Dzerzhinsky spoke about this trend at a plenary session of the Central Committee of the Central Control Commission of the All-Union Communist Party (Bolsheviks):

> Where do private traders have a strong position? In bread-making, leather-working – namely in those sectors where Comrade Kamenev is in charge. He comes to us and whines that everything in our country is going badly, that peasants are growing richer and their prosperity is on the increase. Comrade Pyatakov is also saying that the villages are richer than before. What a disaster! Those working in state administration and representatives of trade and industry are shedding tears over the prosperity of the peasants. What kind of prosperity are we talking about? – 400 million. The peasants have saved four roubles per person. (Laughter and shouts of 'Even less than that!')[12]

Even the creator of the torturous Cheka could see the absurdity of these complaints. 'Iron Felix', it seems, had forgotten the lessons of Lenin, who had taught that the peasantry was the main enemy of the proletariat, a bastion of petty-bourgeois ideas.

Just like Pyatakov and Kamenev, Goloshchekin was worried that the peasants in the *auls* would grow too rich. He repeatedly argued that the *bais* were on the increase and called for attacks against their prosperity.

At the Sixth Conference Sadvokasov was given the floor, probably for the last time: 'Comrades, Filipp Isaevich [Goloshchekin] devoted almost half of his speech lasting six-and-a-half hours to accusations against me. I shall confine myself to the main matters raised …'. Sadvokasov believed that policy in relation to the Kazakh *auls* was flawed. The middle peasant was, in his opinion, the key figure and he felt that the middle peasants were being underestimated and ignored:

> Goloshchekin has been demonstrating that expropriation is necessary because the *aul* in our country has been a feudal phenomenon. I do not consider that correct … Four years ago

126

Vainshtein was talking about expropriation ... This question was raised not so much for revolutionary considerations as for the enhancement of his own revolutionary credentials.[13]

Sadvokasov was the last person who tried to reverse the economic ruin which was closing in on the Kazakh *auls*.

By this time Khodzhanov had sent a semi-repentant letter to the Area Committee. It was read out at the conference. He had drawn the conclusion that it was necessary to 'root out the feudal clan leaders'. He considered that Zhandosov was mistaken when he sought to 'apply that liquidation to all the *bais*'. He also thought Sadvokasov was mistaken when he denied the need for resolute measures 'in relation to the feudal clan leaders'.

After a well-prepared attack, Goloshchekin succeeded in defeating his political opponent once and for all. In his concluding words he mocked Sadvokasov again, saying: 'You realize that Comrade Sadvokasov has been saying he is more of an internationalist than I am (Laughter) ... not only you laugh at this, but chickens will be laughing. (Laughter.)'

Then Goloshchekin delivered his final cutting sentence: 'We find ourselves up against the nationalism of the *bais*, that of Alash-Orda and Sadvokasov.'[14]

Goloshchekin and his supporters continued to criticize Sadvokasov and his supporters for a long time, licking their lips as they went.

Objections such as those raised by Sadvokasov to the First Secretary's views, even the tiniest ones, which appeared in the pages of the press or at various political meetings were immediately branded as nationalist outbursts or regurgitations of Sadvokasov's views.

When such objections appeared, Goloshchekin's close associates went out of their way to demonstrate their loyal devotion to their leader and to flatter him. When they got going, there was no holding them back. For example the Second Secretary of the Area Committee, Uraz Isaev, wrote in the newspaper *Soviet Steppes* on 26 February 1928:

The stench from the direction of Sadvokasov is like that from the most despicable of liberals, when he speaks about science, labour, co-operatives and so on. Comrade Goloshchekin was quite correct when he declared that Sadvokasov and his like are in favour of the socio-economic structure of Kazakh *auls* being left untouched.

The Kazakh 'camel' will follow, in fact is already following the path to socialism. He will crush with his mighty feet the Sadvokasovs encountered en route.

Isaev goes on to denounce the 'nationalists' who expressed doubts about the expediency of resettling Ukrainian and Russian 'landless' peasants in Kazakhstan, calling them 'frogs standing guard by the sea'. He declared that: 'While Stolypin had wanted merely to organize "Kirgiz steppes" and Sadvokasov merely to organize the "Kirgiz", we shall organize both the Kirgiz and the Kirgiz steppes.'

At this time the dire consequences of these words were not clear: all-out collectivization had not yet begun. The great resettlement took place later, when hungry crowds of *kulak* families were forced at gunpoint to leave their homes (to this day nobody knows how many people were involved) and pushed out of rail trucks in the middle of the bare steppe, clustered in dozens of specially designated settlements (or rather where settlements still needed to be built). Later, when collectivization was underway, there was a drive to reorganize the nomads of the steppes; they were forced to remain in one place and their livestock was taken away. As a result, many fled, running wherever their legs would carry them.

Ignorant of these brutal consequences, Second Secretary Isaev slandered Sadvokasov for accusing Goloshchekin of 'colonialist violence' and presenting himself as a 'martyr to the Kazakh cause'. 'Let us attack the Sadvokasov supporters in the margins of our land!' came Isaev's rallying cry.

Goloshchekin of course poured oil on the flames of this struggle at regular intervals, accusing Sadvokasov and his associates of intending to push Kazakhstan onto a path of a dangerous 'closed economy'...

On 23 May 1928 Goloshchekin reported to Party activists in Kzyl-Orda on how the Central Committee of the All-Union Communist Party viewed the work of the Kazakhstan Party organization. He told them that its political line was recognized as correct and the activities of the Area Committee as satisfactory: 'Comrade Stalin, when addressing the Politburo, started out by saying that our main achievement has been precisely to expand the number of Kazakh Marxist cadres, admittedly at a rather slow and weak rate.'[15]

Comrade Stalin.

Comrade Goloshchekin.

Eltai Ernazarov, Chairman of the Kazakh
Central Executive Committee, referred
to as the 'Kazakh Kalinin', 1928.

Dosov, Rykov, Stalin and Goloshchekin (*on the right*) among delegates
to the first session of the Supreme Soviet. Moscow, 1929.

All-Russian Congress of Soviets. Among the delegates are Kalinin in the centre, Goloshchekin (*to his left*) and Ernazarov (*to his right*), next to whom is Ilyas Dzhansugurov. Moscow, 1929.

M. Dulatov.

Zhusupbek Aimautov.

Izmukhan Karamysov: Second
Secretary of the Kazakhstan
Area Committee, 1933.

M. Shokaev.

Magzhan Zhumabaev.

Turar Ryskulov.

Leaders of the national-democratic party 'Alash Orda': *(from left to right)* Akhmet Baitursynov, Alikhan Bukeikhanov, Mirzhakyp Dulatov.

At the Akmolinsk District Conference of farm labourers and poor peasants. This was how the 'Presidium' looked in 1928.

Gabit Musrepov, 1932.

Sabit Mukanov, 1934.

Mukhtar Auezov (*on the right*).

Conference held in connection with the confiscation of *bais'* property, 1928.

Sharing out the *bais'* property, 1928.

Livestock was confiscated from Zeliev, a *bai* from the Akmolinsk District 'distribution point' in the aul of Akkol, October 1928.

A group of reapers in the 'Labour' commune.

The Politburo approved the decision of the Sixth Conference to confiscate livestock and to evict the most powerful *bais*. Goloshchekin declared:

> While we still have the opportunity in theory and even in practice to use the phrase '*Soviet bai*', in the future this will not exist and *bais* will engage with us as class enemies. They will attract many people to their ranks (members of Alash-Orda, the so-called intelligentsia, which is vacillating, and perhaps even some people from the ranks of the communists).

Goloshchekin went on to denounce local Party members who felt themselves to be more Kazakh than communist:

> We are bound to come up against obstacles within those groups, who are themselves interested in creating obstacles ... It turns out that the working masses are no better than the *bais*! A logical paradox emerges: those who should be interested in confiscating property will soon start obstructing it ... We are currently experiencing an exacerbation of the class struggle ... resulting from the pursuit of a correct proletarian policy. We are entering a phase of cleansing.

From this solemn announcement Goloshchekin moved on to self-criticism, as he was occasionally wont to do:

> When addressing a commission from the Politburo, I suggested a description of the current situation to the effect that we had got rid of opposition groups. Yet the members of the Central Committee and the Politburo suggested that we should merely say that they 'had significantly decreased in size'. The Central Committee was right to suggest this, very much so, and I was wrong.

Indeed the comrades in the Central Committee thousands of *versts* away from dusty Kzyl-Orda understood the situation in Kazakhstan better than Goloshchekin himself.

After this revelation there was a wave of exposures of group intrigue and though the newspapers did not mention anyone by name, their implications left little doubt. On 4 June 1928 an article appeared in *Soviet Steppes* declaring that: 'Members of the various political groupings are forming alliances and blocs, informing, making promises and urging each other on – doing anything to vanquish dictator Goloshchekin and the Kazakh communists who have sold their souls to him.'

✢ ✢ ✢

But what about the central question regarding October in the *auls*? Party historians provide the following account:

> In the autumn of 1928 the Kazakhstan Party organization successfully executed another very important socio-economic move – the confiscation of livestock and property belonging to 700 powerful semi-feudal *bais*, who were active enemies of Soviet power. All the confiscated property (150,000 head of livestock, agricultural tools, means of transport and so on) was made over to the Kazakh working masses. This made it possible to consolidate more than 20,000 farms of former farm labourers and poor peasants, set up 1000 collective farms, create 293 small production units and five state farms.
>
> The confiscation undermined to a considerable extent both the economic and the political influence of the *bais* in the *auls*. This in its turn provided more favourable conditions for the further development of economic activity in the *auls* and for their socialist reorganization.[16]

Worrying rumours had been sweeping through the steppe the summer before to the effect that property and livestock would be confiscated not just from the *bais*, but also from the middle peasants. People began selling their animals, and making ready to decamp. Things even went so far that the Kazakhstan Central Executive Committee was eventually obliged to appeal to all the working people of Kazakhstan and explain to them that the spreading rumours were a provocation, that there would not be any campaign against the *kulaks* and that any confiscations would only affect the most powerful of the *bais* 'from among the descendants of former khans and sultans'.

Plans had been made to confiscate 1,500 farms, but the Central Committee, as Goloshchekin explained, 'set restrictions for us'. Individuals categorized as semi-feudal landowners were those who owned 100–400 head of cattle and/or horses. The day after this decree was published, Kuramysov wrote that the time had come 'to freshen the *auls* with a revolutionary breeze', since for as long as semi-feudal *bais* existed – 'the worst exploiters of the masses living in *auls* and the fiercest enemies of socialist construction' – the poor peasants in the *auls* would not be able to escape dependence on the *bais*, poverty, squalor and disease.[17]

We must however question the number of people actually being oppressed by these so-called exploiters. According to the evidence provided by the Chairman of the Kazakhstan Central Executive Committee Eltai Ernazarov, who was later to speak at a session of the All-Union Central Executive Committee, the average Kazakh *bai* would have a number of farm labourers working for him:

> For example, a *bai* might have ten to fifteen so-called *konsy* [poor peasants]: all those poor peasants would be working for him but wages would be paid to one of them, while the rest would just be given leftovers.

This meant that there were between seven and ten thousand farm labourers who were not subjected to exploitation, and the number of oppressed peasants in the steppe was not in fact overwhelmingly large. Moreover, though they were being fed on leftovers, no one was dying of hunger. Two or three years later, when the *bai* oppressors had long since been sent into exile far away from their homeland and the liberated peasants of the steppes had had collectivization thrust upon them, there was death from hunger everywhere.

The news coming in about the implementation of farm confiscations was contradictory. Telegraphs came in from the Alma-Ata District for instance, reporting that the day the decree about the eviction of the powerful *bais* had been announced had been turned into a celebration. The peasants around Semipalatinsk had embarked upon confiscations even before the Area Committee had given them the green light and they had seized 'not merely *bais*, but middle peasants as well and that was their political error'. Sometimes however, a *bai* was given a special paper testifying to the fact that 'he is a good man and does not cause any harm to the local population'. The opposite could also happen: some demanded that *bais* who had fled should be caught, declared bandits and then 'destroyed on the spot', fearing that their former masters might take vengeance later on.

At the Sixth Conference, the now discredited and disgraced Sadvokasov had called for a close examination of the *bais'* ideas and for the handing over of their agricultural implements and supplies to the poor peasants. How much property was taken away from the *bais*? Historians do not give precise figures, but suggest that it was a large amount. Some details may be found in the periodic press. *Soviet Steppes*, for instance, reported on 13 November 1928:

CONFISCATIONS ARE COMPLETE

Aktyubinsk District

According to the preliminary figures sent in from rural areas, 14,839 head of livestock (calculated in terms of cattle and horses) were confiscated from sixty semi-feudal *bais*. In addition, agricultural implements and various other kinds of property were removed: sixteen *yurts*, eleven dug-outs, six hay-mowers, four horse-drawn rakes, seven harvesters, three barns, twenty-six carpets, twenty-six felt mats and so on.

From this we can see that not every semi-feudal exploiter possessed a hay-mower and a harvester, and even carpets and felt mats were in short supply. They did, however, all own livestock.

Soon afterwards Goloshchekin began to sum up the results of the confiscation drive, publishing a report in *Kazakhstanskaya Pravda* and another in *Soviet Steppes*. He entitled his article of 3–4 December 'October in the Kazakh *Auls*'. It would seem that, after gaining confidence in his abilities, Goloshchekin could, by this time, write in all seriousness: 'This experience is also interesting in that *for the first time in history* [my italics] we are confiscating livestock, which is far more difficult and more complex than simply confiscating land.' For Goloshchekin this seemed like a truly historic achievement, though throughout the many centuries in which nomadic peoples had existed, they had been seizing each other's herds of horses and flocks of sheep, without suspecting that this activity might be referred to as robbery or confiscation.

In the same article Goloshchekin went on to write:

The whole campaign was carried out by the Kazakh members of our organization. Kazakh communists have passed a revolutionary exam and have stood firm at their revolutionary post.

Some of the *bais* said: 'We used to be in a position of authority, but the Soviet regime has proved more cunning. It won over the poor peasants with promises of our livestock and has destroyed our authority.' In actual fact the situation had been very different. The *bais* were using livestock for bribes.

If this is the case, the poor peasants were in fact bribed twice: once by the *bais* and secondly by the Soviet authorities; they were used to carry out the expropriation of the *bais* and as a reward were given the *bais*' livestock, which they immediately ate or gave back to the authorities a year or two later when complete collectivization was implemented. This second bribery was of course more successful because the Soviet authorities, unlike the *bais*, had no emotional ties to the livestock.

The method employed far back in the War Communism period in Russia (which proved an effective destroyer of the stable and reliable commodity economy) was at once implemented in accordance with a government decree; poor peasants were given 25 per cent of the grain confiscated from the *kulaks* as a grain subsidy. This had been taken from hidden reserves, of which the vigilant poor peasants informed the authorities: instead of working, they had been keeping an eye on their hardworking and thrifty neighbours.

On 3 October *Soviet Steppes* printed a short article from Chelkar entitled 'The *Bais* are Petitioning':

> *Bais* due to be evicted sometimes engage in passive resistance, distracting the attention of the farm labourers from the conference for poor peasants. Some of the semi-feudal *bais* seem to have reconciled themselves to the confiscations, but keep petitioning the authorities to be allowed to stay on in their former homes. These requests are rejected.

According to this, the confiscations had not led to any resistance and were implemented without any bloodshed, aside from several attacks on the officials carrying it out.

In an article written for the eighth anniversary of the founding of the republic, published on 4 October 1928, Goloshchekin used the exclamations 'a dizzying leap forward!' and 'the last are turning into the first!' to describe the success of the confiscations.

Two weeks later he addressed a meeting of Party activists in the capital and once again launched into long theoretical explanations regarding the unstoppable intensification of the class struggle:

> Many people imagine the situation to themselves as follows: each new step in socialist construction and in the broadening of its base will reduce class contradictions. That is an incorrect picture of the situation: every step we take will unavoidably at the same time serve to exacerbate class contradictions, the class struggle within the Union against the Nepmen and in particular against the *kulaks*. This is what we need to appreciate, Comrades.
>
> The *bais* have been fighting to defend their position with every means at their disposal. The *bais* have been misleading the poor peasants. They're saying: 'First they'll rob me and then it will be you' ... The confiscation drive has given rise to extremely bitter class struggle in the *auls*. This is understandable: the confiscation campaign is, I would say, the class flame, which will temper the Kazakh section of our Party organization.[18]

At the Kzyl-Orda Party town membership meeting in December 1928 Goloshchekin was asked whether the class struggle had come to an end after the confiscation of the 700 semi-feudal farms. He replied: 'No and indeed more bitter class struggle is to be expected now because there are still some *bais* out there.' He went on to address rumours that Kazakh *auls* had been rendered impoverished, dismissing them as blatant opportunism:

> It is perfectly possible that some farm labourer, who was given fifteen of those sheep, might eat one or two after dozens of years without enough to eat. (Laughter.) Yet be so kind as to tell me what kind of sin that really is. Naturally there will be some problems, but we shall quickly overcome them, if we provide the poor peasants' families with credit, help and advice.[19]

By this time the first Kazakhs who had fled the country were on their way to the Astrakhan steppes, to Siberia, to Uzbekistan and other regions. Not just *bais* were leaving; many of the so-called prosperous animal breeders (who were told they would not be touched) went with them. For the time being those promises were being kept, but no one knew what tomorrow would bring. Immense pressure was put on peasants with animal herds to deliver grain, pay taxes and subscribe to peasant bonds. If you did not deliver, pay or subscribe, then you were an enemy of the Revolution. Extreme measures gradually became an all too common phenomenon. Those guilty were of course exposed, but they were dealt with gently and leniently, as if what they had been doing was just overhasty, but that their intentions were right as far as their class awareness was concerned.

Indeed how could extremes be avoided by over-zealous young people imbued with new powers, who had been convinced that 'everyone is equally responsible with regard to World Revolution'[20] and who were hearing in their Party cell everyday or reading in the newspapers exhortations of the following kind: '*Kulaks* and speculators are the most dangerous and bitter of enemies. In the struggle against them nobody should stand on ceremony. We cannot now allow a small group of inveterate enemies of Soviet power to fill their pockets by exploiting disruption of grain stocks.'[21]

Regarding peasant bonds they were constantly reminded: 'The slogan for this campaign has already been launched by Comrade Kalinin: at least one bond per peasant farm. This can perfectly well be applied, even in Kazakh conditions.'[22] The press was indefatigable in its efforts to paint a picture of the enemy. Headlines shouted: '*Kulaks* harm the poor!' 'The *kulak* nest' (this word, conveying the idea of home and family, inspired particular hatred), '*Kulaks* hide grain!' 'Extreme exploitation at the hands of the *kulaks!*' 'Jackals of the Hungry Steppe!' (this was used when the trial of the association of *bais* and *kulaks*, known as 'Earth and Labour', was just beginning), '*Kulaks* and *bais* driven out!' 'Continue the struggle against Sadvokasov and his men!' and 'Strike at the grain-hoarders!'

Many enemies of world revolution were discovered in Kazakhstan and they had to be upbraided, exposed and rooted out. Meanwhile, far away beyond the Kazakh borders there were just as many friends and comrades languishing in capitalist prisons, who so badly needed support. The Central Committee of the USSR's International Organization to assist Fighters for the Revolution called upon its Kazakh Area branch to establish links with thirty-six prisons in Germany, Poland, Rumania, Estonia, Bulgaria, Italy, Yugoslavia, Spain, Hungary, Greece, Turkey, Syria, Palestine, India, Korea and China – a total of sixteen countries.

In their own country the authorities of the USSR squeezed their farmers for grain, coerced them to buy bonds, destroyed their farms and so paved the way to famine, while 'rescuing' the communists abroad with food parcels.

In *Soviet Steppes* on 27 April 1928 Goloshchekin wrote:

> Extremes and distortions are a great evil and it is typical that the most extremes were to be noted in those places where not enough work had been done, where Party organization lagged behind the peasants, where nobody had been sorting out questions of grain for procurement before January. There were cases when pressure was even brought to bear on poor peasants, particularly during the campaign for selling bonds, when in some places those who did not take out subscriptions were branded as enemies of the Revolution.

This is an example of how extreme measures were denounced as evil and where steps were taken to ensure 'a firm line against [such] extremes', but where the rectifying measures turned out to be neither hard nor fast, hardly helping at all. The fight went on while more and more extremes emerged.

It is telling that those guilty of extreme measures were not referred to as class enemies and, however violent their actions, they were not punished by eviction to districts far away from home, as the *bais* had been.

At the end of 1928 nobody openly argued with Goloshchekin anymore: his opponents had been routed or, more likely, silenced. However, in Moscow at a session of the All-Union Central Executive Committee, Turar Ryskulov criticized the confiscation drive. Goloshchekin immediately retaliated, quoting the words Ryskulov had used at the Party meeting for the town membership in Kzyl-Orda:

> If we regard every step taken as bringing the October Revolution to the *auls*, we shall be deluding ourselves. Approximately 250–300 thousand animals of the 35 million are being handed over to the poor peasants. That is not a large percentage. The *bais* as a

social stratum would appear to account for no less than 6–7 per cent of the whole population and this will affect 700–800 farms.

Goloshchekin summed up the situation by saying that Ryskulov had donned leftist attire: 'He had described the situation well, but had not expressed himself reasonably or sincerely.'

In fact Ryskulov's fears were reasonable. He saw that extreme measures needed to be limited for political reasons, as people might renounce their activities as animal breeders altogether, heavily impacting the country's economy.

Goloshchekin went on to declare that 'Ryskulov has virtually come out against confiscation'. However, he attempted to prove this by citing an instance when Ryskulov had voiced the opposite view:

> I support this measure [confiscation] and am not inclined in the slightest to defend those *kulaks* [Goloshchekin however said that Ryskulov had transformed 'semi-feudal landowners' into *kulaks*], but probably hardly anything is being done to set up those 700–800 farms at the new sites.

It seems that Goloshchekin could not forgive Ryskulov for daring to talk about the Kazakh people not in the abstract but in specific terms and still referring to the *bais* – the class enemies. It is perhaps ironic that Goloshchekin himself came from the ranks of the petty bourgeoisie and had never belonged to the proletariat. 'Ryskulov knows that the *bais* were given plots of land and part of their livestock," pointed out Goloshchekin and then went on to conclude: "So now you see Ryskulov stripped bare – the former revolutionary leader in a new situation!'[23]

This was probably the last time that a prominent figure at Party and state level attempted to defend the *bais*. After that the word *bai* became a derogatory label and was used abusively to describe class enemies. This political label took its place among others of the same ilk: 'bourgeois', '*kulak*', 'priest', 'mullah' and so on.

Eight years previously, Anatoli Lunacharsky, the People's Commissar for Education, asked writer and humanitarian Vladimir G. Korolenko to correspond with him, promising to answer every one of his letters and to make their correspondence public. He did not, however, keep those promises and Korolenko's letters were not published in the USSR until 1988:

> The course of historical destiny has played a magic and very evil trick on Russia. In millions of Russian heads, in a matter of a mere two or three years, some kind of logical screw seems to have turned: our people has switched from blind veneration for the autocracy and complete indifference to politics right over to communism or, at least to its communist government.
>
> The essential feature of the peasantry as a class was not its drunkenness, but its hard work – work which was badly paid and offered no hope of a reliable improvement in the situation. All the politics in the last decades of tsarism was based on that lie. Now I raise the question as to whether everything in your new order is truthful? Are there no traces of a similar lie in what you have now succeeded in making the people believe?
>
> It is my profound conviction that there is such a lie and even, strangely enough, that it is one of a broad, class-based nature. You have impressed upon the insurgent and excited people that the so-called bourgeoisie is a class consisting simply of good-for-nothings, robbers raking in the money and nothing else.
>
> Is that the truth? Can you say that sincerely? In particular I ask: Can you, the Marxists, say that?
>
> You, Anatoli Vasilievich, no doubt can remember most clearly the recent period, when you – the Marxists – were waging the most bitter of disputes with the Narodniks. You were demonstrating that it was essential and beneficial for Russia to pass through the 'capitalist stage'.
>
> At that time you saw the capitalist class as the class organizing production, whether badly or well was not the issue.
>
> So why has that foreign word 'bourgeois' – an enormously wide and complex idea – been transformed by you at one fell swoop, in the eyes of our uneducated people who still knew so little about it, into an oversimplified picture of a bourgeois, who is nothing but a good-for-nothing, a robber doing nothing but raking in money?

You have sacrificed your duty regarding the truth to tactical considerations. Tactically it was advantageous for you to fan the people's hatred for capitalism, just as a detachment of soldiers might be stirred up before attacking a fortress. You did not stop at distorting the truth though. You have taken the fortress and are now letting events take their course and the looting start. You have forgotten, however, that the fortress is the people's heritage, created in the course of a 'beneficial process' and that in the edifice created by Russian capitalism there is much that needs improving and further development rather than destruction. You have convinced the people that all that was only the result of robbery, which in its turn should be stolen back.

Through your slogan 'Rob back what was robbed' you have created a situation, in which the robbing of the villages, which has destroyed an enormous amount of agricultural property without bringing any advantage to your communism, is now moving into the towns.[24]

Of course the Kazakh steppes had never reached the beneficial stage of capitalism.

An order based on clan relations existed in the *auls*. When destroying the *bais*, the peasants were not only destroying the organizers of commodity-based animal husbandry, but also their own elders. The gap between the goals of the proletarian state and the 'inert' working masses was even greater in Kazakh than in Russian villages. However well or badly he happened to be doing it, the older relative was not only 'exploiting' other members of his clan but also taking care of them. Indeed prior to the age of social upheavals linked with the Revolution, there was no general hunger to be seen in the steppe, although conditions were difficult for the poor in years fraught with bad harvests or natural disasters.

Goloshchekin's period in office was later compared with the Dzhungar onslaught hundreds of years earlier, when whole crowds of Kazakh people were taken into captivity and the whole steppe was set alight by fire and brought low by suffering. Perhaps that comparison can convey in part what happened in our times.

The days of Lenin's New Economic Policy were over. Food taxes based on the size of holdings and households were replaced more and more by the requisitioning of grain and other goods. Those in charge grabbed the peasants by the scruffs of their necks and dragged them into the 'radiant future' of collective labour, asking no questions, seeking no agreement.

Tragedy was inevitable.

❖

VII. Tragedy of a Nation

Not a single Kazakh family was left untouched by the tragedy. Everyone encountered pain and suffering. Even sixty years later it is hard for people to speak about it, sometimes impossible.

The old Kazakh writer Alzhapar Abishev did not want to share his memories about those years. He listened to my question, gave me an absent-minded smile and shrugged.

'I can't, it's grim …'

After some minutes of silence, he did finally began to speak: 'My father was called Abish, his father Zhumatai, Zhumatai's father Zholdybai. In 1931 there were ninety-four of Zholdybai's descendants. That was our family. After collectivization there were seven of us still alive.'

After another silence, Alzhapar Abishev went on: 'I had made my way to Karaganda before all that: I sensed that disaster was on the way. I had taken my mother and my wife and my youngest brothers with me to Karaganda. We five survived. But back in the *aul* only two others did.

'I remember that there was a hut made of branches next to our wooden cabin. There were three young workers living in it, who worked the same shift as I did. Once, when the temperature had gone down to minus forty, they did not appear for the night shift. Our foreman was a German called Haron. When we came home with him the next morning, we decided to look into the hut of branches. It was the second day of the snowstorm and there was a snowdrift up against the hut door. We managed to clear it away with our boots and went inside. Near a fire which had gone out there lay a dead woman and at her breast a baby of six or seven months. It was trying to suck, but there was no milk left. It was sobbing desperately. Haron realized what had happened straightaway. He closed the eyes of the dead mother, picked up the child, wrapping it in his coat, and rushed off.'

❦ ❦ ❦

Mekemtas Myrzakhmetov, a well-known literary historian, spoke of an extraordinarily tragic case: 'As a child when I used to get up to mischief and romp about, my mother was always coming out with the same mysterious words: "It would have been better if I'd left you behind ..." She used to say that in such a strange voice that I could not help but quieten down. I could not understand what she meant: where might she have left me, and why me? For some reason I could not pluck up the courage to ask.

'Later when I was older and about fifteen I asked my mother one day, why she always used to come out with that phrase I had never understood. Mama looked at me pensively, wiped her tears away and told me the story.

'It had been in the early spring of 1933, the most terrible time, when hunger had wiped out almost the whole of our *aul* (we were living in the Tyulkubas District of South Kazakhstan). In an effort to escape certain death my mother decided to go to our relatives in a neighbouring village. She carried my little sister, while I – at the age of two and a half – walked along beside her, holding on to the hem of her dress.

'We left when it was nearly evening. At the edge of the *aul* the collective farm's melon fields began. Just as we set out on the path, a pack of wolves appeared moving towards us. By this time there was no domestic livestock left within a radius of a hundred *versts* and the hungry animals came together in packs and started attacking people all over the place, something which had never happened before.

'Mama called out and started to scream for help, but there was nobody nearby. The wolves had surrounded us. They were standing, whining and tearing at the earth with their claws. My mother was faced by a terrible choice: either the wolves would tear us all apart, or she would leave one child to the wolves and try and run away with the other.

'The principle that if you save a son you are saving a whole clan is deeply rooted in Kazakh consciousness. Mama took her decision. She placed the little girl wrapped in a cloth on the ground, then grabbed me by the hand. Although I could hardly shuffle along, as I was so emaciated, she ran forward pulling me behind her.

'When she returned later with other people – some had brought guns and others sticks, there was nobody there any more. Just the cloth was lying there, covered in blood.

'So I owe my life to my younger sister.

'Then I asked my mother – there were many things I still did not understand! – why had she not left me behind? She answered: "A son was more important." It is terrible to imagine what she had gone through, what she had been thinking to herself all her life long.

'She had cried her heart out then and had no tears left.'

Galym Khakimovich Akhmedov witnessed many deaths and much human suffering in the course of his long life. In 1921, at the age of fifteen, he was at school in Orenburg; he remembered seeing the railway station platforms piled high with corpses and carts heavily laden with the dead, rattling along the streets from early morning. Somehow, what he saw ten years later was even worse.

'There were so many people dying at that time,' Galym Akhmedov told me. 'There was an orphanage in our street in the town of Aulie-Ata and they used to take away children's bodies in carts every day. They collected them up in the mornings.'

On three occasions in 1932, Akhmedov, who was then working as the director of a technical school, had to take part in a commission investigating cases of cannibalism.

'A man from the GPU, by the name of Petrov, came out from Alma-Ata. He looked very much like a Kazakh. I started talking to him in Kazakh. He shook his head to show he did not understand. He turned out to be a *yakut*. There were four diamond-shaped badges on the lapel of his uniform jacket [indicating high-ranking office]. He had been sent to investigate a situation after a letter of complaint had been sent in.

'We set off to one of the *auls*. One of the women had hidden a human skull and pieces of meat under a pile of ash. She had killed someone. Security guards led her away, I have no idea where to.

In the last *aul*, not far from the town, where the Sverdlov collective farm was, a young lad was the only person still alive there. He had survived because he had eaten human flesh. He had killed a woman with a knife. We started interrogating him, but he would not confess. "No, I didn't touch anybody!" That was impossible because we had found all the evidence in his house. Someone said: "You should fear Allah, because you will face death soon!" Indeed, by this time he was already lying on the ground with a swollen stomach, not moving. He could keep it up no longer and in the end confessed. He started crying and said: "I was out of my mind with hunger and I knifed her." The third case involved an old man from a nearby *aul*. He had been living on human flesh for a whole month.

'It is terrible to think back to those times, but we should not remain silent any longer. It would be impossible to forget how in the winter of 1932, when it was desperately cold, people walked from the Sarysuisk District to Aulie-Ata [now Taraz]. "Walked" is not the right word – they could hardly drag themselves. Women, children and old men – they were dirty, half-crazed with hunger and in rags. Did they manage to survive? After all the people in the town were starving as well.

'What struck me most of all was what seemed like an insignificant episode. At the very beginning of the famine I came to the bazaar. There was noise and shouting and bloodstains on the ground. I turned back and, not far from the empty stalls, there was a pit which was quite deep. There was a small Kazakh boy sitting at the bottom of it. He was lying on the earth on his side, clutching his head in his hands and shivering. His head was all covered in blood. There was a frozen look of terror and inexpressible suffering on his face. He had been starving and in the end had tried to steal a flat loaf from one of the women traders, but unsuccessfully. He had been caught and then beaten round the head.'

Archivists and historians tell us that virtually no official documents concerning the hunger at the time of collectivization have survived; according to recorded history, the famine in Kazakhstan never happened.

I spent several days looking through files in the Central State Archive of the republic, which contained documents from the 1930s – materials from various People's Commissariats. They were empty. It was as if someone had deliberately removed everything, even indirect mentions of the tragedy. It seems that those who caused the famine took care to sweep away its traces.

However, among the thousands of documents in the archive I found evidence of the looming universal famine. On 28 May 1931 the Health Department of the Karkaralin District reported to the People's Commissar for Health about the dire public health situation:

The position with regard to food at the present time is deplorable, if not catastrophic. In the 'Sheep-breeder' collective farm the families of all the farm workers and office staff are no longer being supplied with food. The bread ration is only given to the farm workers and half a litre of milk to each one of them, but absolutely nothing else, although the farm worker might have a family of five to ten people. No sugar and no cereals are being issued.

In the town 300 prisoners have not been issued any food in the last few days and they are only surviving thanks to food parcels, if these are brought in for anyone.

In March and April white-collar workers were issued with 7 kilograms of inferior millet for them and their families, regardless of the number of family members. Some of them did not receive anything at all.

Many health workers are leaving. One by the name of Glebenko left for Semipalatinsk although it is 360 *versts* away. If the picture does not change most of the health workers, including the doctors, may have left for good by the autumn.

In the prison there is scurvy and tuberculosis is growing more serious. There is scurvy in the orphanages and 80 per cent of the mothers in the hospital have scurvy.

Signed, Stanitskii.[1]

This was where the large clan of Zholdybai, great-grandfather of Alzhapar Abishev, was living at the time.

Many have forgotten the confiscation of property and livestock belonging to 700–800 prosperous semi-feudal *bais*. Dana-bike Baikadamova is one of the few who still remember:

'I can remember my father from the time I was five or six. He was a stocky man of medium height and with a tanned complexion. He used to come home at twilight and sit down wearily at the table. Then he would take off his glasses with their blue lenses and sit drinking tea for a long time in silence. I used to go and sit beside him and ask: "Papa, what kind of glasses are those and why do you cover your eyes with them?"

'He would answer: "Little daughter, I have to cover my eyes. When I was just a bit older than you I used to have to copy out lots of papers in an office. At night I would draw plans on thick white sheets of paper. The oil lamp was dim and I could hardly see what I was doing. When I went outside in the mornings, the bright light would hurt my eyes. It damaged my eyesight. That's why I wear glasses now, so that my eyes do not hurt out in the sun."

'My father would sleep soundly and then set off for his work once again.

'To the south beyond Turgai people were damming the Kabyrga and Tokanai rivers under his supervision. They were building dams and canals to irrigate waterless land. My father looked like someone who was strict and reserved. Being a very modest man, he did not say a word at home about how important those dams were for the poor peasants. Later on I learned that he had undertaken an exhausting journey to Moscow and, according to an official memorandum, he, Baikadam Karaldin, Chairman of the Turgai District Executive Committee, was granted 1,720,000 roubles for the construction of those dams. He worked hard in the land-amelioration department of the USSR People's Commissariat for Agriculture. Hunger had already begun in the steppes and if they had not built those dams in time, there is no knowing whether the people of the district would have survived or not. My father set up the "Kenzhetai" cooperative and people began to sow millet in irrigated fields. There were more than 143 families in the cooperative – 840 mouths to feed – and they survived. They also helped large numbers of other people to survive the unprecedented famine.

'No one had taught my father to build dams. He worked out everything for himself. As a fifteen-year-old, after completing two years at the Turgai Russian and Kirgiz elementary school, he started straightaway working in the district administrative office. He worked as a copyist, bookbinder and accounts clerk and later on he became their translator. He subscribed to journals, was friends with the local vet and was probably the most educated man in the district. He was thoughtful in his approach to everything, a serious and conscientious man. At the age of twenty-eight, Baikadam Karaldin, a Grade III clerk, was awarded a medal "for zeal", to be worn round the neck on a ribbon of the Order of St Anne. He was also decorated for building a dam at Kyrkhan, designed to hold back the waters from the melting snows. Thanks to that the people of Turgai were able to sow waste ground with wheat. Since then the local people felt deep respect for my father.

'Mama was a fine singer and played the *dombra* remarkably well. She had inherited her gift for music from my grandmother who was renowned throughout the Turgai steppe for her voice and her compositions. Papa, incidentally, also played the *dombra* with great skill but preferred listening to Mama. Before the Revolution Mama used to sing and play in the Turgai amateur theatre, and was highly successful. Naturally she had very little time for music, because there were plenty of family duties at home. Before I was born in 1914, my parents had had seven other children who had died in infancy. They looked after me with great care and even hired a Russian nanny for me – Grunya. Perhaps it was that young girl who kept me alive; I grew up to be healthy and strong. Papa found a husband for Grunya and he gave her away when she married the fine young man, whose name was Kolesnikov. The children born to my parents after me also survived and soon I had four brothers and three sisters; there were also two other children whom my parents had adopted.

'In 1928 everything was ruined. In the autumn the campaign to confiscate large farms belonging to *bais* began and Papa, although only the son of a middle peasant, was suddenly classified as a semi-feudal landowner from the steppes. Those who had no less than 400 head of livestock were considered *bais*. We, of course, did not have as much livestock as that on our farm, but unfortunately, not long before the confiscation drive my father's mother had bequeathed us all her livestock. Even so the total did not come to 400, but that did not seem to bother the authorities. They suddenly forgot about everything, including my father's involvement in the uprising of 1916 – as a comrade-in-arms

147

of Alibi Dzhangeldin he had been sentenced to death and was only saved from the noose by an amnesty of the Provisional Government – and his service to the Soviet regime. After 1918 my father had worked as chairman of the local Soviet and later he had been the People's Commissar for the Turgai District and Chairman of the District Executive Committee. He had held other important posts in addition to these and during the 1920s had set up dozens of small production units and cooperatives.

'In September 1927 he set off to Kzyl-Orda to submit a complaint about the illegal actions of those carrying out the confiscations. However, when he got there he did not find his former comrade Alibi Dzhangeldin, the then deputy chairman of the Central Executive Committee, and Goloshchekin refused to accept his complaint. After that Baikadam Karaldin set off to Moscow to seek justice from M.I. Kalinin, whom he had known since 1919. At Chelkar station, however, my father was arrested by GPU men and locked up under guard. Soon after he was tried as a saboteur and fugitive. He was sentenced to eighteen months and taken to prison in Semipalatinsk.

'Mama now had a difficult choice to make: either to go into exile with her many small children or to turn her back on our father. There was no one to whom she could turn. Our livestock had been taken away, there were only sixteen animals left – the number specified by law – and the family had been driven out of the house where they usually spent the winter. I, the eldest of the ten children, was only fourteen and my youngest brother Murat was only six months old. Where could she go with that crowd of children? Far away, where there were no friends? Mama decided to ask for a divorce. That was how we lost Papa's surname and began to use Mama's maiden name – Tulebaev – and a name derived from our father's first name – Baikadamov.

'We moved from Turgai to Kabyrga where we had relatives. In January 1928 a Party *belsende* (activist) well known in the district turned up on a sleigh. His name was Khamza Zhuzbaev. He was insolent and always shouting. He had shameless little eyes and a pockmarked face. He was always up to no good and causing quarrels. On that very day an alarming rumour spread round the *aul* about some kind of confiscation. Although I was only fifteen at the time, I was working as a tally clerk at the stockpiling depot; my father had taught me the principles of bookkeeping and accounts. When I came home from work, Mama was not there. I managed to find out from my grandmother that Mama had been taken away on a sledge to the neighbouring *aul,* 20 *versts* away. It was the Party man with the pockmarked face who had taken her off. I was alarmed because that beast was capable of anything.

'In that *aul* there lived an elder held in profound respect by the local people and whose name was Bizhan; in his youth he had been a well-known narrator of folk tales. He was a member of our tribe: a strong and kind man. Whenever he came to visit us, he would immediately gather us children around him and we would sit on his lap or at his feet; then he would stroke his beard with his enormously long fingers and tell us ancient legends, fairy-tales, stories and poems. We were all very fond of him. When I found out the news about Mama, the first thing I did was to rush round and tell him. The old man was heartbroken; it turned out that he had not known that Mama was in their *aul.*

'I eventually found the shed where Mama was being held. They let me go in to see her, but our poor mother was deathly pale. She looked thin and her complexion had become yellow since Papa was arrested, but now new troubles had befallen her. She said nothing, but tears trickled down her face. "Mama, what's the matter?" I asked. – "It's all over, daughter. Soon we'll have to say goodbye." – "But why?" – "They're starting to confiscate girls now."

'I sensed that someone was looking at me from over by the door of the house. I turned round to find a stranger in a round hat trimmed with fur – the kind people from Kustanai used to wear. He looked me over greedily from head to toe, his little round eyes like fresh sheep pellets. The pockmarked Party activist came over. "Well, how d'you find the bride?" he asked the stranger. He then turned to me and said: "Well, dearie, d'you know what's in store for you? If you are so foolish as to play stubborn, you'll be taken off to the Chinese border to a tribe of little men – Lilliputians. Out there you'll be married off: they need *bais'* daughters very badly to improve their stock." He burst into loud guffaws.

'I saw that my mother had fallen silent, nodding meekly while tears poured down her cheeks. Was I really to be married off to that man with sheep pellets instead of eyes? Never! I took Mama's hand and led her away from them. Zhuzbaev blocked my path. He stood there grinning. "You'd do better to agree; you won't regret it. What a fine bridegroom! Not just anyone – he's from the district finance department! We only want the best for you."

'Suddenly the rattling of hooves could be heard and my uncle Kenzheakhmet came galloping into the yard on a frisky horse. He jumped down to the snowy ground, pushed Khamza Zhuzbaev aside with his shoulder and signalled that he should follow him. The activist was about to start shouting threats at my uncle, but my uncle did not say a word, merely brandished his whip.

'It turned out that my uncle's daughter had recently gone missing. Neighbours had told Uncle that there was a new drive to "confiscate" young girls. He rushed to the houses of his relatives and found that my mother and I were no longer at home. He rushed to the *aul*, thinking that his daughter would be here as well. It transpired that she had already been taken and married to someone. If it had not been for my uncle, I do not know how everything would have turned out for us. Mama had been so badly frightened by those villains that she had no strength left to resist their orders and in our household there were no men left.

'A few days later we learned that almost all the girls in the *aul* had been married off in the course of a single night – at top speed, with no bride money, to escape slavery with a tribe of so-called Lilliputians. This of course had been thought up and carried out by devious activists. There was no such tribe.

'Many years later I ran into my designated "bridegroom" unexpectedly. In 1944 in a cold, hungry, wintery Alma-Ata I was collecting water from a standpipe. I turned round and there he was. With the same little sheep-pellet eyes, he stood there shivering and holding a bucket. What's more he recognized me. He shuddered for a moment and then turned away, hiding his gaze. I shall not mention his name; why should I bring shame on his children and grandchildren? Later I was to discover that he had been teaching at the Party school in Alma-Ata in the war. He had made good.

'At the end of that year we first heard about collective farms. We were strictly forbidden to leave the *aul* and ordered to wait for further instructions. We were told by those in charge: "You'll soon have a settled life and all work together." Nobody understood what a collective farm was. We were told that it would be a farm for all of us and that everything in it would be common property. We would sleep under shared blankets and even the children would be communal property. People believed everything they were told and were scared.

'In November 1929 a so-called uprising took place, though in reality there was no sign of an uprising that I could see. Three *belsende* led by Khamza Zhuzbaev galloped in from Kustanai to Batpakkara. It was as if they had been specially selected – slippery customers with a murky past. As it later emerged, they not only engaged in scheming and extortion, they were secret informers for the GPU. They announced that there was no more Soviet power; rule by khans was to be reinstated. With a few accomplices, they drove the communists into the mosque, shaved their hair and beards and forced them to pray. They burned the papers in the militia office, looted the shop and broke down the fence, behind which the jointly owned livestock was kept. Then they embarked on endless *toi* [feasts]. Every day they would slaughter horses and sheep and stuff themselves with the fresh meat. For six days they celebrated the reinstatement of the khans, until two lorries of soldiers arrived from Karsakpai and seized the "insurgents".

'At the very beginning of the disturbances I sensed things were going wrong. Our confiscated horses, which had been handed over to the poor peasants, came running into their familiar stables, neighing, clearly missing their former home. My brothers and I tried to drive them away but to no avail. Anyway, how could children hope to control such large, intelligent animals? Mama and I were afraid; if we failed to drive the horses out from our yard, those in charge would arrest us for re-assuming ownership of our livestock.

'Soon the militia arrested all men in the settlement aged over sixteen. In Kustanai the instigator of the disturbances was forced to give evidence about those who "had taken part in the uprising".

However, anyone who had stood in the crowd that gathered and listened to the leader's tirade was branded a participant in counter-revolutionary activity. Everyone had been part of that crowd! Who could have avoided it, when Khamza Zhuzbaev and his friends had forced all the old men to go the rally and made the young men wait on them at the well-decked table? Now everyone was guilty. The three ringleaders of the unrest – it is still not known whether or not they had been *agents provocateurs* acting under instructions from the GPU secret police – were shot and some of our young men paid with their lives for their mischief. The rest were tried as a group all together; some were given five years, others three, and they were all sent to various prisons.

'That was when our real suffering began. Soon after those events our mother was arrested and taken to Kustanai. She was accused of supporting the insurgents, of allegedly giving them horses. I rushed over to the scene of the trial. No documents were produced at the trial, just one statement. We managed to extract her from prison.

'I told her that we needed to leave. There was nothing for us here but suffering. Yet where could we go without internal passports? We managed to make our way to Alma-Ata via Karsakpai and Kzyl-Orda and we told Dzhangildin everything. He promised to settle my younger brothers and sisters into the Alma-Ata children's home. After that I went home and reregistered the farm in my name, although I was only sixteen. I kept two little sisters with me and sent Mama with the other children to Karsakpai. There at the mine they should be able to sell their horses and then hitch a ride to Dzhusaly station and from there travel to Alma-Ata.

'After that I entrusted my small sisters to our grandmother, while I myself went to the Batpakkara District, where I found a job as a bookkeeper. Then a young man appeared on the scene, keen to find himself a wife without having to pay any bride-money. He was the head of the district police. His plan did not work out, but, in refusing him, I lost my job. This "bridegroom" sent in a complaint to the District Party Committee saying that the daughter of an Enemy of the People had succeeded in penetrating a Soviet institution in order to engage in sabotage.

Without waiting for the ensuing purge, I went back to my own *aul.*

'During my absence still more good-for-nothing activists had appeared. They would wander about all day on horseback, spreading rumours to scare the inhabitants. At night they would slaughter livestock, drink and gorge themselves. Without hesitating, I went to the Rural Soviet making sure I was not seen on the way; a former classmate of mine worked there as a secretary. When he saw me, he burst out laughing and asked: "Where have you sprung from?" I asked him to give me a paper so that I could leave the *aul.* "A paper for you?" he exclaimed in surprise. Then he pointed in the direction of the mosque and said: "Go and listen to what they're saying."

'I obeyed and walked quietly through the dark towards the open door, through which bitter tobacco smoke swirled. Our activists were in the middle of a discussion. Suddenly I heard my name mentioned. "Karaldin's daughter should be put on the list!" – "Yes, she's got sixteen animals! She's a real *Shoshai-bai!*" The chairman asked: "Who wants to put that proposal to the vote?" The rest of them started shouting "*Shoshai-bai! Shoshai-bai!*" and altogether they raised their index fingers. [In those days Kazakhs voted not by raising their right hand, but simply by raising their index finger. Hence the phrase "*Shoshai-bai*", which in the language of those eager activists meant Enemy of the People: a person who should be stripped of their property. The word translated literally as the person who has been shown a finger.]

'Oh God, I thought to myself. They're going to arrest me! I rushed back into the *aul* Soviet and said to my former classmate Bokan: "Help me out! They've put me on the list!"

'He laughed again: "You're a fool, why did you ever come back from Alma-Ata? All right, I'll help you. Leave your sisters behind, your grandmother will look after them; you must run as fast as you can to the ravine by the river. My father's down there with horses. He too is down on the list as a *Shoshai-bai.* Make sure you don't set foot in this cursed place again."

'That night Bokan's father and I travelled as far as the *aul* through which the road to Karsakpai passed. Almost immediately the door was flung open and the messenger from our *aul* Soviet came in – one of the men who had been discussing me in the mosque. He grabbed my arm and said: "So this is where you got to! I thought you were up to something. We realized what was up as soon as we saw the hoofprints. So you were planning to run off were you? No, it's not going to work. Every *Shoshai-bai* must answer to the law. You're coming with me!"

'By now I was frozen with fear. Surely he wouldn't take me back to the *aul* to be punished by those jealous activists, thirsty for revenge? They would put me in prison for trying to escape and my little sisters would be reduced to begging.

'Suddenly the silence was broken by the strong and commanding voice of the master of the house we were passing by, Absemet: "What are you going on about? How do you dare give orders here? This girl is my guest and I do not allow anyone here to harm a hair on her head! You've probably been at the vodka, if you're so insolent that you've insulted the master of the house! Come on lads," he said turning to the young men sitting at a nearby table. "Tie him up and throw him in the shed. Let him sleep it off and freshen up that no good head of his!"

'A group of young men took the messenger firmly by the elbows and led him out. Absemet winked at me and said gently: "Don't be frightened, I'll sort everything out. I'll see you out to the edge of the village myself. Not far from this *aul*, on the well-trodden track leading to the mine, there's a gate guarded by soldiers. They say that they've been catching bandits. Who knows what kind of bandits they're talking about; it's just herdsmen on the run. No one could drive past them without being stopped. You'll need my help to get past them."

'Absemet kept his word. He spoke to someone at the guard-post and after that we were able to get past the barrier without any problems. We travelled another *verst* and then he pulled up his horse. "Now my dear, I can't go any further. Ride on boldly; there are no bandits here. May Allah look after you!" He kissed my forehead by way of farewell.

'I continued on my way alone. Absemet had sent Bokan's father back, saying that otherwise his son would suffer.

'Karsakpai looked unusual in that autumn of 1931. There were hundreds of huts made of branches and with pointed roofs all round the mine. Emaciated sick people were wandering around between the frail-looking dwellings like lost souls. "What's going on?" I asked one of the people I encountered. "Don't you know? It's a disaster out in the steppe," came the reply. "They're starving. All their livestock has been taken away."

'The fugitives had been hoping to find work in the mine, but most of them had been hoping in vain. I looked at the sunken eyes of the people crowding round me; without saying anything they were asking for bread. But where could I get bread to give them? I myself only had food when people I met on the way took pity on me. The weather was frosty by now and people had no food and no fuel. They were living in drafty shelters, in which their hungry children lay suffering from the cold. They covered the children in felt mats and winter coats but they could not really shield them from the cold. Those were the people whom the activists had stripped of everything they could find – bais' children. I listened to their stories. Some of the starving people had fled south to Pakhtaaral and Saxaul, hoping to find food there, but they had soon been in such a desperate predicament that they started giving their daughters to old men, just to keep themselves alive. Girls were given away as wives for a mere pail of millet.

'In Karmakchi I managed to find my mother. She had sent two of the children to Alma-Ata and arranged a place in the Kzyl-Orda orphanage for my brother Bakhytzhan. Her long wait to find me was over. Karmakchi was a settlement on the banks of the broad rushing waters of the Syr-Darya. To this day I cannot comprehend how that once mighty river dried out, almost down to its very bed.

'The situation in Karmakchi was getting worse by the day. Hundreds of hungry people had flooded into the small dusty settlement. They were brought in by lorries from Karsakpai. In the canteen, where a watery soup was handed out twice a day, these destitute people argued and fights broke out when food was not shared out properly. In the bazaar there was always a hungry crowd, although nothing edible was now sold from the empty stalls.

'On a wooden bench at the station two very old men used to sit in their dusty and ragged army jackets, gazing distractedly into the distance. Suffering and a wish to die seemed frozen in those eyes. I did not recognize the old men reduced to helpless beggars at first; they were highly respected elders, over ninety years old and famous throughout Turgai, members of a most noble clan of heroes in our part of the world. They did not pay attention to anyone, just sat and gnawed away at dried watermelon skins. Somehow it was only then, as I looked at those old men, that I finally realized what a terrible tragedy had befallen us Kazakhs and what suffering still lay ahead.

'Mama and I were already despairing over our lack of shelter, when suddenly someone called out to us in the crowd at the bazaar. In amazement I looked at the fair-haired woman with a pleasant open face, who was smiling at me: "Don't you recognize me? You were, I suppose, just a tiny wee girl at the time. It's me, Grunya, Grunya Kolesnikova, your nanny!". The woman came rushing towards me and kissed me three times. It turned out that Grunya had recognized Mama and only afterwards realized that I was her former charge. That was how, surrounded by strangers and people unfamiliar to us, we found "our people", a roof and a piece of bread.

'Grunya and her husband took us back to their home. They shared their meagre rations with us and helped us find somewhere to live and work. In the spring of 1932 the family of my Uncle Amirali also turned up in Karmakchi with other people who had been forced to decamp. We hired a *yurt* and all lived together as one big family.

'When it grew warmer, our uncle suggested that we should move to an island which was situated between the Syr-Darya and the Kara-Uzek rivers. By this time it had become dangerous to stay on in Karmakchi; the canteen had been closed, food issues had stopped and the hungry often attacked each other with knives. They might wound or kill someone for the sake of a piece of flat bread; everyone suspected everybody else of hoarding food somewhere. Uncle got hold of a boat and soon we travelled to the island. In the mornings he and I would go to work, while the women and children spent the whole day catching fish. The ones we caught most often were large long silvery fish, known locally as *lakha*. If they caught one or two, then they would boil them up in a cauldron and throw some millet in with the fish. We never ate on our own, secretly keeping food from others; Uncle always brought back hungry people on his boat. Usually they were people he did not know; he simply collected up from the streets those most in need and brought them back with him.

'More and more people swollen from malnutrition were brought into the settlement from Karsakpai. Among them there were many people we knew from Turgai who had abandoned their *auls*. They told us about the terrible hunger in the place we thought of as home. We used to look out for people from back home, trying to find out anything we could about the fate of our relatives.

'One day I met someone from back home in Karmakchi – a venerable old man by the name of Tursunbek. In Turgai he had been a most respected figure – a kind, just man of impeccable behaviour. His wife had recently died from hunger and disease and his son had been lost in the crowds. When our uncle found out that Tursunbek was in Karmakchi he told me to find him and invite him back to our island. It was with considerable difficulty that I eventually found Tursunbek. He was sitting completely alone on the bank of the Syr-Darya, overlooking the steep drop to the water's edge. He was wearing a carefully cleaned military jacket and had a round black cap on his head. He was looking down at the fast-flowing yellow waters of the mighty river with an air of detachment.

'"*Agai!*" I called. "Come and have supper with us tonight. My uncle invites you!" On hearing my voice Tursunbek looked round listlessly and I caught sight of his thin face, furrowed with wrinkles. His eyes, which had always been clear and intelligent, were now bloodshot and cloudy. When had he managed to age like that? "All right, I'll come," he said after a long drawn-out silence. – "But you don't know the way, how will you find us?" I asked with concern. "We have a boat. I can come and fetch you …" – "Off you go now, I shall come without fail," said the old man in that slow, flat tone. There was something about his voice that made it impossible to disobey. Stumbling as I went I started to walk back, but a few moments later I could not help turning round when I heard people shouting. There was nobody sitting on the riverbank. I rushed back to the place where Tursunbek had been sitting a few moments before and looked down into the fast current. The powerful torrent was carrying along a familiar jacket spread wide against the surface and a little further down I could see the little black cap against the water, yellow from the clayey soil.

'In August 1932 I was dismissed from my job once again after someone informed on me. The daughter of an expropriated *bai* was not allowed to work in a Soviet institution. This meant that we had to move somewhere else. There were five of us: me and Mama, two sisters and my youngest brother. Fortunately, Kolesnikov had found out that in the town of Merke, a man who had trained under my father and was our distant relative, Burkutov, worked as the Chairman of the Executive Committee. We went there by train, feeling confident that he would help us. Indeed Burkutov really did help our family settle in. We found shelter in an Uzbek hovel and he came round before winter set in to bring us saxaul wood and – what was an unheard-of treasure in those days – a sack of flour. "Now I hope you'll be able to get through the winter. I can't take you in myself. We have a houseful and there isn't even enough space on the floor for everyone to sleep on it."

'Soon after that starving people came flooding into Merke from the west and north, from eighteen different *auls* in the Batpakkara District. I remember them appearing in an enormous crowd in the local bazaar – in half an hour they bought up all the food there. The next day the bazaar was looted and people did not dare to go there to trade after that. Robbery and plunder became the order of the day; a chicken would be stolen in one place and a flat loaf in another. Just before the winter set in, everyone started looking for shelter. It is difficult to imagine the terrible over-crowding there was then. The settlement could not possibly take in everyone who was trying to escape hunger and cold. Among the people who had turned up there were many from Turgai and sooner or later, of course, someone made a complaint about Burkutov saying that he had helped a *bai's* family. A commission turned up and our defender was sacked from his job. Mama and I were crossed off the list of the hungry.

However, we had to be thankful for at least having a roof over our heads in the cold winter months.

'Hardship forced us to move still further south. Burkutov and Dzhangildin helped us leave Merke, thanks to their friend, Georg Schmidt. We moved to Andreyevka, to the motor-vehicle depot. I began to work there in the accounts department and after that I found a temporary job in the Chimkent regional distribution office depot.

'One day when I was in the Chimkent bazaar I met Ziyauddin; he had been a mullah in Turgai and in his day had accompanied the rebel detachments under Amangeldy Imanov [one of the leaders of the uprising in 1916], sending them into battle with his blessing. Squatting down, eastern style, he would throw dice on to a little mat, telling the fortunes of passers-by. This was how he made his living and fed his three small children, who would sit nearby huddling close together. I went over and greeted him. When the former mullah heard that I had work, he forgot all about his fortune telling and begged me to help have his children accepted at the boarding school.

'"But who would listen to me?" I asked. "I'm only eighteen myself."

'"Please go and ask! You'll bring it off!"

'The boarding school was bursting at the seams. After numerous efforts and visits I managed to persuade the director – Heaven knows how – to take the mullah's two little daughters aged seven and eight. She did not take the little boy, as it was a girls' school. After that Ziyauddin used to lay out his little mat for fortune telling near the gates of the boarding school. As evening drew near, his daughters would come running out and bring the little boy two small pieces of a flat loaf. They ate the gruel they were given at the school, but kept back their bread for their father and brother. This went on for about two weeks. In the end the director demanded that Ziyauddin ply his trade further away from the school.

'"They're not eating a single crumb of their bread!" she would protest. "They'll die of hunger! It's a mystery how they keep going as it is."

'The mullah said nothing, just lowered his eyes. One day when I went to see him, I used the occasion to persuade the director to take in the small boy as well. In the end she said: "All right, we'll take him, but his father must stop sitting around out here." After that Ziyauddin disappeared. Neither I nor his children saw him again. He probably starved to death.

'In 1986 I visited Arkalyk, where celebrations were in progress to mark a Muslim festival. I noticed that during the service a tall mullah kept looking at me. Afterwards he came up to me with a smile and asked: "Don't you recognize me? I'm Sultan, Ziyauddin's son. Do you remember how in 1932 you saved me and my sisters from starving?"

'There had been no news from their father. Later we learnt that he had been building dams with our father in Semipalatinsk. For that he had been let out of prison; our father had informed our friends about that on a postcard. Later our father was suddenly arrested and then taken to Alma-Ata under heavy guard. The last thing he managed to do was to send a postcard during his journey. When he arrived in Alma-Ata he was hastily tried by a 'troika' and sentenced to be shot. On 25 May 1930 our father was killed. Thirty years later I succeeded in having the case reviewed. In 1960 the Supreme Court of the Republic sent an answer in which it stated that Baikadam Karaldin had been posthumously rehabilitated due to lack of evidence. What a ridiculous document! We already knew that Papa had not been guilty; the difficult hardships of growing up as children of an Enemy of the People were behind us now. No decision of a court could bring back our father.

'In the summer of 1933 Mama left for Alma-Ata. Dzhangildin helped her find a flat and soon after I joined her. My knowledge of bookkeeping, which Papa had given in my youth, came to the rescue yet again and I found myself work as an accounts clerk in the Council of People's Commissars. In August of that year I was sent with a young female Russian doctor to the 'Yntymak' ['Solidarity'] collective farm; it was 15 kilometres from Alma-Ata and sponsored by the Council. It turned out to be an empty, abandoned place. The roofs of the houses had been taken apart for firewood, the windows had lost their frames and glass and there were gaping black holes instead of doors. It was only with difficulty that we found a house we could use to sleep in.

'Later on other employees from the Council of People's Commissars turned up and we got down to work. Emaciated, half-dead people were brought in from the steppe, some on foot and some in vehicles. You could not tell whether they were men or women. Their heads had been shaved to get rid of lice and they were as thin as skeletons. Their bodies were hardly worthy of the name – their flesh had all but vanished. The doctor examined them and I wrote down the data. The doctor asked each of them why they had been out in the steppes and had not come to towns for help. I remember one man's answer: "Hungry people do not go visiting, proud people do not open strangers' doors. They shut themselves away without even the strength to think of God." Most of them replied that they been reduced to following their hungry livestock until the animals ran away.

'Gradually the empty houses began to fill up with people; the former teacher of the local school even returned. In the meantime something strange had been happening to me; I don't know whether it was because of the extreme suffering I had witnessed, but I could not sleep. If I did fall asleep, then I would have the most terrible dreams. I would often wake up feverish and then shiver all night, unable to shut my eyes. During the day I suffered from the most terrible headaches.

'At this time the doctor fell ill and died. She had not been able to understand what was happening to her and just shook her head sadly. Later everything fell into place; the teacher at the farm was visited by some people from his home region and by chance I heard what he told them:

'"The family of the head of the political department at the Machine and Tractor Station used to live in this house. It was a rare instance of a woman put in charge of a political department. She was a Kazakh woman and quite a young one. She used to walk about with a leather belt round her waist and with a holster at her side, in which she kept a revolver. She and her husband had a three-year-old son, who had been seriously ill at the beginning of the famine. What devoted care his parents took of him! Yet they could not save his life. Day and night the parents would take it in turns to sit by the bed of the weak little boy. One night when they were totally worn out, they both fell asleep. The next morning the mother saw that the boy was dead. His stomach had been ripped open and his heart had been removed. It was winter and there was a trail of fresh blood stretching across the white snow outside. Grabbing a revolver, the mother rushed along the trail. It led to a house in the neighbouring street. It was lived in by a man on his own, whose wife and two children were recently said to have disappeared. The mother flung open the unlocked door of the house and saw that the man was sitting on the floor by the stove and cooking her son's heart in a saucepan."

"'I'm going to shoot you!' she shouted."

"'Shoot me, I'm not afraid of anything,' came the answer in an indifferent voice."

"'Then, bending down without any warning, the man put his hand down behind the stove and threw down something from there at her feet. There were three human heads: that of his wife and his two small children."

"'The woman who had been standing there with a revolver in her outstretched hand, collapsed unconscious on to the floor."

'I now understood; the horror of this story had been more than the doctor could cope with. I myself had seen many horrors up to August 1933, but after that story I could not take any more. I lay delirious in a fever for several days.

'In Alma-Ata, to which I returned soon afterwards, the familiar chain of events played out again. People from our former home who had come to the town found out we were there. Someone wrote a lengthy complaint, saying that the children of Enemy of the People Baikadam Karaldin had settled down comfortably in the capital, while the children of poor peasants were dying from hunger. For eight months I could not find work, which meant that I had no right to a bread ration. My small brothers and sisters were driven out of the orphanage. It's a miracle that we managed to get through that time.

'I heard that the organizer of the harassment was a Party worker by the name of Yeleuov. He had come to the capital from the Irgiz District, where everyone had either died or scattered, so he had no longer had any one to order about. Yet I do not condemn him for what he did to our family; fate itself was to punish him. His wife died a tragic death, killed by his brother. The famine drove people to inhumane actions.

'What else is there to tell? In 1935 I married, but my marriage was not to last for long, only three years. My husband, the Secretary of the Regional Committee of the Komsomol, was shot in 1938, leaving me on my own with two small children.

'To cut the long story of my life short, I was dismissed from my work six times on account of my father and eight times on account of my husband. In addition there were many occasions when I was turned down for work at the outset. Efforts were made to destroy our family and to break our spirit. Yet other people – simple, kind people – helped us to cope. All our strength – physical and emotional – was spent on refusing to die. Despite everything, I consider our family a lucky one. As the eldest I supported and brought up my sisters and brothers and my own children as best I could. Our family was a gifted one; my brother Bakhtyzhan Baikadamov became a well-known Kazakh composer, my brother Arstanbek was a magnificent cellist and my sister Aislu became a remarkable singer – a People's Artist of our republic. I myself was unable to complete my higher education. In 1935 I became a shorthand typist and went on to found the Kazakh school of stenography.

'So there we have it. My younger brothers and sisters nearly all died, while I, the eldest, am still alive. I now complete this history of our family and in this account there is not a single drop of fantasy. I remember it all. I remember what we went through.'

✤

VIII. Rout of the Kazakh Intelligentsia

They say that Admiral Kolchak, the governor of Siberia, once casually mentioned that controlling Kazakhs was very easy; all it required was to wipe out the 500 members of their intelligentsia, which the people obeyed and believed in, and the Kazakhs would be conquered. There is no way of knowing whether Kolchak really did say this, but we do know that during his short period in office not a single member of the Kazakh intelligentsia was harmed. The idea, however, is likely to have circulated.

On 1 October 1930 Goloshchekin gave a speech at a meeting of Party activists, expressing similar ideas. He explained the tactical task for Party bodies with regard to former members of Alash-Orda: 'to utilize the Kazakh intelligentsia, bringing it over to our side so as to gain control of the masses from the *auls* and on that foundation build the Soviets.'

He went on to explain:

> The tighter our hold over the masses and the better we organize the poor peasants, the more powerful the blow we can deal at bourgeois nationalism. That would give us the chance to come closer to a period, when we shall have created our own cadres, *when we will be able to cast aside our temporary allies* [my italics]. To eclipse in any way the drive against chauvinism by a struggle against nationalism at that time would have been tantamount to renouncing any hope of winning the trust of the Kazakh masses.[1]

The language Goloshchekin uses here is revealing about his methods: 'utilizing', 'bringing over', 'gaining control of', 'casting aside'. He was careful not to overdo things initially in the fight against nationalism, to shout more loudly about great-power chauvinism; there was the risk that he might not win the trust of the Kazakh masses.

Goloshchekin was however in a position to speak so freely because he had already dealt with the leading members of the old Kazakh intelligentsia: the flower of the people's cultural and spiritual leaders. There was nobody in his way.

It had been easier to sort them out than it had been to deal with the leaders of the 'groups', as representatives of the intelligentsia were not members of the Party and so did not submit complaints about Party members to the Central Committee. They could also always be chided for their sins of the past such as their former connections with the Alash-Orda party (those past sins later became weapons used against them, when the Party had trained its own cadres and gained control of the poor peasants); of course any activity of this sort would be perceived as bourgeois nationalism.

In the beginning Goloshchekin was broadminded in his approach. He called on his comrades to cooperate with the Kazakh intelligentsia, only on the condition that the 'main principles of Party work' remained untouched. At the Fifth Conference in 1925 he announced that the intelligentsia should be brought in line with the rest of the population.

What does reducing a creative individual to the lowest common denominator mean in practice? It means forcing him into obedient compliance, emasculating his spirit or simply destroying him, because no real personality can submit to being neutralized in this way. When ground is to be levelled, hills must be the first to be flattened.

It is unlikely that Goloshchekin ever intended to involve the spiritual leaders and teachers of the Kazakh people in new social construction; he did not remove nationalist labels from any of them. This was part of a tactical trap; for a time he would tolerate the nationalists, but after that they would, in various ways according to circumstance and opportunity, be eliminated. Not for a moment did the Party members set aside the barrels of their guns.

On 27 May 1927 a certain 'S.K.' brought the readers of *Soviet Steppes* news about the writers' organizations of Kazakhstan:

> The political thrust of a work is determined by the particular movement to which an author belongs. On the basis of calculations so far, nationalist authors have brought out fourteen titles, the Kazakh Association of Proletarian Writers sixteen and fellow travellers nine. There is a slightly wider range of authors

from among the nationalists (Baitursunov, Auezov, Dulatov, Kemengerov, Omarov, Abai, Zhumabaev).

The nationalists extol the steppes and the Kazakh people in striking colours but outside any class affiliations, so that for all intents and purposes they are directing their pens against Soviet power.

As we see here, Abai Kunanbaev came under fire for his writing. Although he died before the Revolution he was declared an opponent of Soviet power.

It goes without saying that the re-education of the national intelligentsia had begun long before in October 1917. Sabit Mukanov recalls his first meeting with fellow poet Magzhan Zhumabaev in *School of Life*. It took place in 1918 in Omsk, where Zhumabaev, Mukanov's senior, was holding courses for Kazakh teachers. Zhumabaev was an attractive young man, clean-shaven with a swarthy complexion and wavy hair. After listening to what the young man had to tell him about his attempts to write poetry, he gave what Mukanov thought was a disdainful smile. Yet, despite this, he immediately helped young Mukanov, who found himself in a large strange town for the first time; he found him work as a caretaker and sternly warned him to be a dependable worker:

We had lessons in Kazakh and Russian, geography, arithmetic, nature study, education, history and religion. There were also lessons in singing and gymnastics. Magzhan Zhumabaev taught four subjects – Kazakh language, Russian, education and religion. We not only learnt by heart the principles of Islam, but under Magzhan's personal supervision he taught us the *namaz*, how to pray. The studies would have gone really well if there had not been a sudden change in Magzhan Zhumabaev's attitude to me.

Knowing that I used to write poems, he asked me one day in a rather condescending way to recite to him some of what I had written … He praised my style and presentation, yet, when he read my poems about the poor in the *auls* he frowned and the expression on his face changed completely. When I read him my verse description of my impressions of the road from Zhaman-Shubar to Omsk, he exclaimed: 'Sabit, come to your senses! Your poems are directed against the government. You have probably forgotten the golden rule: "Silence saves men from disaster" or "Those who tread carefully will never go hungry." Burn those poems, but write as much as you want to about love. Please don't argue with me about this. You also need to think about Alash-Orda. That party is the future for the Kazakh people. If you're a true Kazakh you should be dedicating your poems to it!'

I did not recite my poems to Magzhan again, knowing that it would be impossible to make him change his ideas. Yet in my heart I had already began to understand what Alash-Orda was.

Magzhan acquainted me with his own verse. I was most impressed by his lyric poems, yet the ones which extolled Kolchak and Alash-Orda made me indignant, but I kept quiet. On one occasion I could contain myself no longer listening to his rhymed praise for the Kazakhs who had decided to fight against Soviet power in the ranks of Kolchak's army.

'If you talk to me like that again, you'll find yourself not on a course of study but in prison. Do you understand?' asked Magzhan in a threatening voice.

Although I put on a repentant expression, he never recited his poems to me again.[2]

Their second meeting took place a year later, when Kolchak's army had already been routed. It was in Petropavlovsk, in a building known as House of the Romanovs, where courses for Russian and Kazakh teachers had been opened. They had been short of teachers which was probably why Magzhan Zhumabaev turned up there, according to Mukanov:

He was hiding from the Soviet authorities in his *aul* near Petropavlovsk. He had already been invited to join the Alash-Orda people who were setting up their organizations at district level. Zhumabaev was not alone. Among the teachers for our courses there were several other bourgeois nationalists as well.

We used to ask ourselves 'How is it that we're still having to study with teachers supporting Alash-Orda? How will Magzhan

Zhumabaev behave, someone who only yesterday was cursing Soviet power and praising Kolchak and Alash-Orda?'

We decided to talk about the matter with local Party leaders, Sokolov and Gozak.

'We have no other solutions,' said Sokolov. 'It is no easy task, my friends, to find a well-educated Kazakh with a university degree and who also supports Soviet power. Whether we like it or not, for the time being we have to use people like Zhumabaev and the others. You communists need to keep an eye on their work and make sure that they don't introduce Alash-Orda ideas, hostile to Soviet power.'

From the outset most of the students on the course adopted a hostile attitude to Zhumabaev and only a few of them continued to admire him.

At one of the meetings of the Party cell the question was raised as to the activities of the literary circle. A speaker told us that the bourgeois-nationalist works of Baitursunov, Dulatov and Zhumabaev were being recited at literary evenings. Some of their poems had been set to music and the students were singing those songs. It came to light that Magzhan Zhumabaev not only helped put together the programmes for these evenings but used to read his own poems in praise of Alash-Orda.

It was decided at the meeting of the Party cell that all the communist students on the courses – there were twenty of us by then – would attend the next one of these evening recitals.

After the songs had been sung and the poems recited, Magzhan Zhumabaev came out on to the stage and read his new poem 'Fairytale'. In this he sang the praises of Kenesary Kasymov and his son Syzdyk. By this stage none of the communists had any more doubts about the fact that Zhumabaev had remained true to his earlier ideas.

The next day the Party cell of the students from the teachers' courses adopted a resolution at their meeting to the effect that it was impossible for Zhumabaev to continue teaching. The local Party Committee agreed with the conclusions we had drawn and the nationalist poet was removed from his post.

At that time I was a member of the editorial committee for our wall-newspaper. The issue which came out after Zhumabaev had been exposed included a piece I had written entitled 'In a Dream'. Resorting to the rather naïve use of symbols which was commonplace in those days, I brought to the readers' attention the bourgeois-nationalist ideas and activities of Magzhan Zhumabaev.

Now, many years later, when I reread what I had written, I am yet again completely convinced that the path I had chosen then was the correct one. Although I had only had very little political experience at that time, I had embarked upon the true path charted for me by the Soviets and the Party of the Bolsheviks.[3]

Another year went by. Sabit Mukanov, chairman of the local revolutionary committee in Kokchetav, as he himself testifies, took part in armed skirmishes and even shot a prisoner, who had in the past fought for Kolchak: 'It was the first time that I had had to shoot someone and that was probably why I did not carry out my commander's order to the letter. He had told me to shoot one bullet at Kyrchik, but I shot two, although he had fallen over after the first.'[4]

On one occasion Mukanov noticed that poems by Magzhan Zhumabaev had been printed in the Petropavlovsk newspaper *Bostandyk Tuy* (Liberty's Banner): 'I was very surprised that Zhumabaev's work was being printed. I am sure I was not the only person who knew what that man stood for!'

A comrade from the Party explained to the indignant Sabit: 'Worse things can happen. You must know that three of the Alash-Orda leaders – Bukeikhanov, Baitursunov and Dulatov – fought in Kolchak's army against Soviet power. I do not know where Bukeikhanov and Dulatov are, but Baitursunov is currently Kazakhstan's People's Commissar for Education. They say that he is also a member of the RCP (Bolsheviks).' Sabit exclaimed in indignation: 'What is everyone thinking of ... They need to be shot!' However, his comrade reminded him: 'No, my friend! We have no direct evidence.'[5]

Astonishing changes had taken place in the head of this young man during the three years of Soviet power: he was prepared to shoot down his former teacher and another two writers. Mukanov describes further events surrounding the issue of literary resistance in the chapter of his book *On the Leninist Path* which bore the subtitle 'Birth of the New'. At the beginning of the 1920s, according to his memoirs, a grim ideological struggle was being fought out in the literary world. Yet there was nothing new about ideological struggle in this country; a fierce class war had taken shape on the cultural scene and it was based on a well-known principle: 'He who does not sing with us, is singing against us.'

Young Mukanov found himself once again in Petropavlovsk; he had been sent to study at the Soviet Party School. Along with Mukatai Zhanibekov – head of the local militia, known as Ugar by his friends – and three other communists, he was a member of the Muslim Party cell at the Kirgiz-Tatar Club. Another meeting was held, which Mukanov describes in detail:

> Very soon the Kirgiz-Tatar Club became a veritable arena for the ideological struggle. The bourgeois nationalists, Alash-Orda supporters, were not sitting idly by, but trying to exert their influence through literary recitals and concerts. At one of these literary gatherings, the well-known Alash-Orda poet, Magzhan Zhumabaev, began reading his latest poems: they included pan-Asiatic ones such as 'Prophet', Pan-Turkic ones like 'To my Brother!' and nationalistic ones such as 'The Yellowing Steppe'. The majority of those who had come to hear him were Nepmen. We discussed this incident at a meeting of the Party cell. Someone pointed out: 'We could ban Zhumabaev from reciting his poems, that's not difficult. Yet who would replace him? Do we have any good poems on Soviet subjects?'
>
> I mentioned several names of young poets, who had started writing poems in Bolshevist mode.
>
> 'In that case, this is what we shall do,' suggested Ugar. 'I have heard that Zhumabaev is planning to organize another such gathering in the next few days. We need to prepare our poets in advance and organize a recital of their works at the same literary evening. I propose we should disrupt Zhumabaev's recital.'
>
> 'But what if he wants to read his poems?' someone asked.
>
> 'He won't want to!' replied Ugar in a knowing tone.
>
> 'What about freedom of speech?'
>
> 'If you're so worried about freedom of speech, you can unearth Kolchak and bring him to the stage!' said Ugar, sounding angry by this time.

'Kolchak's snuffed it and Zhumabaev's alive!' protested the previous speaker.

'D'you think that there are not many people left nowadays who want the monarchy or the White Guards back? There are plenty of them left, I can tell you! Give them freedom of speech and they'll be no stopping them! No my friend, that's not what our freedom of speech is for! Just remember: there is none for counter-revolutionary propaganda! Freedom of speech is for the working people, not for our enemies!'

Everyone knew what an ardent fiery nature Ugar had. Some people were slightly wary of him, worried that he might get them all into trouble, but most of the cell members liked his proposals and they were duly accepted.

The regular members of the Kirgiz-Tatar Club, including Zhumabaev's admirers, found out from somewhere that the next gathering was going to be out of the ordinary. A large audience turned up. Among them were some of the Petropavlovsk Nepmen. When the bell rang for people to be allowed in, those in possession of tickets, which had been sold out, filled the hall to bursting. Even the aisles between the rows of seats were full. Someone was trying noisily to break down the doors even after they had been closed, but no one paid any attention to the racket.

A few of our young poets, who had been prepared for the occasion as Ugar had suggested, gathered backstage. Magzhan Zhumabaev was also there. He had turned up unexpectedly and was standing apart from the rest, frowning and with his head lowered. He was probably aware that there could be some unpleasantness and his rather handsome face was distorted by a grim expression. I went out into the corridor.

At that moment the outside door of the building opened and our Ugar appeared accompanied by several armed militiamen. He was excited and angry and appeared very resolute.

'Shut all the doors and don't let anyone out!' he instructed the militiamen. They immediately set off to carry out the instructions of their chief.

'Follow me!' said Ugar turning to me and walked over towards the stage.

I hurried after him. Ugar's grim expression had worried not

just the Alash-Orda people, but our young poets as well. Already Zhumabaev's large brown eyes were getting wider by the minute.

'Well now, open the curtain!' Ugar commanded from the frightened manager, who immediately pulled the cord.

The first person who went up on stage was the head man from the militia.

He turned to Magzhan Zhumabaev and said, 'You're the *bai* poet, come over here.'

Not wishing to contradict Ugar, Zhumabaev walked silently out on to the stage.

'And now you, poet from the poor peasants, come out here as well,' Ugar called out to me.

I walked over to him and saw that the lights in the hall had already gone out. The audience was starting to get restless.

'Silence!' yelled Ugar. 'From here I can see everyone and I know you. If anyone is planning to cause trouble here, I'll speak to them after the concert!'

After that there was a tense silence.

Ugar now turned directly to Magzhan and said: 'You Alash-Orda wretch. Stop troubling the minds of Soviet people with your ridiculous counter-revolutionary poems! We don't need poems like that! Can't you understand that songs like yours have had their day!?'

An alarmed Zhumabaev looked at Ugar's face alight with anger and quickly lowered his gaze.

Then Ugar turned to me and said: 'Now let the poet from the poor peasants read his verses. Everybody listen!'

I had great difficulty controlling my embarrassment and agitation but duly recited my 'Son of a Poor Peasant'.

Baimagambet's verses about the October Revolution, the Civil War and the victory of the new Soviet order were read out by his school friend, the communist journalist Abdrakhman Aisarin. Pamphlets in verse exposing the true colours of the Kazakh bourgeois nationalists were recited by Mazhit Dauletbaev. The audience enjoyed the satiric pieces by Baibatyr Erzhanov, making fun of Muslim clerics. In short there turned out to be a whole galaxy of young Kazakh poets and writers in Petropavlovsk. [Does anyone remember the names of any of that galaxy nowadays?]

After that function I and my friends went home feeling we had won the day.

The next day I was summoned to the office of the Secretary of the Provincial Committee of the Party. I was severely reprimanded for showing too much initiative. The Secretary threatened to examine the whole episode at the next meeting of the Provincial Committee, but then he laughed out loud and explained to me in a friendly tone how to wage the ideological struggle on the literature front.

After taking my leave of the Secretary, I went home repeating to myself what he had said: 'In literature there is no room for partisan-style initiative'. Yet I could not help but feel pleased in the knowledge that something new was taking shape in our Kazakh literature.[6]

This lesson in waging the ideological struggle in literature did not fall on deaf ears. Later, in 1923, Sabit Mukanov was studying in Orenburg at the workers' school preparing students for university. A rumour suddenly spread to the effect that there were going to be celebrations for the fiftieth birthday of Akhmet Baitursunov:

The Kazakh students from our workers' faculty and pupils from other educational institutions in Orenburg split into two camps: those who decided to congratulate the poet and present him with a briefcase and a speech were in the minority.

We who were opposed to Baitursunov had a number of meetings and thought through our plan of action. We were well aware that the only people capable of celebrating the birthday of such a 'figure' were those who were not in favour of Soviet power.

I can clearly remember the kind of views which were being formulated at that period. It is true that we had all respected Akhmet prior to the Revolution, when he had been fighting for the rights of the Kazakh people. It is true that all of us who had attended Kazakh schools had learnt our alphabet and grammar from his book. Yet Akhmet Baitursunov could not, by any measure, be compared with those who had brought the Kazakh working people their freedom. Nothing was dearer to us than Soviet power. If Akhmet Baitursunov was against the Soviets, that

173

meant that he was against us – the children of poor peasants – and against the children of Kazakh working people.

We succeeded in disrupting the celebrations. We prepared in advance of the occasion rotten cabbage and other vegetables wrapped in newspaper. Those were our 'gifts' for the man hosting the event, Smagul Sadvokasov.

The main speaker turned out to be a cunning character. Worried that the students might interrupt his speech, Sadvokasov began praising Baitursunov right from the beginning. He used an unusual approach: he started out with a story in order to gradually bring round his audience to his arguments, demonstrating the outstanding role of the poet whose birthday was being celebrated.

According to this speaker, the Kazakh people had five national leaders – Kenesary, Chokan Valikhanov, Ibrai Altynsarin, Abai Kunanbaev and Akhmet Baitursunov. Yet, however hard Sadvokasov tried, as soon as he mentioned Baitursunov rotten vegetables were thrown at the speaker's dais and the table with the presidium. The meeting was so badly disrupted that the birthday celebrations were abandoned.

After seeking advice from Seifullin Saken, I wrote an article which was immediately printed instead of the leading article in the newspaper *Enbekshi-Kazakh* (*Kazakh Worker*, No. 69, 1923). It was entitled 'Speakers, make sure you do not get on the black list!' In that piece I exposed the anti-Soviet activities of Baitursunov.

I finished my article with the following thoughts:

> In short, the gentlemen with white collars, it's up to them if they now want to idolize Akhmet and call him not just *aka* but the Lord God himself. Yet the Kazakh working people are not rallying to Baitursunov's slogans, but to those of men who are calling for the unity and brotherhood of the poor in all countries. The speakers, who had most likely been counting on their own eloquence, had in the end to abandon their vain scheme to present Baitursunov through rose-coloured spectacles. Akhmet has been a father-figure for the *bais*, for chameleons and double-dealers, for men in white collars. For the working people he is neither an *aka*, nor a father, nor a friend. The man who is a Father to the Kazakh working people is he who gave them their freedom and who is the leader of the October Revolution. It is Lenin. We warn those speakers to

look around them and make sure that they do not get blacklisted, when they start praising men like Baitursunov, our deadly enemies.

Subsequent events were to prove how timely that warning had been. The names of Baitursunov and his supporters were blacklisted for eternity in the history of the Kazakh people. The sentence was duly delivered.[7]

Time has also demonstrated that it was impossible to obliterate the names of those poets who fought to bring enlightenment to the Kazakh people. Indeed, political struggle against 'vestiges of feudalism' within the literary arena came to the fore once more thirty years later in Mukanov's memoirs (published in the early 1950s). In them Mukanov singled out what he saw as 'admiration for the past with the *bais*' in lines from songs by Baitursunov:

In our frail boat there are no oars.
We are alone between the shores.
Though storms and mists hide every tree,
Fate sends us on towards the sea.

Also in the following lines:

Where is your gentle voice, Kazbek?
Where are you, mighty Zhakibek?
Come down from your peaks on high
To hear your orphaned people's cry.[8]

(Zhakibek was a hero who fought for his people, well known in the steppes.)

Mukanov recalls that Sadvokasov criticized him as a 'leftist' and indeed he would have problems with the same label later. On 1 June 1932 *Kazakhstanskaya Pravda* took the writer to task for his 'mistaken' slogan: 'Catch up and overtake the literary classics of the capitalist countries.' In general, however, he had a clear grasp of the Party's policy in the sphere of literature and was aware of its nuances.

Earlier, on 1 January 1925, *Pravda* had printed the following exhortation: 'Writers must cast out of literature all that is mystical or obscene and avoid adopting an ethnically biased point of view.'

Labels such as 'vestiges of a medieval past' or 'the *bais* world of the past' hid the fact that ideologists sought to promote the 'national point of view'. The notion of literature associated with a particular national group was painted in a negative light, described using terms such as 'Great-Russian chauvinism' or 'local nationalism', and presented as the enemy of internationalism. There were constant calls for such literature to be uprooted with merciless resolve. The slogan of 'proletarian internationalism' held aloft by Marx was, of course, no more than a demagogic cover for the true goal of communist ideology: to deprive enslaved peoples of national allegiances, to destroy in each one of them its own special spiritual qualities, beliefs, culture and language.

On 18 June 1925 the Central Committee of the All-Russia Communist Party (Bolsheviks) adopted a resolution 'On the Party's policy in the sphere of literature', in which, among other things, it stated: 'There is as yet no hegemony of proletarian writers and the Party must help these writers to earn for themselves the historic right to that hegemony.'[9]

In order to achieve hegemony in literature, the only requirement for writers was to outdo each other in their depiction of Soviet socialist construction. After its Russian predecessor, a Kazakh Association of Proletarian Writers was set up. The chairman of its organizational department in Kzyl-Orda was the writer Saken Seifullin, the secretary was Mukanov and the other members were A. Baidildin, K. Zhusupbekov and O. Bekov. On 4 October 1926 its official platform was drawn up consisting of twelve paragraphs. The main points in this document make clear not just the mood of the times but the importance of literature in the period:

The Kazakh *bais* did not experience the Revolution as such a powerful blow against them as the rich did in Russia. The *bais* still have an influence over life in the *aul*, as do their representatives, the men of the Alash-Orda party. That party speaks openly of this. When the New Economic Policy (NEP) was introduced, the Kazakh *bais* intensified the propagation of their views and ideas. In view of this, in the conditions obtaining in Kazakhstan one of the most important types of struggle is the ideological struggle. One of the most important ideological tools in this struggle is literature [from § 2].

... The October Revolution woke up the Kazakh working people, but the Kazakh working people had not been playing an active part in the cauldron of revolutionary events, as the Russian working people had been, and they had not had the same experience of struggle in class confrontation.

Nationalist writers and pro-*bai* writers, who came out against the October Revolution, put down roots throughout Kazakh lands. Kazakh writers from among the working people who appeared on the scene after the October Revolution but who had only had inadequate education and were not united in an association of their own, have so far mounted only weak resistance to the writers supporting the *bais* ... A permanent Union of Writers is essential, which would unite them and carry out educational work [from § 3].

... In class society there is nothing outside class and literature cannot be outside class either. Class literature extols first and foremost its own class and only then talks about mankind as a whole ... The Association considers that literature which is not capable of helping workers and peasants in their search for a new life is unnecessary [from § 5].

... The literature of the proletariat and peasantry is the counterweight to literature supporting the *bais*. It will wage a tireless struggle against the latter.

We shall write about what nurtures a Marxist-revolutionary ideology in Kazakh working people. We shall write about what is truly happening in the life around us. If we write about the past then it will only be in order to demonstrate its rottenness and to fan hatred towards it [from § 7].

... The class of *bais* among the Kazakhs has not disappeared, it has not been destroyed. This means that its ideologists are still active. Yet as Soviet power is consolidated, the Kazakh *bais* will grow weaker.

With each passing year they will have less land, less livestock and less power. At the time of the most bitter confrontations, the writers supporting the *bais* – together with the *bais* – will be up in arms. That is why our Association must wage a merciless struggle against them [from § 12].[10]

✤ ✤ ✤

Goloshchekin began his attack on the Kazakh intelligentsia only after he had dealt with members of the Party who had nationalist inclinations. By this time the mass of the poor in the *auls* had been dealt with.

At the Sixth All-Kazakhstan Conference in November 1927, Goloshchekin accused the 'academic centre' (i.e. writers such as Baitursunov) of distorting the Party line:

> A special book has been compiled and published containing as many as 5,000 terms in the Kazakh language. The masses have not come to grips with these. There are enormous distortions to be seen: it appears for instance, as we have all come to realize, that the word 'International' has been translated virtually as 'tyrant'. It is quite incredible.

Goloshchekin proceeded to speak at great length about the role of the intelligentsia:

> Comrades, we are quite convinced that in this matter there can be no question of persecution. On the contrary, we must involve the intelligentsia, it must work with us. Yet we must lead it and not the other way round – that is all there is to it. A situation in which the intelligentsia would be *alien and completely hostile to our ideology* [my italics] would be intolerable. It would have a very strong impact on various aspects of our life.
>
> In the midst of the old intelligentsia there is a movement which is reminiscent of the Smenovekhovstvo 'Change of Landmarks' movement. You are probably familiar with the well-known poem by Zhumabaev regarding the '90': he is now writing about the '90', he is on their side and many people mislead themselves in this respect, assuming him to be sincere.
>
> They lost when aspiring to a '100' and so they are aiming at '90'. If they come over to us – fine, we shall welcome them, but at the same time we need to take a hard line, so that the '90' understand that the nationalists are not behind them, but for the time being against them, that they are ingratiating themselves with the '90'.[11]

They stuck to this hard line and struck two years later, so hard that the name of Magzhan Zhumabaev, an outstanding Kazakh poet, was forbidden and his verse was unpublished.

What was it about Zhumabaev's poem that was considered criminal? In 1969 the People's Poet of Bashkiria, seventy-five-year-old Saifi Kudash, addressed a letter about the fate of Zhumabaev to the First Secretary of the Central Committee of the Communist Party of Kazakhstan, D.A. Kunaev:

> From the depths of his heart and with true sincerity born of suffering M. Zhumabaev wrote in that poem ['Voice of the Ninety']: 'In the past, when a bright sun rose above all peoples, I took the wrong path. Yet when I did so, I was serving my fatherland. I did not go the Alash-Orda congress, I did not take part in that party's work. Like certain others I did not enrol as an adjutant for the leaders of Alash-Orda. I realized that the Alash party was not what the Kazakh people needed. Now I have seen with my own eyes and understood that only the Communist Party can provide a correct solution for the fate of the Kazakh people. If the Communist Party represents 90 per cent of the people, then Alash only represents 10 per cent. I defend the 90, because I serve Soviet power, devoting my whole heart to that cause.'
>
> Is that not like a confession? Yet people did not believe him. Why? It is difficult to say, but it would appear that factors of no small importance were personal dislike, revenge and a false understanding of the principles of class struggle.[12]

The letter was never answered. After his rehabilitation in 1960, Magzhan Zhumabaev remained a dubious figure for the communists and his poems were still unpublished.

The Central Committee of the Communist Party of Kazakhstan held strong opinions about the study of the literary legacies of Magzhan Zhumabaev, Akhmet Baitursunov and Zhusupbek Aimautov:

> The poem 'Voice of the Ninety', written in 1927, not only characterizes the poet's political stance, but also shows how far he had advanced as an artist of the new era. In this work the poet

declares frankly that he was a supporter of the Ninety, i.e. the majority of the people, which despite everything was resolutely striving to introduce a new life in their homeland.[13]

This statement was made in 1988; only then did communist experts finally come to trust Zhumabaev.

It would seem that it was not so much the content of the poem, but the desire to deal a blow to the poet, to 'strike' him in Goloshchekin's sense of the word, which led to Zhumabaev's banishment from the literary world. Goloshchekin was well aware that a national poet was inevitably incompatible with proletarian internationalism, which itself was destroying the national spirit; a national poet therefore could not be trusted.

Goloshchekin also seemed to lack trust in the Kazakh people; they hardly had an advanced class – a working class – of their own and they were used to obeying their *bais* and their mullahs. A people like that, in his eyes, required long and painstaking Sovietization, the implementation of which might well involve shedding blood.

In his eyes the whole intelligentsia was suspect, and therefore Goloshchekin kept a vigilant watch on every step it took. From time to time he would insert passages into his speeches pointing out how he had come across various harmful ideas. In his report at the Sixth Conference, Goloshchekin stated:

I came across, by chance, an article in *Kazakh Worker* [Goloshchekin did not read Kazakh; he mocks the Kazakh delegates here] about literature. The article was written so as to give it a Marxist air, in particular on the question as to whether there could be such a thing as socialist culture or not. I shall read you the final image from that article: 'Kazakh nationalism is not of a colonialist character. It does not aspire to command or to subordinate anyone to itself, it only seeks to defend itself, to save itself and, if it is able and has the skills, then to create and achieve equality. Until such time as the masses of the national minorities achieve equality, it will be impossible to root out nationalism.'

For Goloshchekin, this was a dangerous idea:

> The 'nationalism' of the Kazakh worker or poor peasant is to aspire to the same rights as those of the European peasant. This is healthy 'nationalism' of the correct kind. The nationalism of our *bais*, of the bourgeois intelligentsia, what kind is that? Is it an innocent kind? Just watch how the nationalist puppy in the period before the October Revolution and after the Revolution will grow into a very large nationalist dog. (Laughter.) There is 'nationalism' in inverted commas, an aspiration to equal rights, healthy nationalism of the correct kind and we must support it, while we need to strike down the nationalist leaders of the *bais'* ideologists.[14]

The campaign against 'nationalists' was gaining momentum; it is unlikely that those involved in it were aware, as they obediently complied with the directives, what an enormous blow was in store for Kazakh culture.

On 11–12 April 1928 *Soviet Steppes* printed a long article by Gabbas Togzhanov entitled 'Against Nationalism, Philistinism and Unjustified Arrogance in Kazakh Literature and Criticism'. In it the author pointed out that:

> Until quite recently – three or four years ago – our nationalists were demonstrating that art, in particular literature, is not subordinate to politics and that political or – as they expressed it – narrow political interests are alien to it. They maintained that Kazakh fiction serves 'general-national' interests that are above class. That was what the young ideologists of the Kazakh nationalists wrote: Auezov, D. Iskakov, Aimautov and Co. Sadvokasov could not imagine our Soviet literature without nationalists – without Auezov, Aimautov and Kemengerov. He, just like the nationalists, is sure that nationalist writers can provide works most useful on inter-ethnic subjects for the Kazakh working people. What is more, he even protests against the fact that we are exposing the nationalist ideology of the poet Magzhan Zhumabaev – the well-known nationalist and at the same time a rabid counter-revolutionary.

Togzhanov, fuelled by an urge to cleanse Kazakh literature of nationalists, embarked upon the task of exposing one of the leaders of the Kazakh Association of Proletarian Writers – the communist Saken Seifullin – who in his view had no right at all to call himself a proletarian writer: 'Not only is there nothing proletarian about him, but often he is not even Soviet enough.'

The method of accusation Togzhanov used was employed later by Goloshchekin; the critic came down on Seifullin for his old poems, which the poet himself had publicly acknowledged as mistaken. Seifullin was attacked for 'propagation of nationalist ideology', particularly in the poem 'Asia'. In this work the continent of Asia scathingly reprimands Europe:

> Treacherous Europe – a land of violence, exploitation and cruelty.
> Many times I have directed you on to the true path,
> I have sent you many clever minds …
> I sent you my Huns, Magyars, Bulgarians, Moors and Arabs.
> You saw my Tatars, Turks and Mongols.
> The days and years went past, but you did not desist from evil.
> I sent you Semites – Moses, Israel, David and Isaiah.
> I sent you prophets
> And in the end Mahomet.
> So as to cleanse the world of filth,
> So as to soften your cruel and stony heart,
> I sent you many descendants of Semites
> With Karl Marx at their head.
> If you will not listen to these pleas,
> Proud in your refusal to see me as your equal,
> Then, with the words 'Teach through strength',
> I shall send my Mongol with slanting eyes.
> The Mongol has tamed many indomitable men.
> He has broken the spine of many proud men
> And thrown lassos round many a neck
> To drag men over ravines, over plains.
> Many a city has he wiped from the earth,
> Many steppes he has laid to waste,
> As if fire had swept through them.
> He ate raw meat, washed down with blood.

Many infants were impaled on his spears.
The Mongol knows well how to fill men with terror.
His strength can make Heaven and Earth tremble.
Woe to Europe if she does not heed
The voice of justice, the voice of Asia.

This is a literal translation of Seifullin's unusual poem, for which he was eventually accused of nationalism. First Party critics invented a new 'rightist nationalist grouping', which they termed 'Seifullinites'. They then had the poet arrested and he was shot at the end of the 1930s. They failed to 'mould' Seifullin, as the expression went.

As part of his attack on the poet, Togzhanov also criticized Seifullin for having dedicated his book *Dombra*, published in 1924, to Trotsky. The critic had a good memory, for Trotsky had been in Alma-Ata four years before, when banished there after being expelled from the Party. Two months later, on 6 June 1928, Seifullin published his response to Togzhanov's piece in the same newspaper. His answer bore the heading 'Neo-nationalism and Advance on the Ideological Front' and quoted the following from Togzhanov's article in *Kazakh Worker*, published six years before on 21 February 1922:

> The Kazakhs, who in the past lived in luxurious white *yurts*, as happy as could be as they drank their aromatic *kumys*, ate their delicious, fatty horse-meat, horse-meat sausage and owned large herds of horses, camels, cattle and sheep, are now eating all sorts of plants, stinking ants, dog-meat and mice. Although nothing is written in the Russian newspapers about the hunger facing the Kazakh population, it is written about in the Kazakh ones.

In doing this, Seifullin reminded the Party that there had been a time when Togzhanov, together with Sadvokasov, was on the side of Alash-Orda writers; indeed he had called them 'fellow travellers'. Seifullin concluded that 'for as long as the Kazakh class of *bais* exists, nationalism (Alash-Orda) will live'.

Seifullin went on to provide detailed explanations of those works which Togzhanov accused of propagating nationalism. It turned out that one of the offending poems – called 'Eid' – had been composed while he was only a boy, studying at the parish school in Akmolinsk, at a time 'when we would not even have been able to have heard about Marx'. As for the poem 'Letter to a Mother', Seifullin wrote: 'In the first place it is a lie that I regarded a mother's love as higher than all else … Is it not clear from the poem? Do I give pride of place to the mother or the Revolution?'

Togzhanov greatest criticism was about the poem 'Asia'. It had been written in 1922 at the time of the Genoa Conference, when:

> The Asian liberation movement had applauded Comrade Chicherin. In *'Asia'* there was another factor – the references to Semites. Counter-revolutionary elements [nationalists, chauvinists, the petty bourgeoisie] were starting to talk more loudly than before about 'Yids'. I was anxious to come out against that revolting feature of the reactionaries, namely anti-Semitism. It is of course not in keeping with Marxism to threaten imperialist Europe with the peoples of Asia. Nor is it in keeping with the Marxist line to praise Semites for leading mankind to brotherhood. Back in May 1923 I had printed a detailed explanation about that in the journal of the Kazakhstan Area Committee of the All-Union Communist Party (Bolsheviks), *Kzyl-Kazakhstan*, in which I acknowledged the incorrect nature of those ideas.

We see then that Seifullin's explanations and repentance made no difference.

In response to accusations of arrogance, Seifullin made the following statement:

> In Moscow on 30 January 1928 Gromov gave a speech in the Communist Academy about émigré literature. He praised Bunin and recommended to our writers that they should learn from him. Comrade Friche joined in the discussion and said: 'Our lyric poetry is of a higher level than that of the émigrés. We cannot learn from Bunin because he is a mystic. Émigré writers are doomed and they shall be crushed together with their class: they shall be reduced to nothing. In the work of those writers their mastery of form is more and more on the decline. There is nothing our writers should be taking from them' (*In Defence of Literature*, 1928, No. 4). Those were the words used by our most

authoritative Marxist critic, Comrade Friche. Let émigré writers weep at the thought that we do not want to learn from the Alash-Orda mystic Zhumabaev, pupil of Merezhkovsky and Balmont.

This was the level of the literary polemics of the day; it differs little from the battles of today.

Perhaps the most surprising aspect of that period was the almost total disregard of talent; it was not seen as a treasure of the people or as containing a divine spark. Ideology was the only feature within literature that mattered – ideology understood at the most basic and primitive level, at the level where it was of interest to informers. Well-educated pedants like Comrade Friches trained new writers, wielding their 'class whips'. They were escorted to their training sessions in single file, like prisoners; any step to the side was seen as an attempt to escape and those in command would open fire.

Neither Togzhanov nor Seifullin seemed to notice that, in the course of their polemics (consisting more of mutual political accusations than anything else), they trampled on their talented brother writer, Magzhan Zhumabaev, and various other gifted individuals; after such public accusations, official organizational decisions would be made. It was difficult to predict what they would be. The only person who knew was the 'director' steering the newspaper campaign, sitting on high in the Area Committee office. He knew only too well.

The most humane part of Seifullin's article was its conclusion, in which he indirectly complained about the tight constraints facing writers of fiction. In it he defended his right to write on a wide range of subjects, even sad ones:

> When we see a well-organized agricultural cooperative for poor peasants, where a separator is happily singing a song about collective labour and culture, we want to join in that beautiful music of culture and admire the work of the collective concerned. Yet when we see a Kazakh woman dressed in dirty rags and worn out by her heavy labours, bent and wrinkled, walking quietly along behind an emaciated donkey, then our emotional response is bound to be in a sad key. Does anyone think there is a shortage of other sights we can behold in our life today? All these sights are bound to be reflected in our literature.

Guided by all manner of 'Comrade Friches', Kazakh proletarian writers were forced to undermine their national culture; orders were shouted at every turn, reducing all national features of literature to nationalist ones.

Ilyas Kabulov wrote in *Soviet Steppes* on 2 August 1928:

> Our young Kazakhs need to learn not from the poet Abai [Ibrahim Kunanbaev], but from Marx, Plekhanov, Lenin and other classic Marxist writers ... We consider that one of the key tasks for the Party organization in Kazakhstan on the ideological front is to put an end to Abaism just as has been the practice with the usual bourgeois rubbish. In view of this it is essential to mobilize as fast as possible all cultural forces at the disposal of the Party and the Soviets in Kazakhstan against the teaching of Abai and those who share his ideas today.

Goloshchekin, single-minded as ever in harassing the enemy, continued his campaign against Magzhan Zhumabaev and other old Kazakh writers. On 23 May 1928 in a speech at a meeting of Kzyl-Orda party activists he announced:

> In his speech at the Komsomol Congress, Comrade Bukharin cites an extract from a poem by Zhumabaev, which examines the introduction of railways in Kazakhstan (he who really understands what culture is, will develop productive forces) as a loss of everything old. When I was told recently that there is opposition among certain Kazakhs to the Turkestan-Siberian railway, I did not believe it. I could not imagine such a thing to myself. Now, though, after reading about this, I thought to myself that there is such opposition and that its path will lead to slogans calling for self-determination for the bourgeoisie, which will lead inevitably to dependence upon the bourgeoisie.

This objection came from the Party's favourite patron of the arts! Yet had Goloshchekin had the chance to properly survey Zhumabaev's distant literary landscapes – from Moscow to the far-off borders?

A year before he had seen a poem by Magzhan Zhumabaev about which Bukharin had opened fire in *Pravda* on 12 January 1927 in his 'Angry Notes' he virtually gave orders for a campaign to be launched against Russian peasant poets. For this he used the struggle against 'the Esenin way' as motivation – Bukharin described Sergei Esenin's poetry as an unhealthy mixture of raunchy dogs, icons, full-breasted wenches, burning candles, birch trees, the moon, bitches, the Lord God, necrophilia ... and so on. He subsequently grouped all Russian national literature with that of Esenin and unleashed a campaign against it.

Earlier, in March 1926 – long before Stalin's excesses – one of Esenin's friends, the poet Alexei Ganin, had written a poem denouncing Trotsky and was shot as a result. It is worth noting that in 1934 Stalin merely banished the poet Osip Mandelshtam who had written poems against him; it was three years later that he eventually sent him to the camps. This is remarkable in the sense that Stalin was renowned for being vengeful and as such he was unlikely to have forgotten what Mandelshtam had written.

No such term as 'Bukharin's repression' exists, but this powerful political figure – one of the most influential members of the OGPU – destroyed a whole range of Russian writers – representatives of peasant literature – and Kazakh literature. Kazakh writers were first labelled as nationalists and then as counter-revolutionaries, before finally being illegally convicted; this happened from as early as 1929.

The sequence of events that followed is a simple one; Goloshchekin, who to further his own ends 'utilized' the nationalist intelligentsia, now planned to liquidate it. (We might recall his ominous words: 'We can cast aside these temporary allies.' It is clear what this meant in the vocabulary of this executioner.) He supplied Bukharin with a quotation from a poem by Zhumabaev in order to bring fame to his nationalists, that is, to prepare for their arrest and ensure he had support for his activities in the Politburo. Bukharin must have known that no Kazakh would have singled out the political subtleties in the work of the Kazakh poet.

It is possible that Goloshchekin was simply given permission by Stalin to arrest prominent members of Kazakhstan's intelligentsia. What is clear is that Goloshchekin had given the signal for the reprisals to proceed. To all appearances this was the dress rehearsal for collectivization; before the people's or the peasantry's back was broken, cultural leaders who would never have complied with the authorities had to be removed.

On 19 April 1929 *Soviet Steppes* published a letter 'On the Work of Kazakh Writers'. It was accompanied by a short introduction from the editor:

A letter of protest from a group of comrades on the question of errors appearing in the *Literary Encyclopaedia* regarding the assessment of works by certain Kazakh writers has been received by the editors of *Pravda* and the said *Encyclopaedia*. In view of the large-scale public interest in this letter we are reprinting it in full.

Interest in the fate of these writers has not diminished; below are the letter's main points:

Dear Comrades!

In our opinion the assessment of works by Auezov and Baitursunov is not in the spirit of Marxism.

First of all regarding Auezov. It is stated in the *Literary Encyclopaedia* that he is 'an outstanding writer, whose works are distinguished by an astonishing sensitivity and historical truthfulness'. We consider that this opinion reflects at least a lack of knowledge or a failure to understand Auezov himself and his works.

Firstly Auezov at the time of Kolchak, being one of the active members of the Alash-Orda party in the East, could not oppose Kolchak. On the contrary, the whole of Alash-Orda at that time, as is well known, including Auezov, fought in alliance with Kolchak against the Bolsheviks, against Soviet power.

It is true that, after Soviet power had been established, Auezov went over to the side of the latter, joined the Party and at one time held the post of secretary of the Kirgiz Central Executive Committee, but nevertheless, both in politics and in literature, Auezov remained a bourgeois nationalist, an ideologue of the Kazakh *bais*. In 1922 Auezov was expelled from the Party in view of his anti-Party Alash-Orda ideology. He left and engaged after that in literary and educational work. To this day he still continues such work.

In all his works Auezov perceives the Kazakh way of life through the eyes of the Kazakh *bai*, missing what went before and extolling the old Asiatic ways, the Kazakh khans, legendary heroes, the 'wise judges', venerated elders, past and feudal knights. He always portrays such characters in a positive light as men worthy of respect and emulation even today (see: *Karakoz* – or 'Black Eyes' – and his play *Enlik-Kebek*). Not content with this, Auezov propagates this kind of reactionary ideology in his literary 'criticism' as well.

Nor is the assessment of Baitursunov's writings really correct. Admittedly Baitursunov was, prior to the Revolution, one of the leaders of the Kazakh national intelligentsia and waged a struggle against Tsarist policies. At that time he was, objectively speaking, a progressive bourgeois revolutionary in the Kazakh world.

Yet that does not give anyone the right to say that 'Baitursunov is an outstanding Kazakh poet'. He has never been that: he was and remains a political journalist.

Baitursunov remains a bourgeois nationalist – an ideologue of the Kazakh *bais*. He used to propagate counter-revolutionary ideology. The Kazakh public today regards Baitursunov as one of the leaders of the reactionary Alash-Orda intelligentsia, which led and still leads the struggle against our Party and openly defends the Kazakh *bais*.

In order to put right the error made by the editorial board of the *Literary Encyclopaedia*, we ask for our opinions to be printed in the pages of *Pravda*.

With communist greetings,

U. Isaev, I. Kuramysov, G. Togzhanov, S. Safarbekov,
U. Zhandosov, K. Yusupbekov and A. Baidildin.

The slander campaign was drawing to its close by this time. Later not a word appeared in the press about the arrest, trial and sentencing of fourteen Kazakh writers and representatives of Kazakh culture, though other fabricated trials (the Shakhtinsk case and the Industrial Party case for example) were given detailed coverage in the press. To this day the treatment of these writers is only mentioned in general terms. Below are excerpts from the conclusion drawn by the Kazakhstan Communist Party's Central Committee's commission assigned the task of studying the creative legacy of Magzhan Zhumabaev, Akhmet Baitursunov and Zhusupbek Aimautov. On Magzhan Zhumabaev they wrote:

> In 1929 he was sentenced to ten years in prison without any solid evidence, after being accused without proof of creating an association in 1921, entitled *Alka* [circle] allegedly so as to engage in underground activities, although it had been set up by representatives of the Kazakh Autonomous Soviet Socialist Republic under the Siberian Revolutionary Committee to provide wide-scale information for the population of Siberia about the Kazakh Republic. This association, created for purposes of enlightenment during the period of Stalin's repression, was described as a secret counter-revolutionary organization of Kazakh nationalists.

On Akhmet Baitursunov:

> In the late 1920s and early '30s when many prominent individuals from the pre-revolutionary intelligentsia began to be subjected to unjust persecution and repression in our country, large numbers of informers sent in accusations against A. Baitursunov concerning allegedly new facts about the counter-revolutionary activity of the former leaders of Alash-Orda. He was the subject of frequent attacks in the press and in June 1929 he was arrested, sentenced by a board from the OGPU and exiled to the Archangel region. His wife and daughter were banished to Tomsk.

On Zhusupbek Aimautov:

> In 1929 he was again arrested for being a member of an underground nationalist organization and in 1931 he was shot.
> The reason for the tragic death of Z. Aimautov, as indeed for that of M. Zhumabaev, was their involvement in the above-mentioned propaganda organization 'Alka'. To this accusation there was added his former membership of Alash-Orda, but no attention was paid to Z. Aimautov's sincere appreciation of the historic role of the RCP (B) and his practical participation in socialist construction.

In response to a protest from the Public Prosecutor of the republic's Supreme Court, M. Zhumabaev, A. Baitursunov and Z. Aimautov were granted complete posthumous rehabilitation in view of their behaviour not having involved any crime.[15]

That was all; from these short extracts all we can deduce is that Zhumabaev and Aimautov were tried together. What about Baitursunov? They had all been arrested in the same year: 1929. On 1 October 1930 Goloshchekin gave a speech to mark 'Ten Years of the Party's Socialist Construction' at a meeting of the Party's activists in the Alma-Ata branch:

> Comrades, I ask you to note that my speech is not a history of the Party's organization. I do not have at my disposal an exhaustive supply of such material. Yet even if I did, I should not be embarking now on writing history. At this point in time we are making history.

During the speech Goloshchekin focused in great detail on a particular stage of this 'making history' – the rout of the Kazakh 'nationalists'. After a short introduction about the underground activity of Alash-Orda – which had in the early twenties allegedly set itself the task of joining the Party, using their Communist Party membership cards to support the Alash-Orda cause to overthrow the Soviets – Goloshchekin declared:

> Comrades, all the documents which I shall make public are testimony provided by the nationalists of the now eliminated counter-revolutionary organization, the so-called Baitursunov group. (At this point in time another counter-revolutionary nationalist organization is being eliminated – that of Tynyshbaev, Yermekov and Dosmukhamedov).

Goloshchekin mainly cited testimony from Aimautov during his speech, pointing to the fact that the group of writers concerned here – particularly Zhumabaev, Baitursunov and Aimautov – were accused of the same crime and arrested in connection with the same case. Indeed they were accused of crimes committed almost ten years before; their accusers seemed undeterred by the fact that there had been no new counter-revolutionary activity in connection with the case. Goloshchekin seemed confident that conversations which took place ten years earlier constituted weighty proof of guilt and that all the nationalists would have to be eliminated. It would seem that initially there had been plans to have them shot – writer Mirzhakup Dulatov, for example, had spent nine months in death row in Moscow's Butyrskaya Prison and the highest measure of 'social protection' ('death by firing squad') was commuted to ten years in the camps.

First of all Goloshchekin set out to 'expose the intentions of the counter-revolutionaries':

> Gabbasov writes: 'In the spring of 1920 or 1921 there was a meeting in Semipalatinsk, at which the question was raised as to whether we should all join the Party as a group.'

> The nationalist Omarov said: 'Baitursunov led the propaganda work amongst the non-Party workers encouraging them to join the Party. Yermekov supported Baitursunov and Bukeikhanov Alikhan and he shared their point of view. My understanding of the situation was that we nationalists, after joining the Communist Party, would be able to use our legal opportunities in the interests of the Kazakh people.'

> Aimautov: 'In the winter of 1921 Kazakh employees from the town of Semipalatinsk and members of Alash-Orda met in somebody's flat. The question as to whether the Kazakh employees should join the Party or not was discussed. The Alash-Orda people, in particular Dulatov, came out in favour, saying that it was essential to join the Party so that they might use the opportunity to obtain responsible posts in it.'

'Those were their activities,' announced Goloshchekin, though in fact they were nothing but conversations which had taken place ten years ago. He went on:

> Gabbasov states in his evidence: 'Declaring war against the Bolsheviks without the masses, or real strength, at a time when the aggressively destructive forces of Bolshevism were rapidly growing, while the attitudes of Russian society and even the

intelligentsia were unforgivably passive, would have drawn the Kirgiz population into bloody carnage and undermined their economy. It would have allowed the dregs of Kirgiz society to introduce the idea of Bolshevism into the steppes, to stimulate social differentiation within that society and so to ruin the foundation and traditions of our national way of life which had taken shape over centuries. That explains why representatives of the committee joined the Regional Soviet for a time. We assumed that using this tactic we would be able to organize a real force and prepare an anti-Soviet uprising in the steppes.'

Badgambaev stated: 'In Tashkent I met Dulatov and Dosmukhamedov. Beremezhanov spoke of the need to help the *basmachi*.'

Baidildin stated: 'At that time Smagul Sadvokasov was spreading a rumour to the effect that the position of Soviet power was weak, that in Turkestan the *basmachi* were rising up and that we needed to be ready for all kinds of changes. At a meeting in Petropavlovsk it was decided that the work should continue and that we should organize together for the struggle against the colonizers.'

Adilev: 'I remember that one meeting was held with the chairman of the Bukhara Cheka, who was a member of the Alash-Orda underground. They took me into a special room: they were holding copies of the Koran and began telling me phrases which I had to repeat after them. It was a vow that I would never give away secrets and that I should remain loyal to the organization. Validov said that all the prominent representatives of the Bukhara Republic were present.'

Ispulov stated: 'Validov wrote to Baitursunov that there was a large force behind him.'

Adilev stated: 'The Kazakh nationalists expected that liberation would come from the east'.

Aimautov stated: During the II Congress of Soviets, a meeting was convened exclusively for Kazakh delegates, which was chaired by Auezov. The question about the fight against colonizers was raised and a resolution was adopted of a blatantly nationalist kind'

Baidildin stated: 'In 1921 I wrote an article on the occasion of the fourth anniversary of the October Revolution for the newspaper, *Kazakh Worker*. Its editor-in-chief was Auezov. He

summoned me to his office for a dressing-down. The article had
ended with the words: "Long live Soviet power, long live the
Soviet Republic of Kazakhstan." Auezov declared to me that if,
in the following year, I started to attack Alash-Orda, he would
leave the editorial office. After that article he received a letter of
reprimand from Sadvokasov sent from Moscow.

Goloshchekin went on to speak about Kazakhstan's second Five Year
Plan – which would be implemented under his supervision – and about
the Bolshevization of the republic. He said that among the Kazakh
communists there were not a dozen true Bolsheviks. (Only three more
years would pass before Goloshchekin would say, as he took his leave of
Kazakhstan, that there was not a single honest communist there.) Then
he embarked upon his final reading of testimony:

> The accused Baidildin stated: 'Before the Fifth Conference
> in 1925, Sadvokasov said that gross violations were occurring
> with regard to the land question: although Khodzhanov was
> indeed waging a struggle against the colonizers, the method
> used was a Kazakh one, while what was needed was a Genghis
> Khan one. I think that Alash-Orda people – Bukeikhanov and
> Professor Shvetsov – played a major part in elaborating the main
> propositions for the Fifth Conference. I heard via a student
> that a meeting of Alash-Orda members had taken place in
> Dzholdybaev's flat attended by Baitursunov, Dulatov, Yermekov
> and Kadyrbaev. Political questions were discussed at it.'

Goloshchekin concluded his speech with the words: 'There is considerably
more testimony, but I think that this is enough … Fortunately, the
healthy elements in the Party have taken up their Bolshevik weapons.'[16]
From the strength of this testimony (how it was obtained and
its reliability are unknown) it would seem that in reality no counter-
revolutionary activity had been going on. The guilt of these 'bourgeois
nationalists' consisted of the fact that they had been thinking about the
fate of their own people in a way that was different from Goloshchekin's
attitude. He did not know the Kazakh people, did not understand or love
them, preferring to lead them from his office with the help of endless
directives. The actual life of the Kazakhs was deeply alien to him. His

only concern was to 'master the *aul* masses' by 'utilizing' the national intelligentsia, eventually 'cast[ing] aside those temporary allies'. Cast them aside he did – banishing them from Kazakhstan or sending them to their deaths. As we have seen, along with the national intelligentsia, he also cast aside Kazakh national culture.

❖

IX. The Beginning of Universal Collectivization

O n 15 February 1928 *Soviet Steppes* published an article entitled 'Country Notes' by a journalist named Tomilov. In it he wrote:

> The slogan about the collectivization of agriculture proposed by the XV Congress met with a warm response in the countryside, particular among the poor peasants ... Those who oppose collectivization frighten its supporters with examples of the collapse of various collective farms (or communes) which came into being during the period of War Communism. It has to be acknowledged that the question regarding collectivization has not been discussed in sufficient detail in our press yet, or in our propaganda or in the work of our citizens promoting political enlightenment. Thanks to this gap the *kulaks* are able to discuss the slogan about collectivization all over the place, frightening off middle peasants with the prospect of the 'commune'. At one of these peasant gatherings the following question was raised in all seriousness: 'So the Party Congress has decided to introduce collectivization. What kind will it be, voluntary or enforced?'

Tomilov either naïvely or deliberately finds this question ridiculous. However, being used to believing without hesitation everything heard in public speeches or read in the newspapers, of course he could not understand what the peasants were worried about.

Indeed, at first glance there was not much cause for concern. At the end of 1927 at the XV Party Congress, Stalin talked about the gradual transfer of small peasant farms to joint labour, mentioning nothing definite about the pace of collectivization. Earlier, at the Plenary Session of the Central Committee in October 1927, he had again, as at the XIV Congress, criticized the policy for dispossession of the *kulaks* and the establishment of poor peasant committees, referring to it as a 'policy for bringing the Civil War back to the countryside'. On the eve of the XV Congress, when addressing the Sixteenth Party Conference of the Moscow Provincial Committee, Stalin sharply rejected attempts by the opposition to regard the peasantry as a 'colony' to be comprehensively exploited, referring as he did so to the 'indissoluble alliance' with the middle peasants while relying on the poor peasants.[1]

Yet by no means did the rural population believe these assurances; they knew the ways of the Bolsheviks. The peasants were constantly faced with rough coercion of one kind or another. They had been forced to take out government bonds, stripped of grain, shouted at, shamed into obedience and threatened. In the autumn of 1927 prices for grain had dropped sharply; the state, despite its promises, shamelessly began to shift money away from agriculture into industry. In the winter the whole country had been hit by a grain shortage.

People sensed that the policy was changing. On his return from the XV Congress, Goloshchekin spoke pompously at a meeting of Party activists in Kzyl-Orda about a 'new challenge':

> The whole history of Bolshevism can be depicted as moving from one victory to another, but at the same time as a path moving from one set of difficulties to another. The whole history of the Bolsheviks is a history of struggle on two fronts. We need to overcome two enemies. The main one is capitalism. The other hostile force is bourgeois and petty-bourgeois influence on the proletariat.

He continued in more concrete terms:

> The *kulak* farms are developing – as large units – faster than the poor peasants' farms. The offensive against the *kulaks* is first and foremost a course towards large-scale collective farms, towards collectivization for poor and middle peasants.

> Previously Goloshchekin had claimed that 'the *kulaks* were prospering', but this was an exaggeration designed to encourage hostility between the poor peasants and their class enemy. In actual

fact by 1928 the '*kulak-bai*' sector within the rural population had shrunk from 6–8 per cent to 3–4 per cent (in the RSFSR the equivalent drop had been from 3.9 per cent to 2.2 per cent).

It is not possible to form an accurate idea of what the wealth of the dispossessed *bais* had been: there had not been a hay-mower or harvester on every farm and there had not been a carpet in every *yurt*. As for the *kulaks* – a term used by the authorities to cover the most hard-working and efficient peasants so as to make their subsequent elimination easier – they were far from wealthy. In the first wave of confiscations, as is borne out by relatively recent data, the total confiscated property from 320,000 *kulak* farms in the first six months of 1930 came to 400 million roubles. Such property included houses, farming implements, livestock and so on – even down to feather beds and pillows. The average value of the property of a single *kulak* family (and these were large peasant families not like modern urban families) came to 1,250 roubles, equal to the annual salary of a skilled worker. They were not so rich after all.

The campaign for confiscating grain soon began. On 17 January 1928 *Soviet Steppes* published a leading article entitled 'Smash the Speculators'. Readers were told: '*Kulaks* and speculators are the most bitter and the most dangerous enemies. In the struggle against them no one should display restraint. We cannot allow a small group of inveterate enemies of Soviet power to fill their pockets, and exploit the disruption in grain supplies.'

Anyone who did not hand over grain was classified as a speculator. Moreover, all grain had to be handed over for a ridiculously low price; the threat of punishment for speculation was laid out in Article 107 of the Criminal Code and would be enforced whether or not the accused had not been buying up and reselling grain.

At the end of April Goloshchekin addressed the assembled Party membership of Kzyl-Orda:

We have finished taxing the *kulaks*. We have moved against them. The main brunt of self-taxation fell on the *kulak* farms. We clipped the *kulaks'* wings using Article 107.

The application of extraordinary measures and the work of our Party to implement grain collection have shown how capable our Party is of revolutionary action, of revolutionary manoeuvres.[2]

These revolutionary activities consisted in new robbery, in new mass-scale lawlessness. An example of Party work was provided by Stalin, who for three weeks (from 15 January to 6 February) was extorting grain from the granaries of the middle peasants in Siberia. At the time he had stated:

> We cannot let our industry be dependent on the whims of the *kulaks*. So we must ensure that in the course of the next three or four years the collective and state farms, as suppliers of grain, can provide the state with at least a third of the grain it requires. This would push the *kulaks* into the background and would provide the basis for a more of less appropriate supply of grain to the workers and the Red Army. Yet, in order to achieve this, it is necessary to develop to the utmost the construction of state and collective farms, without sparing manpower or resources. It is possible to do this and we must do it.

> Stalin insisted on the wide-scale application of Article 107 by public prosecutors and the legal authorities. On returning from Siberia he signed a directive 'To all organizations of the All-Union Communist Party (Bolsheviks)', in which it was written that '25 per cent of the grain surpluses legally confiscated from speculators and from speculating *kulaks* should be given to poor peasants as long-term loans to satisfy the needs of their families and – where necessary – their consumption requirements.'

> Villages were places where everyone knew everything about everyone else. However well someone might hide a pit of grain for a rainy day from vigilant 'proletarian' eyes, sooner or later the envious gaze of a neighbour would light upon it. 'Socially aware' poor peasants were encouraged to inform on prosperous middle peasants who were hiding surpluses and would then obtain a quarter of those surpluses without breaking sweat behind a plough. This was how the Bolsheviks once again divided rural populations into informers and victims, into those hoping to benefit from other people's property and those whom they would need to impoverish, see off to prison or drive from their homes.

At the end of April, despite various 'excesses and distortions', which as usual Goloshchekin would blame on low-ranking Party members, the grain procurement targets had not been reached. Collectivization was only just beginning and yet the First Secretary of the Area Committee had set himself the goal of creating large state farms for animal breeding and land cultivation. This was in a region where animal breeding was nomadic or semi-nomadic and where there already existed large numbers of small farms where land was cultivated.

A small newspaper article printed in *Soviet Steppes* on 14 May 1928 provides some idea of the commitment to collective farms at the time:

COLLECTIVE FARM FUNDS SQUANDERED ON DRINK

(Village of Burno-Oktyabrskoye in the Syr-Darya Province)

The poor peasants of Burno-Oktyabrskoye decided to organize an agricultural co-operative. The greediest of the peasants decided to join, not those supporting the collectivization of agriculture. They were given a tractor, grain and credit. Citizen Shigalyov was sent to buy horses, but he only got as far as the vodka stall and spent all the co-operative's cash. Naturally he says it was stolen.

Things were no better regarding the tractor. The peasants decided to try it out.

'Does it plough?'

'Yes, it ploughs!'

'Can it pull a cart?'

'Yes, it can!'

They tried it out for all sorts of tasks.

Then someone had a thought: 'It can't swim through water'.

'Who? Him? The tractor? It can't just swim through water, but through air as well if you fix balloons to it'.

They started to test it and took the tractor down to the water. The tractor held out for a long time, then it ran into stones, damaged itself and surrendered to the strength of a dozen fine oxen, who pulled it out up to the bank.

Now the tractor is waiting hopelessly to be repaired, while the fields are waiting just as hopelessly to be ploughed, since the money for horses has gone on drink and the tractor has been sent to an early grave.

This is a lesson to our Party and Soviet bodies to show how carefully they need to set about creating co-operatives. A hastily knocked together co-operative can only cause harm. It can swallow up money and undermine the very idea of the collective-farm movement.

In the meantime, party activists examined corn bins, declaring indignantly that reserves of grain were hidden not only in *kulak* households but also in those of middle peasants and poor peasants. They exposed rumours allegedly spread by the *kulaks* about war and the abolition of NEP, though the risk of war was something the authorities feared more than the *kulaks* and it was obvious to anyone with common sense that NEP was being wound up. The requisitioning of food stocks was in full swing in the villages. It was hardly surprising that people were alarmed and laying in grain stocks, fearing hunger in the future; very little time had passed since the hungry years of War Communism. Yet the well-fed and prosperous authorities were indignant about peasants who had dared to keep back their grain instead of selling their 'surpluses' at cheap prices. The newspaper pointed out:

> All the work for grain procurement consists in persuading peasants to sell all their grain surpluses to the state as quickly as possible. If every middle peasant were to sell just 240–320 kilos, the plan targets for grain procurement would be met. So far there has been no breakthrough.[3]

In *Soviet Steppes* there was a regular column entitled 'How to strike at the wreckers of grain procurement':

> 'Who is whining about hunger?' was the question in a headline in the issue for 12 June. It turned out that four ordinary citizens, taken out of a queue during an inspection, were found to have 'large reserves of grain'. These 'speculators' (the people standing in the queue were arrested for no valid reason, searched and then termed 'speculators' into the bargain) were creating panic, spreading rumours that there was no grain, that people would starve and they ought to save themselves and lay in reserves!

Soon afterwards the so-called 'speculators' realized where the revolutionary manoeuvres were leading the people. Those who realized soonest were persecuted and imprisoned first of all.

Let us turn once more to *Soviet Steppes*. On 18 June 1928 they published an article entitled 'Let us also turn to the scaremongers warning of famine':

> (From our Akmolinsk correspondent) The village of Voznesenskaya in the Voroshilov District. At a meeting of the poor peasants, the organized *kulaks* made energetic speeches against the grain procurement, filling people's minds with rumours of hunger. As a result of pressure from the *kulaks* the meeting drew up the following resolution: 'As we are hungry and Soviet power is condemning us to death through hunger, we are not handing in grain and the grain already stored we shall keep for ourselves.'
>
> How do you like that? Once a *kulak*, always a *kulak*! The inspection revealed that there were more than 30 tonnes of unthreshed grain.
>
> This opposition must sooner or later be broken.

More followed on 22 June:

SEVEN KULAKS HAVE BEEN ARRESTED
Semipalatinsk. (Our correspondent) A group of *kulaks* from the village of Aleksandrovka in the Pozdnyakovsk *volost* of the Bukhtarminsk District organized an attack against the chairman of the Soviet – a former Red Army soldier, who was actively involved in grain procurement. Seven *kulaks* have been arrested and brought to trial.

Then on 25 June:

ONE DOZEN TRUMPED ACES
Petropavlovsk. In the Internatsionalnaya *volost*, twelve *kulaks* have been brought to trial for hiding grain surpluses.

ALLIANCE OF KULAKS AND PRIESTS
Semipalatinsk. In the village of Sekisovka, in the Krasnooktyabrskaya *volost*, the priest was found to have been concealing large grain reserves. He has been deprived of his liberty for one year. The grain surpluses were confiscated.

Later on 7 August:

ARE THE KULAKS STORING GRAIN?

(From our correspondent in the Syr-Darya region) It is out of the question that a Kazakh, regardless of what kind of farm he has, would not put some grain by to feed his family.

The newspaper clearly urged farmers in the steppe not to store surplus grain, as if its staff had forgotten that two weeks previously it had printed a resolution from the USSR Council of People's Commissars banning the use of extraordinary measures, such as: 'Walking round holdings and searching them in order to confiscate grain surpluses, extra-judicial arrests and other sanctions and also making peasants legally responsible for delays in taking their grain to market.'

Goloshchekin had given party activists leads so that they would know where and in whose farms they should look for hidden grain. On 29 April 1928 he wrote in *Soviet Steppes*: 'We should not ignore the question of the relations between the *auls* and the villages. The *bais* and the *kulaks* have a common goal. The *kulaks* are hiding grain with the *bais* and the *bais* are forming a common front with the *kulaks*.'

Pressure on the peasantry was growing; both animal breeders and farmers growing field-crops had their backs to the wall. The authorities made no secret of this. In July 1928 Stalin stated at a Plenary Session of the Central Committee of the All-Union Communist Party (Bolsheviks):

In this instance the situation with the peasantry is as follows: in the first place it is not only paying the state the usual taxes, direct and indirect, but also paying comparatively high prices for manufactured goods and, in the second, it is not being adequately paid for agricultural produce.

This is an additional tax borne by the peasantry in the interests of the drive to industrialize, which will be of benefit to the whole country, including the peasantry. This is what we might call 'tribute', an extra tax.

This is an unpleasant state of affairs, there is no denying it. Yet we would not be Bolsheviks, if we concealed this and closed our eyes to the fact that our industry and our country cannot for the time being manage without this additional tax on the peasantry.

Despite this 'Bolshevik directness', Stalin did not admit that this tribute was being paid by enslaved peasants and did not say how long 'for the time being' would last. Not only were the peasants paying 'tribute' but they were still regarded as the authorities' most bitter enemies.

Mutual distrust and antipathy, like that which existed during the Civil War, grew like a cancerous tumour and was fanned daily by propaganda. Newspaper headlines grew all the more raucous: 'Push the Offensive against *Kulaks* and *Bais*!' – 'In the Hands of the *Kulak* Gang!' – 'In the Grip of the *Bais* and *Elders*!' – 'Drive Out the *Bais* and the Criminals! – 'Strike Harder at the *Kulaks* and the *Bais*!' – 'Into the Attack Against *Kulaks* and *Bais*!' A short article – 'Bestial Husband' – about the murder of a wife for removing her veil reflects particularly clearly this wave of increasingly bitter feelings.

Women, public organizations and schools (which meant children) demanded that 'Uzbek Almyshbaev' be shot.[4] This 'war' unleashed by the Party leadership needed enemies, the number of which was constantly growing. The shedding of innocent blood (five 'saboteurs' from Shakhtinsk had already been shot) only fanned the tension. The *kulaks* and *bais* were presented as the main enemies – miscalculations and mistakes in the economy were all blamed on them.

The article entitled 'Questions of building Collective Farms in Kazakhstan' printed in *Soviet Steppes* on 3–4 July 1928 reveals much about the situation. The author had noticed serious shortcomings in the collective farm movement. In the Zhanybek District of the Syr-Darya province, for example, sixteen of the twenty-eight collective farms had failed. They collapsed at the beginning of autumn and so were unable to deliver grain to the state. In the Petropavlovsk District more than half the collective farms turned out to be 'non-viable' and as a result of re-registering they were dropped. The method the author used to shed light on the collapse of these collective farms was simple and had proved successful back in the days of War Communism – he blamed the *kulaks* and the *bais*:

> If we look in detail at the composition of the existing collective farms we often find that they included a significant percent of *kulak* or *bai* elements, disguising themselves with the title 'middle peasants' or 'poor peasants'. It is not rare to come across '*kulkhozes*' instead of '*kolkhozes*' [*kulak* farms instead of collective farms].

According to the author the *kulaks* crept into the collective farms for their own financial gain, in order to make profits for themselves and at the same time undermine the farms. How they achieved this, however, the author did not relate. In order to gain profit a peasant first needs to toil, since if nothing grows there is no money to be made, so the logic behind the article is far from clear.

He went on to single out other factors to explain the collapse of the farms: there had not been enough planning, the land use was not properly organized, there was little help from agricultural experts and no proper guidance on establishing collective principles. All this, however, is blamed on the wicked intrigues of the *kulaks* and *bais*. He reaches the following conclusion: 'What can be done? Naturally the attack has to be concentrated on the *kulak* and *bai* elements already in the collective farms or trying to penetrate them. The slogan for our work to this end must be: "Keep the *kulaks* and the *bais* out of the collective farms!"'

The Soviets' principal method of control – the purge – was gaining ground. It was used from the very first days of the Soviet regime and appeared to be universally powerful. The poet Vladimir Mayakovsky had extolled it in his day, writing the now ironic lines: 'I purge myself to be more like Lenin, to swim further into the Revolution.'

They purged the Party of deviationists and nationalists, the collective farms of *kulaks* and *bais*, the plants and factories of socially alien cadres, the villages and *kishlaks* of churches and mosques, the universities and institutes of alien class elements and schools of *kulaks'* children. They may have gone as far as kindergartens and crèches in some places. Lenin and Stalin's periodic table of socially alien elements was far more complex and far-reaching than Dmitri Mendeleyev's scientific original. Everything was worked out, checked and tested: the purge, the resulting struggle against its extremes and then the next purge.

The newspaper *Soviet Steppes* published two articles on 24 January 1929 entitled: 'The Disenfranchised Change their Skin' and 'Lessons to be Gleaned from Extremes'. In the first of the two, sent in from Pavlodar, readers were told that many requests had been sent to the electoral commissions asking for the re-instatement of electoral rights. The author here seems indignant that class enemies, in doing this, were so bold as to express their value as citizens; he writes them off as *bais*, mullahs or *kulaks*. In the same vein the second article, from Kustanai, told how, after checking the situation in the Zatobolsk District to establish who had been deprived of their electoral rights, two-thirds of the potential 1,222 voters had been dropped from the list and among those there were 'middle peasants'. The reporters from both Kustanai and Pavlodar seemed concerned about only one thing – how best to over-fulfil the purge plan. The people were being reminded once more that they consisted of two groups – the pure and the tainted – and that the criterion for purity was social origin.

On 22 February 1929 *Soviet Steppes* published an article under the heading: 'An Exam for Proletarian Students':

> The latest decision taken by the Kazakhstan Area Committee of the All-Union Communist Party (Bolsheviks) regarding the purge of socially alien elements from educational establishments is a fact of enormous importance: it is an extension and consolidation of the political course adopted by the Kazakhstan Area Committee, which is currently being implemented firmly and consistently.

This historical decision, formed on the basis of a stereotyped Party directive issued from the Centre, had been signed by Goloshchekin; he himself was originally a member of the bourgeoisie – albeit the petty variety – but did not, of course, regard himself as a socially alien element.

On the previous day the newspaper had printed a letter from Tashkent about how students 'on the make' – already recognized as socially and ideologically alien individuals – had been thrown out from various faculties of the University of Central Asia (and at the same time from the Komsomol). In an issue dating from 10 March a headline exclaimed: 'No Place in our Schools for the Sons of *Kulaks!*'

The Soviet poet Vasily Lebedev-Kumach declared later in 1937 that 'He who searches, shall always find!' Indeed saboteurs were found everywhere, even in light entertainment; when two entertainers by the name of Ryazanskii and Karelskii arrived in Kzyl-Orda to perform in the town's cinema, they had not changed their repertoire from the days of NEP – perhaps they thought this would not bother a provincial audience. Their performance was scheduled for International Women's Day, which was known to have major political significance. They sang some ironic couplets before they began:

If a maiden marries now,
She will be a lady.
If she doesn't marry now,
She'll still become a lady!

They then moved from the official theme of the event to more political matters:

How sad it is when work we must
Out in the field with a mare!
First she'll yawn, then she'll stop
And I'll shout: 'Don't you dare!'

They also sang the following:

Communism is beyond me,
P'raps you can grasp the meaning?
O brother, even Chamberlain
Found it so demeaning!

One journalist was so offended by this that he wrote indignantly: 'There is no place for cultural saboteurs in our Party apparatus. Why does the Trade Union for Arts Workers not come out resolutely with sharp attacks against insolent people who bring the very name "Soviet artist" into disrepute?'

These short rhymes were the last gasp of fresh air in the republic's four-page newspaper; many stories had been crushed by official directives for the press. The time was drawing near when nothing else would appear apart from merciless class struggle.

The previous year had seen a poor harvest in northern Kazakhstan, yet the plan targets for grain procurement had not been reduced and demanded a third more than the peasants could deliver. Goloshchekin announced to the party activists in Kzyl-Orda on 9 March 1929:

The class struggle is intensifying. I have just been travelling all over Kazakhstan and so far 800,000 tonnes of grain have been procured. Seventy-five million roubles' worth of commodities have been delivered, but grain worth only 50 million roubles has been purchased.

According to him forms of class struggle had changed significantly:

> Until now the main methods for the struggle against the *kulaks* and the *bais* were bribes, group manoeuvres, clan-based regroupings and so on. This year, after confiscations a wave of terror began. The *kulaks* and the *bais* do not want to open up opportunities for the poor and middle peasants, who are gradually taking charge of their own destinies more and more.[5]

The real situation was entirely the opposite. The newspapers bent over backwards to find any trace of '*kulaks*' and *bais*' machinations', but there was no such material available. Their pages were, however, flooded with news about state terror. On 8 April 1929 *Soviet Steppes* demanded: 'More Repressive Measures against *Kulak* Grain-hoarders!' Then on 26 April they declared: 'We shall drive *kulaks* and *bais* into a corner and fulfil the grain-procurement plan using revolutionary laws and through organization of the poor peasants in alliance with the middle peasants!'. That same day the paper informed its readers: 'In various parts of Kazakhstan over ten cases are being investigated regarding political crimes committed by *kulaks* and *bais*. We are convinced that the Soviet courts using stern sentences will be able to stem any desire on the part of elements hostile to the working class to engage in terrorist attacks.' Of course the authorities were already skilled in this area thanks to considerable practice.

In an article entitled 'From the Standpoint of Truth', modern historians B. Tulepbaev and V. Osipov describe the situation as follows:

> Armed with stern instructions and far-reaching powers 4,812 officials from area and district Party organizations were sent out into the villages and *auls*. The distinctive characteristics of their actions were cruelty and a readiness to resort to any means. The main focus of their attacks was to be the *kulaks* and the *bais*. Yet those entrusted to carry out this work were often ill-informed about the situation in the field and used to attack middle peasants or even poor ones.

Administrative measures did not prove economically effective: just over 10,000 tonnes of grain and 53,400 head of livestock were confiscated from the 34,121 'bais and kulaks' found guilty of various offences. This amounted to about 1 per cent of the grain-procurement plan and 3.5 per cent of the plan for meat procurement. In the meantime the Kazakhstan Area Committee of the All-Union Communist Party (Bolsheviks) reported in the spring of 1929 that it had succeeded in fulfilling 84.3 per cent of the grain-procurement target, while the amount of meat collected was one-and-a-half times greater than in the previous year with regard to cattle and three times greater for sheep.

It is clear that the heaviest demands regarding grain procurement were those made on the middle and poor peasants. In many cases those peasants were stripped of all the grain they had, down to the very last ear. Kazakh nomads were also required to deliver grain for the procurement programme, although they were not engaged in any kind of land cultivation. They were forced to sell their livestock and then buy grain.[6]

In connection with around a dozen 'bai and kulak crimes' 34,121 people were convicted. This number, however, required further clarification and more details.

The authors of the above article express doubt as to whether the 'representatives of state bodies provoked the intensification of the struggle in the rural areas'. We would suggest however that there is little room for doubt; unleashing class war or, to be exact, war within a specific class, was the basis of Bolshevik policy – activity of this kind was practised from the very first days of Soviet power. In Kazakhstan these tactics were employed more actively once Goloshchekin appeared on the scene. We have seen proof of this and there is further evidence from 1929.

The new chairman of Kazakhstan's Council of People's Commissars, Uraz Isaev, signed a decree on 11 September, according to which the farm of every bai, kulak or prosperous peasant would have to deliver grain surpluses no later than 1 November 1929. For those who did not comply there would be a fine of five times the value of the grain delivery or a criminal conviction as specified in Article 61.

Two weeks later Goloshchekin lent his support to those engaged in grain procurement:

So, the *kulaks* are not delivering and the communists are failing to organize the poor peasants to confront them. We say to those communists: learn to cope, organize properly and oppose those *kulaks*. (Applause.) This is after all organization of the class struggle and that is an enormously important class objective. The organization of a red caravan of a thousand red carts moving towards the towns, where they will be greeted by industrial and white-collar workers coming out to support the peasants – surely that is a class goal?[7]

Goloshchekin instilled inspiration by promoting the image of red carts transporting the confiscated grain and happy townspeople coming to meet them, abandoning their machines and counting-house desks. It was with this spectacle that he wished to attract the officials charged with grain-procurement targets. He was not interested in the fate of the thousands of families whose seed corn would be taken away from them, who would therefore hardly be able to make ends meet and who would probably go hungry. With this glorious vision he sought to inspire those assigned to grain-procurement tasks: the drawing together of the robbers and those rejoicing at the plunder.

Charged with encouraging the collective spirit and spreading propaganda, the newspapers started printing short information bulletins about grain procurement every day, as if they were military reports coming in from the front. On 27 September they wrote: 'Not for a minute shall we relax the struggle against the *kulaks* and the Right-deviationists. (The class struggle in relation to grain procurement out in the provinces is gaining momentum by the minute. The *kulaks* are growing bolder by the day).' There followed:

THE FIGHT HAS BEGUN

The *kulaks* hiding grain are baring their teeth as they refuse to co-operate with grain procurement activity. A new aspect of the campaign – to bring the procurement plan to the household of every *kulak* and prosperous peasant – has met with fierce resistance from the anti-Soviet sections of the rural population. Class battles are flaring up in the villages with regard to the new harvest.

Then on 16 October:

ON THE FRONT LINE OF THE CLASS STRUGGLE

It is reported from Semipalatinsk that in the village of Kabanovo in the Shemonaikhinsk District the *kulaks* are engaging in systematic beatings of Party activists and farm labourers. To that end the *kulaks* have organized their own special detachment of thugs. The visiting assizes from the District Court has reached the following decision: the *kulaks* Yevdokim Sinarov and Zotei Bogatyryov, main instigators of the beating of poor peasants, are to be shot.

Later on 5 December:

EXECUTION OF KULAK TERRORISTS BY FIRING SQUAD

The Petropavlovsk regional court has sentenced a group of *kulaks* to the highest measure for the protection of society, to be shot: they beat up activist officials, members of the Soviet authorized to procure grain.

The Urals regional court has sentenced the influential *bai*, Rakhman Omraliev to be shot. He had made an attempt on the life of Comrade Khankhazhin, a member of the commission in charge of grain procurement.

The *kulak* Ivan Vaganov attempted to drown farm labourer Sayanin – an energetic social activist – in a stream. The Urals District Court sentenced Vaganov to be shot.

All these sentences have been put into effect.

The authorities did not take a life for a life; blood was often shed in response to a mere blow with a fist. The attempts at murder cited above came to nothing; neither the *bai*, Omraliev, nor the *kulak* Vaganov succeeded in their attempts to kill or drown activists.

How many 'terrorists' of this kind would be brought forward and wiped out just to provide warnings, to frighten potential grain hoarders?

❧ ❧ ❧

Loyal Leninists headed by 'the finest Leninist, Comrade Stalin' succeeded in burying NEP. Goloshchekin, together with the newly elected Second Secretary of the Area Committee, Izmukhan Kuramysov (aged thirty-two, from the family of an Aktyubinsk farmer, former farm labourer and worker in Orenburg slaughterhouses, Party member since the age of twenty-five) and the new chairman of the Council of People's Commissars, Uraz Isaev (aged thirty, from a farm labourer's family in the Urals, former militiaman and Party member since the age of twenty), was contemplating ways to bring in more grain and fulfil the planned targets, to drive nomads into collective farms and to force them to embrace a settled way of life.

Plans had been drawn up for the 'Great Breakthrough', which would ultimately break the people's back; there was a great deal of work ahead. The plan for the advance of the collective farm movement in Kazakhstan specified that in 1929 the number of collective farms must be increased from 2,315 to 3,215, bringing 18,668 families – 34,000 more mouths to feed – into the sphere of collective work. By the end of the year there was to be a total of 41,700 families – 194,490 mouths to feed – in collective farms; that was 3.1 per cent of the whole population as opposed to 1.6 per cent in 1928.

Initially the plan was to double the number of collective farms over the period of the Five Year Plan so that by 1933, 4 per cent of the peasant farms would be collectivized. Yet high-ranking echelons of the Party considered that pace too slow and soon the plan called for 16–18 per cent of the farms to be collectivized – in other words a ten-fold increase in the number of collective farms. There was no longer talk of a voluntary or gradual building up of collective farms.

The pace of collectivization was particularly unrealistic where Kazakhstan and other regions like it were concerned – regions in which half the population led a nomadic or semi-nomadic life. Yet no thought was put into the practicalities of Party-issued directives. As early as 1929 the original Five Year Plan had been over fulfilled by 100 per cent and 6.9 per cent of agriculture had been collectivized.

Soviet Steppes came up with a militant headline of the usual kind: 'At the Front Line of Kolkhoz Construction'. On 11 September the following information was provided in an article entitled 'Collectivization of Poor Peasant Farms': 'In the Sarkand District near Alma-Ata a special fund has been set up for the collectivization of poor peasants. It comprises 25 per cent of the property confiscated in the course of grain procurement.' This is vague: what kind of property might have been confiscated during the grain procurement drive? On the same day it reported: 'In response to the seizure of the Chinese Eastern Railway, peasants in many settlements, containing a thousand households and more, are organizing large collective farms.'

On 14 October the paper's leading article almost spluttered with joy:

HARVEST DAY AND COLLECTIVIZATION

The growth of collective farms in Kazakhstan is advancing at a rapid pace, overtaking certain other areas in the Soviet Union. We had 2,315 in 1928, while in 1929 there are already 4,348 collective farms.

In previous years the harvest holiday was celebrated on different days in different districts. Now the working people will celebrate it every year on 14 October as 'Harvest and Collectivization Day'.

On the same page another article stated:

The growth of the collective farm movement is accompanied by intensified resistance on the part of the *bais*, *kulaks* and clerics, which is manifested in violence, killings, arson attacks and the undermining of the collective farms from within.

In response to this the pace of collectivization was accelerated further, bringing no less than 80,000 new holdings into the collective farms. More than half of these would 'involve the Kazakh population'.

A mere ten days later, on 24 October, a resolution of the Area Committee 'On the Results and Next Tasks for Building Collectives' was published under the headline 'Collective Farms – Oases of Socialism in the *Auls*'. It had been decided, as Goloshchekin duly noted, to set up larger collective farms than before. In 1929–30 it was planned to incorporate up to 140,000 holdings into collectives (there were approximately 80,000 at the end of 1929) and to increase the sown area almost threefold. The pace was heating up, almost hour by hour.

The ninth anniversary of the founding of socialist Kazakhstan was celebrated as usual on 4 October. On that day a poet, calling himself simply 'P-3', published an 'Ode to the Steppe's Celebrations':

In the steppe tears have left their mark.
Alash-Orda's sharp flagstaff green
Has pierced its breast with message dark,
Beloved of elders behind the scene.
Barbarous famine stalked the land,
Sheets of ice brought cold and pain.
Gruel was not passed from hand to hand:
They counted millet by the grain.
The felt-roofed *auls* they groaned in pain,
Deep gorges ringed them all around.
The *dombra* wept its quiet refrain.
The people's tears fell to the ground.
The years passed by and many a moon
Shone down from the star-filled sky.
The steppe, once wild, now reaps a boon:
Thistles make way as trains draw nigh
Over the tracks of iron and steel
To humble *auls* along the line.
October's train with its rattling wheels
Shall mark the republic's Year Nine!

Meanwhile from the higher climes of those issuing directives, a snowball was rapidly growing in size, set in motion by the 'Kremlin's mountain dweller' – Stalin – and his cronies. There was no stopping the avalanche of collectivization – the 'Great Breakthrough' – which would bring disaster in its wake.

X. Anti-religious Repression

Surviving on their last reserves of grain from corn bins and granaries, a new horror was bestowed upon the Kazakh people; they were now deprived of opportunities to worship their Lord God. In the collective farms and towns no place was provided for religious worship. The chief atheist by the name of Emelyan Yaroslavskii (originally Gubelman) ran this campaign from Moscow, supervised by none other than Lazar Kaganovich. Freedom of conscience, as they understood it, meant if not actually destroying places of worship, turning such buildings into trading stalls or community halls. For leading Leninists the main goal was to do away with the religious beliefs of the Russian people, in particular those of its largest social class – the peasantry. Ironically the Russian word for 'peasant' was derived from the word 'Christian'. Before breaking the peasants' bodies the authorities decided first of all to crush their minds.

At the beginning of 1929 Kaganovich sent out a directive in which religious organizations were declared as the only legal counter-revolutionary force still in existence. Yaroslavskii proclaimed the introduction of a Five Year Plan for atheism aimed at banishing religious belief from the country once and for all. Work then began on the widespread closing down and destruction of churches, chapels and icons – everything which had survived the days of War Communism.

The Party's henchmen were already straining at the leash. Mikhail Koltsov Fridlyand came up with a plan to blow up the Simonov Monastery in Moscow – a monument of national and world culture which had stood for over six centuries. He fanned propaganda in the newspapers, after which GlavNauka – the Central Department responsible for scientific and artistic institutions and museums – removed its protection from 6,000 of Russia's 8,000 architectural monuments. The purpose of this pogrom against Russian national culture and the Russian Orthodox

Church is made clear in Koltsov's report regarding the destruction of the Simonov Monastery:

> Guncotton slabs were laid out ... then there was a blast ... less powerful than had been expected ... Another bang ...
>
> A clean, shining white 'mountain' soared up into the air. We were tempted to run up to it. It was amazing. The cathedral was blown up into a shower of totally separate intact bricks. They lay there like a mountain of lump sugar. (The monastery was blown up on the night of 21 January 1930).
>
> On the sixth anniversary of Lenin's death, Stalin and the whole Party laid out a new round of guncotton slabs *under the old village, under the remains of its countless small-scale capitalists* [my italics] and between the deepest roots of its old ugly way of life, so as to create a new socialist collectivized order.
>
> The XV Congress was behind us and we were sailing forward across the open sea, our path lit up by the lights of the XVI Congress. There will be new explosions and with those a whole class will be swept off the earth, which till now has been strong and tough, just like the walls of this monastery.[1]

The anti-religious press brought out hundreds of thousands of copies of their propaganda-driven publications, contributing to the effort to ensure that nothing of that 'whole class' remained – only 'liberated molecules'. Between 1929 and 1930 journals such as *The Anti-religionist, Atheists Poised at their Machines* and *The Atheist* brought out materials like those below:

> Anyone who propagates religion is furthering the counter-revolutionary cause, since religion is an implacable enemy of communism. Even the most 'innocent' of sermons on such subjects as 'brotherly love' is counter-revolutionary.

> The ignorant, they make their way
> To church through incense smoke.
> Clever people out today
> Enjoy the sun and joke.
> Churches all we soon shall close,
> While building factories new.

The working people forward goes,
To claim its rightful due.

Unknown author

I have sorted grains of wheat,
Discarding those which will not sprout.
ABCs we'll sow and eat:
God's word, however, we'll throw out.

S. Gorodetskii

'Socialism is the natural enemy of religion ... The entry of socialism is, therefore, the exodus of religion' [Karl Marx]. This is why there will be no religion under communism. We have embarked on the path of atheism and must continue along this path to the end. What we need is not incense, but burning sulphur and oil, what we need to do is not lift our eyes to Heaven, but bring them down to the Earth and drain swamps. We do not need the support of the clergy but fish, ducks and bats.

The crematorium movement is the ally of proletarian free-thinking.

(Sivers, member of the 'German Alliance of Free-thinkers')

I am glad that the Iversk Chapel with its miracle-working icon has at last disappeared from Revolution Square, that the tasteless Cathedral of the Annunciation and many other dens of priests are being demolished and turned into 'Leninist bricks'.

Günberg, a German worker

Thousands of proletarians buried Christmas on 6–7 January [when Russian Orthodox Christmas is celebrated]. Many churches were empty ...

At the 'Hammer and Sickle' Plant all the workers to a man turned up for work on 'Christmas Day'. At a meeting for the whole workforce devoted to the anti-Christmas campaign it was decided that they would 'organize a collection of icons' [to burn them in the furnaces], shut down two nearby churches and hand them over to the Young Pioneers.

In the club 'Red Pond'
Maria spreads revolution!
She has called her son 'Farm Bond',
Her daughter 'Constitution'!

The active involvement of the lads is on the increase and advancing further in that direction (groups of young atheists are appearing everywhere and conferences on atheism are being convened for children and so on).

The ringing of church bells jars on our ears, disrupts public quiet and disturbs people at their work. Three thousand workers and working women from the 'Red Moscow' factory have decided first to put an end to bell-ringing throughout the whole USSR and secondly to take all bells out of churches and hand them over for producing tractors.

Atheist towns cooperating with the collectives in the countryside will make them godless as well. Atheists! Off to the collective farms! To the countryside! Oppose the *kulaks*, the priests and religious sects! Away with obscurantism!

I was sent from the provincial centre to give lectures and practical explanations for the creation of the world and other matters and also to involve the masses in opposition to Christ and the Mother of God, because she was no virgin but a degenerate element, which means hostile to the working people!

Workers' Correspondent, Issue 11

The struggle against religion not only came into being but also produced such results as the mass destruction of icons. In Tver more than a thousand icons were collected for burning. Thousands of icons were handed over to the Union of Militant Atheists in Moscow, Tula and Serpukhov. Podolsk declared itself to be an atheist town. A campaign is underway to have Kolomna declared an atheist town. In the last year alone ninety-three priests' propaganda bases have been shut down. There is a campaign underway to turn Moscow into a true centre of international atheism. Moscow must be atheist! In Samara atheists are conducting six-day debates on the subject of immaculate conception. The workers of Noginsk are handing in icons for burning. Fourteen thousand cripples are demanding that a church be closed down and turned into a club for the disabled. Recently an association of former political prisoners raised the question of closing the 'Church of the Saviour on Spilled Blood' erected on the spot where Alexander II was assassinated and handing it over to them, so they could set up a museum.

In the course of seven months after the death of my mother I saved up my earnings in order to build a monument over her grave. Now I have realized that it was foolish. I do not wish to behave like a savage. It is better for me to buy a book with the money I saved and then I shall understand everything.

Woman worker from the 'Red October' factory, Maria Z.[2]

This was how the 'Great Breakthrough' began on the religious front.

Much later, as the Germans held a knife to the throat of the nation, former seminarist Dzhugashvili remembered his 'brothers and sisters', whom he had harassed, brought low and plagued with hunger. At this point Stalin (who needed to save his own skin) wisely reduced the pressure on churchgoers. For the time being however, chief atheist Comrade Yaroslavskii was given a free hand. Many shootings had already taken place, for by the end of 1919 only 40,000 of Russia's 360,000 priests remained. At an anti-religious meeting of the Central Committee in 1929 Yaroslavskii formulated the main thrust of the military action:

In the next few years, here in the USSR, we shall be able to root out capitalist elements of a kind different from those on which attention was concentrated in 1917–21. While previously we were up against tens of thousands of landowners and tens of thousands of capitalists, now we are confronting three to four million *kulaks*, who constitute the most active members of religious organizations. The struggle against them is not an easier one than that against landowners who support church organizations, probably one that is even more difficult.[3]

In the Bolsheviks' language, the phrase 'root out' meant annihilating three to four million people and their families – this was a more difficult task than wiping out just tens of thousands.

✢ ✢ ✢

As modern political journalist I. Achildiev writes in the popular magazine *Youth*, 'Stalin opted for the path of political struggle against the Church, replacing the debate about world views with political confrontation.' In Lenin's day however 'Soviet power had elaborated a carefully thought through policy that was loyal with regard to the Church and believers.'[4] Let us consider Lenin's debate about world views within its context of a loyal political policy that had been carefully thought through.

Lenin and his teacher Marx used to grind their teeth at the very mention of God, as can be seen from even the most cursory examination of his 'legacy'. Reading Hegel he would add comments of his own, filled with strong emotions, in the margin: 'The materialist raises the importance of knowledge of matter and Nature by casting God and this philosophical rogue into the rubbish pit.'[5] In the margins of his notes amidst a whole cluster of question marks, he exclaimed: 'the idealist swine is sorry for God!!'[6] Elsewhere his comments were similar: 'This trite priestly idealist talks about the greatness of Christianity (with quotations from the Gospels!!). It's revolting, it stinks!'[7] In a letter to Maxim Gorky he even claimed that: 'every little god is a necrophiliac – even the purest and most ideal variety … Every religious idea, every idea about any godlet is unspeakably revolting, the most dangerous kind of idea, the most hideous of plagues …'[8] It is not difficult to imagine the things Lenin said out loud to his comrades-in-arms, given the nature of his writing.

Fanatical hatred of religion and the Church did not stop Lenin deceiving the 'ignorant' people with feigned tolerance towards religion, though this was for tactical reasons. Before the October Revolution he called upon the workers to struggle against 'religious fog … using ideas as weapons and only ideas'.[9] He even permitted priests to join the ranks of the Social Democrats on the condition that they carry out Party work conscientiously. What else could he do? There were still so many believers and he had to take them into consideration, though presumably it pained his materialist heart. This was why the right to engage in religious propaganda was included in the 1918 Constitution. In practice however, this right soon gave way to merciless annihilation of priests and believers.

Lenin forbade the engagement of the Church in charitable works, advocated 'complete freedom in marriage' and discouraged 'church marriage'. He maintained that morality consisted of 'discipline based on united solidarity and conscious mass struggle against the exploiters'.[10] In practice this meant he supported unrestrained killings and the suppression of all those whom the Bolsheviks called exploiters. Lenin 'heartily supported the initiative of those working people, who suggested that "holy relics" be opened up, so as to expose the deceit by the clerics'.[11] He ordered a wide campaign of sacrilege designed to insult Russian Orthodox believers, who made up the majority of the population. As a result, relics in more than sixty of the most venerated Russian shrines were defiled, starting with that of Saint Sergius of Radonezh.

Whether the revolutionary Russian poet Vladimir Mayakovsky knew the saying 'With a prayer on your lips and work for your hands' we cannot know, but he succeeded in translating it perfectly into Bolshevik language: 'With Lenin in your head and a gun in your hands.' Priests were reported 'drowned', 'stabbed by bayonets', 'beaten with rifle butts', 'shot and left to freeze', 'hacked to pieces by sabres'. Yet what were they were being killed for? For preaching, for ringing bells ...

In the Land of the Soviets new men were necessary, men of a quite different breed. They would be non-believers, obedient, their heads full of Lenin and Party slogans and with a gun in their hands ready when called by the Party to destroy, plunder and kill. The song in their throats – the 'Song of the Destroyers' was set to a tune similar to the popular 'Dogs' Waltz'. That was the name first given to the Party's anthem – the 'Internationale':

All shall be burnt or destroyed,
Wiped from the face of the Earth.
Let's cast the old Sun into the void
And cheer at the new Sun's birth!

Not even the old sun was acceptable for the new world. The Bolsheviks knew what they were doing; it would be easier to manage a people that no longer believed in God. It could be led anywhere, even to its own demise, as long as it was given the appropriate precepts, if it was made to believe that its bright future lay in a gulf of barefaced materialism devoid of spirituality.

Atheism and the fight against God were harbingers of religious war – something as old as the world itself. In several towns soon after the October Revolution, the Bolsheviks erected monuments to Judas – the first to betray Christ. Ex-Chief Procurator of the Synod, the Prince N.D. Zhevakhov, wrote in his memoirs that the pre-revolutionary atmosphere in Russia came about because of the mistakes made by the Tsar and his government. Zhevakov also believed that Christian leaders of all states, throughout all eras, just like whole peoples, had been caught up in revolutions, had fought against them and often fallen victim to them.[12]

Indeed modern historian and émigré M. Bernshtam shares this last conviction of Zhevakov's, namely that Christian peoples oppose revolutions and do not participate in them. After using strong evidence to dismantle widespread perceptions of the 'Russian revolution', Bernshtam concludes that:

> It is probable that there have never been so few representatives of a people involved in bringing about any revolution in history anywhere or so many representatives of a people opposing a revolution. The concept of the 'Russian revolution', in our opinion, should be removed from scholarly writing, just as the idea of a so-called workers' and peasants' revolution in Russia should be dropped.[13]

Looking to Christian teaching may help us understand the Bolsheviks' stance on religion. Saint John Chrysostom, the Golden Mouth, appealed to his followers: 'May there grow within us the fruit of the Spirit, which is love, joy, peace, long-suffering, mercy, compassion, faith, gentleness and abstinence.' He also reminded them of what was 'pernicious and hateful to God and cursed in the Holy Scriptures – lies, slander, quarrels, fighting, self-glorification, pride, mercilessness, envy, hatred for our fellow men, malice, grudges, conceit, hypocrisy, disobedience, defiance, bribery, indignities, blame, drunkenness, gluttony, adultery, theft, larceny, disregard of God's commandments, robbery, sorcery, blasphemy, diabolical songs, tinkling bells, pipes, psalteries, obscene dancing and playing and Rusalii [ancient Slavic spring festival to commemorate the dead] – all of which were pleasing to the Devil.' Not one of these accursed activities was missing from 'truly revolutionary morality'. It is no wonder that the true Leninist, Trotsky, defined this morality as follows:

> Leninism is militant through and through. War is unthinkable without cunning, traps and deceiving the enemy. Victorious militant cunning is an essential element of Leninist policy.

At the same time, however, Leninism is the highest form of revolutionary honesty before the face of the Party and the working class. There can be no fictions, no illusions, no false values.[14]

The highest form of revolutionary honesty, then, involved keeping many secrets from the Party and its class. On 19 March 1922 Lenin wrote a letter to the members of the Politburo, a letter that was strictly secret and which did not find its way into his *Complete Collected Works*. It was on the subject of the confiscation of Church valuables:

> The larger the number of representatives of the reactionary bourgeoisie and the reactionary clergy we are able to shoot in conjunction with this offence the better. We need to educate the public in such a way that it should not dare to contemplate any kind of resistance for several decades.[15]

This 'most humane of individuals' was giving no thought to helping the hungry; desperate hunger merely provided a convenient pretext for looting, humiliating, frightening and crushing the Russian Orthodox Church or, to be more precise, its remnants. Soon the masses would be confronted with a new slogan implying that churchmen did not want to help the hungry.

With the fierce zeal of a looter, Lenin hurried to seize the moment and strip the Church bare. As for the 'resolute and merciless war' which he waged against the 'extremely reactionary clergy', he seemed motivated not so much by logic as by his instinctive and ineradicable hatred for Christianity. At this stage all that remained of the Russian clergy was a mere handful of priests.

By this time there was virtually nothing left to strip from the Church; Trotsky complained to fellow Party member Pyotr Krasikov that the main Church valuables had 'gone missing during the years of the Revolution' and all that remained was 'bulky silver'.

❧   ❧   ❧

As we can see, Vladimir Lenin did not allow any 'debate about world views' with the Russian Orthodox Church. His instinctive hatred of

Christianity had become deep-rooted and was growing. It would seem that Soviet political journalist I. Achildiev was mistaken, unless he was deliberately deceiving readers of the journal *Youth*. Stalin had not chosen the path of political confrontation with the Church, he was merely continuing Lenin's work of destroying it:

> Indeed what is there to say today about the trainloads of Church gold and silver which were taken off to be melted down and then sold cheaply abroad, about the way religious shrines and church buildings were shamelessly robbed, stripped bare and destroyed with the sole purpose of turning the people into a crowd of impoverished Ivans (or Amans), who did not remember or know about God, and of enabling capitalist enemies, who for some reason turned out to be the close friends of the Land of the Soviets, to stuff their pockets, their own personal museums and the museums of their countries already corrupted by wealth, with our valuables, pictures and artworks. Of course that was the work not just of the hands, 'mind, honour and conscience' of Emelyan Yaroslavskii, but of the whole Party leadership. What was the result?

The historian O. Platonov writes: 'By the end of the thirties, the organizational work of the militant atheists had achieved "striking success".' Only a few hundred of the 50,000 Russian Orthodox Churches were still able to function; this meant that between 98 and 99 per cent of the churches had been closed 'at the demand of the working people'. While in 1928 around 400 churches had been closed and in 1929 the number was around 1,000, between 1930 and 1940 the figure had risen to tens of thousands. At least thirty per cent of the churches were blown up and the building materials dismantled down to the last brick. Millions of icons and books were burnt and around 400 thousand bells and much other church property destroyed. Never before had world civilization seen a cultural pogrom on this scale. It was for these 'successes' that Yaroslavskii was awarded an Order of Lenin.[16]

Icons were burned on bonfires or cut up for firewood. Hunters of gold which could be removed from the faces of saints appeared on the scene; they would dip the icons into vats of acid and then the gold would settle on the bottom. A new kind of gold-mining was perfected by chemists, who would peel off the precious metal from the sheathing of church domes. The domes of the Cathedral of Christ the Saviour in Moscow, which Kaganovich had had blown up, brought in 422 kilograms of gold for the state. Moscow churches all together were 'washed clean' of several tonnes of gold.

What was the scale of the loss of cultural valuables in Russia as a whole? According to the most modest of estimates, between 25 and 30 thousand churches and cathedrals, around 500 monasteries and at least 50 thousand valuable Church buildings in towns (used for housing the clergy and Church administration) were destroyed or reduced to ruins, along with approximately 2,000 country houses. In Moscow alone around 700 architectural monuments and around 3,000 historic buildings were destroyed. Hundreds of thousands of works of applied art were lost, tens of thousands of frescoes, wall-paintings and no fewer than 20 million icons. If the value of these lost cultural treasures from Russia is assessed in terms of money, the total would come to at least a trillion roubles; such a sum is on a par with the value of the cultural heritage of any large European state.[17]

The atheist besiegers had had their fill of desecration; the role of German fascists in the destruction of Russia's cultural heritage pales in comparison – a mere 3 per cent of the Party's total.

The turn of the Muslims also came. Kazakh educator Chokan Valikhanov has written that 'the Kirgiz prior to becoming Russian citizens were Muslims only in name'. Modern opponents of 'the religious influence of Islam' often cite these words in their writings. It is possible that Valikhanov is right, although this particular aristocrat with his marked sense of irony sometimes came out with rather sweeping statements. It is not our task to determine the degree of religious devotion among the Kazakhs back in the times of Ablai Khan, but it is clear that after the Kirgiz became Russian citizens, belief in the teachings of the Prophet Muhammad among the people of the steppes became a good deal stronger. Even the atheists admit that:

> After the failure of attempts by the Russian autocracy to propagate Christianity among the Kazakhs, it switched to open support for

Islam, which the tsarist authorities saw as a reliable ally, while they pursued their colonial policies. Special decrees were issued regarding the building of mosques and provision of mullahs for these and a council of muftis was set up in the region. After the Eastern Printing House had been moved from St Petersburg to Kazan, it became the leading centre for the propagation of Islam. Religious literature began to be published there in large editions and this was distributed in, among other places, Kazakhstan.

On the eve of the October Revolution there was a fairly widespread group of Muslim clerics in Kazakhstan, which, in the main, adhered to conservative views, seeing themselves called upon to 'defend Islam and Sharia law' and oppose the revolutionary transformation of society.[18]

Later it was announced with treacherous, Party-inspired fervour, that 'it was necessary to help the faithful to understand the class essence of religion, its power and its traditional links with the exploiter classes.'[19] Little was said about how the Bolsheviks had 'helped' believers – helped them with 'Lenin in their heads and a gun in their hands'.

The so-called 'policy of freedom of conscience' masked by hypocritical rhetoric eventually led to the destruction of both freedom and conscience. Lenin, so violently opposed to religion, initially donned a mask of religious tolerance. An address to the Muslim population drawn up by the Council of People's Commissars of the RSFSR, signed by Stalin and Lenin on 3 December 1917, stated:

Muslims of Russia ... all those whose mosques and prayer halls have been destroyed and whose customs have been trampled on by the tsarist authorities and the oppressors of Russia!

From now on your beliefs and customs and your national and cultural institutions are declared free and inviolate. You should understand that your rights, like those of all the peoples of Russia, are upheld by the full force of the Revolution and its administrative bodies.[20]

Of course, freedom of belief was by no means staunchly upheld. Of the 25,000 mosques which had existed in the Russian Empire, by 1986 only 376 still survived. Within the territory of modern Kazakhstan, where there were once mosques in every town and settlement, only rare examples still existed – all the rest had been destroyed.

Lenin was irritated by the fact that he could not immediately embark on wiping out the Muslim religion, as he had tried to do with Orthodox Christianity. This is clear from the report he delivered to the VIII Congress of the RCP (B) on 19 March 1919:

> What can we do in relation to such peoples as the Kirgiz, Uzbeks, Tadzhiks or Turkmens, who are still under the influence of their mullahs? Here in Russia we have a population which, after long experience of priests, helped us get rid of them. You will remember how difficult it was to push through the decree regarding civil marriage. Can we approach these peoples and say: 'We shall get rid of your exploiters?' We cannot do that because they are completely under the influence of their mullahs. We need to wait for these indigenous peoples to advance, for the proletariat to emerge as something separate from the bourgeois elements, and that advance is bound to happen.[21]

However they did not intend to wait long; the same VIII Congress resolved to stop any attempt at counter-revolutionary propaganda disguised as religious preaching. It was impossible for an honest priest or mullah not to fall foul of the vaguely worded resolution, as 'revolutionary practice' in the provinces and outlying regions was soon to confirm.

Methods used to curb such 'counter-revolutionary propaganda' varied, from direct violence to the undermining of religion 'through the spread of literacy, the opening of schools, community halls, reading rooms' and so on, as recommended by the Central Committee of the Party.[22] In a circular dated 10 June 1920 the People's Commissariat for Internal Affairs of the RSFSR instructed its readers that, in keeping with a Leninist decree, churches and prayer halls had been acknowledged as belonging not to the community of the faithful but to the people as a whole. This would mean that: 'there would be nothing illegal or offensive from the religious point of view if such buildings, given that public premises were in short supply, were also used for cultural, educational and socio-political functions.'[23]

Anti-religious 'work' proceeded at two different levels; secretly punitive detachments arrested and sentenced clerics (sometimes even shooting them), while publicly, noisy campaigns were waged by atheists, instituting all sorts of Komsomol 'Easters' and 'Christmases' and Komsomol 'Ramadans' and 'Eids'. At the same time mullahs were criticized and exposed.

Resolute attacks against Islam began at the time of the 'Great Breakthrough'.

On 24 December 1928 the *Zhetysu Infidel* reported:

MOSQUE FOR A COMMUNITY CENTRE

The inhabitants of the *kishlak* Bolshoye Ochinakho in the Dzharkent District have decided to use the only mosque, which is no longer visited by anyone, as a community centre and to spend 200 roubles to equip it from self-taxation funds.

Despite the fact that in most of our *kishlaks* no systematic cultural-educational work is carried out, these recent events show that our *kishlak* is forging ahead.

And in similar vein:

ANOTHER MOSQUE RECAPTURED

Peasants in the village of Kuram in the Chilik District recently resolved to set up a community centre in the mosque. The Kuram peasants have decided to hold educational gatherings rather than waste time praying.

All we can say is 'Well done!' and invite other *kishlaks, auls* and villages to follow their example.[24]

The author of the second article was justified in using the word 'recaptured' for the mosque which had been seized. There was a real war going on. Oral instructions and secret orders were issued by district party committees and the secret police (GPU) and the newspapers provided reports from the 'fronts', firing from their propaganda artillery.

On 25 January 1929 *Soviet Steppes* published a photograph of an enormous mosque standing isolated in a bare space. The headline read 'A Co-operative Instead of a Mosque'. This was followed by a short text: 'The mosque in the village of the Akmolinsk District has been made over to the co-operative shop in accordance with the wishes of the local population.' On 29 January another short article was sent in from Aktyubinsk entitled 'Church Used as a School', which read as follows:

'A meeting of local residents greeted with applause the news that two churches in Aktyubinsk are to be used as cultural premises in accordance with a decision of the working people.'

The following article from Uralsk bore the date 6 March:

SIXTEEN MOSQUES TO BE USED AS SCHOOLS

As a result of a cultural campaign led by the Komsomol, sixteen mosques have been handed over to the population of sixteen Kazakh *auls* to be used as schools. In three of these lessons are already being taught.

Handed over – just like that. The Pharisaic essence of the Party made it indulge in euphemisms even in the most obvious situations.

On 21 April 1929 the Kazakhstan Area Committee, in accordance with a resolution adopted by the All-Union Central Executive Committee, 'banned forthwith the teaching of Muslim doctrines throughout the territory of the republic and prescribed immediate termination of the right of local authorities to issue any kind of permits for religious schools to be opened'. It was demanded that district committees of the Party, particularly in Southern Kazakhstan, should embark 'on preliminary work for mobilizing public opinion, so as to achieve resolutions drawn up by local assemblies calling for the closure of religious schools'.[25]

With each passing day the newspapers would print such slogans as: 'Join the Grim Fight against Religious Deception!' or 'Wipe Out the Poison of Religion!' On 6 May 1929 *Soviet Steppes* published an atheistic piece by a certain 'G':

WE ARE BURYING RELIGION

(Komsomol Carnival)

When Komsomol members from the printing-house were carrying a coffin to the Railway Workers' Club in the twilight, a frail old woman stopped and devoutly crossed herself as she hurried along to have her Easter cakes blessed.

'May you rest in peace. Lord …'

Realizing a moment later what was going on, the old woman spat with gusto. Her dry lips were shaking with indignation: 'Devils! Monsters!'

Homemade torches were being carried along. In their light could be seen the excited faces of the carnival revellers.

In the front there was a coffin on which was written: 'We're burying religion!' Behind the coffin there were 'priests', 'deacons', a fat, imposing figure of a 'mullah', a 'Rabbi', paid mourners, '*kulaks*', 'officers', 'monks' and 'members of sects'.

The faithful of Kzyl-Orda could even get a glimpse of 'Jesus himself' dressed in white vestments, seated upon a lop-eared, friendly-looking donkey and surrounded by 'apostles' in similar white vestments. This very same 'Jesus' was puffing away at a cheap cigarette blowing out bluish smoke.

There were torches on Lenin Street, in the city park and on Engels and Karl Marx Streets. All this was accompanied by the energetic, throbbing music of a local band.

The Komsomol members were burying religion to the mournful accompaniment of singing from the 'priests' very much out of tune.

On 17 September 1929 the Union of Militant Atheists (Kazakhstan) sent a letter to its cells in the provinces demanding that 'the pace of anti-religious propaganda be stepped up'.[26] On 1 November *Soviet Steppes* announced that the demand from the working population of Alma-Ata for the cathedral and the mosque to be closed had been satisfied. The report implied that this had long been a cherished dream of the working people.

The newspaper accompanied this announcement with a short but very cogent explanation. Its author expressed his thoughts on the subject in a short article entitled 'Why the Cathedral and Mosque have been Closed':

What use was a mullah to any of the working people? Clearly none, he only brought them deception. An agronomist, livestock specialist or vet, on the other hand, explains how to increase yields, use livestock better etc. (something everyone has since come to understand).

The closing of the cathedral and mosque were the best present to the working people on the occasion of the twelfth anniversary of the October Revolution.

It cannot be denied that the Bolshevik regime offered what it regarded as the most valuable thing of all – godlessness.

On 24 November, in an article entitled 'Red Flag on the Minaret', the newspaper told its readership:

> In the old days the muezzin called the faithful to prayer from the minaret of the main mosque. His mournful long drawn-out call '*al-la-il-lya-Bismillya-a-a*' was a eulogy of Allah and his Prophet Muhammad.
>
> The Revolution has inflicted a deep wound on all religions. The cultural advance of the masses has now hammered a final aspen stake into the coffin of religion. Thousands of churches, synagogues, mosques and prayer halls are now being used for cultural purposes. This movement has now spread to the whole of the Soviet Union and our region. There are fewer and fewer religious fanatics to be found.
>
> The victorious march of millions advancing to take religion by storm, seeing it as a means of oppressing the masses and ensuring their ignorance when they are striving to assert their rights to culture, cannot be drowned out either by the ringing of bells or calls of the muezzin from their minarets.
>
> In accordance with the will of the people the mosque is to be used for cultural purposes. An association of national minorities meets there and all the wide-scale cultural work among people from the backward eastern indigenous peoples will be carried out there.
>
> This community centre was opened on 7 November.

On 10 December the Kazakhstan Area Committee of the Komsomol announced 'an anti-religious offensive throughout Kazakhstan' timed to coincide with the beginning of the 'anti-Christmas days'.[27] Close on the heels of this wave of coercive measures against religion, presented in the newspapers as a long-awaited joyful carnival, there now followed a drive for obligatory collectivization and persecution of the *kulaks*, at a time when 'in certain places' – as Goloshchekin informed Stalin in a secret letter in the spring of 1930 – the work involved stripping them of absolutely everything, even their last piece of bread.[28] ('Everywhere' would have been more an accurate term than merely 'in certain places'.)

As a result of this, another wave of popular resistance surged. Armed uprisings began in September 1929 in Karakalpakia and the Syr-Darya region. On 1 November Batpakkara in the Kustanai District rose up, on 7 February 1930 the Suzak District in the Syr-Darya region, on 25 February the Irgiz District in the Aktyubinsk region and so on. One of the slogans used by the insurgents was 'In the name of Islam!'

The authorities were retreating by this time. Naturally the 'just, clear and well-defined' general Party line was not up for discussion; it was of course 'quite indisputable'. The central authorities declared that local organizers were the guilty parties; they had gone too far and committed 'leftist excesses'. One such excess was the 'administrative confiscation of mosques and prayer halls'. Such moves had allegedly been used 'by elements hostile to Soviet power to fan unrest and to offend the religious sensibilities of believers'. This criticism of atheists had, of course, been for the sake of appearances. As soon as the unrest was suppressed and the people curbed into submission, the atheist onslaught resumed. The Guriev newspaper *Workers' Truth* reported on 17 April 1931:

THE MULLAH AND THE KORAN HAVE BEEN DEALT WITH

MOSQUE NOW USED AS A 'RED READING-ROOM'

Fishermen and farmers from the 'Urtakshil' Cooperative living in *Aul* No. 15 have completely turned their backs on all kinds of religious drugs. On the eve of the Kurban Bayram festival the collective farmers resolved at their general meeting to turn the premises used as a mosque into a Red Reading-Room. An initiative of this kind from the fishermen should be welcomed. May culture flourish and take root where the drug of religion once held sway. May drug dens turn into centres of culture! Let that be the slogan of the day.

Caspian.

A few days later on 5 May 1931 the same newspaper published an article entitled 'All-out work for Kurban-Eid':

We have left Kurban-Eid to the priests and mullahs. On the morning of 27 April a rally was held in the Kamenny suburb, attended by up to 250 Kazakh workers, who unanimously rejected the mosque as a centre promoting religious deception and ignorance. The festival of Kurban-Eid was turned into an inspiring celebration for the workers in the Kamenny suburb.

✤

XI. The 'Great Breakthrough'

The rural population was promised land in order to win it over to the side of the 'progressive' but extremely small working class. Having played its part when power was initially seized, the slogan 'Land for the Peasants' began almost immediately to sound suspect. The question arose: what does the peasant need land for? To become a 'little master', get rich, and nurture a remnant of the past that was essentially petty -bourgeois? In fact the opposite happened and the Party soon started to take land away from peasants.

First of all, land had been taken away from rich peasants in 1918. Not from middle peasants, who ten years later would be labelled *kulaks*, but from farmers who had already put down firm roots, farmers, who – if we disregard labels – had moderate-sized plots; in Western Europe they would simply have been referred to as farmers, pure and simple, who, as they went about their days growing corn and vegetables and breeding animals, were allegedly seeking to undermine what was most precious for their state: the dictatorship of the proletariat. After the elimination of those wicked exploiters of the working peasantry and the work (undertaken with the help of pistols) of stripping bare seed stores was completed, hunger walked the land in 1921–22. It was the first famine created by the new regime and it carried off seven million lives. Writer Vladimir Korolenko wrote to Party member Anatoly Lunacharsky in 1920, not long before the peak of those famine years:

> You probably accept that I love our people no less than any Bolshevik. Yet I love our people not blindly, as a sector of the population conveniently available for this or that experiment, but as it is in reality.
>
> You have won out over the capitalists, who now lie at your feet, maimed and crushed. One thing you have not noticed is that in

killing them you have also killed off production. Carried away by the blind urge to destroy the capitalist order, you brought the country to the brink of disaster. Back in the past I tried to describe the sad situation to which autocracy had reduced the country, in my book *In the Year of Hunger*: enormous parts of Russia's grain-growing regions had been reduced to starvation and hunger strikes were growing more frequent. Now things are much worse and the whole of Russia is subject to hunger, starting with Moscow and Petrograd, where there have been instances of people dying in the streets. Far greater areas are now in the grip of hunger than had been the case in the provinces in 1891–92. Most fateful of all, you have destroyed what was an essential part of relations between town and countryside, the natural link of exchange.

Each tiller of the land sees only that what he has produced is being taken away from him for remuneration that is definitely not the equivalent of his labour. He then concludes that he needs to hide grain in pits. You search him out, carry out requisitioning and march through the villages of Russia and the Ukraine with a red-hot sword, setting whole villages on fire and relishing the successes of your food policy![1]

Korolenko went on to quote a Ukrainian folk rhyme of that time:

In olden days, dim Nicholas reigned
And bread was hard to find.
Clever communists we have since gained –
No food now of any kind!

He went on: 'What might all this lead to? I would not like to play the prophet, but my heart is filled with a premonition that we are only on the threshold of calamities which will make everything we are experiencing now pale into insignificance.'[2]

Lunacharsky did not answer Korolenko's letters, although he had promised to do so; he also failed to publish those letters together with his replies, as the two men had agreed. (They were published in 1921 in Paris and read by Lenin not long before his death.) After letting down the trusting old writer, Lunacharsky shrugged in a gesture of exaggerated surprise: 'These "righteous men" are horrified at the thought that our hands are stained with blood.'

Korolenko was quite right; despite the millions of victims, the economic collapse and famine, the country was still only on the brink of disaster. Then came a new onslaught: the peasants started demanding their land back. The second collectivization drive of 1929–33, the significance of which Stalin compared to the October Revolution, became the main operation of this peasant country, which was now stripped of its peasants. It was much like the operation to wipe out the Cossacks, which had reduced four million Cossacks to just 2.5 million – an organized and merciless slaughter. The first to fall were the most intelligent, honest and hard-working of the peasants.

We might ask why the Bolsheviks sought to destroy the peasants who fed them and why later the peasantry was viewed by Lenin and his comrades-in-arms as the 'chief enemy of socialism' and, consequently, of World Revolution. There was no end to the labels Lenin pinned to the peasantry; 'petty-bourgeois', 'bloodsucker', 'profiteer' and 'speculator' were all frequently used to describe individual peasants. These owners of minimal property (a hut, a plough, a horse and a small plot of land) were for Lenin 'the force behind the country's petty-bourgeois element' and therefore his most determined opponent. For the sake of the victory of World Revolution the peasantry, which made up the bulk of the Russian population, had to be destroyed or enslaved.

Long before the Revolution Lenin had defined his tactics for handling the peasants: 'We shall first of all support them against landowners by every means possible before confiscation starts but, afterwards, [in reality this happened at the same time] we shall support the proletariat against peasants in general.'[3] In other words, let the peasants rob the landowners (the large commodity-based estates) and then reduce them to poverty by sending in the factory workers from the towns.

After the October Revolution the stage of enslavement was to begin: 'Soviet power must move on from labour conscription for the rich, to the task of applying similar principles to most of the workers and peasants or even do so simultaneously.'[4]

Lenin's ideas were developed by his pupils and comrades-in-arms.

Leon Trotsky (who referred to the peasantry as 'a shapeless fragment of the Middle Ages in modern society') stated at the IX Congress:

> Now that we have gone over to wide-scale mobilization of the peasant masses in the name of goals which need to be pursued on a mass scale, the militarization of the peasantry is an undeniable priority. We are mobilizing the power of the peasantry and shall mould from that workforce workers' units, which shall resemble military units. In the military world there is a system set in motion to ensure that soldiers carry out their duties. This mass-scale workforce must be highly mobile, ready to embark on assignments and obey orders just like soldiers. The mobilized peasant must feel like a soldier of labour, who is not free to deploy his energies as he might wish: if the order comes for him to be sent somewhere, he must comply and if he fails to obey then he will be like a deserter liable for punishment.

At the same Congress, the 'Party's favourite', Nikolai Bukharin, theorized as follows: 'Proletarian coercion in all its forms – starting with the firing squad and ending with labour conscription – is, however paradoxical this may sound, a method for moulding communist mankind from the human material of the capitalist era.'

The implication of this and similar statements was always the same: free working men were being turned into slaves of communism. Human beings as such did not exist for the Bolsheviks – they were simply part of 'human material'. Given that the 'material' was 'inert' – it did not wish to be subjugated – the Bolsheviks used the most effective of all means of suppression – the policy of hunger.

In 1891 Vladimir Ulyanov, an assistant counsellor-at-law, was living in Samara, the centre of the Volga region then struck by famine. Young Lenin, just over twenty at the time, 'was the only representative of the local intelligentsia, who not only did not participate in public efforts to help the hungry, but was categorically opposed to such help on principle.'

Ulyanov's friend Vasilii Vodovozov recalled:

> At the end of 1891, conversations about combating hunger led to the creation in Samara of a special committee to help the starving. Members of the committee were from all walks of life,

ranging from officials in high posts in the local administrative hierarchy to individuals who were blatantly dubious, even people under surveillance. At meetings and gatherings of young people Lenin conducted systematic and determined propaganda against the committee.

Vladimir Ulyanov, as Vodovozov remembered,

Had the courage openly to declare that the consequences of hunger – the emergence of the industrial proletariat, the grave-digger of the bourgeois order, constituted a progressive phenomenon, because it promotes the growth of industry and brings us nearer to our ultimate aim of socialism via capitalism.

Hunger, while it destroys peasant farms, is at the same time dispelling belief not only in the Tsar but also in God and over time it would without doubt push the peasant on to the revolutionary path and bring nearer the victory of revolution.

Ulyanov would become Chairman of the Council of People's Commissars in 1917. According to his friend's testimony, the Lenin of the future expressed his response to the committee to help the hungry – those who were trying to hold back the 'progressive phenomenon' – clearly and simply. He felt that there was only one way to talk to the peasants: 'with your hand at his throat and your knee on his chest'.[5]

Lenin may have been young at the time, but he was a quick developer. The people who stuck in his throat, of course, were Pyotr Stolypin and the Tsar who had succeeded in leading the people to an abundance of grain. How he must have rejoiced when Stolypin was assassinated. Kerensky and company also approved; despite the 'mountains' of grain in Russia, they managed to create shortages in Petrograd and engineer revolution.

Once Soviet power had been introduced it was possible to focus close attention on the progressive significance of hunger. Soon class-based rations were introduced in the towns. 'These came in four categories: (1) for workers engaged in heavy manual labour; (2) for all other industrial and white-collar workers; (3) for representatives of the free professions; (4) for social elements who did not work.' In June 1918 the last two categories comprised 13.9 per cent of the population in Petrograd. In September the following decision was made: 'The People's Commissariat for Social Welfare hereby confirms the need for all *kulaks* and bourgeois elements in towns and the countryside to be deprived of rations; the resulting surpluses will be used to increase the rations of the poor in towns and villages!'

From the very first days of the Revolution, the Soviet government assumed the right to decide who should be fed and who should receive nothing. It was officially announced that the right of all men to be acknowledged as equal when faced by hunger and death through starvation was not recognized.[6] While one group was accorded additional rations, the other was sentenced to a slow death through hunger. Yet other people's suffering makes nobody replete. Only the Bolshevik elite was living in clover; in Petrograd the loyal Leninist Grigorii Zinoviev was eating himself silly and became indecently fat, while elsewhere the poet Alexander Blok was slowly dying of hunger.

In the meantime Lenin had hit upon a socialist method for combating hunger: he announced a grain monopoly. While the capitalist method of combating hunger consisted in simply supplying the population with grain (just as the feudal, slave-owning and primitive-communal methods that had gone before), the socialist method involved fighting over it. Using the excuse of the hunger, which they had themselves orchestrated, the Bolsheviks fanned that fight in every way they could. They did not plough or sow; they robbed and caused deprivation. Lenin hardly had time to send out the necessary telegraph messages to his food commissars. On 10 August 1918 instructions were sent to the Saratov province for the authorities to collect together: 'in every grain–growing district twenty-five to thirty hostages from among the rich members of the population, who will answer with their lives for the collection and storage of all surpluses'.[7]

On 19 August instructions were sent to the Oryol province demanding that the uprising of *kulaks* and socialist revolutionaries be ruthlessly suppressed through 'confiscation of all grain from the *kulaks*'.[8] On 1 October the Party officials in all provinces were told

'to multiply their efforts tenfold to procure grain, to clear out all reserves both for us and for the workers of Germany'.[9]

As described by the historian Mikhail Geller, Lenin 'was behaving like an aggressor in an occupied country using food-procurement detachments as his troops'.[10] This description is too tentative: Lenin was not 'behaving like an aggressor'; Lenin was indeed a real aggressor in the country the Bolsheviks had occupied.

In response to this policy of artificially created hunger, peasant uprisings began all over Russia. Some armed with rifles and some with pitchforks, they attempted to save their families from starving. The Soviet authorities labelled them bandits and regularly sent troops to subdue them. Mikhail Tukhachevsky, after being driven out of Poland but having gained experience in fratricidal offensives in the Civil War, suppressed uprisings of the Tambov peasants with the help of soldiers armed with 35,000 bayonets and 10,000 sabres and equipped with hundreds of machine guns and sixty cannons. In some cases the insurgents were mowed down with cannons; they were tied up, made to stand in front of their own houses and fired at. In Siberia in the same year a peasant 'revolt' was suppressed using two infantry and two cavalry regiments, infantry cadets, a cavalry brigade, an infantry division, four armoured trains and auxiliary troops. These are just some of the examples of the Bolsheviks' all-out war against a country of peasants.

Lenin was well aware that hunger could rule the world more effectively than bullets. However good machine guns and artillery might be, lead could only bring down the enemy in their thousands. Hunger on the other hand could bring down millions. The fewer 'enemies of socialism' that remained, the closer final victory became. Everything that was useful for World Revolution was deemed morally acceptable.

Approximately a million Kazakhs perished from hunger in Turkestan, but the 'Kremlin dreamer' appeared not to notice. Unprecedented hunger threatened to befall Russia as well. As early as the spring of 1921 it was clear what the terrible drought would lead to, given the total lack of grain reserves in an impoverished country. However, Lenin appeared to give no thought to the matter. He was preoccupied with maintaining power by all possible means and aimed to achieve World Revolution using funds that had been illegally obtained in Russia. One thing however did not escape his dreamy gaze: the attempts of the Russian public – those sections of it which had not yet perished in Bolshevik pogroms – to try and assist the people condemned to hunger.

In June 1921 a number of economists, co-operators, specialists in agriculture and doctors offered the government their co-ordinated efforts to help the hungry. A delegation was selected to go to the Kremlin, but neither the Council of People's Commissars nor the People's Commissar for Agriculture agreed to receive the delegation. However, when a committee to help the hungry was created, another humanitarian, Semashko – the People's Commissar for Health – came out in support of its existence. As a joke, individuals from the Kremlin put together the first syllables of the surnames of the committee's leaders (Prokopovich, Kuskovaya and Kishkin) to form an offensive name – the *Prokukish* or *Kukish* (Cock-a-Snook) Committee. Lenin was happy to use the names of those leaders when approaching the Americans to discuss food aid. After establishing relations with capitalist countries in this way, Lenin then proceeded to have the committee broken up and arrested all its members who did not belong to a 'communist cell' – sixty-one out of the total seventy-three. On 26 August 1921 he instructed Stalin and the other members of the Politburo:

> To disband the 'Kukish gang', to have Prokopovich arrested today and to print tomorrow five lines of a short, dry 'government announcement' that it has been disbanded for its unwillingness to work. We shall instruct the newspapers to start deriding the 'Kukish' people from every possible angle. Those fine young gentlemen and White Guards had been planning to slip off abroad and were not prepared to go to the provinces. They must be ridiculed and harassed at least once a week in the course of the next two months.[11]

The joint 'propaganda team and agitator', consisting of Demyan Bednyi, Yakov Zub and various others, was happy to oblige.

The writer M. Osorgin recalled:

> A few days were enough for trains loaded with potatoes and vegetables and tonnes of rye to set off to the hungry provinces from the Centre and Siberia, when money started flowing into the coffers of the public committee, money which people did not want to entrust to an official body. The members of the committee visited Patriarch Tikhon who blessed their activity and issued an appeal for help for the hungry. The Soviet regime had to put an end to the committee, before it could start taking its work further. Five million people died in the Volga region during that famine, but the political situation had been saved.[12]

While in 1891 Vladimir Ulyanov, then an assistant counsellor-at-law, had merely encouraged the people's hunger, after 1917, when he was chairman of the Council of People's Commissars, he drew attention to the opportunities to be found in that 'progressive phenomenon' and led Russia towards the most terrible famine in the thousand years of her history.

Maxim Gorky, who acknowledged that he agreed with Lenin's theory (there was a small difference of opinion between them on the subject of the intelligentsia), wrote an article 'On the Russian Peasantry' in 1922, just after the terrible pestilence that befell Russia. Historian M. Geller describes it as the most pitiless condemnation of the Russian people ever penned by a Russian writer. In it the 'stormy petrel' looked into a far-off radiant future: 'the semi-savage, foolish and ponderous people from Russian villages – all those almost frightening people will give way to a new tribe of literate, sensible and cheerful people.'[13] Gorky, who had once immortalized figures of tramps but later took a millionairess as a wife, regarded Lenin's policy towards the peasantry as excessively flexible.

It seemed that Joseph Vissarionovich Stalin, who has justifiably been called 'the finest Leninist of all', was planning in 1929 to make a few amendments to his teacher's policy.

Sixty years ago teletype did not yet exist and provincial journalists, with their ears pressed to their radio receivers, picked up directives straight from 'Radio Moscow' without having to wait for the telegraphic version; they could then relay to the people, languishing without all important Party instructions, fresh resolutions from the Centre.

That explains why on 7 November 1929 *Soviet Steppes* published the following disclaimer at the end of Comrade Stalin's article, 'Year of the Great Breakthrough', in which every word and every comma were vitally important: 'Comrade Stalin's article was relayed to us by radio. The transmission was of very poor quality. It is possible that there are certain omissions or distortions. The articles will be printed for a second time after receipt of the telegraphic version.'

In this article Comrade Stalin prophesied 'a great future' and 'astonishing growth' for the collective and state farms:

In the history of mankind for the first time on earth, power – Soviet power – has appeared, which has demonstrated in practice its readiness and ability to provide the working masses of the peasantry with systematic and long-term help for production ... The new and decisive feature of the present collective-farm movement lies in the fact that peasants are joining the collective farms not in isolated groups, as was the case earlier, but joining it in whole villages, *volosts*, districts and even regions.

Stalin's artificial optimism, designed to inspire the people, went hand in hand with top secret directives for Party officials at local level, which called upon them to drive people by force into the collective farms – whole villages, *volosts*, districts and regions at a time. This article addressed to the people, which ignored the possibility of negative responses, instructed everyone to delight in the violence that would follow and to view the 'breakthrough' as 'great'; they were encouraged to follow meekly their leader's example and refer to it as an 'unprecedented success' and 'the most important achievement of Soviet power'.

Stalin's November article provided the signal for the unleashing of violence.

At a meeting of Party activists held two weeks later in Alma-Ata (which had by then become the capital), Izmukhan Kuramysov, the Second Secretary of the Area Committee, sought to push into the background those people who feared the worst in the forthcoming campaign. His report was published in the newspaper under the heading 'We Stand Firm on both Feet on the Party's Leninist Platform'; the subheading was even more revealing: 'Great-Power Chauvinism and Local Nationalism Dovetail with Right Deviationism'. In the article, Kuramysov contested the arguments put forward by an anonymous Party member calling himself Sarman, who had sent a letter from Tashkent. 'Sarman' objected to the best lands having been given over to the state farms in order – as he saw it – 'to safeguard the Russians who had found themselves in difficult circumstances'. He then asked: 'What difference is there between the current leaders of the Kazakhs who are opening up the way for resettlers and Abulkhair Khan [who defeated the Dzhungars] in the eighteenth century?'

Of course, nobody volunteered to move to Kazakhstan, indeed a special category of resettlers was driven into the Kazakh steppes at gunpoint by militia-men and Cheka staff. They were sent not to the best lands, but to dig for coal or metal ore in the mines, to build roads and factories.

Sarman's next question was aimed at the very crux of the new campaign: 'The laws of history give rise to classes, which pass through a specific stage of development. To what kind of fate are you leading the Kazakhs who are still beset by vestiges of the clan order?'

What answers did Kuramysov provide?

> Comrades, it is very awkward for me to quote Lenin himself in an argument against such a scoundrel and to have to demonstrate the truth to him relying on Lenin. I am reluctant to do so, it makes me seem disrespectful to Lenin. I prefer to leave that to members of the right wing as they go out of their way to present Lenin and mould him to appear like Bukharin. It would seem to me that the Kazakh working masses, the poor and middle peasants, have already made clear their opinion on such matters, going of their own accord into the collective farms and building the foundations of socialism.

The arguments provided here are even less substantial than those of Comrade Stalin.

The co-ordinator of the collectivization of agriculture in the country as a whole was Kaganovich; he caused the starvation of millions of people, while he himself lasted to a ripe old age before his death in 1991. He delivered a speech in Moscow on 21 November 1929 summing up the results of the November Plenary Session of the Central Committee of the All-Union Communist Party (Bolsheviks) (incidentally the letter 'B' in brackets, standing for Bolsheviks, was still in use, although it had long ago lost any real meaning; not only had the Mensheviks been disbanded, but they had been imprisoned or sent to Siberia. The distinction between the two parties was therefore unnecessary): 'At the Plenary Session of the Central Committee a number of comrades stated openly that they had not foreseen such a rapid pace of collectivization, as that currently experienced and which without doubt is going to be further accelerated.' The pace had not been foreseen, yet it was going to be accelerated! Perhaps Kaganovich had said too much.

On 3 December Goloshchekin gave a speech to the Party activists of his Area, reporting back to them after the Central Committee's

Plenary Session. He pointed out that the number of collective farms had grown considerably in the last few months and emphasized one extremely important aspect of recent developments – 51.8 per cent of the newly created collective farms were 'exclusively Kazakh'. He went on to tell them: 'I came across those who thought that the collective-farm movement in our republic was progressing more slowly than in other parts of the USSR, but I consider that opinion incorrect.'

In such statements Goloshchekin talked about peasants, who had lived a settled way of life for centuries, in the same breath as those who had been nomads for centuries. While for the first group, universal collectivization threatened untold dangers, for the Kazakhs, who were at the same time forced to make an immediate transition to a settled way of life, it represented a catastrophe of unprecedented proportions. These groups of peasants were not regarded as people by their leaders, simply as 'human material' – ignorant, hostile and inert material rooted in an earlier age, material which did not and could not understand what it needed for happiness.

Goloshchekin's speech went on: 'In the Kazakh economy collective-farm construction is the main "lever" with the help of which it will emerge and is already emerging from that centuries-old situation of abject poverty, in which it had found itself.' After expressing his concern in view of the fact that 'livestock and other means of production had only been collectivized to a very slight degree' Goloshchekin concluded his speech like a true Bolshevik with an optimistic assertion: 'We are at a new stage, we are at the stage of new dizzying victories.'[14] Within a mere three months Stalin was referring to 'dizziness from [the] success' of these victories, victories achieved through violence and genocide. If anyone was feeling dizzy it was the people who had been rounded up into collective farms, who were dizzy from malnutrition and exhaustion, from the first signs of starvation.

A week later Goloshchekin delivered a speech at the Fifth Plenary Session of the Area Committee and once again issued instructions for the rate at which nomads needed to make the transition to a settled way of life: 'The main way to resolve the agricultural issue here in Kazakhstan is through the development of enormous expanses of land, first and foremost by the native Kazakh population after collectivization. In this regard it is essential *to ensure a settled population within the shortest possible period*[my italics].'[15]

During the discussions Kuramysov delivered a report and specified that in five years' time nine-tenths of all Kazakhs would have a settled way of life. He informed his audience of the Area Committee's decision to achieve the complete collectivization of the Petropavlovsk and Kustanai regions and to ensure that the same goal was achieved in approximately fifteen districts in each region through the course of the year. (It seems there was nothing voluntary about these transitions after all.) With great enthusiasm he announced the slogan 'Let us advance from miniature collective farms to whole districts and regions of complete collectivization!' and went on to say that:

> Such a rapid advance of the collective movement has only been possible thanks to the mass-scale influx of the middle peasants into the collective farms. This breakthrough means that with regard to the collectivization of agriculture we can now advance at an incomparably faster rate. A significant feature of the current situation is that, when it comes to this rate of collectivization, the Kazakh districts are moving at almost the same speed as the Russian villages.
>
> The state farms now being organized in Kazakhstan are also playing an enormous part in accelerating collectivization. In this respect Kazakhstan can achieve spectacular results creating what at this point in time will constitute model regions of the USSR.

After this, feverish attempts began to speed up the rate of collectivization. Party officials made numerous promises and worked hard to achieve the highest possible rates of collectivization in record time. This disastrous race for ever higher percentage figures was made even worse by a decision taken by the Central Committee of the All-Union Communist Party (Bolsheviks) regarding rates of collectivization:

> The Central Committee of the All-Union Communist Party (B) stresses the need for a resolute struggle against any attempts to hold back the advance of the collective movement because of a shortage of tractors and complex machinery. At the same time the Central Committee sends a serious warning to Party organizations against 'directives' from above issued to the collective movement, which might create a risk of genuine socialist emulation in the

organization of collective farms being replaced by mere playing at collectivization.

Kuramysov clarified Goloshchekin's main ideas for those carrying out collectivization:

It is quite possible that collectivization of animal-breeding farms is somewhat more complex and difficult than the collectivization of grain-growing farms. This does not, however, mean in the slightest that we have reconciled ourselves to a slower pace of collectivization in respect of such farms than that specified for farms growing grain.

The Fifth Plenary Session of the Area Committee obediently voted in favour of those principles proposed by Goloshchekin. In a resolution about the development of collective farms it was duly noted:

In every way possible the collectivization of animal-breeding farms should be encouraged at the same rate as those used for farms growing grain. So as not only to cover districts where grain is grown but also those where cotton is grown and animals bred, we are specifying rates for collectivization aimed at involving the whole population within just one year.

On 17 December 1929 a decision was taken at the Plenary Session stipulating that 30 per cent of all farms should be collectivized by the spring of 1930.

Those present at the Plenary Session threw up their arms in delight, clapped and shouted their approval of the measure. At the same time as this feverish excitement, the great round-up of the rural population into a hungry and cold collective future began, where Death was waiting for them on the very threshold, no longer just holding a scythe but at the wheel of a wide-span harvester.

1929 was drawing to an end and as a parting gesture Toktabaev, the People's Commissar for Agriculture, brought the All-Kazakhstan Congress of Veterinary Party Workers the cheering news that at the end of the Five Year Plan there would be not 38 million head of livestock in Kazakhstan but 58 million. In reality things turned out rather differently. At the end of the Five Year Plan only 4 million head of livestock remained according to official estimates (which are bound to have been exaggerated). What the real livestock figures were nobody knows. Those who survived collectivization say that the real figure was far smaller.

The era of stagnation – the mid 1970s to 1982 – which was to prove dynamic when it came to corruption, robbery, awards and political anecdotes, left us one interesting example of oral popular creativity, which may well have been of local origin. On one of the public holidays in the Soviet calendar, Napoleon stands among the guests in Red Square reading the newspaper *Pravda*. The military parade passes through the square.

'Sire!' whispers one of his advisors. 'Look at those cannon! If we had had cannon like that, France would never have been defeated at Waterloo!'

No response, Napoleon does not lift his gaze from the newspaper.

'Sire!' whispers the advisor slightly louder. 'Look at those tanks! If we had had tanks like that, France would never have been defeated at Waterloo!'

Silence; the tricorn hat tilts at an even deeper angle.

'Sire!' exclaims the advisor. 'Look at those rockets!! If we had had rockets like that, France would never have been defeated at Waterloo!'

Napoleon raised his eyes, hands the newspaper to his advisor and says with a sigh: 'If only we had had a press like that France would never have even known about Waterloo.'

It cannot be said that at the time of the 'Great Breakthrough' there were no opportunities to make your opinions known; however they were only within the limits of official directives. The essential and immutable rule to ensure self-preservation was, as we know, deeply embedded in the timid hearts of censors and editors. Later in that same garrulous era of economic stagnation this was expressed – albeit in a way which showed little respect for what had gone before – in the idea of revolutionary vigilance: 'Better too much vigilance than not enough!'

There is no need to expound what "insufficient vigilance" might have led to in those times. It is therefore extremely difficult to find in the newspapers of the day the truth about how collectivization was implemented, as opposed to how it was reflected within the limits on openness to which the press was then subject. That is why we are obliged to piece together that truth, in retrospect. When one campaign was succeeded immediately by another in order to put right any 'errors' or 'excesses and distortions' as they were called at the time, a few details – tiny particles of the truth, pathetically small – did emerge among the torrents of fervent self-criticism, but only ever within the limits duly permitted.

Truth was not necessary for the 'human material', neither during the collectivization period nor in subsequent generations. It was best forgotten and eliminated. Criminals, regardless of the guise in which they appear, have never liked leaving any traces behind them.

So how was the first wave of collectivization introduced in Kazakhstan? In the spring of 1930, in response to the signal given by Stalin in his article about 'dizzying speeds', Party officials were called upon to reveal their transgressions. The key transgression was that they had beaten the backs of the people but proved unable to break them; bodies were reacting to pain and resisting the violence. Armed 'anti-Soviet actions' began to take place on all sides.

In June Goloshchekin delivered an enormously long address – lasting for two days – at the Seventh All-Kazakhstan Party Conference. He attempted to justify the exaggeratedly fast pace of collectivization; this was not in front of the people, the victims of collectivization, but in front of his seniors in Moscow. There was no threat to him personally; this was an unavoidable, tactical subterfuge by a regime engaged in deceiving its people. Yet, as usual, since the order had been given, someone had to be accused of inappropriate behaviour. Rather than implicate Party leaders, over-zealous Party workers at grass-roots level were made examples of: 'Mistakes in the sphere of collectivization can be classified as failures to understand the Party line, as distortions of the Party line, as departures from Leninism. Mistakes made in the field do not in any way result from Central Committee directives.'

Goloshchekin then turned to his audience and asked: 'Was the pace correct in 1930 when 30 per cent of the farms were collectivized? Was it correct to set the goal of complete collectivization within two years in two regions (the Petropavlovsk and Kustanai regions), the two economically strongest ones?'

'Correct!' shouted the disciplined Party members, guessing what would now be demanded from them.

'If we were acting correctly, then you working in the field did everything completely wrong,' noted Goloshchekin in a gentle, humorous tone of reproach. The delegates responded to him with laughter.

Here is the detailed excerpt from the shorthand report, which aroused the conference delegates' uncontrollable laughter:

> Comrades, the collectivization rates within the Area were: 24.5 per cent in January 1930, 25 per cent in February, 45.1 per cent in March and 51.3 per cent in April. You moved forward with gigantic strides! (Laughter.) Do those rates resemble those which we had planned together with you? Perhaps we were being opportunists then?
>
> If, however, Comrades, you examine the data region by region, you will see ever more gigantic strides. In the Alma-Ata region only 17 per cent of farms had been collectivized in January, but in April the total was 63.7 per cent (Laughter); in the Petropavlovsk region 38 per cent of farms were collectivized in January and 73.6 per cent in April; in the Semipalatinsk region 18 per cent of farms were collectivized in January and 40 per cent in April; the same figures for the Kustanai region are 36 and 65; in the Karkaralin region the figure was 48 per cent in April (you know that region is the key one for grain and now has thousands of tractors); in the Guriev region the figures for January and April were 1.5 per cent and 36.6 per cent; in the Urals region the April figure was 72 per cent and it was 60 per cent in the Pavlodar region. In Karakalpakia where the economy still depends on primitive wooden ploughs, where the social order is still based on semi-feudal relations and where the *bais* and the *ishans* [Muslim community leaders] still enjoy considerable influence, the January figure was 12.5 per cent and the April one 52 per cent (Laughter); in the Syr-Darya region the figure was 64.4 per cent in March and finally when we come to the most forward-looking region of all – the Kzyl-Orda region – the figure is now 61 per cent as opposed to 14 per cent back in January.
>
> I turn to you now, here at our conference, to request that you tell me with complete, Bolshevik honesty: is that mistake the result of the line pursued by the leadership of the Area Committee and their leadership as such?

How should we explain, Comrades, that from 5 February if not the end of January even, the Area Committee had been ringing the alarm bells and that the Central Committee had already issued firm instructions regarding the need to correct mistakes, while we were unable right up until April to achieve any slowing down of the pace? How can that be explained? Some people say it was a miscalculation, but it would seem to me to have been a failure to understand the seriousness of the mistakes.

If the Petropavlovsk and Kustanai regions carried out in the course of two months what was meant to have taken two years, what can be said about other regions such as the Uralsk, Aktyubinsk, Alma-Ata and Syr-Darya ones? Particularly striking is the fact that the more backward a region in its economic development, the faster the rate of collectivization: for example in the Karkaralin and Syr-Darya regions ... (Comrade Isaev called out: 'They're easier to administer!') Quite right, Comrade Isaev, administration in such regions is easier. In the Karkaralin region, 84 per cent of the farms in the animal-breeding Berkalin District have been collectivized, 76 per cent of those in the Abralin District, 70 per cent in the Shoroshevskii District, while in the Uralsk region up to 73 per cent of the farms in three districts engaged in animal husbandry and field cropping have been collectivized and so on and so forth. As soon as it is a matter of an animal-breeding district, there is an immediate leap in the figures!

One comrade, struck by that situation, wrote in: 'A serious step underway is the forced pace of collectivization in our animal-breeding districts, where the authorities insist that an obligatory condition for joining a collective farm is that all livestock be handed over for collective ownership.' This is also clear from the fact that the largest percentage of collectivized farms is found in the animal-breeding, nomadic and semi-nomadic districts (Zhanybek – 95 per cent, Slamikhin – 85 per cent, Chizhin – 82 per cent, Chelkar – 86 per cent, Taipak – 82 and the Dzhambeyty District – 80 per cent and so on).

That comrade wrote all this, forgetting just one 'minor detail', namely that in those districts political groupings were particularly numerous and indulged in the worst outrages. (Laughter.)

How much laughter was to be heard in the hall, how much merriment! Goloshchekin's audience behaved as if he had been describing oafs from the lowest echelons of Party officialdom, who in their devoted zeal had overdone things when it came to the collectivization percentages. Yet behind those figures lay the practical experience of collectivization well known to everyone in the hall: the confiscation of livestock and property in the icy cold of winter and the chill days of early spring, rounding peasants up into groups with threats and promises, stripping farms bare and disrupting the familiar patterns of working life, condemning people in the process to hunger and cold. Goloshchekin conveniently forgot the directives he himself had issued at that stage; his subordinates had been obliged to put them into practice rigorously, as if they were military orders.

Back in January of that year Goloshchekin had sent some agricultural workers from Kazakhstan off to a Party congress with the following exhortations:

> When it comes to setting up collective farms the rates we have achieved are on a par with those in the most advanced parts of the Soviet Union. This wide scale of collectivization and its rapid pace have enabled us to set a target for complete collectivization of agriculture for the whole of our population here in Kazakhstan if not by the end of the current Five Year Plan, then at least at the beginning of the second one. Is that a long period of time or a short one? It means we have another four years. 'Pessimists' say that we have given ourselves too long a period to achieve this – pessimists in inverted commas of course – because the process is moving so rapidly that it is overshooting our plans and our proposals.[16]

Goloshchekin of course had ulterior motives when talking about periods set aside for collectivization; in actual fact Kazakhstan had only been allotted three years in the Five Year Plan. He went on to consider the violent 'rapid process' he had organized in response to the sudden pressure from the middle peasants, who were allegedly impossible to hold back as they rushed to join the collective farms. He also hinted that the pressure was such that the collectivization plan would be completed ahead of schedule, encouraging the obedient organizers in the field to overdo things even further.

The newspapers of the day showed no restraint as they fanned the frenzy, calling for still more unreasonable rates for setting up collective farms; they of course did not write about methods of collectivization. The leading articles from *Pravda* were sent from the capital by telegraph and reproduced every day in *Soviet Steppes*. They served as direct orders from the Centre – instructions in print (in addition there were others which remained secret from the general public). Meanwhile the plans drawn up by Area Committees in response to those instructions often went further than the Moscow directives.

Here are some examples from the press of that period:

> January 12, 1930: Petropavlovsk. The rapid growth of the collective farms has made necessary crucial changes in our sowing plans. In the spring of 1929 7.4 per cent of farms had been collectivized and by December 35 per cent. It is proposed that 60 per cent of the farms in the region will be collectivized by the spring sowing. In the Bulaevskii and Krasnoarmeiskii districts collectivization will be complete by then.

In the same newspaper, *Soviet Steppes*, something appeared which had been almost completely absent from its pages in recent years: advertisements. They were from Odessa cooperatives which flooded the Kazakh market with their output in the early days of collectivization:

> IMPOTENCE AND HOW TO CURE IT
>
> Fourth extended edition of the well-known book by Dr N.V. Svetlov, with coloured illustrations. Price including postage: 3 roubles, 25 kopecks. Distributed by the book company, 'Literature' at 64, Tenth Anniversary of the Red Army St., Odessa.

On 13 January the leading article in *Pravda* read as follows:

> LIQUIDATION OF THE KULAKS AS A CLASS IS NOW ON THE AGENDA
>
> Total collectivization spells the death of the *kulaks* as a class. The collective farms must declare war unto the death against the

kulaks so as finally to remove them from the face of the earth. The Party is developing an effective Bolshevik offensive against the *kulaks* with the direct goal of their liquidation.

Death, war and liquidation ... Another article published that same day reporting from Aktyubinsk reported that:

> A gang of bandits which had been operating in the region has now been eliminated. The gang had been robbing the population, stealing livestock, preparing to derail an express train and was engaging in terrorist acts. An OGPU board has sentenced the bandits Shcherbakov, Aimbetov, Irzhanov, Kunakov and Arstanov to be shot. The sentence has been carried out.

Later, on 14 January:

> Rostov-on-Don. A congress held to discuss the implementation of universal collectivization is sending a telegram to its friends and comrades Voroshilov and Budyonny: 'In fields where decisive battles with the White Guards took place, and in fields where the blood of fighting men from the First Cavalry Army was shed, the red poppies of our collective farms are now blooming.

Then on 21 January:

> KAZAKHSTAN'S COUNCIL OF PEOPLE'S COMMISSARS APPEALS TO YOU
> Let us whip up the anger of the mass of poor peasants, farm labourers and middle peasants against the *kulaks*, the *bais* and their henchmen who are squandering livestock!

On 22 January:

> THE FIVE YEAR PLAN IN A SINGLE YEAR
> Aktyubinsk. Four enormous districts are now making the transition to complete collectivization: the Akbulak and Martuk districts (both Russian) and the Ileksk and Mugodzhar districts (both Kazakh).
> *Semipalatinsk.* The Samarsk District has now been totally collectivized. This campaign has been promoted using the

slogan: 'By April 1930 100 per cent of the population will be in collective farms.'

On 24 January an article by Comrade Stalin was printed: 'On the Question of the Policy for Liquidating the *Kulaks* as a Class.' This advertisement was published on the same day:

> Jolly stories, little scenes, parodies, verses, tales and ironic articles to read or declaim are all to be found in our interesting collection: 'Satire and Humour'. Price for the bound edition including postage: 2 roubles, 30 kopecks. Distributed by Literature, 64, Tenth Anniversary of the Red Army St, Odessa.

On 31 January nineteen chemical workers arrived in Alma-Ata to rally the collective-farm movement. A short meeting was held and a local peasant by the name of Berezovskii delivered a brief speech:

> We peasants from the Alma-Ata District – poor and middle peasants – fervently hope that progressive proletarians have come to us with open fraternal hearts and that they will help us embark on a new life, putting all that was dark and outdated behind us, much of which still has to be rooted out in our village.

This was reported in *Soviet Steppes* on 2 February. That same day it was reported from Kharkov that workers from the 'Hammer' factory had held a meeting about getting rid of the *kulaks* as a class:

> A worker who was not a Party member but had thirty years' experience of industrial labour behind him announced: 'I am happy that I live in times when the last remnants of the capitalist classes are being crushed [note that peasants are referred to as capitalists here]. We shall knock the last aspen stake into the grave of the *kulak* class! I am joining the Party ranks so as to fight under its banner for Lenin's cause!'

We might wonder at the size of the aspen stake needed for a grave of millions of Ukrainians who, incidentally, had fed this man during the thirty years he stood by a machine in his factory.

In the same issue the newspaper brought the people's attention to a resolution drawn up at a session of Kazakhstan's Central Executive Committee: 'The session considers that the collectivization of 47.4 per cent of all farms planned by the People's Commissar for Agriculture for 1929–30 is the *minimal target* [my italics] and proposes that the Council of People's Commissars should review this figure with a view to *possibly raising* it [my italics]'. After all that, Goloshchekin, who was in charge of the whole campaign and had goaded those engaged in implementing collectivization plans, now expressed surprise at the grass-roots Party workers' achievement of high collectivization figures. On 3 February he took the floor:

> Now on the basis of collectivization a transition is taking place – from a nomadic or semi-nomadic economy to a settled one. We are on the point of being able to put an end to small *aul*-type settlements consisting of no more than five or six *yurts*, indeed put an end to the very existence of *yurts*. At the same time opportunities are emerging for doing away with the archaic, backward way of life and for creating conditions for the cultural advance of the masses. There exists a misconception to the effect that the creation of collective farms in Kazakhstan is proceeding more slowly than elsewhere. This is incorrect.

After repeating that statement, Goloshchekin went on to reiterate his principles with regard to accelerating the rate of change. He drew attention to the 'intensified class struggle' and then went on to conclude: 'The backward sleepy land of Kazakhstan will be transformed into a progressive country where life is *seething with activity*, a country at the forefront of the socialist offensive [my italics].'

On 6 February the leading article in *Pravda* read as follows: 'The rural bourgeoisie, the *kulaks* "who have drunk blood from the peasant's heart" [Marx] have put up frenzied resistance to the movement of the main masses of the peasantry in the direction of socialism and continue to do so.' Stalin followed in the footsteps of his teacher Marx. All over the country the finest representatives of the peasantry were being annihilated and threatened with hunger; in the meantime, however, nothing seemed to deter the buoyant mood of the Odessa book merchants or reduce their desire to make money: '135 jolly tricks and riddles in a single

Collective farmers setting out for the fields, early 1930s.

Morozov, a shock worker from the Akchuk collective farm of the Red Partisan Rural Soviet, sowing corn. Eastern Kazakhstan, 1935.

A caravan bringing farming tools to the 'Balyams' collective farm, 1931.

Using camels to bring in the harvest.

Fetching drinking water, 1930.

Grain handed over to the State.

Horsepower.

Beggars in the early 1930s.

Peasants accused of cannibalism under arrest – victims of hunger themselves.

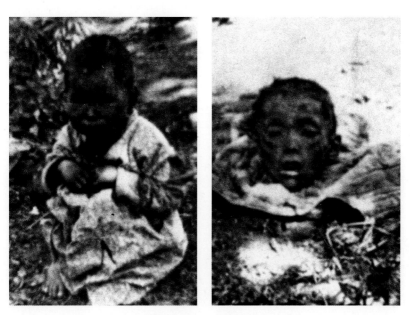

These children they managed to save.

Peasants decamping to town after the Great Disaster, 1930.

The text reads: 'A small girl still alive discovered in a pile of hay after being seized to be used as food, town of Tokmak.'

'The Great Disaster' by M. Kisamedinov.

After the Great Disaster. 'Yaroslavskii' collective farm,
Alma-Ata Region, 1932.

'Legend' by M. Kisamedinovers in the 'Labour' commune.

book: "Physics for Entertainment". Price including postage: 1 rouble, 70 kopecks. Distributed by Literature, Odessa, etc.'

What was really taking place while the newspapers overflowed with directives, threats and joyful promises from politicians? While the Odessa book company advertisements attempted to entertain the public and turn a profit? The press did not report on the realities of everyday life and people hardly mentioned the collective farms. What happened was this: a single meeting was enough. Collectivization was announced and a vote would take place straight away. The officials in charge were not concerned whether an individual wanted to become a collective farmer or not. A single question would suffice : 'Who's against collectivization?'

In many districts people were warned that those who did not join the collective farm would be allotted the worst land, out in the desert or up in the mountains. They would be driven away from irrigated land and have their property confiscated. Others who did not want to work alongside the rest would be driven out of their *auls* and villages. Such explanatory work, which left little room for doubt, was carried out in the Talas District in the Syr-Darya region and in many other places besides.

In that same Talas District enormous collective farms, incorporating several hundred smallholdings scattered over an area with a radius of 500 *versts*, were set up; however, they were virtually impossible to administer. The nomads, forced to live in the semi-desert areas, had all their livestock and property confiscated apart from essential items for domestic use. The new people in charge forbade them very strictly from selling or buying anything without first obtaining a special permit.

In the Iliisk District near Alma-Ata, peasants were pressured or threatened into the collective farms, with no chance to acquaint themselves with the charter for the new collective. If anyone asked whether it was possible not to join, he would be told in no uncertain terms that it was not. In one of the *auls* in Kzyl-Orda the official in charge of the collectivization drive was a foreman by the name of Uteshev. He warned people straightaway that those who refused to join a collective farm would be considered enemies of socialism and Soviet power. Those unwilling would be threatened with eviction and confiscation of property, deprived of electoral rights and arrested. He did indeed arrest people, even farm labourers.

A letter was sent to the Area Committee of the Party asserting that: 'the mass of peasants is brought into the collective farms using only administrative measures. Those in charge at district level consider the collective farm successful and exemplary.' The Regional Committee from Karakalpakia telegraphed its superiors at the next level (Karakalpakia at that time was part of Kazakhstan) to report that each district official had assured the local authorities that they would create a 'specific' number of collective farms and that this 'gave rise to unhealthy competition, blatant coercion, the use of scare tactics, additional tax burdens and the arrest of ninety peasants on a single occasion after they had declared their reluctance to become part of the collective farm'.

People were deceived at every turn; they were told that as soon as the collective farm was set up, it would be flooded with manufactured goods and machines and tractors would be supplied. In the Zatobolsk District of the Kustanai region middle peasants had their property confiscated and they were deprived of their electoral rights: 'If you do not join the collective farm you will be regarded as a *kulak* in the village because you are an opponent of collectivization.' Some officials even declared: 'Either you join the collective or you're in for the chop.' This particular threat had a proverbial rhythm about it – one born of the life 'seething with activity'. In that same district 'cattle and sheep were all declared shared property in most of the collective farms and in some of them poultry and even seeds for growing watermelons, cucumbers and so on'.

Cossacks from the Sixteenth Cavalry Regiment, who lived on the banks of the River Ural, were ordered to join collective farms no later than 23 March, otherwise they would lose their right to vote and they would be excluded from the regiment. In the Petropavlovsk region where there were plans for total collectivization, Fedotov – the official in charge – threatened those refusing to join collective farms with extra taxes, with incarceration in Houses of Corrective Labour and so on. The fishing communities living round the Aral Sea, scattered over a distance of 200–300 *versts*, were incorporated into a single collective farm. The Aral Sea was still full of water in those days, because the waters of the Syr-Darya and Amu-Darya rivers were not yet treated as state property. Near Alma-Ata orchard-keepers were also made to join collective farms.

Let us return to the Talas District; the collectivization there was described in a detailed note from a man named Asylbekov:

On 15 March livestock was collected together for the farm as a whole and 'small towns' consisting of *yurts* were set up. After instructions had been issued by the local authorities, activists were sent out to all parts of the district. They wore their hair long (a sign of ruthlessness) and issued instructions for an immediate switch to arable farming. Those *belsende* activists forced the peasants to move on twice a day (once in the morning and once in the afternoon), but they did not pay attention to the fact that the camels were terribly thin and that the lambing season had begun. As a result of this excessive movement for the animals, large numbers of camels and lambs perished. When the farmers had eventually moved to the planned destination, then a small town of three or four hundred households would be erected ... Some *yurts* were used to keep livestock in: the owners of those *yurts* would then be forced to go and live in *yurts* that were the homes of other families. The part of the farm where the peasants lived would be divided into several sectors, for example that of the sheep breeders who looked after the sheep (given the shortage of food the population was drinking sheep's milk by this time). They lived in more favourable conditions, while the remaining farmers were literally going hungry.

This note was made public by Goloshchekin at the Seventh Party Conference in June 1930 and it was one of the few – there were only two or three in all – indirect allusions to the famine which was beginning. Those few mentions only made it into the press because the disaster was closing in on Kazakhstan at that time. Later neither the press nor officials breathed a word about the hunger and disease that befell the whole people. Any hint of it was strictly forbidden right up to the death of Stalin and in some ways right until the present day.

Goloshchekin, had conveniently forgotten the way he had urged on those pushing through the collectivization programme a mere six months before. He read out the note sent in by Asylbekov and went on to expose those guilty of excesses: 'So you see, Comrades, what have been the consequences of "communomania" out in the countryside.' Yet what else could it possibly have led to, when on the very eve of those events – 13 February 1930 – the Area Committee had sent out a directive entitled 'On the Creation of Conditions for the Transition of Collective Farms from their Lowest Form to the Highest', the basis of which was the *real* and complete socialization of all the means of production.

Goloshchekin went on:

> Don't forget that when we collectivized the 'little cows' owned by individual families, which peasant women would use to feed their children, they would then have to go along with their earthenware jug to plead for a glass of milk. That incidentally disrupted the farms' fodder base. A peasant's wife would feed her 'little cow' or goat with what was left over from her family's table, but now those animals would have to be fed from what was used to feed the farm's working animals. Surely that approach meant we were undermining animal husbandry?

Goloshchekin did not refer here to peasant women and their children because they were in need, but because the food base of the collective farms was being undermined. This was also blamed for the enormous losses in animal herds.

Let us once again consider that life – 'seething with activity' – in Kazakhstan during the first wave of collectivization. In the villages of Alekseyevka, Yurevka and *Aul* No. 8 in the Syr-Darya region those middle peasants who did not hand in their seed corn had all their property confiscated. In the village of Kantemirovka they collected clothes and domestic crockery to be shared out within the collective and a local agronomist by the name of Frosov even 'collectivized' dogs and cats.

In the Semipalatinsk region officials working in the districts and certain Party district committees provided the following logic: 'If the middle peasant is the *kulak* of the future, then all the measures that can be applied to the *kulak* can also be used in relation to the middle peasant.' The methods used were familiar: first a military-style state of alert would be announced so that labour conscription might be introduced (Trotsky had dreamt of free peasant labour giving way to labour conscription) and all family seed stocks would be taken away (they might use the terms 'take away', 'confiscate', 'requisition' or 'expropriate', but it was simply robbery). By this time it was not a question of what had been taken from landowners and capitalists – it was peasants' own property, which they had acquired through labour.

The dictatorship of the proletariat had trained its activists in robbery extremely well. Middle peasants were made to sow larger areas than before, they were subjected to threats of confiscation and eviction, they were arrested and the courts would demand the confiscation of their property even down to their underwear. In the Enbekshi-Kazakh District *yurts* were made collective property, in the Irdzhar District it was hunting rifles and sewing-machines and in certain others ducks and geese.

In the Issyk District near Alma-Ata people were rounded up to attend a meeting where it was announced that there was to be a 'total collective farm'. The slogan which accompanied this collectivization was: 'Those not in the collective farm are enemies of Soviet power and the fate of the banished *kulaks* awaits them.' At the meeting, one peasant from the village of Turgen asked in astonishment: 'When everyone has become a commissar, who's going to do the work? There isn't much food produce as it is and if people are only going to work 8–10 hours there'll be even less.'

Officials operating in the Iliisk District intimidated the devout peasants with the threat that those who observed Ramadan would have to pay an extra tax of 20 pounds of grain. In some *auls*: 'the question was raised as to the need for a transition to shared family and domestic life.' It seems that the 'rumours spread by the *bais*' implying that 'wives and children would be shared property in the collective farms' were not groundless after all.

On 20 May 1930, at the height of the campaign to avoid excesses, *Soviet Steppes* printed an article by Ilyas Kabulov entitled 'Hero of the Balkhash Abscess'. The subheading of the article announced: 'Agents of the class enemy, using mandates from executive committees as cover, have started attacking poor and middle peasants in the *auls*.' According to instructions from the Area Committee, *bais* and *kulaks* were now considered as the main parties responsible for the excesses. Kabulov related how grain procurement was carried out in the nomad districts – the Iliisk, Balkhash and Chokpar districts. He cited the text of one of the local directives, which had followed the Area Committee's instructions relayed by telegraph:

For *aul* Soviets Nos. 1 and 2. The District Executive Committee insists that no later than 15 February of this year a compulsory Red Caravan of camels be organized and placed at the disposal of the peasants in collective farms. Chairman of the District Executive Committee.

Kabulov went on to explain:

> In order to carry out the instructions of the local authorities, Kazakh animal breeders were obliged to buy grain in neighbouring districts. Nobody sells grain just for money – it is too precious. They would exchange a sheep for 15 pounds of grain; a cow for 24 kilos of grain; a bull for 48 kilos of grain; a good horse for 64 kilos of grain and a female camel for 72 kilos.

The author, with good cause, referred to this as the destruction of animal breeding:

> Some of the farms – mainly those of middle and poor peasants – were ruined. Many families were reduced to utter poverty and started going hungry. The district and regional authorities explained that those who did not come into the collective farms would be deprived of the best lands and privileges and then declared enemies of the movement to set up collective farms. All those who did join were strictly forbidden to carry out any religious rituals in the home. That was how the thirty-eight collective farms were set up.

Musaev, one of the officials in the region, announced that in 1930 agriculture would be 100 per cent collectivized.

The frightened population started selling and slaughtering livestock. By the middle of the winter the whole population was made subject to a new tax: each holding had to deliver 10 kilograms of wool. The animal breeders were obliged to shear their sheep and goats in the winter. After that the animals started dying. Holdings in the Iliisk and Chokpar districts had to deliver by way of tax 16 kilos of skeleton-weed [in the 1930s wide-scale campaigns were initiated to find, procure and cultivate wild rubber-bearing plants in order to overcome the 'rubber boycott' against the USSR introduced by the West]. It was proposed that one hectare per person should be sown with skeleton-weed. The Kazakhs, who had never grown skeleton-weed before, were obliged to go out looking for the roots in the desert during the winter cold. Those who did not obtain these roots were fined.

Baiga [long-distance horse races], wedding parties and suchlike were not allowed and could also be subject to fines.

Mosques were closed. In these parts there was a custom known as *keregekyu*. In accordance with this tradition, parents would send their young daughter to entertain their 'dear' guests. This was one custom the custodians of the new life – influential Party workers and all those in authority – chose not to abolish. They instead made wide use of it.

A commission was sent from the Kazakhstan Central Executive Committee to sort out the problems introduced by over-zealous collectivization, after which the Balkhash District, for example, lost 40 per cent of its livestock. It was headed by Eltai Ernazarov, known as the Elder for all Kazakhstan. He had previously been referred to as the *aksakal* of all Kazakhstan, until the authorities began to regard that word as reactionary and therefore unacceptable. This commission disbanded a number of *aul* Soviets, declaring that they were in the spirit of the *bais*, and released various poor peasants, farm labourers and middle peasants, who had been arrested.

Yet a handful of dismissed officials did little to compensate for the many months of violence which had held sway over Kazakhstan. The 'criminal distortions', which came to light in the Balkhash District were not an exception to the rule; they were everywhere. Directives, as before, led to ruin and destruction. It was not by chance that three years later Uraz Isaev, when he delivered a speech to the Area Committee, expressed sincere astonishment: 'While several good and correct decisions were not implemented, it is clear that various incorrect decisions were implemented with incredible speed.' Such decisions included, among others, one taken by the Area Committee on 17 December 1929, stating that during the first year of collectivization all agricultural tools and working animals were to be collectivized in the grain-growing collective farms, as were all the animals providing milk and meat in the animal-breeding collective farms.

In his diary of 1907 Leo Tolstoy wrote: 'Personal selfishness is a small evil, family selfishness a large evil, the selfishness of a party is an evil larger still and selfishness of the state is the most terrible of all.' While this may be correct in general, Tolstoy had not seen as far ahead as selfishness beyond a single state; it was based on old historical experience. He could have hardly foreseen the state selfishness of the 'proletarians'.

Party apparatchiks not only believed in the power of the directive, but enforced it with generous use of legal punishments, armed force, rifles and machine guns. In February of 1930, when the people were agitated throughout the country, realizing that they faced death by hunger or banishment, Bukharin, who had recently called upon the peasants to aspire to more prosperity, wrote in *Pravda* that 'the language of lead was what was needed when talking to *kulaks*'. And talk they did.

On 14 March 1930 an article appeared in *Soviet Steppes* telling readers that in the Kaskelen collective farm at least half the livestock had been slaughtered:

> At that time when the government was organizing a month's campaign for the development of animal breeding, in reality a month of destruction was in progress. The collective farmers admitted: 'Yes, we killed a fair number of animals. Everyone killed at least one cow and of course a whole number of sheep.' The herds of sheep from that farm were more or less completely annihilated. They had originally numbered several thousand and the surviving animals could be counted in hundreds. The yields of the dairy cows were low, as they were being fed on nothing but straw.

The most surprising feature of the article is its subheading: 'Livestock herds must not just be replenished but increased!'

The nomad economy had been torn up by the roots and those who had composed the Party directives continued to nag, to expound, to goad and to formulate new tasks. L. Roshal, one of the secretaries of the Area Committee, wrote in *Soviet Steppes* on 20 March: 'The real situation regarding the collective farm movement has exceeded all proposals contained in the Plan: over 40 per cent of the farms in Kazakhstan have now been brought together in a *kolkhoz* [collective farm]. All in all this movement is proving most positive ...'

Roshal, newly arrived in Kazakhstan, had come to help Goloshchekin introduce collectivization and he quickly began to produce a rich array of directives and circulars. Soon after his arrival, the new functionary signed a resolution from the Area Committee in which criticism was levelled at 'the extremely unsatisfactory pace of grain collection and parasitical attitudes' in regions which had been impoverished by 100 per cent collectivization. Most revealing are the measures with which the officials intended to correct the situation. Their instructions were as follows:

- to organize competitions among farm workers in the voluntary collection of grain from hidden reserves;
- to disband as false collective farms those in which the majority of members are known to be maliciously refusing to hand over their seeds for the farm stocks;
- to reduce to a minimum trips outside the farm on horseback and so on.[17]

As Roshal understood it, only the most inveterate of *kulaks* would be unwilling to collect grain voluntarily at a time when economic ruin threatened, everything was in chaos, there was a wave of legal and punitive reprisals underway and the threat of hunger hung over them all. (He himself had of course never worked in the fields.) This was why Goloshchekin's new assistant made an appeal for '*kulak-bai* sabotage' to continue, insisting that 'work aimed at eliminating the *kulak* class in districts where total collectivization was in place should not slow down for a moment.'[18]

A team from *Pravda* arrived from Moscow to support the journalists of *Soviet Steppes*. They visited the Iliisk District, observed together where everything had been collectivized and expressed their amazement:

> Could there really be 100 per cent collectivization in a district where a semi-nomadic way of life has survived, where the transition to permanent settlements is only just starting and where the population has never seen agriculture based on the *kolkhoz*? Despite all that, we are assured that collectivization has been complete. How could such a miracle happen?

It turned out that it could – as usual, with the help of heavy-handed violence.

The journalists from *Pravda* described very cautiously, in evasive terms, the methods used for introducing collectivization, turning their attention to funnier moments as, for example, when a teacher who was not a Party member, by the name of Beisembaev, created a 'paper' cooperative in his own name; it was perfectly evident that the teacher merely wanted to imitate his leaders. Disregarding any kind of logic, but keeping in step with Party discipline (which was, of course, far more important than logic or common sense), the *Pravda* journalists drew the most incredible conclusion: 'Despite distortions of the Party line, the idea of collectivization has taken firm root among the Kazakh population.'[19]

Meanwhile 'life seething with activity' continued to flourish. In the capital's first 'East-Kino Theatre', a play in seven parts was shown every day; it was called *Love at Sixteen*, though children under sixteen were not admitted. Indignant at the behaviour of the Pope, Leningrad academicians Oldenburg, Fersman and Shcherbatskii submitted an application to the atheist cell in the Academy of Sciences asking to be accepted as members of the Union of Militant Atheists. A woman worker from the Turkestan-Siberian Railway wrote a threatening letter to the newspaper: 'In 1914 the Pope blessed the World War. Now he is preparing a crusade against the Soviet Union. I am subscribing one rouble for the creation of an air squadron "Our Answer to the Pope".'

On 20 May *Soviet Steppes* published an appeal by Togzhanov 'calling for the *bais* to be brought down from their last hideouts'. He explained the distortions in the collectivization campaign with reference, in particular, to 'ridiculous provocative rumours' which had been circulating in the steppe since the very beginning of collectivization. These rumours are cited below, clarifying what was said among Kazakh nomads, among whom the idea of collectivization had allegedly taken firm root. Togzhanov also listed certain pieces of news, which were doing the rounds:

- collective farmers' wives and children will become social property;
- collective farms will share out all the women among the men;
- in order to improve future breeding stock in the collective farms Kazakh women will be allotted special 'thoroughbred' men, 7 feet tall, from the central regions of Russia, in particular gypsies (in the Alma-Ata region);
- children will also be social property, because expensive medicines for export will be made out of their flesh and then sold for high prices in China;
- livestock will be confiscated and Kazakhs will have to eat grass [vegetables] and the like.

Since time immemorial the people of the steppes have trusted what they hear on the 'grapevine', rather than the written word. It is hard to imagine what kind of threats and punishments Party officials had to use as they sought to introduce collectivization, in order to round people up and send them into the collective farms, in the face of all those rumours.

✤ ✤ ✤

On 9 April 1930 *Soviet Steppes* printed a speech given by Goloshchekin when the first congress devoted to Kazakhstan's history was opened:

> If we consider Kazakhstan before the October Revolution, I should have called it pre-historic Kazakhstan. In fact Kazakhstan as such did not exist then. It was not a united country and was incredibly backward. Its economy was archaic, nomadic and there were no cultural institutions – even traces of the same – and relations between the different indigenous peoples were tense …
> I must stress that it is precisely the socialist reconstruction of agriculture, collectivization and the organization of state farms, which has been of exceptional importance for Kazakhstan, providing a way out of a backward, archaic economy for a backward, impoverished people.

Let us concentrate on the essence of this speech rather than its sociological rhetoric. What did the reconstruction of agriculture, which had not been properly planned, give to the people of Kazakhstan? If we keep simply to economics, then according to the official data collected by Uraz Isaev's commission, during the first few months of the initial wave of collectivization livestock numbers in the republic dropped by 30 per cent – or 10 million head.

It would have been naïve to expect any other outcome. Even in the collective farms, which were set up before the others and were carefully nurtured by the authorities, complete chaos reigned. One such farm was a commune named after Goloshchekin himself, which had been set up in the southern part of the republic; it was used as a model and praised more than once in the newspapers. In the year of the 'Great Breakthrough', extensive correspondence about this exemplary farm was made public:

LESSONS FROM THE GOLOSHCHEKIN COMMUNE

All the work and life in this commune is intrinsically haphazard. The commune does not know how much land it has. In the course of a year it has squandered twenty-four cattle, *yurts* and their contents, six horses, 185 sheep – the total value of which amounts to 13,076 roubles.

What has been wasted by the members of this collective would have been enough to set up four medium-sized collective farms. When it rented a bazaar, the commune suffered losses totalling 13,429 roubles. Buildings are falling apart. Windowpanes have been broken. Doors are dilapidated. No repairs have been done over a long period. Sewing machines are left out in the cold, in the open air. They no longer contain any shuttles; they are broken and the lubrication in them has frozen. They are covered in hoar frost and children play about with them.

In the course of a year the commune was given 30,000 roubles in advances and loans. Where are those 30,000 roubles? Where are the material results of that year, the tools for the forge, the mill? The commune has swallowed them all.

The question of the commune's stomach has become a key issue and current attitudes reflect that. Comrade Utemisov, one of the leaders of the commune, when asked how it would continue to survive, replied: 'If the worst comes to the worst, we can dismantle the roof and sell it for firewood.'

The commune used to employ hired staff (a baker, cook and two unskilled workers). They found themselves being treated like the commune's farm labourers. *Bai* ideology penetrated the commune and built itself a nest there. Comrade Baizakov, one of the ordinary communards, gave an extremely succinct assessment of the situation: 'We have food to eat. We do what we're told. We keep silent.'

❧

XII. Peasant Uprisings

Complete collectivization petered out in popular uprisings. Stalin retreated for a whole year.

Such was the way writer Boris Mozhaev summed up the situation at that time.[1]

Official historians keep silent without breaking ranks about the events which took place in Kazakhstan; if they do refer to them they restrict themselves to a few vague phrases. It is understandable; the Institute for Party History affiliated to the Central Committee of the Communist Party (the custodian of secret Party documents) concerned itself with the history of the Party intended for public display rather than with its real history. When referring to 'anti-Soviet outbursts' in his book of 1957 entitled *Victory of the Collectivized Order in Kazakhstan*, historian A. Tursunbaev only mentions in passing the '*bai* revolt' in Suzak and the 'armed action by the *bais* in the Adai region, in the Alakul District and elsewhere'.[2] *The History of the Kazakh SSR* makes no mention of such events at all. *Essays on the History of the Communist Party of Kazakhstan* has little to say on the subject:

> The enemies of Soviet power were quick to make use of leftist excesses in the collective-farm movement. They encouraged the peasants to engage in anti-Soviet activities, organized attempts on the lives of Party and Soviet officials and those of activists from the *auls* and rural areas. So, at the beginning of 1930, twenty-three top officials in the Suzak District of the Syr-Darya region were ruthlessly killed by *bai* and *kulak* elements. The class enemies goaded on the peasants to slaughter livestock on a mass scale before they joined the collective farms.[3]

Even writers of an article on academicians B. Tulepbaev and V. Osipov on
'the complex questions of collectivization' entitled 'From the Standpoint
of Truth', written during the recent era of *Glasnost,* sidestepped this
issue[4]. They acknowledge that it is impossible to blame everything on
the 'ill will of the *kulaks*' but, 'while not denying the definite role of
the *kulaks*', these researchers from the same Institute for Party History
affiliated to the Central Committee of Kazakhstan's Communist Party
(which now calls itself the 'Institute for Political Research') consider that:
'to a certain degree the situation was made worse through clumsy and
sometimes criminal actions by representatives of state bodies'. It is clear
from whose 'standpoint of truth' these evasive conclusions with their
bureaucratic flavour were drawn.

Little light is shed by the short passage cited below, which was originally
drawn up by loyal defenders of 'Leninist principles':

> In 1929 in Kazakhstan, according to data from OGPU [the
> Joint State Political Directorate – secret police], there were
> thirty-one 'gang formations' involving 350 people, in 1930
> there were already eighty-two such formations involving 1,925
> people and, in 1931, eighty such formations involving 3,192
> people. Apart from that a further 2,001 'hostile groups' had
> been identified in the villages and *auls* involving a total of 9,906
> people. In addition 10,936 'individual saboteurs' had been
> arrested. As a result of their activity in 1929–31, 460 Party and
> Soviet representatives were killed, 372 hostile anti-Soviet acts
> were perpetrated and there were 127 cases of grain burning and
> damage to livestock.

OGPU failed to include (or the historians chose not to mention) in its
report either its own punitive actions in response to the above, or their
degree and scale. Yet even if we merely rely on the newspaper reports
quoted in earlier chapters, it is clear how ruthlessly these 'bandits' and
'saboteurs' were treated; those guilty of physically harming Party activists
would be sentenced to the 'highest measure of social protection' and
shot, while all manner of acts could be classified as 'sabotage'.

The scope for openness in 1930 was of course not wide enough
for the press to report on popular uprisings at the beginning of
the collectivization drive. It was only six months after the Seventh

Conference that Goloshchekin admitted 'anti-Soviet activity on a mass scale had taken place in our republic'. It was the first and last time he would publically acknowledge this. Other leading officials would not have been allowed to speak in that way. He cited several details, which until recently had been the most complete set of facts recorded. For the next sixty years this particular subject was a closed one for historians; this did not stop them defending numerous theses on 'the victories of the collective order' in the meantime. What did Goloshchekin actually say at this conference?

Firstly we experienced anti-Soviet activity on the part of the Russian peasants in the Zyryanovsk District of the Semipalatinsk region (which they were already preparing for a year ago). It was headed by outright *kulak* elements who had involved an extremely small number of middle peasants.

Secondly, there were anti-Soviet outbursts in six districts inhabited mainly by Kazakhs in Central Kazakhstan, which those involved had been planning since the spring of last year. All this activity is of significance in that it provided an opportunity to analyse the struggle waged by the semi-feudal elements to retain the old order (their activities began with the election of a khan). Their main demands were in the name of religion and they were against collectivization and taxation for individuals. They were also demanding the return of the livestock confiscated in 1928 and that a stop be put to class struggle in the *auls*.

As you can see, Comrades, the main issue in this unrest was the struggle of the semi-feudal elements and the *ishans* to retain the semi-feudal, patriarchal way of life in the *auls*.

They succeeded in winning support within the *auls* from the poor and middle peasants only because of the serious distortions and errors in our previous work.

In those districts mistakes were made during grain collection and in particular during the collectivization drive, which meant that instead of weakening the position of the *bais* we made it stronger. It is revealing to note that where we had got through to the poor and middle peasants, they themselves handed over the leaders of the unrest to us, who had spoken out against people from the Party, saying that collectivization would mean the same kind of confiscations but this time involving middle and poor peasants as well and that all the outrages were the result of the general policy under Soviet power.

Finally another typical aspect of this situation was that unrest occurred in the *auls* of nomads and semi-nomads in Central Kazakhstan and that the nomads in Kazakhstan were the least Sovietized sector of the population.

The uprisings in the Suzak and Alakul districts and in the Adai region were not even mentioned.

At the same time, in his report he did state that the Adai region no longer existed as such. Why should that have been?

We set ourselves the task of involving Kazakhs as workers for Karabugaz, in fishing and for Embaneft, where oil was extracted [this 'involvement' was the realization of Lenin, Trotsky and Bukharin's dream to introduce labour conscription and the mobilization of a peasant workforce in labour units]. The second objective was to resettle that sector of the population, which was unable to prosper economically in the *auls*, in districts set aside for land cultivation. So far it has proved possible to transfer 374 holdings to collective farms, where the newcomers did settle, but it required a great deal of effort. Three times, Comrades, we organized everything and gave them money; they travelled a hundred *versts* from the Adai, where they gave an adequate amount of hares to the person in charge and then went back again. (Laughter.)

Three hundred and seventy-four farms would house only a small number of *auls*: where were the tens of thousands of other people living in that region? Goloshchekin said nothing about them. Ordinary people know all too well that the people from the Adai set off in large numbers into neighbouring Turkmenia after the uprising. Over there they continued their armed struggle in the ranks of the *basmachi*.

In reality popular uprisings occurred all over Kazakhstan – from Mangyshlak to the Altai and from the steppes of Aktyubinsk to the banks of the Syr-Darya River. The unrest began in September 1929 in Takhtakupyr in the Kara-Kalpak region and in Bostandyk in the

Syr-Darya Region. On 1 November Batpakkara in the Kustanai region flared up, as did Irgiz in the Aktyubinsk region on 7 February, Sarkand in the Alma-Ata region on 26 March and so on. The slogans used by those in revolt were 'Down with Soviet power: Long live Free Labour!', 'In the name of Islam' and 'Away with Soviet Laws against the *Bais*'. Where in the past Soviet historians blamed everything on the '*kulak* and *bai* elements', they have now begun to acknowledge that 'what caused the uprisings was enforced collectivization, and the confiscation of property from middle and even poor peasants.'[5] Goloshchekin, who in June 1930 had depicted the popular movement as a fight waged by semi-feudal landowners and *ishans*, knew full well the real reasons for the uprisings. In the spring of the same year he had informed Stalin in a secret letter, that the measures against 'alleged' *kulaks* had gone so far as to strip people of their most essential possessions, down to their last scrap of bread.[6]

Gradually details of those events are entering the public domain. The situation in Suzak is outlined below, in a notification sent out to rural areas in January 1930 by the Party Committee of the Syr-Darya region:

In conjunction with the decision to liquidate the *kulaks* as a class, we are embarking upon practical work to this end. In the region three people have been selected for this purpose: the Secretary of the Regional Committee of the All-Union Communist Party (Bolsheviks), the Chairman of the region's Executive Committee and the head of the regional branch of OGPU. Their task involves immediate evacuation of the *kulaks* from where they are currently living, first and foremost in districts where total collectivization has already been completed.

It is also essential now to embark on drawing up a register of *kulak* farms. This will be carried out by OGPU bodies in strict secrecy and will not be based merely on materials from the taxation and accounting bodies. It is permissible to collect additional details about various *kulak* farms at the same time. When the register of *kulak* farms is being drawn up, it is important not to lose sight of those *kulaks* who have come in from other districts and had their property confiscated before settling in your district. Those former *kulaks* need to be registered, just as all former *kulaks* still resident in your district, whose property has already been confiscated.

273

The task of drawing up this register of *kulak* and former *kulak* elements is to be undertaken immediately, but this register needs to be as complete as possible with precise details regarding why each farm has been classified as belonging to the *kulak* class. Ten days is the allotted time for the completion of this task and do not send the materials duly collected to us. This letter is to be returned to the Regional Committee of the All-Union Communist Party (Bolsheviks) no more than twenty-four hours after it has been read. Kulsartov.[7]

Underestimated by Marx but duly identified by Lenin and Stalin, the '*kulak* class' now became the object of urgent registration; then its representatives were arrested. At the same time 'a high percentage of poor peasants, farm labourers and middle peasants' landed up in prison. All this took place in a district which was the 'most backward, both as regards its economy and also its culture and way of life', where 'a single-share plough was seen as an innovation' and the 'main means of production for working the land were the wooden plough and the hoe'.

In some places as much as 99 per cent of the population was illiterate. The poor peasants and farm labourers there were the most downtrodden and lived in the worst conditions, as a result of which a large proportion of the population suffered from all manner of social diseases.

A report drawn up by the Area Committee's commission, after the uprising had been suppressed, informed it of the following:

Some *auls* are going hungry (Nos. 6, 8, 9, 12, 13, and 14), as a result of which they have started eating edible roots and it is possible that mass-scale slaughter of livestock has been taking place. On the other hand this situation is reflected in the political mood. In some places there have been instances of administrative penalties, particularly with regard to the collection of seed grain (for example in some *auls* the very last pound of flour has been confiscated from the poor peasants). In many places the wrong approach has been used when goats, sheep, cows and so on were made the property of the collective.

As witnesses later recounted, insurgent Suzak was first bombarded by cannon set up at the top of Kok-Tube Hill. Before that a small spy plane had flown low over the settlement at which the locals had thrown stones and sticks; a regiment of Chonovtsy (special punitive detachments) had riddled the crowd with bullets. The insurgents had all been tried in a single group. Each adult was sentenced to ten years, provided he had been born in Suzak. People were also tried in neighbouring villages; a court would be set up in a red *yurt* and those arrested would sit on the ground outside it. The story goes that in one settlement everyone was called out by their surname and sentenced to ten years, but one shepherd was forgotten. He sat and waited for a long time and then, without waiting for his name to be called out, went into the red *yurt* of his own accord: 'Why aren't you calling out my name?' he asked. 'You? Oh yes ... Well, ten years for you too.'

Materials are also available from the archives of the Chimkent Cheka. The following report from Aulie-Ata was sent in to Chimkent, to the regional OGPU office:

> There is no doubt that actions were prepared here, but over an extremely short period. What brought them forward were the arrests which you carried out. It is possible that the ringleaders assumed that the arrests were connected with illegal work having been discovered, so they reasoned that they were going to be arrested anyway and therefore spoke out.
>
> The local population viewed and still views all the steps we take as 'only a question of taxes' or what is going to be 'taken away' and so on.
>
> It seems to me that we shall not establish Soviet power in Sarysu without a good deal of bloodshed. The more *bais* that are wiped out in this district the better. When all is said and done, up until now the *bais* have been in charge of the situation and the power was in their hands. The rout of *bais* in 1928 did not go far enough and can even be seen as insignificant.

The penetrating eye of the Cheka singled out the very essence of Bolshevism: 'We shall not establish Soviet power in Sarysu without a good deal of bloodshed.' The following passage was contained in Operational Intelligence Summary No. 3 dated 13 February 1930:

On the morning of 7 February 1930 the Suzak *kishlak* was taken over by a gang of bandits numbering some 400 (this needs checking) on foot and on horseback. The gang had been organized in the neighbouring Sarysu District and consisted of *bais* from *auls* a long way from Suzak on the River Chu (120–150 *versts* from Suzak) – *bais* of the same clan as those in the Suzak District, who had been arrested in connection with actions carried out in the *aul*, after which some of them had been imprisoned in Suzak.

The aim of the gang had been to set the members of their clan free and take revenge on the representatives of Soviet power. The weapons of the band varied widely. As far as firearms were concerned they had 30–40 rifles of various kinds and some hunting weapons (the exact number has not been established). As regards cold steel they had sabres, daggers, axes and the like.

In reports submitted later, more detail was provided:

In view of the fact that the bandits were short of arms, the khan-led gang embarked on urgent manufacture of cold steel, which was used to arm the rest of those drawn into the venture. Three forges were adapted to make these weapons; apart from repairing firearms, on special instructions from the khan, they made blades with wooden handles out of 200 scythes seized from the local co-operative, pikes, iron spearheads and the like. In part this shortage of weapons was made up for by weapons taken from those of our men whom the bandits killed or took prisoner; they captured 2,160 cartridges, twenty-two .38 calibre rifles and five revolvers. These numbers are incomplete, because when they took Suzak the bandits also seized weapons belonging to the militia and other people.

Home-made blades and pikes against machine guns and cannon. A middle peasant named Shonakov had been chosen as the khan; in their reports the OGPU men referred to him as a former member of the rural administration.

The khan turned to the clan leaders and semi-feudal landowners with a special appeal, calling upon them to help his cause: with propaganda, men, livestock, weapons for their equipment and with the organization of his armed force. All these appeals by the 'khan' had religious and class-based implications. The Muslim clerics, who were not generally on the side of bandits, played an important part in encouraging the population to support this action.

What had led the mullahs to take action was that it had been decreed by local officials that one of the largest and finest mosques in the *kishlak* of Suzak was to be used as a community centre; the crescent had already been taken down from its roof and riddled with bullets. In order to set up this centre carpets and felt mats etc. had been confiscated from prominent community leaders. The mosque building had not, however, been used as a community centre yet, but a grain-delivery depot had been set up in the main prayer hall and it was there that the peasants had to bring in their grain for the seed stock. When Suzak was taken, the bandits immediately started repairing and clearing out the mosque.

Soon after the uprising had been suppressed, the Eastern Department of the OGPU representation in the Kazakh SSR summarized the 'Results of the Suzak Actions' in Operational Intelligence Report No. 8:

The bandit movement in the Syr-Darya region, in particular in the Suzak, Turkestan and Chayan dDistricts, has for the most part been eliminated thanks to the measures duly taken. In the Suzak District, in the fighting between 6–12 February, 125 bandits were killed. On 16 February, when Suzak was taken, 200 were killed in the fighting and approximately 200 active bandits (those captured with weapons in their possession) were shot on the spot.

A total of 389 people were arrested and taken prisoner thanks to the swift action taken: bandits, their accomplices, stirrers and scouts. While the band was being crushed, 'Khan' Shonakov and other ringleaders were killed.

During the Suzak operations the following 'trophies' were captured: 290 horses, 20 camels, around 150 firearms of various kinds and approximately 100 cold-steel weapons. In the Karnak *kishlak* of the Turkestan District sixty-three people were seized, including those who had killed the secretary of the Party cell and those who had seized the seed stock. In the Karasae *kishlak* thirteen of those who had played an active part in the banditry were seized.

Our losses during these operations in the Suzak District were as follows: twenty-four Party and Soviet workers were killed including some members of their families; one in Karnak *kishlak* and one in the Achi-Sai District, fifteen during the fighting; five men were seriously wounded and eight slightly.

The 500 odd 'bandits' who were killed during the fighting and shot on the spot, had had in their possession 150 firearms and 100 cold-steel weapons; in other words half of those killed had not even had a homemade blade or pike. This is why the lovers of Party truth within the historians' establishment 'affiliated to the Central Committee of the Communist Party' maintained their silence. It was a massacre let loose by the authorities against people reluctant to avail themselves of happiness in the collective.

In the section of OGPU intelligence summary No. 8 headed 'Our Measures' it was stated: 'Operative groups and detachments in the countryside plagued by banditry are continuing to eliminate bandits and their accomplices in hiding and any other counter-revolutionary elements and also to seize their weapons.'

The old Kazakh writer Galym Khakimovich Akhmedov assured me that was how things were, more or less. The leader of the Area Youth Committee was returning home in the spring of 1930 after the uprising had been crushed. He and his companions were travelling in several cars; there were about fifteen men altogether. During the journey an old Kazakh appeared on the road coming towards them. One of the passengers called him over and when he was close the man shot him at close range, without saying anything first.

'Why did you do that?' the others asked him.

'But he's a bandit!' came the answer.

'What do you mean bandit? He didn't say a word.'

'No, he was a bandit, I tell you!'

Then came the final act of the Cheka operations – the traditional Bolshevik plunder:

Preparations are now being made for confiscating the property of the bandits killed and also those who were shot, all those who took part in the counter-revolutionary action and the powerful *bais* who have been leading the counter-revolutionary work in the districts plagued by banditry.

In June 1930 Goloshchekin acknowledged that in a number of places the collectivization movement had been compromised and that a good deal of time would be required in order to rally the movement again. At the Seventh Communist Party Conference Goloshchekin opened his report with a rhetorical question: 'We need to ask: "Whose fault was it?" There is no doubt whatsoever that the Party line and the Central Committee directive were *absolutely correct* [my italics] and could not have caused those mistakes. As for the practical leadership of the Area Committee, I am sure that the committee pursued the Party line correctly and followed the directives of the Party's Central Committee. Yet at the same time we cannot clear the Area Committee of all responsibility for what happened out in the rural areas.'

Party logic was unchanged: the Centre was always right, while out in the provinces people might sometimes make mistakes. Goloshchekin began his report with the following words: 'You would, I am sure, agree that there were no preconditions to be built on for collectivization in the *auls* of the nomads and that it had not been prepared for in advance by our people?' In other words, according to Party logic, no preconditions were essential before embarking on collectivization and the people had not been prepared for it in the slightest. All that was necessary was to follow the Party line.

Nowadays official historians, when describing the extremes resorted to in the first wave of collectivization, still use data provided by Goloshchekin in 1930 in his report to the Seventh Party Conference. According to his testimony, the middle peasants had been unfairly treated on a wide scale; how wide a scale can be judged from the 'figures relating to corrections'. Property was returned to 9,533 middle peasants' holdings, 4,073 middle peasants were released from prison (known in those days as Houses of Corrective Labour), 1,618 people had their electoral rights restored and

1,160 middle peasants were allowed to return from banishment. To this day total figures have not been made public; how many people were arrested, how many banished and how many shot.

As A. Tursunbaev writes in his book *The Kazakh Aul in Three Revolutions*, '*kulak-bai*' farms were divided into three categories: people assigned to the first category were banished beyond the borders of Kazakhstan, those in the second category beyond their home region and those in the third category outside their district. In 1967, when this book was published, there appeared to be a reluctance to remember that the *kulaks* or *bais* assigned to the first category, or classified as belonging to a counter-revolutionary group, were to be imprisoned or shot immediately, in keeping with instructions issued on 4 February 1930 by the Central Executive Committee and the Council of People's Commissars of the USSR; their families were banished to remote regions. A nationwide plan existed for assigning 60,000 former *kulak* farms to the first category and for approximately 150,000 farms in the second category to be banished to remote places outside their home region. Finally, the Party instructions classified 800,000 smaller farms as belonging to the third category, while those to whom they had previously belonged were forced to resettle outside the confines of their *kolkhoz*. At this point no mention was made of the one million sub-*kulak* prosperous families in the plan for eliminating the *kulak* class; those new categories of class enemies appeared later, thanks to the inventiveness of those practised in the acquisition of the property of others.

At the time plans were announced by the Party with the firm intention that they would be over-fulfilled. Roy Medvedev wrote:

> As early as 1930 far more *kulaks* than 'planned' had already been arrested, shot or banished to the northern parts of the country. In 1931 repression was on a still greater scale. In all probability the total number of 'dispossessed' *kulaks* was around one million families and at least half of them were banished to northern or eastern parts of the country.[8]

Medvedev was well known for his cautious approach to figures and so the data he provides are likely to be underestimates. He goes on to write:

In many regions and districts, blows from the authorities were also unleashed against 'less prosperous' middle peasants, poor peasants and even farm labourers, who for various reasons refused to join the collective farms; for the sake of convenience they were listed as 'sub-*kulaks*'.

The cruel directive calling for the banishment of dispossessed *kulaks* and their families was bound up with the fact that in 1930–31 the state did not possess the material or financial resources to support the collective farms which were being set up. For this reason it was decided to hand virtually all the property of the *kulak* farms to the collective farms. As early as May 1930, *kulak* property accounted for 34 per cent of the collectives' indivisible reserves in half the collective farms; enforced collectivization resulted in excessively cruel methods of dispossession.

Hundreds of thousands of peasants including women, old men and children were sent east in cold, unheated rail trucks heading for remote regions in the Urals, Kazakhstan and Siberia. Thousands of these people perished en route from hunger, cold or disease. An old Party member, E.M. Landau, recalls encountering one such train in Siberia in 1930; it was in the depths of winter and a large group of *kulaks* and their families was being taken in wagons 300 kilometres away into remote parts of the region. Children were crying from hunger. One of the peasants could not bear to hear his baby crying any longer as it sucked at its mother's dry breast; he took the child from his wife's arms and shattered its head against a tree.

Large numbers of former *kulaks* and members of their families perished during the first years they spent in the sparsely populated parts of the Urals, Siberia, Kazakhstan and the north-east of the European part of the USSR, where thousands of special '*kulak*' settlements were set up. The position of these deported families only changed in 1942, when the young men from those special settlements began to be called up into the army. By the end of the war, supervision of these settlements by special commandants came to an end and the inhabitants of the special settlements were granted relative freedom of movement.

It is not known precisely for what Goloshchekin was responsible in Kazakhstan, but even if 'figures for corrective measures' are taken as a basis, it can be assumed that tens of thousands of people were the victims of repressive measures while he was in post. At the Seventh

Party Conference he self-criticized somewhat, perhaps insincerely, saying that it would have been better not to make public the resolution of 17 December 1929 which called for complete collectivization, because in rural areas it had been interpreted as a directive:

> In that resolution despite all the work of the Area Committee and counter to the thrust of that work, we forgot about the diversity of our economy, about the difference between villages and *auls* and about the special features of Kazakhstan.
>
> There is another mistake, which could well have influenced the leadership in our region. In January a directive was received by telegraph: 'In this connection we are faced with the task for immediate implementation throughout Kazakhstan to evict *kulaks* from current dwellings especially where there is total collectivization.'
>
> This directive was cancelled three or four days later, but there was no holding back the momentum, people were carried away with the idea of eliminating the *kulaks* in general, not just in connection with collectivization. Initially the Area Committee was thinking in terms of almost fifty to sixty districts. That too was cancelled after three or four days (later the go-ahead was given for just sixteen districts) but those errors may well have influenced the regional leadership for a period.

Goloshchekin tried to shift all the blame on to 'the mass-scale effort to present middle peasants in the same light as the *kulaks*'. One detail here is of particular interest: Goloshchekin believed that the most serious distortion of the Party line in the practical steps taken to eliminate the *kulaks* as a class was the fact that 'taking away the *kulaks*' essential clothes and household possessions and all their food stocks arouses sympathy for the *kulak* families and their children among the middle peasants and even the poor peasants, who start giving them food.' This actually annoyed him! Here sympathy was being shown not to people in the abstract, but to real human beings.

An enormous resettlement of people was going on in the country by this time. Long before the banishment of 'ethnic minorities' from the Northern Caucasus carried out by Stalin in the 1940s, the cream of the Russian and Ukrainian peasantry – of Russians and Ukrainians in general – were being sent into the tundra and swamps of the north and Siberia, into the deserts and steppes of Kazakhstan. The country's best animal breeders were driven one way or another beyond their homeland or across thousands of *versts* within their own enormous republic.

Transferring, banishing, resettling – behind all this there was a hidden agenda with implications that were not just economic and political. If we think back to the numerous moves of whole ethnic groups and indigenous peoples within Kazakhstan during the years of Soviet power, we begin to understand that peoples were being deliberately and consistently mixed together; this reduced them to a collective of grey, faceless dust, ensuring that not one of those groups retained their natural spiritual and historical identity – this was in their own homeland, where an individual's links with his *aul* and his own house were so strong. This was how 'Soviet Man' was being created from living 'human material', robbed of all that was natural and special and rooted in the individual by the engineers of the radiant future.

At the time when the 'Great Breakthrough' was beginning, three-quarters of the Kazakh population were leading a nomadic life, tending their livestock in open pastures. Of the 119 administrative districts in the republic, nine had a nomadic population and eighty-five a semi-nomadic one. The planned transition to a settled way of life was starting. It was proceeding slowly and with enormous problems, made worse in December 1929 at the Fifth Plenary Session of the Area Committee when Goloshchekin insisted that a ridiculous decision be taken; the settling of the nomads was to be speeded up, based on total collectivization of their herds and farms. In practice this meant that all livestock belonging to the Kazakhs was to be rounded up in special 'settlement centres' and, whether they liked it or not, the nomads would have to live there.

Then came the question – where would these 'settlement centres' be? There was nothing but bare earth in the 'centres', yet orders had been given for proper villages to be built. Goloshchekin based his plans on the idea that collective farms with nomads were impossible and therefore, so as not to lag behind more 'advanced' parts of the country in terms of introducing collectivization, all livestock needed to be made collective property straightaway. Given that these plans were being implemented in the winter months and there was no feed for animals in the new 'settlement centres' (there was no chance to prepare for this type of resettlement), animals soon began to die.

Later the commission set up by the Council of People's Commissars under Isaev came to the conclusion that livestock numbers in 1930 had fallen by 30 per cent – a total of 10 million animals. We must ask however, was this really the case? At the Sixth Plenary Session of the Area Committee, which took place in 1933, Nurmukhamedov from the state planning body – Gosplan – accused the leadership of double bookkeeping: 'When registering numbers of livestock in 1930, the People's Commissariat for Finance gave a figure of 20 million, while Comrade Isaev maintained it was 30 million. That amendment by Comrade Isaev played a major part in bringing about the catastrophic situation which we are faced with today.' In other words the plan for meat procurement in the hungriest years was based not on the real figure (20 million animals) but on a fictitious one (30 million animals), meaning that during the first wave of collectivization herds were halved without the authorities' knowledge. Even wars had not resulted in such devastation.

These unprecedented losses did not distress Goloshchekin. At the Seventh Conference in June 1930 he stated:

> How can this be explained? Some of the nationalists say that it is the result of the Area Committee's policy, others – I don't really know what to call them ... (Voice from the floor: 'Kulak leaders!') ... say that the reason for this was our grain-procurement plan. It is probably bound up with the fact that declining herds are a phenomenon to be found right across the Union.

It goes without saying that Goloshchekin laid most of the blame on the *kulaks* and *bais* who, as they could not destroy the land, reduced sown areas and started to slaughter livestock extensively. Goloshchekin also blamed 10–15 per cent of the drop in livestock numbers on 'gross distortions and errors'.

In previous times, before total collectivization and forced rapid resettlement, the *kulaks*, *bais* and middle peasants did not attack their animals with knives. It was lucky that they were able to do it at this stage; at least they had some meat to eat. By then the animals were not being looked after properly and were suffering from inadequate food and the cold. The livestock was bound to become emaciated and die.

After much popular unrest Stalin conceded to permit peasants to leave the collective farms if they wished; within a single month the level of collectivization in Kazakhstan fell from 51 per cent to 32 per cent and in certain districts and in the Karkaralinsk region collective farms vanished altogether.

Thousands of the country's finest animal breeders and tillers of the land were reduced to ruin or banished to places where they later died. Many were killed and within a matter of months Kazakhstan's herds of 40 million animals were halved in size. Goloshchekin assured delegates to the Seventh Party Conference that 'enormous successes' were being achieved.

> Can these successes lull us into sleepy contentment? Not in the slightest. We need to aim higher; from the point of view of socialist construction they are insufficient with regard to the task of raising the prosperity of the masses. We have not yet brought the masses to that state of socialist awareness of which Lenin spoke, socialist awareness at the level where 'the commune begins'.

Goloshchekin saw only one danger on the horizon: out in the rural areas people might start worrying about excesses – 'once bitten, twice shy' – and they might decide that it was time to leave the *bais* and *kulaks* in peace. He reminded his audience: 'We must arm ourselves against that danger. There are still battles to be won.'

When arguing about Goloshchekin's report to the Seventh Conference Uraz Isaev, Chairman of Kazakhstan's Council of People's Commissars, made a sober speech, saying that in the animal-breeding districts it was difficult to find a Kazakh who appreciated the 'advantages' of the collective farms and that therefore it was wrong to hurry with collectivization: 'It is necessary that the middle peasant, as he attempts to increase his herd to seventy, eighty or a hundred sheep, should not fear that he will be labelled a *bai* or eliminated.' On the other hand Comrade Opershtein (whose office it has not been possible to establish) declared: 'The positions we have achieved in the building of collective farms need to be consolidated.'

At the closing of the conference Goloshchekin once again expressed his 'concern' to protect the living standards of the working people: 'At this point we feel a great sense of Bolshevik anxiety – the anxiety of people responsible for the welfare of the masses ... We feel anxiety, but not panic.'[9]

This was followed by a short Bolshevik interlude entitled: 'Five Years of Bolshevik Work'. Speeches were made 'In Celebration of Comrade Goloshchekin'; at the end of the elections to Party posts Comrade Isaev took the floor:

I have been called to speak on behalf of a group of comrades. The enormous merits of Comrade Goloshchekin as the leader responsible for the Bolshevization of our Party organization (Applause), for our international training and the nurturing of truly Marxist cadres are indisputable and clear beyond any doubt.

To mark the achievements of Comrade Goloshchekin the Seventh Party Conference proposed:

To publish in Russian and Kazakh all the works of Comrade Goloshchekin to mark the tenth anniversary of the founding of Kazakhstan (Applause) [and] to name the Kazakh Communist University now being organized in the town of Alma-Ata after Comrade Goloshchekin. (Applause.)

Both proposals were unanimously approved.

All this was followed by Goloshchekin's reply:

Comrades, we have now completed our work. It would be as well to concentrate our attention on the decisions which have been adopted. You have, however, deflected me from the true path and compel me to respond to the honours you have shown me. Are they truly deserved?

We are all soldiers of the Party and each one of us does what the Party demands of him.

There are two dangers: the first is – and you know this already – that they can have a dizzying effect. What might happen if your salutations were to make this head spin and I were to start thinking: 'What a great leader I am ...'

(Voice from the floor: 'Your head is not spinning. You deserve this honour!')

The second danger is that I shall remain here another five years and you will have to tolerate that! (Enthusiastic applause.) See to it then, Comrades, that you do not depose me! Each one of us does what he can.

XIII. The Second Wave of Coercive Collectivization

On the eve of the second wave of collectivization adult males, devoting careful thought to children, composed slogans for Young Pioneer rallies in the hope that among the young citizens more might grow up to be like Pavlik Morozov, the Soviet boy-hero who denounced his father to the secret police. A newspaper then, in all seriousness, printed their appeals: 'Recruit to your unit all the children of poor peasants!' – '*Bais* and *kulaks* are the Pioneers' enemies!' – 'Since a very young age we're for the Soviets!' – 'Don't let children be hooligans so mean! Take all that is rotten from the cinema screen!' – 'We shall not bare our backs to canes, just listen to good advice for our pains!' – 'Do away with the slavery of old, bring out from the kitchens our mothers now bold!' – 'Tell us brother, what you have done to help poor peasants' children, now that we've won!' – 'Let us raise the harvest yields, bring fathers into *kolkhoz* fields!' – 'When we are all among Pioneers, to ethnic hate we close our ears!' – 'We shall help bring in the grain – failing crops were in the past! Our collectives wealth shall gain, Pioneers, march forward fast!'

Only three years passed before Goloshchekin was recalled to Moscow; his place was then taken by Mirzoyan. Party members assembled in Alma-Ata for the Sixth Plenary Session and delivered speeches, but not about economic collapse in the villages and *auls* or about the unprecedented scale of livestock deaths. Not a word was said about the hunger which had been raging for two years – after all, none of the speakers were going hungry. They did not speak about the deaths of almost all children under the age of four or the fact that nearly half the Kazakh population had died. Those subjects were taboo. In any case there was no time for all of that; they were too busy repenting, justifying themselves and criticizing

288

each other. They promised never to commit such errors again. The Plenary Session came to be referred to as historic.

Eventually, one of the delegates could bear it no longer and said: 'We are all talking about putting a stop to the slaughter of livestock, while we are forgetting the main element among productive forces – human beings. The population in some districts is in a very bad way ... In Kazakhstan we have as many as 80,000 homeless children.' It is clear that he was aware of the inadmissible nature of his outburst, of its seditious implications. In response to this, Nurmukhamedov went on to speak of human beings as the main elements among productive forces; human beings as such meant nothing, but if presented as part of productive forces they might still mean something. The speaker's heart must have been in a very sorry state if he could not stop himself from mentioning human beings, from mentioning children. That was Nurmukhamedov from Gosplan.

His words were not met with applause. The subject was not taken any further. The hall remained silent as if nobody had noticed his words. The silence continued until Comrade Pinkhasik went up to the speaker's dais. He was Secretary of the Urals Regional Committee of the Party (and soon to be elected Secretary of the Area Committee). Born in Odessa, Pinkhasik had joined the Party at twenty-one and at the same time – in 1918 – had been made Public Prosecutor of the Trans-Baikal tribunal. In 1919–21 he served with the Cheka in the town of Omsk and was the deputy chief of the Cheka of the Far Eastern Republic. It would appear that he had been knee-deep in blood since the early stages of his career (in Siberia Cheka officials were responsible for particularly harsh brutality). It was he who sternly rebuked Nurmukhamedov:

> Comrade Nurmukhamedov tells us that animal breeding is not the most important issue. The most important thing in his eyes is that here in Kazakhstan there are 80,000 homeless children, that people look ill, that their faces are of a kind that make it terrible to look at them. I consider that it is wrong for this Plenary Session to adopt such a medical viewpoint. We are politicians and cannot embark on a bourgeois-philanthropic path of that kind.

None of the delegates dared to say a word about the hundreds of thousands of people who had died from hunger. It was something beyond the comprehension of Comrade Pinkhasik, whose children were not roaming the streets looking for scraps; they were living off the special rations accorded to Party members.

In response Nurmukhamedov apologized:

> I provided too much detail, when I described the calamitous situation of the decamped nomads. This led my comrades to conclude that I was taking a philanthropic view of the situation. In this respect I accept the negative comment that Comrade Pinkhasik made. I should like to point out, however, that I did it in order to draw the Plenary Session's attention to our fight against the consequences of the decampment.

In 1922 there were 7 million homeless children roaming the country; most were the children of peasants. Nobody knows how many orphans were created by the collectivization of the 1930s. Its destructive impact was worse than that of the Civil War or War Communism. Later moves were made to take care of the homeless children; a campaign was even initiated. On 16 August 1933 *Kazakhstanskaya Pravda* printed an article on the subject entitled 'The Fight against Homelessness – a Concern for the Whole of Soviet Society in Kazakhstan'. The author of the article, V. Shmatkov, considered that this phenomenon was 'to a considerable extent' the result of the errors and excesses of the former leadership and the local Party and Soviet bodies:

> The period of the unstoppable increase in the number of homeless street children is over; homelessness is now of a more stable kind. The key task today is to support children's homes and to put an end once and for all to the presence of homeless children on our streets.

This would imply that, as in Lenin's day, mothers and fathers were eliminated through bullets or starvation while the children, who would become homeless as a result, were not even considered. They were only thought of afterwards; it was, of course, no longer possible to put an end to the children's orphaned state.

The journalist continued in the following vein: 'It is necessary to collect up the remaining vagrant children from the streets, from railway stations, from bazaars and other places.' He also commented that the children's homes were overcrowded and in a revolting state. This was true even in the country's capital. In a children's reception centre in Malaya Stanitsa or in the 'children's village' in Kaskelen, they were using: Slop-buckets as there were no lavatories, no washbasins; the children were not being washed and they slept in rows on the floor. In many orphanages there were no stoves or roofs, the ceilings were in need of repair. There was no fuel and a whole number of other problems although winter was just round the corner.

It is possible that among the residents of those children's homes and among the homeless children from the streets there were some who had recently heard slogans at Young Pioneer rallies such as:

> For Kazakhstan as beacon bright,
> Home of progress and of joy,
> Let us all now join the fight
> For settled farms – each girl and boy!

Not six months had passed since the first devastating wave of collectivization when a new directive was sent from Moscow; Goloshchekin addressed all the district committees in the grain-growing areas with an article entitled 'Let us mark the Eleventh Year of this Area with an Appeal to the Collective Farms!' In it he no longer accused private farmers of refusing to hand in 'grain surpluses', but collective farms. He demanded:

> The *kulaks* and *bais* should be driven out of the collective farms immediately and with complete ruthlessness. People seem to have forgotten about collectivization, although work to develop collective farms cannot be deferred for a single day. Inadequate work to implement collectivization or a total absence of any activity is the result of people 'allegedly' fearing excesses and this fear is used by many to justify merely letting events take their course. Such cowardice is not characteristic of a Bolshevik, it is the most pernicious opportunism.[2]

291

On 7 November 1930 *Soviet Steppes* appealed to its readers: 'Let us wipe out the *kulaks* as a class! ... Let us unfold the banner of total collectivization!' On 17 November the same paper exclaimed: 'The era of the collective farm has dawned. Let us organize a new appeal for this new wave of collectivization!' By now sown areas were reduced, harvest yields were down, there was not enough grain available and yet those engaged in procurement were still demanding the handover of 'surpluses'.

On 8 November the headline in *Soviet Steppes* read:

A CLASS ENEMY WITH A PARTY CARD

Aulie-Ata. (From our correspondent). Sagindyk Rustembekov, member of the All-Union Communist Party (Bolsheviks), stated at a meeting of a council for the poor peasants' group in *Aul* No. 55: 'We have no grain, we cannot fulfil the grain-procurement plan.' The women of the *aul* with Rustembekov's encouragement beat up three local officials. Communists like that need to be driven out of the Party. Soltybai.

On 12 November Goloshchekin addressed the Komsomol Conference for the Area:

Rooting out clan-based, semi-feudal and patriarchal relations, the elimination of the *bais* as a class in the context of total collectivization – this is what will bring us out on to the final wide path leading to a bright future and banish memories of the accursed past in the Kazakh *auls*.

The fact that Goloshchekin's recent words about collectivization had been discredited 'in a number of places' and that considerable time was said to be needed to promote the movement had already been forgotten; it had been no more than a tactical withdrawal prior to a new, massive and still more cruel round-up of peasants.

People were now only talking about complete collectivization and the hands of the zealous Party workers had already been untied. 'Pace will decide everything!' proclaimed Goloshchekin and all the apparatchiks, promulgating the directives and engaged in propaganda, repeated that maxim day in day out, turning it from theory into practice. The inspired delegates, bearing in mind the role of Goloshchekin in the 'Bolshevization of the Party bodies in Kazakhstan', elected him as an 'honorary member of the Komsomol', presented him with a Komsomol badge and sang the *Internationale* twice over.[3]

On 13 November the Area Committee adopted a decision to accomplish an immediate breakthrough in the collective farm movement. *Soviet Steppes* in the meantime exposed 'saboteurs disrupting the agriculture of Kazakhstan': agronomists Donich and Sirius and the deceased Professor Shvetsov. They were accused of having put into practice the principles of the discredited economist Kondratiev 'with the malicious zeal of saboteurs'.

Particular venom was directed at the favourable statements the researchers had made about the economy of the nomads:

> Today's Kazakh farming is so well adapted to the natural environment, that it is particularly in tune with the latter and should be recognized as the most productive type of farming in the given conditions. The nomadic way of life, typical for most of Kazakhstan, had endured not because the Kazakhs and their kind of farming had not yet attained the level of the settled population. The Kazakhs were animal breeders and nomads because it would have been impossible for them to be anything else given the conditions in which they lived: their natural surroundings demand it.

These profound thoughts about the compatibility of any truly indigenous method of farming with the farmers' natural environment were unacceptable for the politicians of the day, who were at the time intending to destroy all that was natural – the way of life which had taken root in the land, in the Kazakhs' economy and in their spiritual and domestic life.

E. Fyodorov, author of the article, accused the agronomists of defending the interests of the *bais*:

> According to Shvetsov, 'professor of sabotage', destruction of the nomadic life in Kazakhstan would not only usher in the demise of steppe-land animal breeding, but also turn the dry steppes into uninhabited deserts.

Donich's ideas about the gradual nature of the development of the Kazakh middle peasants' farms to a productive level and about natural growth from the small-scale to the large-scale co-operative forms of labour were dismissed by Fyodorov as 'blatantly great-power-chauvinist principles in the struggle against the nationalities policy of the All-Union Communist Party (Bolsheviks)'.[4]

Yet by this time it should have been clear that the enforced creation of giant collective farms and communes caused the economy nothing but harm. The new wave of collectivization, moving relentlessly towards Kazakhstan, was ready to sweep everything before it. Turar Ryskulov attempted to soften or deflect the blow. In an article entitled 'Attention drawn to Animal Breeding in the Nomadic and Semi-nomadic Districts', he wrote that Kazakhstan was reminiscent of Argentina as far as its size, population density and the nature of its economy were concerned.[5] He went on to point out that Kazakhstan's production could and should be developed in a similar direction:

> To this end help should be given to the nomads' districts where three-quarters of the country's livestock are to be found. We need to take as a model not just Denmark or Germany (with regard to the care of livestock indoors) but also Argentina, Australia and the steppe regions of North America, where natural pasture resources are used for livestock wherever possible.

Ryskulov's proposals were, of course, too late; animal breeding had already been half ruined. In addition nobody would have listened to such advice at a time when the whole country, regardless of any special local conditions and features, was being shaped to fit a single economic model.

The newspaper's editors provided commentary to accompany the article, explaining the author's errors. Their most weighty argument was the formula underlying socialist economics, which had been expressed simply and intelligibly by Stalin: when resolving the animal-breeding issue 'we need to follow the same path, along which we advanced when resolving the grain problem'. Ryskulov was accused of seeking 'to break the resistance to the *bais*' forgetting, as he did so, Stalin's 'rebuilding of socioeconomic relations'.

In the republic's main grain-growing regions, which had been laid to waste by the first wave of collectivization, hunger had already set in. People living in the towns were also having to tighten their belts, while the communists were still 'fighting the *kulaks*'. On the same day all the newspapers printed Maxim Gorky's article 'If the Enemy does not Surrender – he should be Destroyed': 'Inside our country extremely cunning enemies are orchestrating famine, the *kulaks* are terrorizing peasant activists through murder, arson and other kinds of villainy.' According to this logic, hunger had appeared in the land not as a result of economic collapse caused by the proponents of collectives but because of the activities of traders and suppliers, who were imperialist agents.

In another of his articles addressed 'To Humanists', which was also printed in many newspapers and journals, Gorky wrote: 'The organizers of the current famine, which has aroused the anger of the working people, against whom they engineered a base conspiracy, have been executed in accordance with the unanimous demands of the workers. I regard these executions as perfectly legal.'

On 19 December 1930 *Soviet Steppes* printed the following headlines on its front page in large letters: 'Long Live the Unsheathed Sword of the Dictatorship of the Proletariat!' – 'OGPU has been Fighting its Battles for Thirteen Years' – 'The Working People of Kazakhstan Demand that OGPU should be Awarded the Order of Lenin!' It was a perfectly appropriate award.

As before in the year of the 'Great Breakthrough', the Area Committee went out of its way to increase the pace of collectivization. Percentages for each month were calculated in advance and every effort was made to rise still higher, like mercury in a thermometer. The economy was not just red hot, it was gripped by a fever. All the indices reported to them did not seem to satisfy Goloshchekin and his henchmen: 'Pace will Decide Everything!' – 'The Pace of Collectivization is not Fast Enough!' – 'Push the Wave of Collectivization still Higher!' These were typical headlines for 1931.

By June 55 per cent more of Kazakhstan's agriculture had been collectivized than during the first wave of sweeping collectivization. People were no longer wary of excesses. Just as it had in the previous year the newspaper happily reported: 'As regards the rate of collectivization the Republic of Kazakhstan is neck and neck with the advanced fraternal republics.' In those same 'advanced' republics hunger had already set in.

Soon afterwards it was the newly arrived Secretary of the Area Committee, Mikhail Kakhiani, who began supervising collectivization. It seems he was no less of a specialist in rural affairs than Roshal before him. On 17 June *Soviet Steppes* printed his speech delivered at the Second Area Congress for Collective Farms. Kakhiani, who had spent the whole of his working life as a Party functionary, explained that animal breeding was an important part of efforts to supply the working class with food products and to raise its wages in real terms. Yet saboteurs were making it difficult to raise those wages in practice. What was to be done?

> Major successes can be achieved here in Kazakhstan with regard to animal husbandry. At the XVI Party Congress Yakovlev [USSR People's Commissar for Agriculture, 1929–34] cited examples illustrating how it is possible to make a big difference to dairy farming. If a cow is given one portion of fodder, a specific yield will be obtained, but if that fodder is increased by 30 per cent twice the milk yield will be obtained. If the amount of fodder provided is 60–65 per cent more then three times the milk yield will be the result.
>
> Here you have a simple example of how we need to work in the animal-breeding sector. We can and must make sure that more meat, more milk, more wool and more leather are produced. The same needs to be said with regard to the development of sheep and pig breeding (if of course the pigs are not treated swinishly).
>
> We can achieve major success with regard to the development of these sectors. In the next one or two years we need to resolve this problem.

Such was the advice handed out to the exhausted collective farmers by Yakovlev and Kakhiani.

While those deliberations were in progress, the poet Demyan Bednyi cheered up the cooperatives with his little verses, which – like the articles by Maxim Gorky – appeared in all the newspapers. One of his 'masterpieces' of that period was 'In Support of Bolshevik Haymaking' (a subject also written about later by Gorky):

If we don't shirk,
Through our hard work
Food stocks will start to grow,
While we all reap and mow.
If state farm cows,
Collective sows,
And even our own beasts
Enjoy their food and feasts,
The republic shall have meat,
Fresh milk and butter to eat.
It will be strong and hearty,
Trusting in the Party.

U. Isaev, the Chairman of Kazakhstan's Council of People's Commissars, noted with alarm that in the previous two years there had been 'an unremitting reduction in livestock numbers'. He of course drew his own conclusion from this, that there was only one route for the successful development of animal breeding, namely collectivization. It is probable that livestock herds dropped in size by half (to 20 million), but the Council of People's Commissars hid this fact, professing in its reports that there were still 30 million head of livestock and deliveries of meat were calculated on the basis of that figure. The targets the collective farmers were set meant that the ruin of the animal breeders occurred even sooner than might otherwise have been the case.

Goloshchekin, who had of course known about this, insisted that the plan targets should be met come what may:

We must in the most ruthless and resolute way (and I assure you that the Area Committee was able in the past and is still able to do this) organize things so that the objective for animal breeding should be achieved, just as was the case with grain procurement.

Goloshchekin declared this on 16 August 1930 at the Third City Conference in Alma-Ata.

Zeinulla Toregozhin from the People's Commissariat for Supplies was bold enough to object to what Goloshchekin had said. He predicted that, if things continued in the same way in 1932, the republic would only have 275,000 head of livestock left. There was no end to the labels hung round Toregozhin's neck after that: slanderer, opportunist, enemy of socialism and industrialization, whiner, nationalist and so on.

The procurers confiscated everything they could possibly find. In Turgai the Party officials worked using the slogan: 'Avoid excesses, but leave no sheep and goats behind!' If anyone tried to protest at this lawless behaviour, he would quickly be arrested or frightened with the threat of prison. To make things clearer the procurers explained: 'Under socialism there will not be a single person without a conviction.'

In districts where grain had never been sown, people were forced to hand over their livestock for a pittance in exchange for grain; any crops would later be removed. The slogan at the time was as follows: 'Take from wherever you can, shake out the sacks right to the bottom.'

The Plenary Session of the Area Committee held in February 1931 called upon the Party workers to collectivize all productive livestock. The Plenary Session made it clear that reference to the 'special features of the *aul*' would not be accepted as a pretext for relaxing targets. Activists in Turgai were given very clear instructions: 'Collectivize all the livestock, not leaving even a single puny goat behind for individual ownership.'

Not only did the officials strip the farmers bare but they lectured them in the process: 'In order to eradicate the small-proprietor mentality of the collective farmer, livestock from one collective farm should be transferred to other collective farms in an *aul* of a different administrative area.' In addition to everything else, ordinary collective farmers were forced to contribute to collections made for all sorts of items, perhaps a car for some district chief or the building of a house for one of the local Party leaders and so on.

The slightest reluctance to come forward with the goods demanded by the unrealistic plan would be regarded as protest against the Soviet regime. 'Protests' of this kind were ruthlessly suppressed without any inquiries being made.

One of the many cases of this kind was the 'unrest' in the Shetskii District of the Karaganda region. In 1931 there were 80,000 head of livestock there but the plan target was 120,000. Initially the plan contributions were calculated in numbers of animals, so people had to hand in their very last cows (most people had handed in their sheep earlier). The local officials in charge of the proceedings, who were better off, kept back their cattle and handed in sheep and goats to the state. When the authorities realized what was happening they started calculating plan quotas in tonnes. The poor peasants, who had already been stripped bare, had their quotas raised; who else was there left to make up the plan targets?

That was when the unrest began. Moreover it was provoked by an outsider – for his own ends rather than anything else – the chairman of the Soviet from *Aul* No. 15, Isa Babzhanov. This local despot, nurtured by the new regime, had stripped the inhabitants to the bone and punished all those who were not to his liking with exorbitant taxes, using threats of arrest and the firing squad to acquire 'concubines' and much more besides. When the previous chairman of the *aul* Soviet protested at this arbitrary treatment, Babzhanov 'organized' unrest, knowing that the Cheka detachments called out to deal with it would be bound to protect him, Party members and representatives of Soviet power. Indeed, that was what happened.

Two communist detachments hurried to the *aul* from Aksu-Ayuli, the district centre, and from Karkaralin. The 'rebels' – nineteen unarmed individuals – were shot. Babzhanov himself killed his personal enemy – the former chairman of the *aul* Soviet – then went on to kill his father and his brother and rape his wife. Her breasts were cut off and she was thrown on to the body of her husband to die. As a warning to others, the members of the punitive expedition – representing the district's Party and Komsomol activists – forbade the burial of the corpses. 'Insurgents' in neighbouring *auls* were also shot after being accused of refusing to pay taxes and hiding livestock.

In the locality of Berkutty, Cheka officials hacked six people to death and the corpses were not cleared away. In the Abralinsk District, in revenge for the fact that 'bandits' had detained three couriers, a detachment 'rounded up the remaining population of the *aul*, which had consisted almost exclusively of elderly women and children, lined them up and then shot them down with a machine gun'. Similar actions were carried out in other places and soon afterwards the commanders of the relevant detachments were rewarded with specially inscribed revolvers.

When the operational division of the OGPU in Karaganda

subsequently took charge of such work it emerged that 'there had been no armed uprising in the Shetskii District. Isolated unarmed outbursts occurred. No armed gangs had been rallied to operate within the territory of the Shetskii District.' It was further noted that 'the unauthorized shootings of thirty-six unarmed individuals arrested in a number of *auls* in the Shetskii District carried out by certain staff of the Shetskii District Department of OGPU and Party workers of the district had been the fault of Sychov (head of the District Department of OGPU)'.[7]

During the ensuing investigation Sychov justified himself, saying that he had acted on instructions from the head of the Semipalatinsk operational division of OGPU, Bak, who used to bombard his subordinates with directives of the following kind: 'The number of arrested *bais* should not worry you in the slightest. I repeat that you must now adopt the most brutal line.' These were all too familiar words, precisely the kind that Goloshchekin often used that year. In secret telegrams to the rural districts he used to demand that 'brutal pressure be applied' in order to eliminate 'our shameful lagging behind when it comes to procurement'.

The victims of this 'brutal pressure' – shot or hacked to pieces without trial or investigations out in the steppe – are probably still listed in Cheka reports as 'bandits' and 'counter-revolutionaries' rebelling against the collective order.

The farming practised by the men of the steppes had collapsed and hundreds of thousands of Kazakhs had decamped to other regions. They fled as far as they could from the collective farms. According to Gosplan data, 121,200 people moved away in 1930 and as many as 1,074,000 in 1931. Such migrations had never been seen before. Despite all this the Party apparatchiks continued to follow their previous policy and boast of the successes achieved.

In October 1931 Izmukhan Kuramysov, Second Secretary of the Area Committee stated:

> The whining and spineless behaviour of certain of our communists
> – even activists – complaining that all is not well in Kazakhstan,
> that allegedly there are certain elements of degradation and that
> the future of Kazakhstan is unclear are hard to understand and

quite unforgivable. This is empty chatter of the under-occupied. There has indeed been a drop in livestock numbers, but the *bais* are responsible for this. Sometimes the middle peasants as well, in response to agitation from the *bais* and *kulaks*, give way to panic and also start squandering their animals.

Kuramysov ended his report with solemn words:

> We Kazakh communists can and should be proud of the fact that we have participated in a great historical process, that we have made a contribution to this new order, have helped to erect a new pedestal, on to which we have raised up working Kazakhs. We took part in the rooting out of all the nightmarish legacies of the tsarist order, which have now been overcome. Let the various nationalists, like the Alash-Orda people, lament, beat their breasts and declare: 'I love the Kazakhs.' May the results of the very existence of Soviet Kazakhstan and the working Kazakhs themselves demonstrate who has done more for Kazakhstan and the Kazakhs.[8]

By the end of 1931, 65 per cent of agriculture in the republic had been collectivized. The cold weather set in. There were no buildings available in which to shelter the livestock, which had been rounded up. Cows, sheep, horses and pigs died of cold and hunger.

It is hard to understand what predominated in this engineered chaos – bungling or deliberate disregard for common sense, in order to humiliate people.

The Merke meat-producing state farm was driven up into the hills to a height of 2,500 metres above sea level, where previously livestock had only been put out to graze in the summer months. Blizzards raged across that plateau in the winter and the snow would be one-and-a-half metres deep.

The accommodation provided consisted of cold cramped little houses, semi-dugouts and buildings made of turf, through which the winds would blow. Often there were no shelters of any kind for half the livestock. Those animals which did have somewhere to go often froze in sheds full of cracks, huddling together so tightly that weaker animals were sometimes trampled on. One night twenty-eight animals were crushed in this way. In that state farm, and in the neighbouring collective farms the previous year, many animals had died. The winter of 1931–32 was more disastrous still.

Not only had no preparations of any kind been made for the transition to a settled way of life, but it was implemented too rapidly, like mobilization for a war. According to the official plan, the bulk of the settled farms should have been established in 1931 and 1932. The Plenary Session held in February 1931 demanded that when the transition to settled life took place, villages for collective farmers should be built by poor and middle peasants from various clans. In practice the result was resettlements of Kazakhs within the enormous territory of their region. The authorities in charge demanded that collective farms must, without fail, be large and embrace several clans. Naturally each clan tried to ensure that its new home was as near to its former home as possible and this inevitably led to quarrels, confusion and offended sensitivities.

In the Bayanaul District, which had not been generously endowed by nature, people were rounded up on to *solonchaks* (grey, salty soil) and bare stony ground. There was no drinking water, no food for the animals to eat and no sheep pens. The nomads hardly had time to dismount from their camels before the officials announced that another great victory had been scored for the settled way of life. In response, activist Arapov from the 'New Ploughman' collective farm wrote to the newspaper, addressing a message to the public prosecutor of the republic: 'Give us water! There is none left. The earth here is just bare stones. We sank wells down to a depth of 9 metres, but there was still no water.'

That particular collective farm was moved from one site to another four times, but it was the same picture everywhere. A black whirlwind of ruin was raging throughout the steppe, threatening devastation and death. Meanwhile Goloshchekin's only worries concerned the possible failure to implement some plan target or other, laid down by the Centre. His statements of that period are distinguished by even more cynicism than usual.

In the autumn of 1930 Molotov asked him about the reasons for mass decampments from western Kazakhstan. Goloshchekin replied without hesitation: 'It's what the *bais* wanted, that's all there is to it!' In 1931, when hundreds of thousands of Kazakhs had been obliged to flee from the threat of imminent death, Goloshchekin had the audacity to state quite calmly:

The Kazakh, who never used to leave his *aul* and did not know the routes he followed as he wandered, is now moving easily from one district to another within Kazakhstan, joining Russian or Ukrainian collective farms or starting to work on construction projects in the Volga region or Siberia. Naturally transitions of this kind change the economy, change his way of life, destroying old habits and old traditions of farming. Inevitably losses are experienced. The nationalists see only the gloomy side to all this, the disruption of farming, while others – 'leftist' phrasemongers – see this as counter-revolution. What is really happening is the rebuilding of a way of life.[9]

On another occasion, at a meeting held in the Kazakh Communist University, Goloshchekin declared:

Opportunists – voluntary or involuntary agents of the class enemy – say that we are ruining the economy. Yet, if we look closely at any collective farm and compare it not only with farms before the Revolution, but also with farms as they were two or three years ago, we shall realize how nonsensical and also harmful such statements are. We need to remember that there are no class divisions in the countryside now. At the time when landowners, *kulaks* or capitalists used to exploit the peasants, millions of people really were being reduced to poverty and hunger by that exploitation, which enslaved them. There is no more of that today and there cannot be any more in the future.[10]

Over a million Kazakhs had left their homes and, as they left, the paths they moved along were lined with corpses. Goloshchekin seemed to forget this when, at a meeting of Party activists in Alma-Ata, he joked:

In infertile districts poor harvests gave rise to a bumper crop of opportunism. (Laughter.) People gave way to panic and began to compile ultra-opportunist balance sheets for fodder stocks. Are there any grounds for panic? None whatsoever. Thanks to mechanization and collectivization we have rescued our agriculture and our peasantry once and for all from their former situation of inescapable hunger.[11]

But there was no grain available any more. Everything had been cleared out. Even Party workers had succumbed to this robbery.

Staratelev, Secretary of the Mendygarin District Committee, stated that the Area Committee's plan was unrealistic and said it had not been thought through. He was then ordered to hand in grain unconditionally. Staratelev replied: 'If that's the way it is, then I shall have to strip all the collective farms bare, down to the last dough trough and all the farmers will run off.' Izvarin, Secretary of the Ubagan District Committee, gave a similar reply to the Area Committee: 'We can meet the plan targets for grain procurement, but not with grain, only with carp and bustards.' In addition Shumeiko, a member of the Karabalyk District Committee, stated: 'The economy of this district has been disrupted by impossibly high plan targets. The collective farmers and also the poor and middle peasants have no prospects of being able to survive. We have driven the collective farmers away from us; they are leaving.' Goloshchekin expelled them all from the Party and took Izvarin to court.

The second wave of collectivization had now come to an end. In 1931 livestock numbers in Kazakhstan fell by a further 10 million. A famine now began on a scale that even Kazakhstan had never seen before.

❧

XIV. Disaster Throughout the Steppes

From the beginning of 1932, if not earlier, letters, telegrams, and memoranda were sent to the Area Committee, Kazakhstan's Central Executive Committee and its Council of People's Commissars concerning the famine.

A telegram from Ushtobe in February 1932 read as follows:

> All *auls* near Balkhash gripped by famine. In six others only 2,260 of 4,417 holdings extant and 63 per cent starving. Remaining population in dire straits. Starvation started beginning December 1931. Total of at least 600 dead. Starving eating dead horses, remnants of slaughtered animals.

A telegram from Irgiz in 1932 read:

> To Goloshchekin, Alma-Ata Area Committee. 14,000 kilos of grain collected to fulfil plan targets to be exchanged for manufactured goods STOP Given food problems of district COMMA hunger of some degree found in 2,203 households COMMA request authorization to return procured grain to supply farmers who have delivered livestock STOP District Commissar Poktarov.

People continued to send in missives of this kind, even to Moscow. On 1 February 1932 the following statement was sent to the Presidium of the Central Executive Committee of the USSR. Statement:

> Considering ourselves no longer able to remain silent and aloof witnesses to the famine which has befallen the population of the former Pavlodar region, we are compelled to turn to the central

bodies of the USSR government. Refraining from any analysis or assessment of the reasons which gave rise to this famine, we are deliberately confining ourselves to a description of the picture we observe.

In the last six weeks approximately, starving people have been coming into Pavlodar, swollen from malnutrition and dressed in rags – mainly Kazakhs. The town is inundated with them. We are confronted by the most incredible poverty. Dozens of them come into every house every day. Starving people of all ages are coming: young and old and children. Hungry people are scattered over rubbish dumps looking for and eating scraps.

Medical establishments are flooded with people dying of starvation. The famine has given rise to epidemics (a special *troika* [commission] has been set up to tackle typhus). On the outskirts and inside the town we are constantly coming across corpses of frozen, homeless, starving people. There have been instances of people dying from hunger in the town's dispensary in front of patients waiting to be seen by a doctor. We know of houses where the starving who came in to ask for bread have collapsed on the point of death. It is not rare to come across a family of Kazakhs wandering in from somewhere and pulling behind them a sled with their goods and chattels and the corpse of a child laid out on top of them who has died during their journey.

Hungry, half-frozen children get dropped off in children's establishments. Children's homes are crammed full and they are not taking any more in. Children of all ages are to be encountered everyday roaming round the town, freezing, emaciated and with stomachs swollen from malnutrition. They usually tell you: 'Father's dead, mother's dead, no home, no bread.' Some citizens take children in and send them to the militia but the militia will not deal with them and just drives them back on to the streets.

In the end an empty house was given over to those children and they were taken round there. Some of us visited that house. Without going into details about the dying and the corpses found in the yard outside it, in the porch and actually inside the house, we shall report in general terms that the children in this 'refuge' are given a small helping once a day of either gruel or soup with a tiny piece of bread. They are lying around on the floor and on the stove in stinking filth and in total darkness, urinating and defecating where they lie and crying; those who no longer have the strength to cry are simply groaning or wheezing. The scene is so grim, that the woman who was sent by the town Soviet to look after the children ran away the next day.

When one of us went to the town Soviet on 20 January to report on what we had seen in that house, the chairman of the town Soviet found nothing better to do than to call out the militia, have that man arrested and send him to OGPU.

The disaster is only getting worse. The famine is driving more and more starving people into Pavlodar. People weak with hunger are dragging themselves into this town from all directions and dying on the way. According to the accounts of the starving who manage to pick up 'scraps' in the houses they go into, some *auls* and settlements are already completely deserted, others now contain isolated households; instead of hundreds as before, they can be counted in tens at the most.

Some of the population has left for Siberia, but those who have stayed on are being brought down by hunger and dying. In the Pavlodar District the population is only half what it was as recently as in the summer of 1931. The villages of Podpusk and Chernoye are now deserted and *Aul* No. 1 no longer exists. In the *aul* of Zhalybaevsk in the Beskaragai District, which used to be home to 300 households, the only thing still to be found there is the office of its Soviet.

We do not wish to point out which specific measures need to be adopted to help. Our aim is to raise a corner of the curtain concealing these horrors.

[Signed by] Political exiles V. Iogansen, O. Selikhova, P. Seminin-Tkachenko, Y. Podbelskii, A. Flegontov.[1]

From a letter to the Chairman of the All-Union Central Executive Committee, M.I. Kalinin, dated 10 February 1932:

The whole population in Kazakhstan is dying of hunger and in some places whole *auls*: for example, the *aul* Soviets Nos. 9, 10 and 11 in the Pavlodar and Irtysh districts and this also applies to all districts in Kazakhstan.

Recently people have been dying everywhere; the planted crops have not come up and all the livestock has been handed into the state. The collective farmers are not being supplied with grain by the state and the population has nothing to eat. In the collective farms individual families have no livestock of their own and no horses. Trading in the bazaar or among individuals has all been stopped and there is no grain to be had. White-collar workers employed in local organizations, local activists working for the chairmen and members of village *auls*, secretaries of Party cells and groups of those applying for Party membership and also employees of district organizations are engaged in the theft of other people's property. If they see that some citizen or collective farmer has a scrap of bread, a pound of flour or a piece of meat, they will take it off them and use it themselves; they make out it has been handed into the state, but in actual fact eat it themselves. In addition, they take people's money, good garments and any other property; they search people's homes and frighten the population. Also part of the process is their acceptance of bribes; they take from anyone they please. If any person was unwilling to pay bribes, even poor peasants or middle peasants not well off at all, he would lose his voting rights, have his property confiscated and be branded a *kulak*. The population has to put up with sickness, death, confiscations, bribery and theft and then people have to go out and beg in their poverty; they even go as far as other localities or regions. There have also been cases when mothers and fathers have abandoned their hungry children and gone off on their own. This can be explained by the fact that in the future people will not be able to survive in Kazakhstan; it is tough and terrible to live here. Moreover, the local authorities are subjecting this hungry population to campaigns for various kinds of procurement, while the population which has to meet their demands cannot find a single crust to eat for itself.

[From] *Aul* Soviet No. 4 in the Maxim Gorky District.

[Signed] Nurgalii Duisenbinov.[2]

In February 1932 Citizen Melania Dvornikova (née Goleva) from the village of Sarkand in the Lepsinskii District of the former Semirechensk Region sent the following 'comradely letter' to Comrade M.I. Kalinin in February 1932:

Dear Comrade! I am turning to you with a most humble request that you should answer for me, a woman, the following questions. Why are we faced with this situation while collective farms are being built up? The grain procurement was very tough, or – as I see it – intolerable, as for example in the Muslim Kazakh collective farm 'Taras'. All the grain, i.e. the grain sown, has been made over to the collective and each farmer had, in addition, to hand in 160–240 or even 320 kilos. Where can he take them from if he was working all summer on the collective farm? At the present time that hungry crowd is making its way on foot along the roads with small children, looking for something to eat, falling by the wayside and dying like flies. This can lead to terrible robberies and murders; even now such incidents have started. In the village of Ayaguz a woman was hacked to death for a single loaf of bread. The poor are begging and every day dozens of them turn up, but there is nothing to give them, because neither the collective farms nor their workers have any grain surpluses and there is still less fat to be had. In the collective farms rations are distributed according to work-days completed; these are hardly enough for the worker, let alone the members of his family. This is what makes hundreds, thousands of people go abroad, without a thought for what kind of welcome they will receive on arrival – they may even get beaten or killed, but no one gives a thought to that. Most of these people belong to the class of farm labourers or poor peasants. In my personal opinion this is not right.

As for myself I can say that I am a peasant woman from the family of a poor peasant. I was involved in the wave of revolutionary change. I have been a member of the Party since 1924. I am thirty-eight years of age. As a young a woman and until 1929 I worked as a hired labourer, as a delivery woman or a cleaner. In 1929 I was working as a cleaner in the Sarkand People's Community Centre; I took on myself the assignment to sow one *dessiatine* [1 tenth of a hectare] because at the time my salary of 23 roubles was not enough to live on. For that sown area, which had an actual yield of 850 kilos, they demanded 970 kilos [it was decreed that the total yield per *dessiatine* was 1,760 kilos]. A legal document was drawn up, which had no effect and

I was made to walk up and down the roads of the village from one holding to another with a black board on my chest on which was written: 'Enemy of the people, malicious grain hoarder'. As a member of the party and someone who has handed in over 700 kilos, I do not consider myself an Enemy of the People. Apart from me, other women were also humiliated, forced to pay outstanding taxes down to the last kopeck and to wear epaulettes from old tsarist uniforms. They were made to go and live with their two-week-old babies in cold barns and were kept there for three whole days, which caused a good deal of illness.

As a member of the Party, I began to demonstrate that this was not right after the false evidence was collected against me, in particular by Sidorov, chairman of the village Soviet. Although now a Party member, he is the son of a *kulak* – so neither a brother by class nor a comrade who shares my ideas; he, as a member of the Party, raised the question of expelling me from the Party. At the end of 1931 I was advised to hand in my Party card, and this is why I am now turning to you and asking you to reinstate my rights as a member of the All-Union Communist Party (Bolsheviks). This request I now sign.[3]

In April 1932 the Petropavlovsk Regional Committee informed Goloshchekin of the following:

In twelve districts of the North Kazakhstan region 246 cases of death from starvation and 133 cases of bloating from malnutrition had already been recorded by 17 April 1932. In the 'Kalinin' collective farm, Nasachenko and the widow Verumskaya have died leaving two children. In the collective farm 'Volunteers' Rally' everyone is eating the meat of dead animals, digging up the dead bodies of horses and using their meat as food. In the village of Kupriyanovka in the Tonkeri District there were twenty-three deaths and twenty-nine cases of bloating from malnutrition. In the village of Semipolye (the 'Flame' collective farm), sixty-three people are suffering from malnutrition and three have died.

In spring 1932 a short report was sent in after an inspection of the village of Poltavka in the Trudovoi District in the North Kazakhstan region:

None of the people investigated had any grain. All there was to eat was carrion – some boiled and some raw. The meat was the colour of blood and green in places. There were signs that it had begun to rot in the spring heat. In all the households we visited the children looked ill. Many of them had swollen faces. We asked Vasilisa Lyga: 'Why are you sitting on the stove?' She replied that she could not get down because she was too weak and she pointed to a boy of thirteen who was too weak to bring her some of the meat.

A report was sent in the spring of 1932 after an inspection of the 'Kazgorodok' (Little Kazakh Town) settlement:

Most of the people are emaciated. They eat scraps and make soup from bones already scraped bare. Apart from that they use dry leather to eat and sometimes even processed leather. In the district centre there was a family which was eating dog meat. Near the house a pile of dog's skulls were found. Some paws were floating in a cauldron. In the village of Shoky, which had once contained 144 households, there were now around 60. People had left to look for food. Most of the remaining people at the time of the inspection were eating carrion, meat that was rotting, soup made with bones and swill consisting of bran and boiled leather. Fifteen families were completely emaciated and swollen from malnutrition. The collective farms had no emergency funds to support their members. Bigar Kigarin, a construction worker, received rations for one person, while his wife and three children have just swill and water. Kozhan Konzhebaltov had a family of six. When the inspection was being carried out his ten-year-old boy was rummaging in a pile of dung, pulled something out of it and began to suck it. Kuov Sagandykov's family of three is eating dog meat.

Collective farmers Valuev and Kalnikov from the village of Zhuravlyovka in the same region wrote to Goloshchekin in 1932: 'In our district many people are being lost. Thousands are taking to their heels. Children are ill and incapable of work.'

A memorandum was sent in by Dr Kramer from the North Kazakhstan region in 1932:

I have examined 500 children. The correlation between the birth-rate and the mortality-rate is as follows: one woman here has given birth to fourteen children and only one is still alive. Another has given birth to ten and two are still alive. The children as a rule die by the age of two or three. During the winter in some *auls* all the youngsters perished.

A report was compiled by the Kazakhstan section of OGPU dated 4 August 1932:

According to available data, food problems are becoming acute in the Atbasar District. As a result of hunger, deaths and cases of swelling from malnutrition are on a massive scale. Between 1 April and 25 July 111 deaths were registered, 43 of them in July alone.

It was pointed out in a report drawn up by Kazakhstan's Council of People's Commissars that not only were farmers who had decamped suffering from hunger, but also 'around 100,000 Kazakh households in the nomadic districts, which have not moved off anywhere. Among the Kazakh population cases of sickness and death are now on a mass scale.'

On 5 September 1932 a memorandum was drawn up by Zamailov, an instructor in the organizational department of Kazakhstan's Central Executive Committee:

The Kazakh population, currently not engaged in productive work, which has now moved into the vicinity of Balkhashstroi from the adjoining districts, is in dire need of help with food. Because of these food problems, thousands of people are suffering from disease (epidemics of typhus, scurvy, dysentery), but they are not receiving any medical help or help with food. The question of food assistance for the nomads who have recently arrived here needs to be resolved immediately.

In Bertys I myself witnessed corpses of those who had died from hunger and epidemic diseases strewn over the main square and not cleared away for 3–5 days.

An express telegram was sent to the Kazakhstan Central Executive Committee: 'In the Baukovskii *Aul* Soviet of the Bshikaragai District people beginning to die of hunger STOP For your information STOP *Aul* Soviet.' That was how the text read – 'beginning to die'. They informed the Centre, they did not ask for help. They did not expect any.

An extract from the report delivered by Kakhiani at a meeting of Alma-Ata's Party activists was printed in *Soviet Steppes* on 11 January 1932 and read as follows: 'We have achieved even more striking success in agriculture.'

On 15 May 1932 the same paper printed an extract from Goloshchekin's speech at a meeting of the Area Party activists 'On Collectivization in the Kazakh *auls*':

> Firstly, the experience of the last three years has shown that through collectivization the Kazakh *auls* have acquired an optimal form for their economic organization, which will raise the level of prosperity for the working masses in the *auls* to the highest degree and at a rapid rate.
>
> Secondly, it is in the Kazakh *auls* that the most serious violations of Leninist principles in the domain of the collective farm movement have come to light and are still doing so and that there has been a considerable amount of administrative coercion, a mechanical approach to this work without the features of local agriculture being taken into account, a failure to complete certain stages of this transition before moving on to the next in the chase after exaggerated targets and the existence of purely superficial collectivization in certain instances. Yet, despite all this, what has been clearly demonstrated is that the main mass of the poor and middle peasants in the Kazakh *auls* has allied itself voluntarily with socialism as it advances along a wide front.
>
> In confirmation of this situation we can cite the fact that collectivization of the Kazakh *auls* as of 1 April extends to 73.9 per cent of the poor and middle peasants in our Area.

Further on in his speech Goloshchekin pointed out:

> We are asked what advances and achievements have been obtained because, in connection with the current state of animal breeding and some decampments by the rural population, slanderous assertions are being spread about regarding the impoverishment of the Kazakh *auls*. Analysis of the situation shows that we have made enormous advances in the building of socialism.

He concluded his lengthy speech with the following words: 'We are building the socialist Kazakh *aul* at a Bolshevik speed.'

This 'building' in the spring of that year proceeded as noted in documents from the North Kazakhstan Party archive:

> On 30 April 1932 the Chairman of the Nadezhdinka Village Soviet and his deputy broke into the house of collective farmer Supko who had objected about having his cow confiscated; they ordered him, if he did not want to be shot, to stand with his face to the wall without moving. The cow was duly confiscated. At Yeremeyevsk farmstead the same people, together with Maximenko, secretary of the group applying for Party membership, locked up a sixty-year-old woman in a barn, arrested Sivokhina – a sixty-year-old collective farmer – and Ryzhkin – a sixty-seven-year-old collective farmer – and beat up all three of them.

Results of Goloshchekin's so-called 'Bolshevik speed' included the following:

> In the 'Ilya' collective farm in *Aul* No. 5 of the Tonkeri District there are sixty-one working horses of which four cannot stand up, ten are completely emaciated and the remaining forty-seven need extra feed immediately. The *kolkhoz* has no reserves of hay. The livestock is being fed on the reeds which were previously used to cover sheds two to three years ago. Every collective farmer receives on average one teaspoonful of milk per day. There are thirty-six people in the collective farm swollen from malnutrition. Five people died between 25 February and 14 March.

Kazakhstanskaya Pravda, on 22 May 1932 printed a telegram of greeting sent to Goloshchekin and the Kazakhstan Area Committee of the All-Union Communist Party (Bolsheviks):

> To a loyal promoter of the Party's general line, under whose leadership the tsarist colony of not so long ago – Kazakhstan – has turned from a backward region into a large industrial and agricultural centre of the USSR. The Municipal Party Conference of Chimkent sends its ardent Bolshevist greetings. Long live the Area Committee of the ACP (Bolsheviks) and its leader, the veteran Bolshevik-Leninist, Comrade Goloshchekin!

The same paper on 17 June stated that: 'Japanese peasants are starving. *Kulak* farmers are growing rich at the expense of tenant farmers.'

In June 1932 Kuramysov delivered a report on the sowing campaign to the Alma-Ata Party Conference: 'In Taldy-Kurgan people even went as far as declaring the pyramid poplars growing round individual houses collective property. In some cases they cut them down. One woman serving in the Red Army came over and announced that half the poplars round her house had been felled.' Kuramysov proceeded to talk about a newspaper article describing how collective farmers had been forbidden to sow allotments and that the village Soviet had sent everyone notes demanding that they hand in their last chicken or cow. Kuramysov remarked: 'That kind of thing was going on everywhere!'

At that point Goloshchekin, indicating the relevant place in the article, said: 'He's even reporting that all the beehives have been collectivized.' In response Kuramysov exclaimed: 'It's hard to imagine!'

On 20 October 1932 Goloshchekin addressed a meeting of party activists in Alma-Ata. By this time a decision had already been taken by the Central Committee of the All-Union Communist Party (Bolsheviks) regarding animal breeding in Kazakhstan, or what still remained of it. Goloshchekin did not appear put off by the fact that farming was in a state of collapse:

> The Central Committee approves the line adopted by the Area Committee in connection with the restructuring of the Kazakh *aul*! (Enthusiastic applause.) In order to understand why the Central Committee approves the line we have adopted, it is

necessary not just to look back to theoretical principles, but to appreciate that precisely this course of action and the current leadership from the Area Committee have made possible enormous achievements in practice.

The most important positive results we have achieved are precisely in the field of agriculture. Despite the poor harvests of the last three years, the sown area has increased. Yet, at the same time there have been major miscalculations with regard to the qualitative growth of Party organization. There have been considerable setbacks in farming. We are faced by food problems and economic difficulties in some Kazakh *auls*. We are not hiding any of this. Some people, however, such as right-wing opportunists, great-power chauvinists and, in particular, nationalists – those owls who can only see at night, those agents of the class enemy – pick out certain negative phenomena to use against our general line, for their fight against the Area Committee. They exert an influence on some of our ranks, engaging in anti-Party, anti-Soviet agitation.

Former leaders, who in their day fought against the Leninist line in the nationalities question, who started waging a grim struggle against the Area Committee as early as 1925, have since taken up residence outside Kazakhstan (in Moscow, in Tashkent) and present themselves as lovers of the people, liberal nobles who, over their tea and sometimes vodka, sigh deeply at the fate of their people, thus misleading inexperienced, vacillating students, and certain comrades from Kazakhstan; they corrupt them, fill their heads with ideas against the Area Committee, against our line. That is why, while we continue down the proven path of victories, consolidated by the Central Committee resolution of 17 September, we must combat first and foremost great-power chauvinism and nationalism in our ranks, fight against any spirit of compromise. We must eliminate the philistine swamp, which is aiding and abetting the efforts of the chauvinists and nationalists to undermine us. (Shouts of 'Correct!' and Applause.)

Goloshchekin ended his speech with the words:

> The Party's Area Committee, while resolutely pursuing the general line, has achieved major success in developing Kazakhstan. (Enthusiastic applause.) Under its great leader, Comrade Stalin – the first and finest Leninist of them all – we shall stride on from victory to victory. (Lengthy and enthusiastic applause which turns into an ovation. Cries are heard such as: 'Long live the fine Leninist, Comrade Goloshchekin!' or 'Hurrah!' Loud, lengthy applause.)

On 28 October 1932 it was reported in *Kazakhstanskaya Pravda*: 'The enormous successes in the socialist restructuring of the Kazakh *auls*, achieved under the leadership of the Kazakh Area Committee headed by Comrade Goloshchekin, are an undeniable fact of great historical importance.'

Cruel disregard for humanity was the defining characteristic of the exhortations delivered by all members of the Party leadership as they pushed through collectivization. On 8 July 1932 Molotov delivered a speech at the All-Ukrainian Party Conference. He spoke about the enormous victory of the collective farms and called the Ukraine one of the shining examples of the successes so far achieved, as it 'marches in the front ranks of the socialist reshaping of agriculture'. Lazar Kaganovich assured the audience that the Party organization in the Ukraine under the leadership of Comrade Stalin would be able to march even further forward 'to great new historical victories'. These words were greeted with enthusiastic applause.

In the Ukraine at that time millions of people were dying of hunger. Certain regions of the Ukraine were cordoned off by troops. Cheka operatives and the militia held back crowds of half-starved people moving away from their homes, using rifles and machine guns. They stopped them trying to flee to safety. According to the most recent available data, approximately 7 million people died there from hunger.

The cruelty intrinsic to the actions of the Party leadership outstripped even the cruelty of their words. Despite the terrible famine, Stalin insisted on continued exports of grain to European countries. While less than a million hundredweight of grain from the 1928 harvest were sold abroad, in 1929 that figure rose to 13 million, to 48.3 million in 1930 and to 51.8 million in 1931; it dropped to 18.1 million in 1932. Even in 1933, the year when the famine was at its height, approximately 10 million hundredweight of grain was exported to Western Europe.

At the time of the economic crisis in Europe this Soviet grain was sold for very little. Meanwhile even half the grain exported in 1932–33 would have been enough to save the southern regions of the country from starvation. In Western Europe people were calmly eating the Soviet grain which had been wrested from peasants who were dying of hunger. All rumours about people dying of hunger in Russia were firmly rejected. Even George Bernard Shaw, who made a trip in the early 1930s to acquaint himself with the USSR, wrote that the rumours about famine in Russia were a fabrication and he had seen for himself that Russia had never been so well supplied with food as at the time when he was visiting it.

To this day nobody knows how many people died from hunger in 1932–33. Many researchers agree that the figure was 5 million. Others say that 8 million is probably nearer the truth. Historian Roy Medvedev wrote that: 'More people died then than [in Russia] in 1921 or in China during the terrible famine of 1877–88.'[4] This information has been supplemented by other more recent statistics provided by the journalist E. Alexandrov, using materials from the Museum of the Revolution's exhibition 'Land. Hunger. Reforms.' held in Moscow in the spring of 1992. This provided an opportunity for the public to meet leading specialists in agrarian history:

In June 1932, in a letter to the Politburo explaining the repressive measures he was adopting, Stalin complained that 'tens of thousands of Ukrainian collective farmers are still wandering about the country and corrupting the working people'.

In the spring of 1932 the state was compelled to issue subsidies to the grain-growing regions totalling 17 million hundredweight. The grain was duly sown and mass hunger avoided for the time being. Yet people were still in an emaciated state when the new harvest began to ripen. As soon as the ears of wheat began to ripen, so-called 'clippers' would rush into the fields – first and foremost mothers – who went to pick unripe ears of corn at dawn so as to be able to cook some kind of gruel to feed to their children. That was when Stalin's '7–8' edict was issued [dated 7 August 1932] specifying the death penalty for 'theft of socialist property' (or a prison term of ten years if there were extenuating circumstances). Using this edict 'of the five ears', as the peasants used to call it, 56,000 people were sentenced between August 1932 and January 1933 (of the 2,000 sentences to death by shooting more than 1,000 were carried out).

The procurement campaign of 1932 cleared all grain out of the villages. Yet the plan targets were still not reached and indeed could not have been. On this occasion the state procured 180 million hundredweight and then removed 'only' 18 million hundredweight, but not for humanitarian considerations. By now the most barbarian of administrative measures were being used to get hold of the grain. Mass-scale starvation now began. Historians mention various numbers ranging from 3 to 14 million deaths from hunger in 1932–33. Most agree on a figure of between 4 and 7 million. Documents have recently come to light enabling us to say that Stalin and his entourage had been hatching a criminal plan at the time. Moreover there had been reserves of grain in the country which would have been sufficient to save the people affected. The famine had been an organized one in the full sense of that word – possibly the most terrible of all Stalin's crimes against the people of the USSR. It is possible to suggest various motives underlying Stalin's 'cannibalism', but collectivization is not the first to come to mind. After all, the hammer of hunger struck indiscriminately at collective farmers and other groups of people as well. A more likely objective is the final and irrevocable taming of the peasants, who had not yet abandoned the age old habit of deciding for themselves what they would sow, where and when.[5]

At the beginning of the 1930s a new popular saying emerged: 'Hammer and Sickle mean Hunger and Death.'

Let us consider the testimony of the Kazakhs themselves; Sasan Nurgalievich Nurgalymov, a veteran of the Great Patriotic War (1941–45) awarded the Order of Alexander Nevsky, recalls his story:

'I was born near the mountains in the *aul* of Karagash in the Aksusk District of the Taldy-Kurgan region. My father was the same age as Ilyas Dzhansugurov, the future poet, and was one of his friends. They were in the same class at primary school. In 1926 my father died and my mother was left on her own with four children. Two years later, in 1928, our house was confiscated and our livestock taken away, apart from our milk cow and a horse. I can hardly picture my parents' house any more. I was only seven at the time. Soon afterwards we moved to Aksu to live with my mother's family.

'Yet I remember the year 1932 all too clearly. It was a hungry cold year and there was nothing to eat. People started dying in the winter. GPU men were driving around the streets on sleighs collecting up the dead. They used to pour carbolic acid or kerosene on them and then burn them. The remains they used to throw from the steep river banks into the water below. People came to our district from Chubartau, trying to escape hunger. There were large numbers of them and they all perished. Only one woman survived. She used to wander about the deserted streets, tearing at her hair and calling out to heaven knows who: "May you be cursed! May you be cursed!"

'Once we were all sitting at home on a cold February evening. Mother was cooking us gruel made of millet and we were waiting for this food, huddling close to the stove. Suddenly the door swung open and a bundle of rags flew into the room. We unwrapped it and there was a child, a little boy of two or three months. Mother ran out into the street, but outside the house there was nobody to be seen. The baby was given the name Kudaibergen – "gift of God". We were worried that we would not be able to feed him properly, since we ourselves were short of food. Soon he was taken in by a blacksmith, who had a wife but no children. They brought up the abandoned baby and now he is working as a livestock specialist in a state farm and has seven children of his own.

'At the beginning of 1933 I was taken to Sarkand where I went to boarding school. We were fed on nothing but cabbage, oil-cake and boiled water. Everyone walked about with enormous swollen bellies and we fell sick with every disease under the sun. The teachers were not much better off. I remember our Kazakh language teacher, Abdrakhman

Iskakov; he too was swollen from hunger and hardly had enough strength to take his lessons. Things were particularly difficult in March and April. When we went outside in the mornings there would be frozen corpses in the irrigation ditches.

'Later our lessons were cancelled altogether. We spent whole days lying on our beds in the hostel thinking about where we might get hold of some food. The older pupils learnt that potatoes were stored in the cellar of the canteen building. None of them were able to crawl through the gap in the wall and so they made me – the youngest and the thinnest – go in for them. I was frightened, but the leader of the "gang" slapped me in the face and threatened to beat me up if I did not co-operate. I managed to scramble through the gap and climbed down a rope into the cellar. From outside someone threw down a small bucket. There were very few wet, half-rotten potatoes in there. I sent up several filled buckets and while I was groping about in the dark cellar I found half an abandoned barrel of salt herring. I had just managed to put two fish in my pocket, when the lock on the door began to rattle. The caretaker, a one-legged old man, was standing there, holding a bat. I thought to myself that I would be able to run away from him without being caught, but then an elderly cook came down the stairs. I crouched down behind some crates and they walked past without noticing me. The next moment I managed to slip out again and catch my breath. For three days we cooked those potatoes in our room and shared them out fairly with everybody else, complete with pieces of herring.

'In the summer I was sent to herd cows in the Andreyevskii District and in July I was fetched home by my uncle Ablai, my father's younger brother. By then all the pupils had been taken home from the school, back to their relatives to make sure that they did not die of hunger. My mother was worried that something might happen to me and so she had sent my uncle to bring me back. From him I learnt that my seven-year-old sister Siyunbike had fallen ill with tuberculosis that winter and died.

'I was given 5 metres of cotton fabric as payment for my work with cows. Ablai and I sold the cloth and bought a few flatbreads. Then we went to Aksu on foot. We walked along breaking off tiny pieces of the bread. It was hot, the sun was burning down and the route was a long one – 45 kilometres. All around us there were ragged people, each at the end of his tether. They could hardly drag their feet; some of them were going to Aksu, others to Sarkand. Somehow they sensed that there was some bread in our bags! They caught sight of us from a long way off and started following us, forcing themselves forward with their last drop of energy and then falling on to the ground and losing consciousness. So many years have passed since then, but I can still see that July road and the half-dead people wandering along it in a daze.

'Hajji-Akhmet Kulakhmetov was an old retired teacher and war veteran who marched as far as Berlin. He came from the same part of the country as Nurgaliev and was born in the Saga-Biyon settlement in the Aksusk District in 1916, when terrible drought had befallen the Semirechie region and two grim years of famine were beginning. He lost both his parents at an early age and lived with his brother's family until the age of eight. Later he lived in a children's home and after completing his fourth year at school he decided of his own accord to move to another district and he enrolled in the school for peasant children in Koksuisk.

'Akhmet remembered the first collectivization campaign, which he experienced as a twelve-year-old. Old Bekish, who had previously been in charge of the *volost* administration had had all his livestock confiscated; the animals were rounded up in one particular spot and then shared out between all those who had no animals. Kozybaev, the official from the District Party Committee was in charge of everything and rode around on the finest of the horses which had once belonged to the *bais*. He set up a stable in front of a small *yurt* and assigned to each of the poor peasants on his list five sheep, a mare and a calf. Some of the poor peasants set up their own small holdings after that but most of them simply ate what they had been given.

'Those who lived in the district adjoining the border knew all the ravines and paths leading into China very well. Prior to 1917 the shepherds had taken their flocks of sheep up into the Chinese mountain pastures, and young men used to visit Kulja, where they exchanged horses and sheep for tea, manufactured goods and other commodities. In the hungry and troubled years soon after the Revolution, prosperous Kazakhs used to go into Chinese territory with their herds, but in 1921 many of them returned. At the end of the 1920s rumours were spreading about the *kolkhoz* communes, where everything would have to be shared – even children and wives – so the Kazakhs once again fled into China through the Kanalskoye Gorge, through which Ataman Annenkov had withdrawn across the border in his day.

'Kulakhmetov told me that collectivization had been a hard experience for him and his family:

'"Before that people had lived quite well, but the introduction of collective farms marked the beginning of economic ruin. In 1930 the Borte clan rose up in protest against the collectivization of livestock. The young men, who were armed by this time, attacked the district centre, killed the Party activists, cut off the head of the Party secretary and poked out his eyes. They burnt all the papers in the District Committee, GPU and militia offices. A detachment of the insurgents set off towards Kapal, but it was met by troops which had been sent out to suppress the uprising and 300 men fled to China abandoning their families."

'"Up until 1925 it was possible to walk freely into China, nobody stopped you. At the end of the 1920s frontier troops set up border posts. Various skirmishes and shooting incidents followed, but nevertheless the Kazakhs continued to cross over using secret paths. After the autumn of 1931, Kazakhs from the Matai clan were driven by poverty and hunger to seek refuge over the border and they were later followed by others. Heroic Nurmukhamed Zhokeyev from the Kolgei clan, well known for his bravery, formed a detachment of armed men and helped more than a thousand families make their way into China. Nurmukhamed was aged about forty at the time; at the beginning of the 1970s he came back to his homeland and spent the last four years of his life in his native village of Dzhansugurov."

'"The authorities decided to stop people leaving for China and a platoon of NKVD soldiers armed with machine guns was sent to the area. They also had an aeroplane at their disposal. The numbers of refugees still remained constant. Not long afterwards a clash took place beyond Kapal and there was a great deal of shooting; rumour had it afterwards that roughly 1,000 people had perished as they tried to escape into China; they were hemmed into a gorge and mown down with machine guns. I was fifteen years old at the time and living in Kapal, where I witnessed these events. The rattle of machine guns and rifle fire went on for about a fortnight. When the shooting eventually stopped, the surviving refugees collected up the corpses of their dead relatives along with five or six others, dragging them up on stretchers made of willow branches to the local cemetery to give them a proper burial."

'"Despite the new barriers, some of the inhabitants still managed to escape to foreign parts. In 1931 I was sent to the sugar beet technical school not far from Gavrilovka [modern Taldy-Kurgan]. That was where

I experienced the famine which spread through our homeland. The daily ration for students was as follows: two sugar beet, 200 grams of bran and a rotting cabbage. The lads were swollen with hunger and dying. Between November 1931 and March 1932 around forty of the 270 students died. The local river was our salvation. We used to spend whole days fishing for gudgeon in the River Koksu, which we would boil up at once in a cooking pot on the bank."

"'The director of our technical school was a former revolutionary by the name of Vasiliev. He was very worried about the young lads, who were dying like flies. In the canteen they used to boil up half-rotten potatoes in their jackets and each boy would be given a ladleful. The skins would be thrown into the rubbish pit, and starving tramps with swollen stomachs would appear, as if from nowhere, to hurl themselves at what had been discarded. In the morning we might find five or six of their frozen bodies out in the yard. We even had a cart pulled by two donkeys on which the dead bodies would be taken away. The director himself selected boys for that work whom he thought were still strong enough for the task. The corpses would be taken down to the River Koksu and there they would be thrown into the water or pushed through a hole in the ice. Once I was called upon to do this job. In the course of the winter probably as many as 100 corpses were disposed of in this way. I can still remember the place. Opposite it there now stands the village of Krupskoye."

"'In the early spring of 1932 people began searching in the fields and from under the snow would dig up rotten ears of wheat, from which they picked out the grains. They used to fry them on fires, eat them and die. Later on we learnt that hundreds of people had poisoned themselves in this way in Aksu and Kapal."

"'Those who survived the terrible winter of 1932–33 were forced to plant sugar beet in the spring. There were no tractors and the ground had to be dug with spades. Just try digging the earth before sunrise after a daily ration of a bowl of unrefined millet. People used to collapse out in the fields and die. Each sugar beet was treasured and we were strictly forbidden to eat them. Not everyone can control himself though; some people would boil them up in a cooking pot, while others would simply eat them raw. If you were caught, you would be sent straight to the Public Prosecutor. So many people were convicted!"

"'It was only after the summer of 1933 that the situation improved slightly. An order came from somewhere to the effect that each day each working person should be given up to 200 grams of grain for every member of his family. At last people started to feel less oppressed by hunger. At the end of 1933 the technical school was made over to the Moscow Sugar Trust and from then on we were issued with half a kilo of bread, hot tea and soup twice a day."

"'What I remember most clearly of all though is the winter of 1932. It was a terrible time! Director Vasiliev sent a telegram to Gavrilovka asking for help, saying that otherwise all the students would die. The district authorities eased up a bit and issued us a little sugar, jam and sunflower seed oil. However, these riches had to be transported to the school. Once again donkeys were used. Three or four students climbed into the cart and set off, taking the director's Berdan rifle. There was a second shipment a week later.'"

"'My turn to transport the food came round and I set off with two other boys – Ivan Sazonov and Pavlik Voroshilov. The journey which was only a matter of 17 kilometres seemed endless. There were swollen rotting corpses at the sides of the road. We counted fifty-seven dead before we reached Gavrilovka. There were also starving people walking over the frozen snow-crust, swaying as they went. They tried to attack our cart, for they could see what we were transporting. Then we started firing the rifle into the air. One woman shouted after us. 'Oh lads! Dear boys! At least take the child! Perhaps it'll survive?!' We took from her grasp a six-month-old baby and later we gave it to our cleaner, Pershina, a kind elderly woman. She nursed him back to life. I do not know how the boy's life turned out in the end, because two years later I and my fellow students graduated from the school and went our separate ways."

"'Since then I have seen and lived through a great deal: the war from Stalingrad to Berlin. I was wounded twice and on one occasion seriously, so that I had to spend nine months in an army hospital. Yet what I remember most clearly of all is my boyhood years, the technical school and the hungry year of 1932. The mother's desperate cry is still ringing in my ears.'"

Academician Zhabag Suleimenovich Takibaev is known as the first Kazakh physicist; he has had almost 500 individual and joint works in pure and applied physics published, covering a wide range of subjects in the field. He set up the republic's first research institute for physics – the Physical-Technical Institute – where he is currently the Director. He also set up the Institutes of Nuclear Physics and High-Energy Physics, which are internationally renowned. These are his memories of the 1930s:

'I was born in the *aul* of my great-grandfather Takibai in the territory of the former Abralin District of the Semipalatinsk region. Later Lavrenti Beria chose the area for a testing-ground for atomic weapons and I remember the physicist Igor Kurchatov, after he had selected the site, told me that they had passed through the *aul* that was my home on their way.

'Our family was deeply religious; my grandfather had made the pilgrimage to the holy places and as such became a *hajji* [a Muslim who has completed the *hajj* to Mecca] and my father who was a kind, quiet and responsive man, became a mullah. By present-day standards he would have been termed illiterate, but in the 1920s my father was regarded as a learned man and taught children in the modest school in the *aul*. If I remember rightly he was even known as its 'director'. Religious practice was already forbidden in those days, but it is impossible for an honest Muslim not to follow in the footsteps of the Prophet. Our father used to retire to a small empty room in the school resembling a storeroom and pray at the appointed times.

'Yet it is not possible to hide away from prying eyes! Someone caught sight of him praying and reported him to the authorities. They really put themselves out, because somewhere they got hold of a camera and secretly photographed my father at prayer. They protested about his position as director in the school, claiming that a primitive man like that should not be allowed to teach Soviet children! Admittedly on that occasion things only went as far as an oral reprimand in the district office of the GPU, after which our father was allowed home again. Yet in 1930–31 when there was unrest in our steppes in protest at collectivization, insurgents captured the district centres of Kainar and Chingistau. They exchanged red flags for green ones, but were later defeated by a detachment of soldiers sent in from Semipalatinsk. I heard the rifle fire myself and the name of the man leading that punitive detachment, which I had heard from the grown-ups, was etched on my memory. It was Shubin.

'Some time after that they arrested my father, although he had not taken part in the unrest. They simply roped in anyone who had been prosperous in the past and, in my father's case, he was a mullah as well, which in the vocabulary of the day meant 'religious fanatic'. Mother took me to visit my father in Semipalatinsk Prison No. 2 and the last time we saw him was shortly before his death. After spending several years in prison, he died in 1933, three months before his trial. By then only 15–20 per cent of the original population was still living in the Abralin District; some had left for China or elsewhere, but most of them had died of hunger.

'My family moved to Semipalatinsk. I remember one day a sleigh drove past our house loaded up with something covered over with bast matting. I and other local boys ran after it; we wanted a ride. I caught up with the sleigh, jumped on to it and fell down on something hard. When I lifted the edge of some sacking I saw underneath it the frozen bodies of small children.

'Those were terrible times. I would not wish experiences like that on anyone. In the winter of 1933 every morning there would be horse-drawn carts out collecting up the frozen corpses of those who had died from hunger and disease. That was probably the eventual fate of my grandfather who, people say, had been exhausted from hunger and just fell down dead out in the street. Shortly afterwards my grandmother died. She was followed by my mother, driven to despair by all she had lost. I was now an orphan and taken in by the children's home. Or rather homes – No. 2 and No. 5. Thank you for that ...

'Now try and imagine springtime in Moscow in 1941, the glistening Hall of St George in the Kremlin with hundreds of boys and girls from all over the country – winners of Stalin scholarships. Each one of us was sitting at a little desk of his own and waiting in tense anticipation. We waited for one hour, then two and – at last! – quite unexpectedly, not through the main door but from somewhere at the side, men in smart military uniform appeared forming a human corridor. Then, looking intently at us, our leaders, whom we knew from the numerous portraits we had all seen, passed down through the corridor – Kalinin, Voroshilov, Kaganovich, Molotov – and behind them, after a long pause, another man dressed in a field jacket and boots stepped slowly forward. It was Stalin! All those sitting in the room called out in a single shout – "Hurr-rr-ah!"

'The hurrahs and clapping probably went on for several minutes. My desk was very near a place where Stalin stopped. I forgot about everything that had ever happened to me before in those moments. Everything else slipped away; I just looked and looked at him. Yet he did not resemble the portraits I knew; he was heavier, with stooping shoulders and a lumbering gait, while his gaze was tired and apathetic. His voice had an apathetic ring too. He said a few words about our studies and rounded off with a slogan like "Forward to Communism!" I was so ecstatic that I could not remember the words! No one on earth could have been happier than I was! Had I really seen him? Had I been blinded by it all?

'Later in Tashkent, where I was studying at the University of Central Asia, everyone wanted to hear about it; at a meeting in the Tashkent Agricultural Machinery Plant, in some factory or other, in various schools – everywhere there were eager questions, flowers and clapping. To think he'd seen the real, live Stalin! I was taken from one gathering to another until one day, carried away by it all, I blurted out that when Stalin finished a sentence he blinked, he blinked very often, as if he was trying to see more clearly.

'The next morning a car came for me and took me to the NKVD [secret police] building. An important-looking man explained to me at length and in very serious tones that the blinking was a detail I should not have mentioned. There was no point in mentioning insignificant details. After that I was allowed home, but I was not invited to any more public gatherings. Not by anyone, ever again.

'In 1950, when I came to the Academy of Sciences in Alma-Ata to start work after defending my postgraduate thesis, a note was passed to the scholar chairing the general assembly where my candidacy was being discussed. It read: "How has the son of an Enemy of the People managed to slide into your ranks?" Everything could have turned out very badly for me, but fortunately the arrest did not follow immediately. I flew to Moscow and went straight to the head of the personnel department of the Physical Institute of the USSR Academy of Sciences, where I had been studying as a postgraduate. The general from state security listened to me attentively and told me to come and see him the next day. When I appeared, he told me that I could go home as the problem had been resolved. What saved me was that in my CV I had not concealed the fact that I was the son of a mullah from an *aul* who had died in prison. Indeed it was something I had never concealed. Even in the children's home in hungry 1934. This had meant that I had not been accepted into the Young Pioneers by my classmates, just as later I was not accepted by other comrades into the Komsomol.'

Writer Kalmukhan Isabaev recalls:

'I remember that cold autumn day in 1932. At the time it seemed that our whole family had been lying in an unheated room for a very long time. My father, with legs swollen from hunger, my weak mother, holding my little sister Sauken to her breast, and we three brothers – nine-year-old Zarken, four-year-old Babken and me, nearly six. It was half-dark inside the house. Three days earlier my mother had made a soup out of the last handful of bran. She poured it out for us into little bowls and gave us strict instructions to lie still without moving, to save our strength. The next day Sauken and Babken could not hold out any longer and began to whimper. Mama went out into the street after tightly closing the shutters and she came back in with tears in her eyes.

'"My little foals! I have shut out the light from the windows. Nobody shall watch as we die ..."

'The twilight helped us fall asleep. I watched the thin splinters of sunlight shining through the cracks in the shutters, how they crept round the room to the dull side of the *samovar* and gradually everything started going round in circles in front of my eyes – specks of dust in a ray of light, the plump *samovar* and the empty doorway. At that stage I realized I was losing consciousness because of hunger. Each time I came round I felt again that sad gnawing in my stomach. Next to me my younger brothers and sisters were spluttering through their tears, calling their mother. She hurried over to them and then suddenly collapsed face downwards on to the floor. My father crept over to her and called out in an agitated voice: "Makhtum! Makhtum!" Mother did not reply. Then all four of us started crying.

'All of a sudden bright sunlight flooded the room; someone had thrown open the shutters. There was a loud knock at the door. My elder brother rose to his feet. From the threshold a low strong voice boomed out: "Hallo neighbours! Are you all right?"

'It was a familiar voice; it was "Uncle" Ivan – the collective's storekeeper – Ivan Martynov. I don't know where he was from or when the Martynovs had come to live in our *aul* but it must have been a long time before.

'"Have a little treat. I've brought you some flour," he said and held out a small cloth bag.

'It was like a miracle. Mother came to. Almost before she had time to open her eyes, she was holding out her hands for the flour. For the next few minutes she was busy by the stove; she quickly pushed some brushwood inside it and blew on the flames. With greedy happiness we swallowed down the floury broth she had made, worried only that the bowl would soon be empty.

'Later we learned that on that day Ivan Martynov had walked past all the houses and left a small gift of flour in each one. It turned out that in the farm store there had been a sack he had been strictly forbidden to touch. Yet, because people were on the brink of starvation, the storekeeper broke the rules. He had shared out the flour fairly, just giving a little more to the households with the most children.

'From that very day my father began to mend. When he was better, he went to work and a little food started coming into the house after that.

'One day our mother came home crying. I thought to myself: "Someone must have died from hunger." Then our father came in after her.

'"That's enough now," he said to Mother with a frown, trying to calm her.

'"How can you say that's enough? If it hadn't been for Martynov, think how many people would have died! He took pity on us and shared out the collective's flour. It makes it look as if only he was guilty! Can't you behave like real men and stick up for him?"

'"Just try and do that! It would take more than three days to get to the district centre. They wouldn't release him anyway. You know that perfectly well ..."

'"But what did they sentence him to ten years for? For helping the hungry?"

'"That's what it looks like ..."

'Winter began soon after that and Ivan's wife Marfa decided to go and visit her husband, who was languishing in Pavlodar prison. One day all five of the Martynov children turned up on our threshold in their ragged little coats fastened together with string and straps. The eldest of them, my friends Petka and Vanka, were six and seven. Marfa kissed each one of them in turn and hurried off to the cart on which she had hitched a ride. They lived with us through the whole long winter. In the spring a large cart stopped by our house: Marfa had come back for the children, bringing her father with her – a strong old man with a ginger beard. Our mother kissed the children goodbye and they set off – I do not know where.

'In 1951, for my holiday, I came back to my childhood home. The war was over and as a junior lieutenant I had stayed on to serve in the army after our victory. At that time our family was living in the Lenin collective farm in the Bayanaul District. After spending a few days there I took a horse and a double-barrelled gun and galloped off into the steppe.

'A long way away from home I came across a lake I had not seen before. I looked down and saw smoke curling up from a fire; someone was sitting next to it with a fishing rod. I rode over and saw that it was an old Russian with a white beard. I greeted the fisherman and asked which lake it was.

'The old man screwed up his bright blue eyes as he looked up at me.

'"And where are you from?"

'"From Bayanaul."

'"So that's it. We're both from these parts then. You've come a long way. You've reached the Karaganda region here. This is the Osakarov District. The lake's called Shidinda. Who do you know from Bayanaul?"

'"Lots of people."

'"Do you remember Ali Isabaev?"

'"But that's my father!"

'The old man almost dropped his fishing rod. Then he took a deep breath sucking in the smoke from his pipe, put his enormous fishing rod down and stood up.

'"It can't be Zarken?" he asked in excitement.

'"No, Zarken's my older brother. I'm Kalken."

'The fisherman gave a happy laugh and quickly pulled me down from my horse with his strong grip. He started looking at me closely, patting me on the shoulders with his wide hands.

'"Don't you recognize me? I'm Ivan Martynov. You must have heard that name from your parents, surely? Marfa!" he called in the direction of the nearby house, "We have a visitor!"

'A bent old woman came to the door and looked over towards us, shielding her eyes with her hand. Then she clapped them in amazement and came running over. She kissed me on the forehead.

'"You're the image of Makhtum. Welcome! In you come my boy!"

'A tall fair-haired young man came out of the house, whom at first I did not recognize as my childhood friend Vanka.

'Soon we were sitting at the table laid for a special occasion. We remembered Petka who had been killed during the war; we drank a toast to the Martynovs and my parents and for our meeting.'

This was the story told by the writer Zhappar Omirbekov:

'My father, Omirbek Yeralinov, had been working as a coal-miner in the Karaganda coal mines before the Revolution, when the mines still belonged to the British. He was a stocky man of medium height, who had inherited the strength of my great-grandfather Baizak, renowned as a hero in his *aul*. Sometimes he boasted that he earned twice as much as the other miners – a silver rouble a day when he worked a double shift. That was good money in those days; for a rouble you could buy two goats or a sheep. In 1919 the mines were shut down and my father came back to his *aul*, 130 *versts* from Karkaralinsk.

'Our farm was a small one: just a cow, two horses and some sheep. In 1931 our cow was taken away for the collective and we were issued with 16 kilos of wheat for the winter. The Party activists began saying: "Omirbek has two whole horses, isn't it time to sort out this *kulak*?" In the spring my father went away to Karaganda, taking his older son Sharif with him. He made a dugout for them and took up his miner's pick once again. Not long before New Year he sent us a message telling us to follow him.

'We left the *aul* secretly on two sleighs: Mother, my brother Mukhtar, my uncle with his nephew, my sister and I. How much can you take with you on such a long journey? Apart from clothes and blankets, all we took was a small round table and our big round *samovar*. The next day we were caught in a blizzard and it was difficult to stay on the road. Beyond the Narshokken (Sleeping Camel) Mountain, some people travelling on foot caught up with us in the steppe, which was now deep in snow. Those exhausted people carrying small sacks on their shoulders were wearily making their way towards Spassk. When they caught sight of us they walked over and asked if we had anything at all that was edible. Mother gave them some dried curds and a few pieces of dried meat. All the way to Karaganda for three whole days we kept on meeting poor wretches like that who had been driven from their homes by hunger.

'Two well-built brick houses stood out amongst the cluster of miners' dugouts. They had been built long ago by the British; there were also wooden huts used as offices. The dugout dwellings of the miners were crammed with people; each miner would be providing a roof for his relatives flooding in from the *auls*. There were ten people living in our room of 14 square metres and at one time the number even went up to eighteen. There were hundreds of hungry people wandering about among the dugouts who had been unable to find work.

'The rations to which my father was entitled as a miner were as follows: 1 kilo of bread a day, 3 kilos of flour or cereals a month, 6 kilos of meat,

1,800 grams of fat and 400 grams of bread for each of his dependents. Two months after our arrival, however, my father fell ill and he was given a surface job, which meant far smaller rations. That was what our family had to live on, not to mention the fact that, like everyone else, we were helping other relatives. The Kazakhs have a saying: even if there is only one hungry person in an *aul*, everyone will starve. One night our uncle turned up with his family – seven of them. They were frozen and swollen from hunger. My mother gasped, realizing how long they must have gone without food. She said: "First of all we'll give you tea and soup after that. You mustn't eat lots of anything straightaway." Our uncle replied: "We're going to die anyway, so give us soup." He sensed that death was coming and indeed soon four of his family were dead.

'Among those who survived was my cousin Kapan Satybaldin, who later became a well-known prose writer. He was a terrible sight with a swollen face and he could not talk. Mother used to give him sweet tea and wash his face with the water the bran was boiled in. Then she would rub his face with hempseed oil. Two weeks later the swelling had gone down. Kapan came back to life, so to speak, and started talking. He was very advanced and educated for his age. Who could have known that this young hero was going to prove far-sighted as well! When he had left the collective farm where he lived, Kapan had taken with him a few pieces of headed notepaper stamped and all – the kind they used to write official certificates on. Papers like those could be used as internal passports for people who had no rights and who had been rounded up into collective farms. Without hesitating for long, young Kapan wrote out documents of this kind for several people from back home and this enabled them to find work and earn a crust of bread. From that day on people kept coming to our dugout – people we knew and strangers alike. Kapan made a "stamp" out of a damp potato and then on the empty pieces of notepaper, which he had been prudent enough to bring with him from the *kolkhoz*, he created "documents" for everyone. One day someone asked if him if he was not afraid he would get caught out. "Come what may. At least I've helped a hundred people survive."

'In August 1932 our father died. Life became more difficult and it was my brother Sharif who came to the rescue, after becoming a hammerman, as did our uncle Khusain Altaibaev, who used to train young miners. In the autumn I went to school, into the first class. I remember the terrible winter of 1932–33. In the mornings the orderlies on duty used to collect up the dead bodies. Often they would be found on the roofs of our dugouts; homeless people used to sit on dugout roofs huddled up against the chimney pipes from the stoves which turned cool over night. Often they would be covered with snow. Infectious disease also carried off many lives. It was during that winter that my four-year-old sister Batura died of smallpox. There was not a single family that did not lose someone. People stopped crying over deaths – they had grown so used to them.

'Water was a serious problem in the settlement. Crowds of people would cluster round the one and only tap, from which came a trickle of water from the distant Samarkand reservoir (near the modern town of Temirtau). Sometimes you might start queuing at four in the morning and wait till nine to fill a couple of buckets – that would be something to celebrate. Sometimes you would have to trudge home with empty buckets after standing for hours, frozen to the bone. The snow on the streets was dirty from soot and in order to get sacks of clean snow to heat up on the stove, you would have to go out into the steppe beyond the settlement. Once I went out on a sleigh with my uncle the blacksmith to collect clean snow and a militiaman driving by deliberately knocked our sacks onto the ground. The blacksmith could not contain himself and shouted to the heavens: "O Allah, send down a quick death to me and that rogue as well!"

'In the settlement there was a small market – a makeshift bazaar – where a mug of water cost 20 kopecks. Within that tiny market people half crazy with hunger used to wander about looking for anything they could lay their hands on; they were known as "shock-workers". They would grab a loaf of bread from a trader or an inattentive customer, or perhaps just a piece of bread, and then run off. They would stuff the bread into their mouths as they ran.

'In the first three months of 1933 food aid was at last issued to these desperate people. The starving were assembled at midday and given 300 grams of white bread. But is that really enough to survive on? They tried to rob the goods wagons containing food down at the railway station, but properly fed and healthy guards had no trouble driving people away as they fired into the air. On one occasion I witnessed a crowd of hungry people push the guards out of the way and gather round a tank of some sort. Someone managed to make a hole in the bottom of it and sunflower-seed oil began to pour out of it. People began pushing to get nearer and to catch the liquid in mugs, pots or even hats.

'In the summer my mother and brother Mukhtar left to go back to the *aul*, hoping that life would be easier there, but I went to an orphanage. I myself was in favour of going, because I did not want to be a burden to anyone. The orphanage was in the village of Bolshaya Mikhailovka. Life was hard there and many children died of typhus or dysentery. Having to bury small children or youngsters was a frequent task. We took it in turns to dig the graves; we were all reluctant to deal with the dead. The staff in charge of the orphanage added an extra 50 grams of bread to our rations for each person we buried.'

This is what Sagidolla Akhmetov remembers:

'Even nowadays I still recall a terrible episode which occurred in 1932. A thin exhausted woman, with eyes sunk deep from hunger, came over to a street trader, a healthy-looking man, and after grabbing some bread he was selling she rushed off. Nearby her children were waiting – dirty, ragged and thin – just skin and bones. With no difficulty the trader managed to catch up with her and hit her on the head with a mallet. The blow was so hard that the woman fell down dead. That happened in broad daylight in the centre of Akmolinsk.

'I remember how the situation took a turn for the worse in the late twenties. Local leaders and activists began going from house to house and confiscating livestock, declaring that the animals now belonged to the collective farm. How people would cope without their livestock did not seem to worry them at all.

'At that time I was involved in building the railway from Akmolinsk to Karaganda. I moved earth using a wheelbarrow and also had to drag stones. We were preparing the track bed. Then at the beginning of winter in 1930 I went home. There everyone was starving. My father, after he realized that it was not going to be possible to feed the family in the *aul*, decided he would move to Akmolinsk. "We're not going to survive here," he said, "At least there will be some kind of work going in the town." So we left.

'Soon after that, the first ever school for tractor-drivers in the region opened in Kotyrkul. I was able to enrol as one of its pupils. After studying there I worked in what was then known as "Kazzheldorstroy" (Kazakhstan Railway Construction), first of all as a tractor-driver and later as a stoker and assistant train-driver. We worked on the section between Anar and Akmolinsk and Akmolinsk and Akkul. The stretch may not have been a very long one – just six hours – but during that time several tonnes of coal had to be shovelled into the firebox.

'A year later, at the beginning of winter in 1931, our family returned to the *aul*. After that I lost contact with them for a time. It was only in March 1932 that I discovered from one of our relatives, when he came to Akmolinsk, that people in the *auls* were beginning to starve and die. Soon after that my father, mother and elder brother managed to reach the town. They had nothing left apart from what fitted into a single bag. My younger brother Kopei and sister Kadisha had both died from hunger. When they set off to Akmolinsk, my father had borrowed a horse from a prosperous relative. On their way people crazed with hunger had attacked them, seized the horse and butchered it immediately.

'Hungry people were flooding into Akmolinsk from all directions by this time. As soon as the snow began to melt, the most horrible scenes came to light. Wherever we went we saw the corpses of people who had died of hunger. The numbers were particularly bad near the stations of Babatai, Vishnyovka and Anar.

'The work of a stoker is demanding. Each day we were given a kilo of bread. On days when we were travelling we were given an extra 600 grams. After each trip we would take bread back to our families. That was all we had by way of food. What I used to bring home disappeared in the blink of an eye.

'Soon crowds of hungry people were filling Akmolinsk. Between the rail depot and the town in those days there was a patch of waste ground about 5 or 6 kilometres wide. Almost every day I had to cross it with a friend on my way home. It was on that route that we kept encountering dead bodies. We tried to bury them, but the number of corpses was growing by the day. It was the same in the streets of Akmolinsk as well. Then they brought in the mounted militia. Each militia-man had a lasso; he would tie several corpses together and drag them outside the town to the old cemetery. I even had to go there, when we buried one of our men from the railways. The corpses were deposited in enormous common graves. When one pit was full, they moved on to the next.

'There had been eighteen people in the family of our uncle Syzdyk Bizhekenov. We helped them when we could in the beginning, but soon we ourselves were ill with hunger … Not a single member of our uncle's family survived.'[6] L.I.V. (he has asked for his name not to be revealed) also recalls those years:

'Ten peasant families were evicted from our village, yes – peasants, who differed little from the rest of the villagers and were perhaps even poorer. Many of them perished including my parents. My brother, who was still unmarried, and I survived by some miracle, although I was with them at that time. As a minor I was less likely to be stopped on my way, although one time I had to hide and make my way to my village as a homeless child.

'A few words on the special resettlement sites in Kazakhstan: some 60 kilometres from the village of Aktau (now Aktasty) there was a camp near what they called "Rotten Swamp". People used to die of disease there because the water was full of ticks; when they used to filter boiled water for tea, the ticks would be caught in the muslin. When the cold weather began most people were still sleeping in the open air and could see the sky; they had no roofs over their heads, no heating. Up to 150 people a day were dying. They dug a common grave measuring about 7 by 8 metres and 3 metres deep. The bones of my mother are lying in that pit. At the time I was about thirteen. That was in 1930–31. If the bones of those people have not been removed they must still be rotting there. Yet all those people were innocent. They had been chased out of their rural homes, just because some were more competent and prospered in life more than others. I would ask you not to mention my surname because my daughter is well educated, my son-in-law has a responsible post as do my sons and none of them know anything about all this. I am already seventy and retired; I fought in the Great Patriotic War of 1941–45 and was decorated.'[7]

In his book *My Father's Case*, Kamil Ikramov wrote:

'I must have been about six, when our luxurious railway coach crossed the land of the Kazakhs in winter. At a station called, I think, Kazalinsk, the truck stopped opposite a white building. Snow was covering both the track and the steppe like a sheet and near the train stood skeletons with their hands stretched out in supplication. They were living skeletons with child skeletons in their arms. I do not want to invent what my father told me [he was First Secretary of the Party organization in Uzbekistan at the time] or embroider on it or how his face looked then. I do not remember my father at that moment; in fact, I do not remember anything apart from the sheet of dirty snow and people with black faces and black hands raised, not in protest, but begging for a piece of bread. In our coach they were probably frying cutlets and potatoes in sheep fat.'[8]

Goloshchekin often used to travel along that same route on his way to Moscow ...

Kamil Ikramov went on to tell the story of a friend of my own family, Zinaida Kastelskaya, which also dates back to 1933. She told him:

"'I was standing in the garden and may well have been crying. I was in a desperately sad mood. Your father came over to me. He too had not been able to sleep. 'Why are you feeling so sad? Has someone upset you, disappointed you?' he asked."

"'I told him that I had had a horrible dream – such a terrible sad dream – and there did not seem to be any way out. He asked what kind of dream it had been. I replied that at first the sky had been high and wide open and then suddenly the stars began to fall out of it. They went on and on falling – so many stars. Then I looked again and ran over to those stars; when I looked more closely, I saw that they looked like dead sheep – a whole curly dead flock. Then I went up even closer and saw that the stars had turned not into sheep but people, Kazakhs! Terrible dead people were lying there, thin like skeletons and covered in rags."

"'Your father came over all sad and then suddenly said to me: 'Zina, you're such a kind little girl, you don't even realize what all that means ...'"

"'Was that '33?" I asked.

'It was like that in '32 as well, or even '29, but not that bad. 1933 was the worst. People were talking a good deal about the Kazakhs then. All the way along the route from Moscow to Tashkent. It was a terrible sight, those wretched ragged children begging for food and dying as they begged. That must have been when people started talking about the horrors in Kazakhstan. Perhaps it was after Bukharin travelled there, because he came back completely stricken by it all. He gave away everything he had, all his money and used to say: "We did not eat on that journey. It was impossible to look at all that". All the tracks, all the stations were full of dying people, when you travelled through Orenburg. Wherever you looked there were pathetic children lying about in the stations and everywhere in general.'

Nikolai Bukharin's himself did not starve in 1933.

The Kazakh writer Mukhatar Magauin told me:

'In 1944, when I was four years old, we were roaming the steppe. We travelled for twelve days along the ancient routes of our clan, from the southern part of the Semipalatinsk region to the north of the Dzhezkazgan region. We covered a distance of 300 kilometres. I remembered it all: the empty winter pastures, the houses with broken windowpanes and torn off doors. The insides of those houses had long been used as lairs for wolves; human skeletons and skulls lay scattered about the ground and the herds of saiga antelope ran into the thousands. We did not encounter a single human being or a single inhabited *aul* on our travels. Everything had been empty since 1932.

'Later on, while I was still a young boy, I would pray to God, asking him to let me become a writer, so that I could tell people about all that!'

XV. 'Hammer and Sickle' Brings Death and Starvation

The newspapers of 1933 – just as those before them and those from the years that followed, right up until 1985 – kept silent about the starvation and deaths. They shouted instead about the victories of collectivization and socialism. Fortunately, newspapers are not the only source of information for the public.

Tatyana Nevadovskaya, at the age of nineteen, kept a diary in a school exercise book. At the time she was living in the *aul* of Chimdavlet in the foothills of the Zaili Alatau mountains with her father, a professor who had been sent into internal exile. They were both working in an agricultural experimental station. In 1980 Tatyana presented an album of photos dating from the 1930s to the Central State Archive of Kazakhstan, complete with her reminiscences about her father, his colleagues and the life of that time. 'Photo album' is perhaps not the right word; it was an ordinary exercise book with plain pages into which she had glued faded amateur photographs complete with notes. At the end, on the last page, there was a poem she had written. It had the short heading 'Kazakhstan Tragedy' and was dated March 1933.

Nevadovskaya recalled:

'In the period 1932–33 the local population of Kazakhstan was in a situation of desperate poverty. The Kazakhs were leaving their *auls*, whole families were dying of hunger, freezing to death in the winter and falling prey to disease. Later this situation was classified as "distorted", but at the time the whole of Kazakhstan was experiencing major economic difficulties.

'The winter was terrible for us as well, but much more so for the local population. I was very young and impressionable and was moved by what I saw. I was deeply troubled by the terrible hardship, the hunger, the poverty and the vulnerability of the Kazakh people, who in those days were uneducated and downtrodden. I would hope that the current generation of Kazakhs (now a people reborn and educated) will not forget the people who died from hunger, the children and old people, the *kishlaks* and *auls* now empty and deserted, the people who froze to death in the steppe and those who suffered from disease.'

This is the poem she wrote in 1933, when professional poets who had not by then landed in camps were not writing with the same simple directness as this young laboratory assistant:

Heady March is here with notes of spring,
So full of memories – so sad and bleak.
The young grass has a bitter sting
After snows once strewn with bodies weak.
The poverty and dirt I do not see,
Nor the rags and lice of which we read.
What makes me suffer bitterly
Is the fate of all the hapless dead.
Hunger scythed them down, while I could eat.
My feet were shod, while theirs were bare.
I recall a begging granny in the street
And still I hear a mother in despair.
From under her rags she drew her breast
To show us no drop of milk was left.
Her baby's body could not come to rest,
Clutched by his mother of hope bereft.
I do not shudder at this ghastly sight,
Yet gaze on it calmly no one could.
As people fall who have no strength to fight,
Gleaning grains where once ripe corn had stood.
Stacks of straw are still large, intact,
Despite pouring rain, strong wind and snow.
Inside rotten ears of corn are packed,
Covered in mould – poisonous you know …
A helpless infant's little hand
Might still find a rotten ear.
Although he now can hardly stand,
His thin cracked voice you will hear.

Where is their guilt? Why all this pain?
Here in this huge homeland of ours?
Why such thin fingers must rummage for grain?
Why such sick children go begging for hours?
Through their skin poke shoulder blades
And ribs so painfully protrude.
Stomachs swell as the last hope fades.
Why this tragic lack of food?
Winter crops sprout in the warm blue haze.
Larks in the sky are soaring aloft,
As children's hunger blurs their gaze,
A Kazakh's corpse lies on soil so soft.
Who gave the orders? I want to understand.
Who made us sink to poverty and die?
Since ancient times, throughout this land
The nomads have led forth their herds – so why
Make camels and donkeys suffer so long?
Why strip from farmers their very last shirt
And force a whole people once supple and strong
To miserably starve in the cold and the dirt?
Who needed all this – Allah or Our Lord?
To take all they had and give nought in return?
Which despot would brandish so high his sword?
Which lunatic heartlessly take all they earn?
Last wagons, last felts and also last sheep
Are seized without protest or any cries.
Shepherds cannot plough with furrow deep:
With no *yurt* in winter, death is no surprise.
Without a herd or sheep, hunger is their lot:
Neither nature nor the weather is to blame.
We cannot say it is too cold or hot,
Or that harvests did not bring the land great fame.
It should have brought the people meat, bread and tea.
But no! They took away the first-class wheat,
Leaving giant straw stacks in every field and lea;
Round them cluster peasants with not enough to eat.
Neither Jesus nor Allah would invent such a fate,
To leave a Kazakh without wool, without felt,

342

With no skins for his shoes till far too late,
No warm cap, no warm coat and no belt.
He would not know that all around Moscow
The peasants they plant, sow and reap.
It is hard to watch such sorrow
And at night I can no longer sleep.
The lark trills up in the sky so bright,
While down below all is so grim.
Evil and beauty, darkness and light
Blend into one troubling hymn.

In the record Tatyana Nevadovskaya had put together, one photograph was particularly striking. It showed bare lumpy earth and in the distance a small row of pyramidal poplars with bare branches. The trees bordered a field. A fair-haired girl stood there in a cotton dress, not seeming to notice the photographer; she looked over to the side. In the foreground there was a Kazakh boy, perhaps a man rather than a youth – it is difficult to tell. He sat on the ground clutching his knees, with a tired look on his face. Next to him lay a hoe on the ground. His clothes were ragged, his shoes in tatters, and his feet were wrapped in strips of cloth. His face was thin and worn; in his dull gaze there lurked desperation and hopelessness. His face seemed to be gripped in a shudder of suffering, which would not let it go.

Tatyana had written: 'This photograph is a striking document laying bare the period of so-called "distortions".

'In the early spring of 1933 I was walking along with one of the specialists from the lab and I had my camera with me. Next to the road sat an exhausted Kazakh at the end of his tether. He could hardly manage to make his way home from working in the fields; he was drained of strength, groaning and asking for something to eat and drink. I passed my camera to my companion and hurried over to take him some water. He drank greedily. I had noticed that my companion had photographed us. After that I hurried back home to bring him some bread and sugar ... When I came back to him with the bread he was already dead.

'That was how people used to die in that terrible hungry year of 1932–33. In memory of the undeserved and unjustified sufferings of this people at that time I would have erected a monument at that spot, just as obelisks are erected at graves of the Unknown Soldier.'

343

Tatyana's wish is easy to understand, yet a monument can no longer be erected at that spot; it would be impossible to find nowadays within the confines of that *aul* – Chimdavlet. Indeed how can we compare that poor man dying of hunger and exhaustion on his way home through the spring fields with the Unknown Soldier? The soldier would have fought for his homeland, protecting it from its enemies and with a weapon in his hands. That poor Kazakh had had nothing but a hoe to hold. Nor did he know what had befallen his land and why suddenly people all around him started dying of hunger. He did not know the word 'genocide' – the destruction of a clan, tribe or even a whole people. He would not have known that civil wars come in different guises and that sometimes there are no cannon firing, no shots to be heard, although death wipes out more people than on battlefields.

Let us turn to the professional poets. There were more than enough ready to sing the praises of the collective order. At the VI Congress of the Soviets, poet A. Bezymenskii declared himself 'against Rus and for the USSR, creator of powerful socialist industry and a great poem transforming the face of the earth and the hearts of the peasants through its torrent of state and collective farms'.

'Comrades,' he announced, 'Rus of the *kulaks* will not surrender; for our successes, the successes of the Union of Soviet Republics will be measured by the extent to which the image of that enemy is wiped out, the image which is intrinsic to "Beloved Rus".' Naturally he went on to quote his own verses:

I utter those words – 'Beloved Rus' – from the past,
So as never to hear them again.
'Beloved Rus' was the curse meant to last,
With swamps and rivers empty of rain.

Poet Mikhail Svetlov was to write:

Birds sing and acacia rustles,
As the sun pours down like a tide.
The land below gleams as it bustles

344

Towards collectives nationwide.
Rippling wheat now fills the land
As far as the eye can see,
All the way from Dnepropetrovsk
To Kremenchug in this land so free.

Eduard Bagritsky wrote:

We look around and all we see
Are enemies – no friend.
Yet if the times demand we lie, then lying it shall be –
And if they do demand we kill, killing will know no end.

Another poem of his reads:

Over each slope and ravine,
Like wolves, the Cohens roam,
Pushing their noses so mean
Into the clean neat home.
They look to the left and the right,
Sniffling so angrily:
'Dig out the corn you hid last night
In the ditch so speedily!'
Who dares to start a fight?
Brothers, make no noise!
They'll hurl you down with all their might,
Or shoot the men and boys.
Black earth is flooded beyond repair
With the blood and sweat of our despair.

He also had this to add on the subject of class enemies:

The earth sucked at their tender bones,
Thrown into hasty graves.
The sentence was signed amid cries and groans
With the blood of those poor shot slaves.

345

Bagritsky, who wrote about the destruction of class enemies, did not write about the consequences of that destruction.

There is, however, testimony to what went on at that time; in the Ukraine, for instance:

> I went into one of the small houses and froze on the threshold. Next to the wall on a wooden bench lay the almost dried out body of a child aged five or six. Its mother was leaning over it, holding a knife and was trying with difficulty to cut off the child's head. The knife and her hands were covered in blood and the child's legs shook convulsively. For a moment I caught her eye and she looked at me. She was unlikely to have taken anything in, her eyes were dry, the light had gone out of them; they were like the eyes of a corpse, which had not been closed. An hour later we went back into the same house to record this – yet another case of cannibalism – but this time we saw that same woman lying on the earthen floor, her face turned upwards with the staring eyes of the dead. She was holding the severed head of her child to her breast.

Or the Kuban region:

> The most terrible hunger reigns there, people are eating each other, many are dying and the rest are on the move, cutting meat from the dead and eating it. They are dying on the move, simply falling down and expiring. There is nobody to bury them, they lie there until they rot. Then only bones are left; it used to be like that with horses and now with the people.[1]

Or near the Sea of Azov:

> We drove for many hours heading north. Our vehicle moved along a road overgrown with tall grass. The streets in all the villages were overgrown with weeds almost as tall as a man. Those who passed through did not find a single living being in the villages; in the houses lay skeletons and skulls, but no people, no animals, no birds, no cats, no dogs. Everything had perished from total hunger.[2]

Let us return once more to the work of poets:

For failing to sow all the corn
And keep up with the plan,
Wages are small and forlorn –
Just bullets for Berdy-Igan!

Vladimir Lugovskoi, 1932

Like lightning, execution flashes,
Pistons are struck by triggers of steel.
The Chairman sends out metal lashes;
Revolver bullets men's fate shall seal.
This is no fine speech or prose;
The rain of bullets dies down for a while.
The collective's Chairman submits to no foes
Throughout the planet, wherever he goes.

Boris Kornilov, 1932

His rawhide jacket was all worn,
His cap with earflaps encased his head.
He wiped the spittle from lips all torn,
And whispered a plea for some bread.
But then I sensed in him a foe
And took a much closer look.
I caught his gaze so full of woe,
But cunning too, that I could not brook.
If a few grains he might glean with his hand
And then survive – this ginger fox –
The rattling train of my homeland,
With all its proud herds and flocks,
Will come to socialism too late.
So I let the coins of silver fall back
Into my pocket, pulled down by its weight.
I set off again on my homeward track.
Weaving through lampposts in the mist
The chance for a good deed deliberately missed.

Dmitri Kedrin, 1932

347

On a Moscow street Kedrin could easily have encountered not a ginger-haired '*kulak*', but a dark-haired '*bai*'.

Toktabaev, chairman of the permanent Kazakhstan delegation, announced on 2 February 1933:

> In a number of areas in Kazakhstan, 'Sevles' [Northern Timber] has been recruiting collective farmers and labourers. The newly arrived Kazakh workers were exposed to extremely difficult conditions; they were not provided with accommodation or food rations on a par with those of other workers. This has led to dozens of Kazakh workers, farm labourers and collective farmers pouring into Moscow. Having no money they are going hungry, lying around in railway stations and unable to return to their homes.

These poor wretches were also probably forced to beg for something to eat. Who bothered to take a closer look at them, as passers-by decided not to give them anything? Who suspected that they had just one selfish urge – to survive?

Meanwhile what were ordinary people writing? In Russia one of the many anti-*kolkhoz* ditties read as follows:

> In the collective we used to toil
> Collectively all day.
> Of our twenty-five horses so loyal and strong
> Twenty will now never neigh.

A Ukrainian offering ran as follows:

> In nineteen hundred and thirty-three
> People fell as they walked along.
> Neither cows nor pigs could they see,
> Just posters of Stalin so strong.

People in Karaganda who had been resettled used to sing this song born of their experiences:

> We toiled away as peasants
> Working from morn till night.
> As masters of so many skills,
> Near Oryol and the Volga so bright.
> Then came nineteen thirty-one
> And the prison gates opened wide.
> All our wives and children
> Were taunted as *kulaks* and cried.
> They took away freedom and rights
> And our fields in the places we knew.
> They drove us all out of our houses –
> Infants and wives, old people too.
>
> In the railway trucks the slops bucket stank
> And we had so little to drink.
> The cries of the children for water
> Made all our sad hearts sink.
> At that time of suffering
> Another trial lay in wait.
> Sickness cast countless children
> Into graves at a frightening rate.
> Then scurvy tortured us too,
> As we all so desperately starved.
> Typhus thinned out our ranks
> And our falling numbers were halved.
> As honest peasants we used to toil,
> Valuing every hour.
> Why did the land of our fathers
> Punish us with such cruel power?
> We are not guilty of any crime;
> To repent would be a sin.
> One day our story shall be told
> For the sake of all our kin.

❖ ❖ ❖

Kazakh historians B. Tulepbaev and V. Osipov provide the following description of those times:

> The situation of the children was particularly grim. Tens of thousands of children were dying of hunger. They were starving not just in the *auls*, but also in the villages down in the plains, in industrial settlements and the towns of Kazakhstan. In Aktyubinsk, for example, in the spring and summer of 1932 the figures were as follows: 175 child deaths in May, 208 in June, 320 in July, 450 in August. All that was in a town which at the time had a population of only 15–20,000 inhabitants. Construction workers from Kazakhstan also suffered from hunger; this can be seen from the extremely high 'turnover' of such workers. In the mines of Karaganda, for example, of the 37,772 members of the workforce, 33,865 had to be replaced in the course of 1932. This applied particularly in the case of people who had been resettled; 7,545 such workers had to be 'replaced' in 1933.[3]

According to figures provided by historians Z. Abylkhozhin and M. Tatimov, approximately 45,000 families were banished from Kazakhstan in 1931. It is possible, however, that those figures are not complete; there were tens if not hundreds of settlements for the 'specially resettled'.

In Prishimye in 1931, around 3,000 people died in the course of a mere three months in such settlements: camps set up next to railway stations. By the end of that year 'natural wastage' accounted for more than 30,000 lives.

Veteran miners from Karaganda, who had been resettled in this way, spent decades working underground, earning respect and medals, but without having the label *kulak* officially removed from their collective biography. They too have vivid memories:

Grigorii Gerasimov is over eighty now. He was born in the small town of Insar in the Penza region of Russia. In 1931 his family underwent dispossession as *kulaks*. What kind of property had this family of eight possessed? A cow, two horses, and approximately one hectare of land. They were deported to Osakarovka and simply dropped in the bare steppes. In the winter of 1932 Grigorii Gerasimov lost his wife and his eighteen-month-old son to hunger. 'I did not even have the chance to bury them,' he recalls.

Vasilii Zatsepin was born in Russia's Orenburg region. His family also numbered eight. Their farm had included two horses, two bulls and two cows. In the spring of 1930 the whole family was driven out of its house: 'They took away our winter clothes, even our accordion.' First, the family was banished to the bare steppe 100 *versts* from the nearest village of any size and then in the spring of the next year they were all moved to Karaganda. 'You can imagine what we went through there, living in dugouts and later in huts made from peat and earth, with the most terrible overcrowding, exposed to hunger and cold … I lost my father, four brothers and little sister. My mother and I were the only ones to survive.'

Zatsepin's wife, Anastasia, was born in the Saratov region. In 1932 she had lost her mother in the Karaganda area and the following year her sister had died of starvation:

'Our mother fatally strained herself while trying to lift spadefuls of wet clay onto the roof. I ran round to the commandant's office to try and find help for burying my mother. When I got there the door was shut, but there was a tiny window in the door. I looked through it and inside I saw men stripped to the waist and beating someone with a whip, whom they were telling not to shout out. After that I made a quick getaway. I ran to the cemetery. There I found an old railwayman digging a grave for his dead wife. I asked him: "Uncle, please put my Mama into the same grave." "Of course dear, why not. Only you need to help me, dearie." I started straightaway to take earth out of the grave with my bare hands.'

Yakov Lutovinov was born in the village of Bykovo in the Voronezh region. In the spring of 1931, as a ten-year-old boy, he had ended up in Osakarovka. The family had gone on foot to somewhere on the banks of the River Ishim to build the ninth settlement for resettled persons. In the winter, while they were building the railway line, Yakov's sixteen-year-old brother Alexei died. They buried him, like many others, under the earthen railway embankment. Typhus struck the settlement where they were living. Each morning orderlies would go round the huts shouting: 'You, who're still alive, have you got dead bodies in there?'

Whole families were dying. 'In the winter they would collect the dead in piles and cover them with snow till the spring, because there was no way the people there could find the strength to dig the frozen earth. We were all swarming with lice as well. If it had not been for Dr Koch, not a single one of us would have survived.'[4]

In 1932 an OGPU special report was made in the Aktyubinsk region:

> Ivan Gorushka, a collective farmer from the 'Road to Communism' *kolkhoz* in the Sevastopol Village Soviet, has said: 'Soviet power has sunk to such a state that, when you go out into the fields to collect seeds, magpies peck at the eyes of our horses half-dead from hunger. And people are dying of hunger. When will Soviet power and its leaders get swallowed up? Devils have already caught up with Lenin; if only some people could be found who would wipe Kalinin and Stalin from the face of the earth. Never mind, just wait till Japan comes along, then we shall wipe them from the face of the earth straightaway. The people have been tortured long enough; we'll show them how to build socialism!'[5]

✤ ✤ ✤

Did present-day authors N. Mikhailov and N. Teptsov, in their research about collectivization, ever consider the sheer number of people who suffered from repression under Stalin? To ascertain this number, we must turn to Stalin himself. As we know, the 'Great Leader' did not like to leave living witnesses to his crimes; he was even more loath to admit to them. On one occasion, however, he said too much. On 19 February 1933, in a speech at the First All-Union Congress of Shock-Workers from the Collective Farms, Stalin noted that prior to collectivization, out of every 100 village holdings, 4–5 would have belonged to *kulaks*, 8–10 to prosperous peasants, 45–50 to middle peasants and 35 to poor peasants. He announced proudly that, when the creation of collective farms began, 'We managed to put a stop to that mismanagement and injustice, we smashed the *kulak* bondage.'

Now we can start calculating. Stalin worked out that among every 100 peasant holdings there were between twelve and sixteen belonging to *kulaks* or prosperous peasants. At the beginning of the 1930s there had been around 25 million peasant holdings in the Soviet Union. This meant that Stalin blacklisted 3 million of them. If we bear in mind that, on the basis of statistics from the period, each '*kulak*' family had on average 7–8 members, this meant that over 20 million people numbered among those 'liquidated as a class'. A terrifying number.[6]

In his book *Zaual* (The Ordeal), Zeitin Akishev describes what happened to him in May 1934 in a place now known as Akkuduk (in the Maiskii District of the Pavlodar Region):

> We were transporting seed grain: over 1,900 kilos of it. We drove into the settlement. Everything was empty: no people, no dogs. At the edge of the settlement we looked into a house, but there was nobody there. We went in through the curtain at the door, something usually to be found in houses belonging to young families. I took hold of the material and it came to bits in my hands. There were two skeletons on the bed. We realized they must have belonged to a young man and woman, because one had long black hair and the other much shorter hair. Perhaps newlyweds. They had probably decided to die together when the danger of a hungry death hung over them. They had died in a last embrace. That picture has never left me.[7]

In July 1933 delegates to the Sixth Plenary Session of the Kazakhstan Area Committee sent 'a Bolshevik greeting' to Comrade Kaganovich, addressing him as 'Comrade Stalin's finest comrade-in-arms'. The former coordinator of the collectivization campaign almost lived to celebrate his centenary. He had worked hard to send so many people to premature death, while he himself prospered, endured, not succumbing to the strain. He was destined for a long life.

Recently I had the opportunity to listen to an interesting story about him. In his later life Kaganovich began to behave rather oddly; as an old man, he used to go out into the yard, sit down on a bench with a bag of sweets and give them out to children who passed him by. He would sit there until he had handed out all the sweets, with a blissful smile on his face. The storyteller commented sadly: 'He was getting really old by then!'

THE GREAT DISASTER

The Great Soviet Encyclopaedia informed its readers: 'L.M. Kaganovich was awarded the Order of Lenin for the successful development of agriculture.' An award for collectivization; Lenin would have approved.

I heard another story about him recently. In 1937 the Party leaders in the Karkaralin region were brought to trial. Among the accused was Mansur Gataullin; in 1932 he had written, together with four others, the famous 'Letter of the Five' to the Area Committee about the excesses in the collectivization drive which had resulted in mass hunger.

Gataullin was permitted to speak after his other comrades. He pointed at them sitting on the bench for the accused and said:

'They are not Enemies of the People. It is I who am one. So try me, just me. Yet I am not an Enemy of the People, I am an enemy of the Enemies of the People. I became one when I arrived for a work assignment in Kent [the Kent District near Karkaralinsk]. When I got out of the car, there was nobody and nothing to be seen, just a long building for livestock. I opened the door and inside were corpses. The whole enormous building was piled high with corpses. Some of them still had their eyes open but you could see that they would die any minute.

'I went outside again. There was shouting coming from the road. Desperate ragged women were attacking my driver with knives. I shot into the air and they ran off.

'I looked around and a short way off there was a cauldron over a fire. Something was cooking. I walked over and lifted the lid; in the bubbling water a little foot floated up, or a hand or a child's heel.

'That was when I became an enemy of the Enemies of the People.'

❖

XVI. Requisitioning –
Hunger as a Weapon of Terrorism

During the three years of collectivization Goloshchekin did to Kazakhstan what Pol Pot did to Kampuchea. If it had not been for those four years of preparation, however, nothing would have been accomplished; by the time of the 'Great Breakthrough' he was fully in charge of the situation. The 'Bolshevization' of Party ranks had enabled him to dispose of all political opponents and replace 'national cadres' – those Kazakhs who thought independently – with obedient and servile people who would obey orders without question. The flower of the nation – writers and educators – were perishing in prison camps; the great national poet Shakarim had already been shot. Those with religious faith had been brought to heel. The campaign to 'Sovietize the *auls*' was an artificial means for fanning 'class struggle' – for pitting people against each other. Everything had been carefully orchestrated so as to crush the Kazakh people.

A hurricane of incredible strength swept over the steppe. The Kazakhs who used to greet each other with the question 'How fares the livestock?' had now been dispossessed of all their animals – of the very foundation for their way of life.

In 1929 there were 40 million head of livestock in Kazakhstan; in 1933 there were only 4 million left (it is likely that the actual number was smaller still). Moreover, in the main animal-breeding districts, where almost the whole herd had been concentrated in the old days, there were only 300–400,000 head of livestock left, according to the official figures. However, it has not been established how 'true' those figures actually are, whether they are exaggerations or underestimates.

Kazakhstan, which had once been the country's main supplier of meat, wool and leather, had turned into a land unable to feed itself.

Goloshchekin stifled even the slightest note of criticism and mercilessly punished any sign of insubordination, of which there were sadly few.

Death through hunger had claimed the first tens of thousands of victims and was threatening to turn into a calamity for the whole population; at this point a few people in the ranks of the Kazakhstan Bolsheviks were brave enough to mention this to the First Secretary of the Area Committee. On 4 July 1932 five communists sent the Area Committee a letter; they were G. Musrepov, M. Gataullin, M. Davletgaliev, E. Altynbekov and K. Kuanyshev. After the ritual expressions of praise for the Party basing its work on 'the correct Leninist principle' they moved on to the crux of the matter:

> Yet here in Kazakhstan, despite the enormous successes scored in industry and agriculture, with relation to animal breeding there is now a serious shortfall, which is turning Kazakhstan from the Soviet Union's main animal-breeding base into one of only secondary importance.

The 'enormous successes' in agriculture were as follows; after two years of the new policy the herds were 'only an eighth of the size they had been in 1930'. Moreover:

> This enormous loss and the unprecedented slaughtering of livestock took place not only in the holdings of the *bais* and *kulaks*, not only in the holdings of the middle and poor peasants but also – and most of all – in the common herds of the collective farms and the animals owned by individual farmers (this applied in part also to the state farms). We are confronted by a drop in livestock numbers such as never seen before (and since then in animal products) and now there are no grain reserves to be had until the new harvest.

The authors of this letter asked whether this was not just a consequence of 'sabotage' by the *bais*, but perhaps of 'leftist' distortions of the Central Committee line:

> Is our point of view correct with regard to real assistance for those returning to Kazakhstan after banishment, the basis of

whose work has been totally disrupted and who are still dying in enormous numbers in certain districts? How appropriate is it to remain silent about this, which might appear like a fear of Bolshevik self-criticism with regard to the catastrophic decline in livestock numbers and the starvation which has now gripped many Kazakh districts, where there are mass-scale deaths in certain places (since the beginning of the second half of this winter)?

Admitting that this picture appeared extremely distressing, they sought to glean at least some optimism from the profound thoughts of Comrade Stalin: 'Our difficulties are difficulties in which lie hidden opportunities for overcoming them.' They expressed surprise at the fact that:

Major successes scored with regard to the elimination of the *bais* as a class and the liberation of the working people in the *auls* from enslavement at the hands of the feudal *bais* have not, for some reason, been accompanied by rapid growth in animal breeding.

They came to the following conclusion:

It is essential to strike harder at these leftist deviations and also at the rightist opportunists as the main danger and to involve the whole Party organization more widely in this struggle, for we cannot tolerate indefinitely this leftist deviation, this Trotskyism in practice, which has led to rightist results.[1]

Goloshchekin regarded this letter as an attack on his authority and a nationalist manifestation of *bai*-style intentions. He threatened to expel them from the Party and to take them to court. Goloshchekin brought his favourite brutal pressure to bear and a mere week later four of the signatories (at the time Gataullin, the fifth signatory, was away on a work assignment) submitted letters of repentance to the Area Committee. On 15 July 1932, at a full sitting of the Area Committee Bureau and the control commission, the letter in question was dismissed as 'a complete misrepresentation of the socialist restructuring of Kazakhstan and the achievements of its nationalities policy',[2] though its authors were 'spared' and let off with a strict reprimand.

In August 1932, Uraz Isaev, Chairman of Kazakhstan's Council of People's Commissars and Goloshchekin's closest comrade-in-arms, realized both the seriousness of the situation and that Goloshchekin's opinion of himself was unshakeable; as such, he sent a letter to Stalin:

> In ten to twelve districts of Central Kazakhstan a considerable proportion of the population is currently starving. On the basis of approximate figures, 10–15,000 people died of hunger in the spring of this year. Nor have mass decampments to other regions and republics, which intensified particularly in 1931, stopped now. In many Kazakh districts the population has declined by more than half since 1929. The total number of peasant holdings in the region is less now than in 1931, by some 23–25 per cent. Hungry Kazakhs and their homeless children cluster round industrial enterprises or state farms in the Semipalatinsk and Aktyubinsk districts and at railway stations. They are engaged in stealing, they lay siege to the collective-farm fields and cut ears of corn. The hunger, concentration of people and the dirt everywhere have created conditions in which epidemics have been spreading: smallpox, typhus, dysentery and other diseases.

Naturally Uraz Isaev tried to coat the pill:

> The main factor which has led to the current state of animal breeding, must be recognized as the distortion of the Party's policy in Kazakhstan and your repeated instructions to promote collectivization in backward districts inhabited by indigenous peoples.

Isaev would seem to imply that Stalin did all he could to make sure that the nomads, who had been forcibly driven into the collective farms, should not suffer. The Chairman of the Council of People's Commissars went on to criticize his immediate superior:

> The Area Committee did not put right the distortions in a sufficiently resolute way. It believed (or wished to believe) that the Kazakhs had decided to join the collective farms, while only the *bais* and the nationalists opposed collectivization. A mood for

immediate total collectivization of the *auls* had taken hold of the Area Committee.

He went on to say:

> The fashion for total success without any shortcomings provided the soil in which the habit of whitewashing took root. The wish to overtake neighbouring districts and to achieve socialism more rapidly led to the official introduction of collectivization in the Kazakh *auls*. The use of campaigning as a method of work and the introduction of specially appointed functionaries to supervise the district committees created a whole series of so-called 'shock-worker campaigners' in the Area and in the districts and led to the appearance of dozens of *belsende* or activists (inside-out activists, I would say, who constitute a new parasitic stratum in the *auls*).

After going all out to obtain a special decision from the Central Committee regarding 'Kazakh *auls*' – mainly in connection with animal breeding – and suggesting a number of economic measures, Uraz Isaev turned to the most important issue in his conclusion:

> We cannot, of course, place all the blame for our miscalculations at the door of any one person. In this matter the whole Area Committee Bureau has questions to answer. I personally bear part of the responsibility for the miscalculations and errors made by both the Area Committee and in the whole of our Party work in Kazakhstan, since I am the leading Party representative in Kazakhstan. Yet in order to restructure our work boldly and to strengthen the leadership, it is essential to refresh and renew the leadership of the Area Committee. We all know the key role which the First Secretary has played. I myself feel that Goloshchekin, who has carried out such major work in Kazakhstan (the Sovietization of the *auls*, the fight against the formation of political groupings and so on), will not have the necessary strength to bring about the major changes in direction required after the stern criticism meted out regarding the mistakes made by the Area Committee and those he himself has made.[3]

However, the Central Committee's decision regarding animal breeding in Kazakhstan was adopted in September 1932. The Centre back in Moscow had approved some assistance for those nomads who had had to leave their *auls*; crumbs dropped into the hands of beggars which had turned black from hunger. The following winter hunger would kill hundreds of thousands of people. Goloshchekin was called back to Moscow in January 1933 at the height of the food crisis, yet he still managed to take some more leadership decisions.

The newspapers continued to chronicle the situation in the countryside. On 16 September 1932 *Bolshevik Stoker* carried the following article:

TRIAL OF KULAKS FOR SEIZING KOLKHOZ POTATOES

An unusually large crowd of people had come together in the club-house of Tikhonovka village. They had come to watch the show trial of those who had been seizing collective farm property – Grigorii Pogorelov and Vasilii Kosov.

Pogorelov was a defiant *kulak* and was always causing trouble amongst the collective farmers in the village of Tikhonovka, insisting that 'the struggle against losses was not obligatory' and so on. On 25 August Pogorelov decided to seize potatoes belonging to the collective farm so as to go and speculate at the local bazaar. He failed in his attempt. Pogorelov then came up with a new plan for theft, but this time with Kosov. The plan was to seize the potatoes at night on 31 August at around midnight. They stole more than 20 kilos of potatoes, but on the way back they were arrested.

The visiting assizes from the regional court, consisting of its chairman Kartsev and assessors Kovalyk and Balgabekov, reached the following verdict: 'Grigorii Ivanov is sentenced to the highest measure of social protection; he will be shot and his property will be confiscated. Vasilii Kosov is sentenced to ten years to be served in the Karlager prison camp.'

. . . Kirichenko, a kulak, had been working recently at the stone quarry belonging to Sev-Kazstroitrest (North Kazakhstan Construction Trust). On 27 August, on his way home from work, Kirichenko went into the field where potatoes for the collective farm were being planted and began stealing some. He was arrested at the scene of the crime, while digging up potatoes.

A proletarian court, consisting of Chairman Kartsev and assessors Kovalyk and Balgabekov, took into consideration the fact that Kirichenko is a class enemy – an incorrigible one at that – and that his crime had been classified after a decision made by the Central Executive Committee and Council of People's Commissars on 7 August. They reached the following verdict: Maxim Kirichenko was sentenced to the highest measure of social protection and was to be shot. The sentence when delivered met with approval from those present in the packed courtroom.

On 27 September 1932 *Bolshevik Stoker* carried the following article:

HENRI BARBUSSE ARRIVES IN MOSCOW

Moscow, TASS: A delegation of workers from Moscow plants and factories gathered when the train was due, so as to meet Barbusse. Representatives of the All-Union Society for Cultural Links with Foreign Countries, the International Organization for Helping Revolutionary Fighters and Soviet organizations for writers and art publishers were also present.

Henri Barbusse thanked everyone for the friendly welcome he had been accorded. He declared: 'I am burning with enthusiasm to see with my own eyes the enormous work that has been done to build socialism, which has been carried out by the workers and collective farmers of the USSR under the leadership of the Communist Party. Your successes and your enthusiasm warm the hearts of workers and the finest members of the intelligentsia throughout the world. As I set foot in the Land of the Soviets, I sense that there is something worth living and fighting for.

On 6 October *Bolshevik Stoker* published the following speech by Maxim Gorky made at a special meeting held in the Bolshoi Theatre on 25 September: 'Comrades, the invincible strength of our clever Party is an excellent inspiration to us all! I wish that it should only grow greater. (Ovation.)'

> On 12 November 1932 Goloshchekin sent the following telegram:
> Carry out the following measures immediately in these districts: Mamlyutskii, Bulaevskii, Tonkeri, Leninskii, Presnovskii, Stalinskii, Atbasar – stop deliveries of goods and trading. Stop loans for black-listed collective farms. Use OGPU staff to remove counter-revolutionary elements. If sabotage continues, raise the possibility of eviction of collective farmers outside the region into northern areas and their replacement by conscientious collective farm workers.
>
> Use brutal pressure, put an end to shameful lagging behind in grain procurement.

In his book *The Harvest of Sorrow: Soviet Collectivization and the Terror-Famine* (published in London, 1988), Robert Conquest writes:

> In the winter of 1931 it was admitted that the grandiose grain schemes of 1928 had failed. Only a quarter of the planned acreage was in use, and that most inefficiently. Official documents speak of shortages of livestock, seed, implements, construction materials. People were shifted from one *kolkhoz* to another in the (usually vain) hope that more livestock or grain might be available. By February 1932 about 87 per cent of all *kolkhozes* in Kazakhstan and 51.5 per cent of non-collectivized households (the latter almost entirely nomad herders) were without livestock. In 1926 nearly 80 per cent of the Kazakh population had earned their living through livestock; by the summer of 1930 this was down to 27.4 per cent. But agriculture did not provide an alternative, for the area under cultivation only increased by 17 per cent. These figures give some idea of the extent and depth of this man-made disaster.
>
> The disaster was due to economic and political mis-calculation in the narrow sense but even more profoundly to a misunderstanding of human cultures in the widest meaning of

that term. The mechanical and superficial nature of the Party's thought and practice shown in Kazakhstan is extraordinary, and extraordinarily revealing.

The famine in Kazakhstan was man-made, like the famine of 1921, in that it was the result of ideologically motivated policies recklessly applied. It was not, like the Ukrainian famine, deliberately inflicted for its own sake. Indeed in late 1932, 2 million pounds of grain were earmarked for aid to Kazakhstan – less than half a pound per person, but better than what the Ukraine was to get.

Nevertheless it has been suggested that the effectiveness of the unplanned Kazakh famine in destroying local resistance was a useful model for Stalin when it came to the Ukraine.[4]

It seems to me that the British historian is mistaken when he suggests that the famine in Kazakhstan, unlike that in the Ukraine, was unplanned. In both republics collectivization was carried out in the same way over approximately the same period of time. Furthermore, the Kazakh nomads and semi-nomads were forced – at shocking speed – to adopt a settled way of life. This meant that Kazakhstan was exposed to ordeals still more cruel. This may well explain why between a fifth and sixth of the Ukrainian population died, while in Kazakhstan the equivalent figure was a third. In addition the indigenous population of Kazakhstan suffered particularly badly; the Kazakh population was halved.

Stalin well understood the 'effectiveness' of famine as a tool for suppressing the peasantry, even before the collectivization of 1929–32; the finest Leninist of all was bound to have taken on the lessons of his teacher in 1921.

In July 1933, five months after Goloshchekin left for Moscow, Kazakhstan's communists spoke publicly for the first time about his 'mistakes'. They were allowed to voice these opinions for by this time the Party career of their former leader was over.

Goloshchekin was appointed Chef State Arbitrator for the Council of People's Commissars of the USSR in order to sweeten the fact that he had been 'relieved of his post'. We might wonder how the subject of his dismissal was broached; the human victims of his political manoeuvring were passed over in silence.

On instructions from Comrade Stalin, Goloshchekin made sure that nothing was said about the famine. The gang of thieves and murderers controlling the zone – by this time the 'zone' was the whole country – and their ringleaders demanded that their accomplices should speak of their work in eulogies only; however, even these were often viewed with suspicion for being insufficiently lavish. They commanded their subordinates to shout in rapture about the success of collectivization, thanks to which the USSR would soon catch up with and overtake the United States and Europe. Those who observed Party discipline duly shouted, happily and loudly.

The main speech delivered at the 'historic' Sixth Plenary Session of the Kazakhstan Area Committee was that of Uraz Isaev, who had dissociated himself from his former chief in good time. When referring to the disasters which had befallen the Kazakhs, he made the following statement: 'We have been through two difficult years; some people have suffered from hunger, lost a family member or left their original homes.'[5]

The most honest speech was that delivered by Nurmukhamedov from Gosplan, (the State Planning Committee): 'If you were to ask any of us to name exact figures as to how many people, how much livestock or what size of sown areas were involved, we would be unable to do so.' There were no accurate figures available, but surely there was data about the loss of human life? More to the point, nobody attending the Plenary Session had the right to make such figures public. They were strictly secret. However, certain examples were eloquent in themselves. Nurmukhamedov told his audience: 'My brother who had been a farm labourer for twelve years possessed one cow and had never sown any crops of his own, but in 1930 was required to deliver 80 kilos of grain to the state. In order to do so he sold his cow and some of his household utensils. Cases like that were common.'

The Aulie-Ata District had at one time been flourishing; in 1929 it had had 500,000 head of livestock, but in 1933 there were only 7,000 left. In April 1932, when the Karaganda region was set up, 99 per cent of the population was collectivized. None of the collective farmers had so much as a single sheep they could call their own. In the East Kazakhstan region only 15 per cent of the 1926 figure for livestock survived. In the Kegen District virtually nothing survived of their original one million head of livestock by the end of the collectivization campaign. 'Citizen Sarymbaev (in the Sarysu District) had a family of four and was left with just two camels and five sheep, after handing over eighty sheep and four cows. (Laughter.)'

The livestock belonging to the railway workers of the Turkestan-Siberian Railway was collectivized but then handed over to meat procurement authorities. At the Tyulkubas Station all the staff had their domestic animals confiscated. In the Chubartau District there had been 473,000 head of livestock, but in 1933 only 783 remained. Of the original 330,000 head of livestock in the Pavlodar District only 30,000 thousand remained by 1933.

Rozybakaev recalled:

> At the end of January 1932 I witnessed the horrific situation in the *auls*. I sent two telegrams to Goloshchekin saying the situation was grim and help was necessary. By way of reply he asked: 'You're worrying about questions of decampment, but aren't you willing to collect seed stocks?'

In the Kzyl-Orda District forced settlement programmes had been underway. People were rounded up in so-called 'settlement points' where there were no proper conditions for developing agriculture or animal breeding. In the summer any kind of life was impossible there. In the Chuiskii District people living within a radius of 150 kilometres were brought together. A memorandum recorded the following:

> In 1932 the settlement programme was carried out in three days, before the sowing and during it. People were assembled in Dzhaisan (a completely empty spot with no buildings). Carts were sent to the *auls* and militiamen went along too, who then drove people out of their *yurts*, made them get into the carts and then took them off. Four months later they had all scattered (half of them had gone into neighbouring Kirgizia).

The Zhana-Arkinskii and Kurgaldzhinskii districts along with certain others were classified as 'advanced' in terms of grain procurement, at a time when they were actually 'experiencing major food problems'. In 1931 the Turgai District had 100,000 head of livestock and in 1933 no more than 4,000. Shelykhmanov from the Area Military Committee made the following Statement: 'We wrote several memoranda in 1930 and 1931 to Isaev and Goloshchekin about the situation with regard to horse breeding. They did not pay even the slightest attention to our worries. Goloshchekin said that he knew more than I did about all that.'

What could be done when Goloshchekin maintained that the transition from a nomadic way of life to a settled one was impossible without victims? For him, reductions in numbers of livestock were an inevitable condition of that transition. This theoretician could, of course, 'explain' anything, even though he repeatedly uttered statements everyone knew to be ridiculous.

His mistakes also needed to be justified. Goloshchekin came up with a formula, claiming that the most important thing was not the number of livestock but its productivity, 'so that every animal should provide more meat, more fat and more wool'. This was said at a time when tens of thousands of animals were dying every week.

By 1933, in some of the collective farms there were only four or five horses left. There were hardly any draught animals left at all. The last of the cows had to be yoked up when it was time for sowing. Sickles and scythes were prepared for reaping. In some of the *auls* and villages there were no adult men left, so youths had to do the work instead. Any sense of ownership – which now, sixty years on, people are attempting to instil in the rural population, with limited success – had been knocked out of animal breeders and tillers of the land; the Land of the Soviets had needed 'collectivized man' – slaves bereft of any possessions.

An old man, one of the experienced agronomists from the 'Giant' collective farm who had somehow managed to survive the hurricane sweeping through rural Kazakhstan, wrote a petition; it was read out at the Plenary Session: 'I support the sowing campaign, the weeding campaign and the hoeing campaign and I also support this Party, so I am asking to be admitted to the ranks of the Party's supporters.' He was asking for the chance to work on the land.

Other speeches were also delivered at the 'historic' Sixth Plenary Session. Comrade Krist – representative of the Council of People's Commissars and the procurement committee – asked:

When did we begin to use repressive methods last year? It was already near the end of the campaign; by that time grain was already being dispatched (which is why there were not enough widespread repressive measures).

The distinctive feature of the new grain-procurement campaign, involving a strict combination of organizational work with the masses and legal methods of state coercion, was that we shall apply fines for the non-fulfilment of targets at the end of the first month of grain procurement.

By that time there was nothing left to collect and there were hardly any people left in the *auls* and the villages, but this functionary was still thinking about how he might best implement 'legal' repressive measures, informing his comrades about his 'positive experience' of state coercion.

Tulepov, another delegate attending the Plenary Session, 'came out with a proposal':

In the "Red East" commune in the Enbekshi-Kazakh District the communards caught individual farmer Esyutina out in the fields cutting ears of corn. The woman was handed over to the legal authorities, but the militia released her. Esyutina was the daughter of a *kulak* and her husband and brothers had been shot for their involvement with bandit gangs. Here we had an obvious class enemy, who was actively undermining our collective-farm production. We are not meting out sufficiently resolute punishments to class enemies.

People used to speak in cautious terms about the former First Secretary, fearful of the consequences. Comrade Yandulskii said: 'We showed too much trust in the authority of Comrade Goloshchekin. At every meeting of the Bureau, Tulepov used to praise Comrade Goloshchekin, talking about his impeccable Marxism-Leninism and so on.' Comrade Bekker asked the Plenary Session: 'How could we possibly speak out against the authority of Goloshchekin?'

The delegates did not forget about the need for self-criticism. D. Sadvokasov, a member of the Area Committee Bureau, admitted:

It would be ridiculous to think that we did not know that animal breeding was in decline and at a catastrophic speed. We knew that, but I, just like the rest of us and other comrades from the leadership, did not have enough courage to raise our voices and point that out. We feared the labels that would be attached to us.

When Izmukhan Kuramysov came forward to repent, his audience could not hide their amusement:

I deserve more reproaches [than Isaev] for my role was specifically to popularize the line adopted by the former leadership. It was I who raised those questions more than anybody else, more actively, more frequently and more incorrectly than anybody else. (Laughter.)

The Plenary Session finally acknowledged that the main causes of the economic collapse had been neither 'saboteurs' nor 'class enemies', but 'mistakes and distortions in the policy of the Party'. They did not, of course, blame the Party's policy itself; in the eyes of the people and those of the grass-roots Party workers, the 'Party line', just like those who devised it, was raised on an almost sacred pedestal, where mistakes did not exist. The delegates at the Plenary Session showered praise on the Central Committee of the All-Union Communist Party (Bolsheviks), which, through its decision of 17 September 1932, 'resolutely amended the incorrect policy of the Area Committee and charted a correct policy for the development of animal breeding'.

The Central Committee of the All-Union Communist Party (Bolsheviks) only amended the policy after the livestock had been almost completely wiped out, when the rural population had almost entirely died out or moved elsewhere. Kaganovich, who represented the Central Committee in the special commission to deal with Kazakhstan, decided that now, when there was virtually nothing left, it was possible to allow the collective farmers in grain-growing areas to keep more livestock. They were permitted between two and three cows, ten and twenty sheep, ten and twenty pigs and piglets; equivalent figures in animal-breeding areas would be up to 100 sheep, eight to ten cows, three to five camels and eight to ten horses. Why had such permission not been granted earlier when people were still alive and the livestock healthy?

The commentary regarding the stenographic record of the report delivered to the Sixth Plenary Session was written in the spirit of the times. Once again reference was made to gigantic success, to the fact that the consequences of excesses had been completely eliminated, to the fact that hundreds of thousands of those who had decamped were now able to continue farming, that all that remained of resettlement practices was the memory. It pointed out that in the meantime animal breeding in Kazakhstan was already 'moving forward at an unprecedented pace'. Once more people deceived themselves with flowery oratory.

Mekemtas Myrzakhmetov recalls:

> In the spring of 1933 the farmers were not trusted to sow the seed corn themselves. They would simply have eaten it. That year there were aeroplanes flying over the fields; they sowed the corn from the air. At the spots, where the planes turned round, grains of corn would fall into the furrow, people would start scrabbling about on the ground like chickens to pick them up. Large numbers of them.

❖ ❖ ❖

The Party line, laid down by the theoreticians of communism and put into practice by the Party's workers in the field, left strange, complex traces in the very souls of the Bolsheviks themselves.

I remember reading a thick manuscript of the recollections of a former GPU officer, sent to the press for publication. This man of long experience, who lived the last years of his life in a spa in the Northern Caucasus, recalled how in his distant, turbulent youth, bathed in the romance of socialist construction for the good of the whole people, he had stood guard with a rifle over 'enemies of the people', who had been resettled in the Karaganda steppes. A vague sense of dissatisfaction filled the heart of that veteran from the GPU; the people he served knew nothing of his exploits. After all he was called upon to take many risks. On one occasion he was confronted by an enormous hostile crowd; he was in command and there were few other guards. Sometimes there were angry shouts from the midst of the crowd. He had to keep his hand on his open holster day and night. Then he would have to go and search, to ask many careful questions, to find out who in the crowd had been shouting, expressing their disapproval. He would have to summon those disgruntled people to his office, investigate what was going on, interrogate and confront them one-to-one. He would have to prepare files for subsequent legal proceedings. Of course those people would be driven off later, convicted for shouting and later sent to a camp. Nevertheless he had felt insecure and exposed all the time. Those two or three years when he worked as a commander on special assignments in the Karaganda steppes had been a difficult, dangerous time; he had had strict instructions not to talk to anyone about them. Now though (he recorded his reminiscences at the end of the 1970s) it was right and proper to tell the younger generation about his secret assignments. He felt he should let them know how Cheka officers had to serve in those days, let them learn from his experience.

Another veteran of the same service recalled his youth in a filmed interview (the text is reproduced below):

> At that time, we Komsomol members, used to be on watch day and night. We would be on duty at HQ and have to call out people for interrogation: at 11pm, 2 o'clock in the morning, 5 o'clock in the morning. We would keep them under guard, until they collapsed from the strain. When they did, they would hand over the grain they had been hiding: sometimes 10, sometimes 15 kilos. That's what we were reduced to in those days.

One of the letters from the archive, originally sent to the Party's Regional Committee, contained the following:

> It's impossible to work here any more. All the hostile people have their heads held high and are ready to tear us apart. They believe that we are guilty for the fact that they have been left without grain. It's dangerous to walk about here in the evenings. We were sent here without any weapons.
>
> The economic situation in the villages is very grim. The last harvest failed. Many people have left for places where the grain situation is better.
>
> As for our illegal actions, they are not really our fault. The work is extremely difficult. Anyone who is spineless or who has a weak character would not be able to cope. At the same time I

have no wish whatsoever to be arrested for not fulfilling our plan. Please let me have some leave to go to Petropavlovsk! I have a small child there, whom I have had to leave in the care of strangers. While I have been away he has been ill a number of times. I can't bear living apart from him any longer.

[Signed] Lebedeva.

Let us turn to a letter from one of the implementers of the plan – a man of far higher rank than the previous witnesses – from the second level of the leadership: namely Turar Ryskulov, Deputy Chairman of the RSFSR Council of People's Commissars. His was a truly amazing story.

In December 1929 the Central Committee of the All-Union Communist Party (Bolsheviks) prepared a resolution on the subject of collectivization; many members of the Central Committee at that time objected to the rapid pace proposed. Stalin, however, subjected the draft version of the resolution to harsh criticism. He demanded acceleration of the creation of collective farms; he also demanded that all instructions regarding levels of collectivization of livestock, farming implements and so on be dropped from the text. R. Medvedev wrote on this subject:

> In the final variant of the resolution the time made available for collectivization was substantially reduced for the Northern Caucasus and the middle reaches of the Volga. Other sections that were dropped were those regarding procedures for collectivizing the means of production and livestock and those regarding peasants being permitted to keep sheep and goats, poultry and farm implements in their individual plots. Instructions were also omitted regarding methods for eliminating the *kulak* class and using *kulaks* on the collective farms, as long as they recognized the authority of the *kolkhoz* and were willing to carry out all the obligations incumbent upon its members. The final version was aimed at ensuring that collectivization be completed in the main grain-growing areas by the autumn of 1930 or the spring of 1931 and in other regions by the autumn of 1931 or the spring of 1932.[6]

The only person who 'out-lefted' Stalin was the member of the Politburo commission responsible for total collectivization, the Deputy Chairman

of the RSFSR Council of People's Commissars: Turar Ryskulov. Below
follows an extract from the journal entitled *Questions of the History of the
CPSU*:

> On 3 January 1930 T.R. Ryskulov, Deputy Chairman of
> the Council of People's Commissars and member of its
> [collectivization] commission, sent a note to the Politburo
> with amendments to the draft of the resolution regarding
> the pace of collectivization. He suggested firstly that the pace
> of collectivization should be stepped up in districts growing
> industrial crops and engaged in animal husbandry; secondly, that
> the first part of Point 3 be removed from the draft resolution,
> in which it was stated that in districts where collectivization
> was total, the main mass of collective farmers would consist of
> middle peasants [this was motivated by the fact that presenting
> the issue as such would give it an incorrect class orientation, since
> – in Ryskulov's opinion – the dominant role in the collective
> farms would be played by the poor peasants and only the poorest
> echelons of the middle peasantry, and since they supported total
> collectivization, they were bound to impose their wishes on the
> middle peasant masses]; thirdly, that the point be removed from
> the commission's resolution, in which it was stated that when
> joining a collective farm a peasant should be allowed to keep
> sheep and goats, farming implements and a cow and, in exchange
> for all that, there were categorical instructions that everything
> should be collectivized 'without reservation'; fourthly, increase
> the percentage of the deductions to be made over into the
> indivisible fund to a level of approximately 50 per cent of the
> total collectivized funds of the collective farmers and to exclude
> from the draft the point according to which the collective farmers
> retain the right to leave the collective if they so wish.

Ryskulov's amendments pushed the voluntary principle into the
background, putting pressure on the peasant masses as the basis for the
organization of collective farms. In his note to the Politburo Ryskulov
emphasized that the commission sought 'to replace the revolutionary
character of the collective farm by over-riding voluntariness'. In essence
Ryskulov's amendments were heading in the same direction as Stalin's

initial comments; they were aimed at forcing the peasant masses' transition to the path of collectivization using artificial methods.

As Ryskulov and Stalin's amendments were made to the draft, another section was removed, prohibiting Party workers and executive committees from proclaiming districts with a low percentage of collectivized farms as districts with 100 per cent collectivization. In the final version of the resolution, another important point was removed concerning the role of the Soviets in the creation of collective farms.[7] Two days later on 5 January 1930 the resolution was finally adopted.

Surely Ryskulov must have comprehended the monstrous storms he, together with Stalin and his cronies, was inflicting on the land. He must surely have known that this tempest would soon descend on the Kazakh steppes. Of course he realized this; he was aware of what would happen, after all, he was a man who, if nothing else, knew the conditions in which the Kazakhs lived. Had he been keen to show that he was 'more of a communist than a Kazakh'?

It is possible that pressure from Stalin was to blame, or indeed pressure from Ryskulov's immediate superior S.I. Syrtsov, the Chairman of the Council of People's Commissars of the RSFSR (who had been one of the main instigators of the genocide of the Don Cossacks in 1919); he had also demanded that 'the collective movement should be intensified' in animal-breeding districts. Perhaps Syrtsov ordered Ryskulov to send the note to the Politburo on instructions from his own superior? Either way, two days later the resolution was adopted by Stalin, opening the way for arbitrary violence on an unprecedented scale.

Ten years earlier Ryskulov had been helping to save his fellow Kazakhs who had been dying of hunger; now he was involved in formulating the policy for a still more terrible disaster and, worse, in implementing it. His Bolshevik instincts had triumphed over his earlier humanity, though his soul still suffered at the plight of his hapless people (according to his wife Aziza he was deeply troubled by what he had done). After the Northern Caucasus, the Ukraine, the Volga region and the Urals, hunger was to befall Kazakhstan. At the end of 1930 Ryskulov tried to soften the blow dealt to the Kazakhs by the first wave of collectivization, publishing an article in *Soviet Steppes* entitled: 'Attention should be shown to Animal Breeding in the Nomadic and Semi-nomadic Districts.' However, this timid attempt to put the situation right was too late to make any difference and, in addition, was subjected to harsh criticism by Goloshchekin's followers.

Later Ryskulov found the courage to write to Stalin; he attempted three times to lighten the disastrous force of destruction unleashed upon the Kazakh people. His first two letters date from late 1932 and the last from the beginning of 1933, when hunger had already claimed the majority of its victims.

The third letter, written on 9 March 1933, was the most detailed. Its first pages are the most striking:

MOSCOW, KREMLIN, CENTRAL COMMITTEE OF THE ALL-UNION COMMUNIST PARTY (BOLSHEVIKS)

For Comrade Stalin.

Copies to the Agricultural Dept of the CC ACP (Bolsheviks), to Kaganovich, to the Council of People's Commissars of the USSR and to Comrade Molotov.

Decampments of Kazakhs from one district to another and beyond the borders of Kazakhstan, which began at the end of 1931, increased by the following spring but then, followed by the return of some of those involved (thanks to the measures introduced in the interim) in the summer of 1932, are once again on the increase. Deaths stemming from hunger and epidemics in a number of Kazakh districts and among those who decamped are now assuming such proportions, that it is necessary for the central bodies of our administration to intervene urgently. A situation of the kind which has emerged in Kazakhstan regarding a certain part of the Kazakh population is not to be found in any other region or republic. Those who have decamped are taking disease with them into neighbouring regions and along the Tashkent, Siberian and Zlatoust railways. The partial measures drawn up for the Soviets (in particular, by the Council of People's Commissars of the RSFSR) do not resolve the issue. Help provided in good time, based on a resolution of the Central Committee to send food, failed to a significant extent to achieve its goal. Given the great importance of this question I am writing to ask you to acquaint yourself with this letter and intervene in this situation, so as to save the lives of many people destined to die of starvation.

According to the most recent approximate figures obtained on the spot, the numbers of Kazakhs who have decamped into neighbouring regions are at present as follows: 40,000 in the middle reaches of the Volga; 100,000 in Kirgizia; 50,000 in Western Siberia; 20,000 in Karakalpakia and 30,000 in Central Asia. These Kazakhs were even to end up in such distant places as Kalmykia, Tadzhikistan, the far north and so on. Some of the Kazakhs concerned led by *bais* decamped into Western China. Decampment of this kind by Kazakhs is occurring for the first time in Kazakhstan. It is not just a question of nomadic movement, which usually takes place in the summer over small distances – movement of people with animals – but for the most part it involves hungry people fleeing in search of food. In certain districts decampments of this kind involved up to 40–50 per cent of the whole population. Most of the people involved have not been able to find work and they are exposed to very harsh conditions, while the numbers of Kazakh workers taken on in factories, state farms and machine- and tractor-stations are currently being reduced. Indeed the general reduction of the workforce in such enterprises is usually achieved entirely at the expense of Kazakhs, if there are any employed in them (in particular several dozen Kazakhs have now started arriving in Moscow's stations after being dismissed from work in forestry and other projects). The actual process of such decampment serves to weaken the collective farms they leave and often goes hand in hand with the looting of the belongings such families leave behind them, with the sale of their *yurts* (often their only homes) and the wasting or sickness of their livestock, if they have any, in the course of their travels, during which they gradually sell off anything of value they still have left.

Yet the most negative phenomena resulting from these decampments and the undermining of the Kazakhs' farms are the hunger and epidemics among the Kazakhs, which are once again assuming a frightening scale.

Ryskulov suggested that work should be provided for those Kazakhs who had decamped, that immediate help should be given to the starving, that 6,400 tonnes of grain be issued to them as early as March, that houses be built for those who opted for the settled way of life and livestock be procured for the now ruined farms.

❖ ❖ ❖

Our recent history sometimes appears like a monstrous nightmare that defies the imagination. Human life has never lost its value to such an extent before. Never had such enormous torrents of blood been spilled. How could it come about that before 1941, some twenty-five years after the 'Great October Revolution', the population of the former prison of the peoples liberated by the Bolsheviks was reduced by a third through violence and hunger?

For some that state was no more than fuel for stoking World Revolution. Fuel made up of individual men, women and children.

How could that have come about?

Reasons can be sought in many places: in racial conflicts and religious wars, in the transformation or restructuring of world order by both visible and mysterious forces. Some might say that God let it come about, after the people had turned their back on Him and betrayed the Lord's Anointed.

The root of all evil came with this song:

All shall be burnt or destroyed,
Wiped from the face of the Earth,
Let's cast the old Sun into the void
And cheer at the New Sun's birth!

The song was to become the people's anthem. Work began to create 'Soviet man' from the human masses of the accursed past destroying all that was finest, all that constituted the spiritual and physical core and strength of the past thousand years. A 'new sun' was lit in the darkness of slaughter, while the 'new man' was fashioned from raw human flesh. Instead of divine light there came Lenin's lamp.

How had he expressed it? 'Socialism is accountability.'

They say that God remembers each and every one of us, but in this instance it is hard to hold on to such faith. Various calculations have been made, but during the thirty-seven years between 1917 and Stalin's death in 1953 the population of the Soviet Union decreased by between 70 and 90 million. A similar number of people – perhaps even more – were killed in wars, shot during 'peacetime', wiped out by hunger and disease or tortured to death in prison camps. The number of victims is in the region of 10 million if not more.

Between 10 and 20 million people died of starvation during collectivization. The largest numbers of victims were in the main grain-growing and animal-breeding districts – Russia, the Don Valley, Northern Caucasus, Volga region, the Ukraine and Kazakhstan – areas which should have been feeding the whole country. It took five years for the country to make good the losses suffered during the collectivization period. If we bear in mind that it took nine years to restore population numbers after the Great Patriotic War (the number of those killed in the war, using the most up-to-date figures, has been calculated as somewhere between 25 and 46 million), then the scale of the disaster brought on by enforced collectivization is clear.

Nobody knows exactly how many people died of hunger in Kazakhstan in 1931–33; Robert Conquest puts the figure at around 2 million, Z. Abylkhozhin and M. Tatimov state that 'losses directly attributable to hunger' came to 1,700,000.[8] B. Tulepbaev and V. Osipov conclude that hunger claimed between 1,050,000 and 1,100,000 Kazakh lives, along with 200,000 to 250,000 representatives of other ethnic groups living in Kazakhstan.

Looking at population censuses it emerges that it was not until the 1970s that the indigenous population of the republic was restored to its original size.

It is, however, not just a question of the numbers of the dead. We need also to comprehend what had died in their minds and hearts.

XVII. The Demon Flew
Inside the Hurricane

On 4 October 1933, to celebrate the day Kazakhstan was founded, the community of Kazakh students studying in Moscow invited Mirzoyan (Goloshchekin's successor) and Isaev to speak to them; they both happened to be in the capital. Mirzoyan declined the invitation but Uraz Isaev accepted.

After he had finished his speech, questions from the students came thick and fast. Most of them concerned what was currently going on in Kazakhstan, asking why people were in such dire straits. Eventually someone came out with: 'Why are Kazakhs dying of hunger?'

Isaev turned red in the face and shouted: 'that was a question from a *bai's* son!'

The young man stood up, looked him straight in the eye and said: 'I am from Ayaguz. Last summer I was planning to spend my holidays in that *aul*. I sent a telegram to let them know when I was coming. When I arrived nobody came to meet me at the station. I walked home. When I got to the *aul* it was empty. All the *yurts* were there as usual, people's belongings were all in place, but there were no people. No one at all. I started wandering about in the steppe. Then suddenly, right by the *aul*, I saw corpses in a ravine. They were all lying there – my parents, my relatives, all the people from my home. The ditch was full, it had the whole *aul* inside it.'

❖ ❖ ❖

Not far from Kustanai, Gabit Musrepov came across one of the many deserted, though newly organized, settlements made up of *yurts*. This strange installation had its own streets and each *yurt* had a number on

378

it. Everything was arranged as if it was in an ordinary town. Even street signs had been provided: Kuramysov Street, Ernazarov Street, Isaev Street, Roshal Street. Each street bore the name of one of the Kazakhstan 'leaders'. The settlement itself bore the name of Goloshchekin.

There were no people in it: they had all died.

Nettle seeds are tough, one managed to survive even from the days of collectivization. In the Kustanai region there was until very recently a 'Goloshchekino' station. So, Filipp Isaevich's name 'lived on' after all – in the very place where he had driven the largest numbers of people to their hungry death. The people of the steppes used to refer to him as Ku Zhak – a Kazakh version of his surname – which in Russian literally means 'Bare Cheeks'.

He was arrested shortly before the war. The investigation lasted a long time and for unexplained reasons it was never completed. On 28 October 1941 Goloshchekin was shot on instructions from Beria, near the village of Barbysh in the Kuibyshev region. Other Bolsheviks were shot alongside him. They were all accused of espionage in the interests of international imperialism. Was he killed in keeping with the cruel code of the criminal world, shot by fellow criminals careful to sweep away all the carefully concealed traces of his political activity together with its real implications? Did one snake simply swallow another?

In the *Historical Encyclopaedia* his entry reads as follows: 'Illegally executed during the period of Stalin's cult of personality. Posthumously rehabilitated.' Goloshchekin has been recorded as a victim; there is not a single word about him as an executioner. Things like that were not recorded in Soviet encyclopaedias.

In a small district newspaper in the Aktyubinsk region, on the day when the victims of the 1930s famine were remembered for the first time in June 1992, a poem appeared written by one Bakhytgerei Amangeldin; one verse in particular provides a fitting epitaph:

Goloshchekin, may you call out from Hell!
After forcing men to eat each other.
You, cursed monster, with a soul to sell,
So keen to set brother against brother!

379

Let us return a last time to the deserted steppes, just before autumn when all is clear beneath the broad shimmering skies; people left this behind not of their own free will, but because they were unable to survive there. They did not live to tell the tale. They did not leave heirs behind them. No traces of these people remained as they fell silent, somewhere far away in those terrible years. Should not their innocent blood have a voice?

There is a Kazakh folktale about Er-Tostik – a young hero born to Old Man Ernazar and his wife at a time of famine.

A great famine befell the steppe and people began to move away to other regions. The eight sons of Ernazar left with the others. He and his wife remained at home with a stock of food to last a year, which they hoped would enable them to survive the catastrophe.

The year passed and their food was finished. One day, when the old woman opened the hole at the top of her *yurt*, Ernazar caught sight of a piece of cured horse brisket or *tostik*. They boiled the meat, ate it and grew stronger. Then, at the appointed time, a son was born to them by the name of Tostik.

He grew fast and within a year he was of true heroic stature. No one was able to outfight him and he was a finer shot than all other men. When he went hunting, he brought home game and his parents were proud in their contentment. They began to live well and to eat their fill.

One fine day Tostik shot at a goldfinch and damaged its wing. The bird began to hop across the grass and then hopped into the neighbour's *yurt*, followed by the huntsman. Inside an old woman was spinning yarn. The bird hopped through the threads, but Tostik became caught in them.

'Oh, you idle boy!' said the old woman angrily. 'Instead of lazing around, you would do better to go and look for your brothers.'

It was the first time Tostik had heard that he had any brothers. His parents had never mentioned them. He began asking his mother questions.

'That half-witted old woman is lying. You haven't got any brothers!'

A few days later Tostik was playing knucklebones with the son of the peevish old woman. He lost his temper and accidentally almost knocked him for six. The old woman burst out this time even more angrily: 'A curse on you, you wretch! Your strength will be the death of you! You'd be better off going to look for the bones of your lost brothers.'

Tostik thought for a while and then went to ask his mother questions again. She would say nothing.

Then he asked her for something to eat. His mother gave him some wheat grains and told him to prepare some gruel. Tostik started heating the grains and then said: 'Why don't you try it Mother, to see if the food's ready?'

The old mother took some of the hot grains and her son seized hold of her hand and squeezed it with all his might.

His mother started pleading with him: 'Let go my son, it's burning me!'

Tostik responded with a command: 'Tell me all the truth about my brothers and then I'll let go.'

'All right, I'll tell you.'

When Tostik let go of her mother's hand, she began her story: 'You had eight brothers and in the year of the terrible famine they left. They did not come back. Are they still alive? Nobody knows.'

That is the beginning of the story about the hero, who set off to look for his lost brothers.

The most important thing about this story is the way it ends. Heroes are usually kind and would never hurt anyone weak, but this one had to inflict pain on his own old mother. He must have gone through emotional torment to take such a step.

In order to find out the truth we have to conquer our fears when confronted with suffering. It may be painful but we cannot live without that truth. Er-Tostik understood that.

What was that? There was a demon flying in the hurricane. It just went flying, on and on …

Lord forgive us our trespasses, lead us back to the true path.

Glossary

Aksakal – male elder (*Kazakh*)

alka – circle (*Kazakh*)

aul – rural village (*Kazakh*)

azap – suffering, pain (*Kazakh*)

basmachi – from Basmac, a Turkic language, meaning to make a foray, raid; an anti-Soviet uprising against Russian Imperial and Soviet rule by the Muslim, largely Turkic peoples of Central Asia. The movement's roots lay in the 1916 violence that erupted over conscription of Muslims by the Russian Empire for service in World War I. In the months following the October 1917 Revolution, renewed violence developed into a major uprising centered in the Ferghana Valley, soon spreading across all of Soviet Turkestan. Guerrilla and conventional warfare lasted for years in various regions, and the violence was both anti-Soviet and anti-Russian.

baza – base (*Kazakh, Russian*)

bai/bais – class of affluent farmers (*Kazakh*)

belsende – activists (*Kazakh*)

dashnaks – members of the Armenian National Party known as 'Dashnaktsutyun'

dombra – Kazakh national musical instrument: a long-necked stringed instrument from the lute family. They have been used by Kazakhs and their ancestors for more than two thousand years

dzhigit – a brave young horseman (*Kazakh*)

ishans – leaders of Muslim communities

keregekyu – tradition whereby parents sent their young daughters to entertain guests (*Kazakh*)

kishlak – rural settlement of semi-nomadic people (*Kazakh*)

kolkhoz – Soviet collective farm (*Russian*)

konsy – poor peasants (*Kazakh*)

kulak – affluent Russian farmer

kumys – fermented mare's milk (*Kazakh*)

kurbashi – head of defence (*Kazakh*)

lakha – large silvery fish

namaz – Islamic prayer ritual
omul – fish; species of the salmon family
pelmeni – dumplings consisting of a meat filling wrapped in thin, unleavened dough; from cuisines of the indigenous Siberian and Turkic peoples (*Ugric, Mansi*)
perestroika – restructuring (*Russian*)
samovar – a metal vessel traditionally used to heat and boil water
taiga – the coniferous evergreen forests of sub-arctic lands, covering vast areas of northern North America and Eurasia (*Turkic*)
toi – feasts (*Kazakh*)
tundik – ventilation hole in the roof of a *yurt* (*Kazakh*)
ulems – Muslim theologians and lawmakers
verst – unit of distance: 1 *verst* – 1.067 kilometres (*Russian*)
volost – a rural Soviet (Russian)
yakut – Turkic people who mainly inhabit the Sakha (Yakutia) Republic
yurt – a traditional nomadic tent

Terminology
AUCP (B) – All-Union Communist Party (Bolsheviks)
Cheka – secret police
Gosplan – body responsible for economic planning within the Soviet Union
Great-power chauvinism – the policy and politics of the ruling body, of which great-Russian chauvinism is one manifestation
Kirgiz – the term was a Russian invention, intentionally introduced to erase reference to the Kazakhs and Turks as independent and separate peoples
Komsomol – the All-Union Leninist Young Communist League
New Economic Policy (NEP) – response to War Communism implemented by Lenin; known as 'state capitalism', it allowed small private enterprises and abolished state grain acquisition
Nepmen – entrepreneurs who took advantage of New Economic Policy; later looked upon with disfavour by Party leaders
NKVD – the People's Commissariat for Internal Affairs (secret police)
OGPU – Joint State Political Directorate (secret police)
Orgburo – body responsible for organizational decisions within the Soviet Union
Politburo – central governing body of the Soviet Union
RCP (B) – Russian Communist Party (Bolsheviks)

RSFSR – Russian Socialist Federal Soviet Republic (Russia)

War Communism – strict system adopted during the Russian Civil War (1918–21) to control the circulation and distribution of commodities; it included the nationalization of industry and state acquisition of food surpluses

Weltpolitik – world policy

Notes

Introduction

1. Other important publications of this period include: Abylkhozhin, Z. B., Kozybaev, M. K. (1989) 'Kazakhstanskaya tragediya', in *Voprosy Istorii* (1989) 7, pp. 53–71; Abylkhozhin, Z. B. (ed.) (1991) *Istoriya Kazakhstana. Belye pyatna*, Alma-Ata.
2. Davies, R. W. (1989) *Soviet History in the Gorbachev Revolution*, Bloomington: Indiana University Press, p. 1.
3. Interview with Valeriy Mikhailov (9.12.2008). http://rus.azattyq.org/content/Valeriy_Mikhailov/1357347.html. Retrieved last: 29.8.2013.
4. Ohayon, I. (2006) *La sédentarisation des Kazakhs dans l'URRS de Stalin: Collectivisation et changement social,* 1928–1945, Paris; Pianciola, N. (2004) 'Famine in the Steppe: The Collectivization of Agriculture and the Kazakh Herdsmen, 1928–1934', *Cahiers du monde Russe*, 45 (2004) 1/2, pp. 137–192.
5. Cameron, S. (2010) *The Hungry Steppe: Soviet Kazakhstan and the Kazakh Famine,* 1921–1934. Ph.Diss., Yale; Payne, M. (2011) 'Seeing Like a Soviet State: Settlement of the Nomadic Kazakhs, 1928–1934', in Alexopoulos, G., Hessler, J. and Tomoff, K. (ed.) *Writing the Stalin Era: Sheila Fitzpatrick and Soviet Historiography*, Houndmills, pp. 59–86; Kindler, Robert (2014, forthcoming) *Stalins Nomaden: Herrschaft und Hunger in Kasachstan*, Hamburg: Hamburger Edition; Ayagan, B. G. et al. (ed.) (2012) Pravda o golode, 1932–1933 godov, Almaty: Litera-M.

Chapter II

1. *Kazakhstanskaya Pravda.* 7 November 1932.
2. *Soviet Encyclopaedic Dictionary.* Moscow, 1987. Fourth edition.
3. *The Civil War and Military Intervention in Russia.* Moscow, 1972.
4. *Greater Soviet Encyclopaedia.* Vol. 7. Moscow, 1963.

5. *Soviet Historical Encyclopaedia.* Moscow, 1963.
6. N.K. Krupskaya, *Reminiscences of Lenin.* Moscow, 1968, pp. 197–8.
7. Quotation from: *Questions of the History of the CPSU.* 1966, No. 8.
8. *Correspondence of V.I. Lenin and the Editorial Board of the Newspaper Iskra with Social-Democratic Organizations in Russia. 1900–1903.* Vol. I. Moscow, 1969, p. 302.
9. *History of the Communist Party of the Soviet Union.* Vol. 2. Moscow, 1967, p. 411.
10. Y.M. Sverdlov, *Selected Works.* Vol. 1. Moscow, 1957.
11. Quotation from: Y.P. Plotnikov, *Y.M. Sverdlov in Exile in Turukhan.* Krasnoyarsk, 1976, p. 20.
12. K. Lisovskii, *In Exile in Turukhan.* Novosibirsk, 1947.
13. Y.P. Plotnikov, Op. cit.
14. Ibid.
15. Ibid.
16. Ibid.
17. Ibid.
18. Ibid.
19. Ibid.
20. K.T. Novgorodtseva-Sverdlova, *Yakov Mikhailovich Sverdlov.* Moscow, 1976.
21. Ibid.

Chapter III
1. *Questions of the History of the CPSU.* 1966, No. 8.
2. *Questions of the History of the Urals.* Sverdlovsk, 1967.
3. K.T. Novgorodtseva-Sverdlova, Op. cit.
4. Ibid.
5. N.A. Sokolov, *The Killing of the Tsar and his Family.* Moscow, 1991, p. 39.
6. E. Gorodetskii, Y. Sharapov, *M. Sverdlov.* Sverdlovsk, 1981.
7. P. Gilliard, *Emperor Nicholas II and his Family.* Vienna, 1921, p. 237.
8. Ibid., p. 237.
9. E. Gorodetskii, Y. Sharapov, Op. cit.
10. Quotation from: I. Nepein, 'After the Shooting', Urals News. 1988, No. 11.
11. Ibid.
12. N.A. Sokolov, Op. cit., p. 147.

13. Ibid., p.149.
14. Ibid., p. 58.
15. *Ogonyok* (Little Flame). 1990, No. 22, p.25.
16. Quotation from: I. Nepein, Op. cit.
17. N.A. Sokolov, Op. cit., p. 187.
18. E. Gorodetskii, Y. Sharapov, Op. cit.
19. Ibid.
20. N.A. Sokolov, Op. cit., p. 241.
21. Ibid.
22. Ibid.
23. Ibid.
24. Quotation from: *Literaturnaya Rossiya* (Literary Russia). 1990, No. 38.
25. I. Nepein, Op. cit.
26. *Ogonyok* (Little Flame). 1989, No. 21.
27. *Literaturnaya Gazeta* (Literary Gazette). 4 October 1989.
28. *Molodaya Gvardia* (The Young Guard). 1990, No. 7.
29. Quotation from: I. Nepein, Op. cit.
30. E. Gorodetskii, Y. Sharapov, Op. cit.
31. Ibid.
32. Quotation from: N.A. Sokolov, Op. cit.
33. P. Gilliard, Op. cit.
34. See: *Ogonyok* (Little Flame). 1990, No. 22, p. 26.
35. Quotation from: *Rodina* (Homeland). 1989, No. 5, p. 89.
36. Ibid.
37. L.D. Trotsky, *A History of the Russian Revolution.* Moscow, 1990, p. 191.
38. *Ogonyok* (Little Flame). 1989, No. 39.
39. Quotation from: *Nash Sovremennik* (Our Contemporary). 1990, No. 4, p. 158.
40. *Kazakhstanskaya Pravda.* 12 January 1927.
41. Quotation from: I. Nepein, Op. cit.
42. Ibid.
43. Ibid.
44. *Nash Sovremennik* (Our Contemporary). 1989, No. 11, p. 166.
45. *Ogonyok* (Little Flame). 1990, No. 2, p. 26.

Chapter IV
1. *Ogonyok* (Little Flame). 1989, No. 1.
2. Ibid.

3. *Questions of the History of the CPSU.* 1958, No. 2, p. 73.
4. T. Ryskulov, *The Revolution and the Indigenous Population of Turkestan.* Tashkent, 1925, p. 35.
5. *Foreign Military Intervention and the Civil War in Central Asia and Kazakhstan.* Alma-Ata, 1963, p. 90.
6. Quotation from: T. Ryskulov, Op. cit., pp. 39–40.
7. Ibid., pp. 41–2.
8. Ibid., p. XIII.
9. Ibid., p. 9.
10. Ibid., p. 58.
11. Ibid., p. 72.
12. Ibid., p. 77.
13. Ibid., p. 83.
14. Ibid., p. 100.
15. Ibid., p. 101.
16. Quotation from: M. Chokaev, *Turkestan under the Regime of the Soviets.* Paris, 1935.
17. T. Ryskulov, Op. cit., p. XII.
18. Quotation from: *Yunost* (Youth). 1990, No. 1, pp. 83–4.
19. *Questions of the History of the CPSU.* 1958, No. 2, p. 76.
20. Ibid., p. 77.
21. V.I. Lenin, *Complete Collected Works,* Fourth edition. Vol. 30. p. 117.
22. Ibid., p. 134.
23. Ibid., p. 138.
24. Ibid., p. 139.
25. Ibid., p. 140.
26. V.I. Lenin, *Complete Collected Works.* Vol. 53. p. 190.
27. A. Azizkhanov, *The Turkburo: Authorized Body of the Central Committee of the Russian Communist Party (Bolsheviks).* Tashkent, 1977, p. 41.
28. *Yunost* (Youth). 1990, No. 1, p. 82.
29. *Questions of the History of the CPSU.* 1958, No. 2, p. 81.
30. A. Azizkhanov, Op. cit., p. 35,
31. *Questions of the History of the CPSU.* 1958, No. 2, p. 79.
32. Ibid., p. 82.
33. Ibid., p. 84.
34. Ibid.
35. V.I. Lenin, *Complete Collected Works.* Vol. 41. p.435.
36. *Kzyl-Uzbekistan.* Tashkent, 9 April 1925.

37. *Soviet Steppes.* 3 December 1925.
38. Ibid., 4 December 1925.
39. Report of the Kazakhstan Area Committee of the Russian Communist Party (Bolsheviks) to the Fifth All-Kazakhstan Conference of the RCP(B). Kzyl-Orda, 1926.
40. *Soviet Steppes.* 3 December 1925.
41. Ibid.
42. Ibid.
43. Ibid., 4 December 1925.
44. Ibid.
45. Ibid.

Chapter V

1. *Soviet Steppes.* 25 December 1925.
2. See: *Questions of the History of the CPSU.*
   See also: V.N. Alexandrov, Y.N. Amiantov, Filipp Isaevich Goloshchekin. 1966, No. 8.
3. *Essays on the History of the Communist Party of Kazakhstan.* Alma-Ata, 1963, p. 242.
4. Ibid., p. 259.
5. *Soviet Steppes.* 26 February 1928.
6. Ibid., 29 November 1926.
7. Ibid., 4 December 1926.
8. Ibid., 6 May 1926.
9. Ibid., 30 November 1926.
10. Ibid., 5 May 1926.
11. *Soviet Steppes.* 6 December 1925.
12. Quotation from: *Novyi Mir* (New World). 1988, No. 5.

Chapter VI

1. *Soviet Steppes.* 24 October 1928.
2. Ibid., 5 May 1926.
3. *Essays on the History of the Communist Party of Kazakhstan.* Alma-Ata, 1963, p.261.
4. S. Mukanov, *The School of Life.* Vol. 2. Alma-Ata, 1961, p. 401.
5. Ibid., p. 402.
6. Ibid., Vol. 3. p. 171.
7. *Soviet Steppes.* 20 November 1927.

8. Quotation from: *Molodaya Gvardiya* (The Young Guard). 1989, No. 10.
9. *Soviet Steppes.* 21 November 1927.
10. Ibid., 23 November 1927.
11. *Kazakhstanskaya Pravda.* 26 January 1989.
12. *Soviet Steppes.* 9 August 1926.
13. Ibid., 22 November 1927.
14. Ibid., 25 November 1927.
15. Ibid., 30 May 1928.
16. *Essays on the History of the Communist Party of Kazakhstan.* Alma-Ata, 1963, pp. 272–3.
17. *Soviet Steppes.* 6 September 1928.
18. Ibid., 23–4 October 1928.
19. Ibid., 19 October 1928.
20. Ibid., 30 May 1927.
21. Ibid., 17 January 1928.
22. Ibid., 18 January 1928.
23. Ibid., 19 December 1928.
24. See: *Novyi Mir* (New World). 1988, No. 10.

Chapter VII
1. Central State Archive of the Kazakh SSR, Collection 82, Subdivision I, File 821, Section 61, Sheet 47.

Chapter VIII
1. *Soviet Steppes.* 18 October 1930.
2. S. Mukanov, *The School of Life.* Vol. 2. Alma-Ata, 1985, pp. 64–5.
3. Ibid., pp. 217, 221–2.
4. Ibid., p. 330.
5. Ibid., p. 356.
6. Ibid., pp. 365–8.
7. Ibid., pp. 415, 418–20.
8. Ibid., p. 418.
9. See: *Outline of the History of Kazakh Soviet Literature.* Vol. 3. Alma-Ata, 1958, p. 27.
10. Quotation from: S. Mukanov, *The School of Life.* Vol. 3. Alma-Ata, 1966, pp. 180–84.
11. *Soviet Steppes.* 21 November 1927.
12. Quotation from: *Druzhba Narodov* (Friendship of the Peoples). 1988,

No. 12.
13. *Vechernaya Alma-Ata* (Alma-Ata Evening News). 28 December 1988.
14. *Soviet Steppes.* 21 November 1927.
15. *Vechernaya Alma-Ata* (Alma-Ata Evening News). 28 December 1988.
16. *Soviet Steppes.* 18 October 1930.
17. Ibid.

Chapter IX

1. *The Collectivization of Agriculture in the USSR: Paths, Forms and Achievements.* Moscow, 1982.
2. *Soviet Steppes.* 25 April 1928.
3. Ibid., 11 June 1928.
4. Ibid., 1 March 1929.
5. Ibid., 16 March 1929.
6. *Kazakhstanskaya Pravda.* 14 January 1989.
7. *Soviet Steppes.* 22 September 1929.

Chapter X

1. *Kazakhstanskaya Pravda.* 22 January 1930.
2. Quotation from: *The Moscow Church Bulletin.* 1992, No. 2.
3. Quotation from: *Moskva* (Moscow). 1990, No. 4, p. 157.
4. *Yunost* (Youth). 1989, No. 10, p. 51.
5. V.I. Lenin, *Complete Collected Works.* Vol. 29. p. 158.
6. Ibid., p.267.
7. Ibid., p.287.
8. V.I. Lenin, *Complete Collected Works.* Vol. 48. pp. 226–7.
9. Ibid., Vol. 12, p. 145.
10. Ibid., Vol. 41, p. 313.
11. L.I. Emelyakh, *Lenin's Critique of the Russian Orthodox Church.* Leningrad, 1971, pp. 27–8.
12. N.D. Zhevakov, Op. cit., Vol. 2, p. 5.
13. See: *Bulletin of the Russian Christian Movement.* Paris, 1979, No. 128.
14. L.D. Trotsky, *A History of the Russian Revolution.* Moscow, 1990, p. 192.
15. Quotation from: *Nash Sovremennik* (Our Contemporary). 1990, No. 4, pp. 168–9.
16. O. Platonov, *Journey to Kitezh-grad.* Moscow, 1990, No. 4, p. 159.
17. Ibid., p. 166.
18. *Overcoming the Religious Influence of Islam.* Alma-Ata, 1990, p. 6.

19. Ibid., p. 7.
20. *Decrees of the Soviet Regime.* Vol. 1. p. 114.
21. V.I. Lenin, *Complete Collected Works.* Vol. 38. pp. 158–9.
22. *Overcoming the Religious Influence of Islam.* Alma-Ata, 1990, p. 33.
23. Ibid., p. 37.
24. *Zhetysuiskaya Iskra* (Spark of Zhetysu). 24 December 1928.
25. *Overcoming the Religious Influence of Islam.* Alma-Ata, 1990, pp. 192–3.
26. Ibid., p. 194.
27. Ibid., p. 206.
28. Party Archive of the Central Committee of the Communist Party of Kazakhstan, Collection 141, Subdivision 1, File 2948, Sheet 9.

Chapter XI

1. P.I. Negretov, V.G. *Korolenko.* Moscow, 1990, p. 255.
2. Ibid., p. 256.
3. V.I. Lenin, *Complete Collected Works.* Vol. 11. p. 222.
4. Ibid., Vol. 36, p. 144.
5. M.S. Geller, '"First Warning" – Lash of the Whip', *Questions of Philosophy.* 1990, No. 9, pp. 39–40.
6. Ibid., p. 154.
7. V.I. Lenin, *Complete Collected Works.* Vol. 50. pp. 144–5.
8. Ibid., p. 154.
9. Ibid., pp. 185–6.
10. M.S. Geller, Op.cit., p. 41.
11. V.I. Lenin, *Complete Collected Works.* Vol. 53. pp. 140–42.
12. Quotation from: M.S. Geller, Op. cit., p. 52.
13. Ibid., p. 63.
14. *Soviet Steppes.* 6 December 1929.
15. Ibid., 15 December 1929.
16. Ibid., 16 December 1929.
17. Ibid., 15 January 1930.
18. Ibid., 23 March 1930.
19. Ibid., 27 March 1930.
20. Ibid., 23 March 1930.

Chapter XII

1. *Kazakhstanskaya Pravda.* 24 February 1989.
2. A. Tursunbaev, *Victory for the Collective Order in Kazakhstan.* Alma-Ata,

1957, p. 155.
3. Ibid., p. 303.
4. *Kazakhstanskaya Pravda.* 14–17 January 1989.
5. See: *Hunger in the Kazakh Steppes.* Alma-Ata, 1991, p. 143.
6. Ibid.
7. For information on the Suzak Revolt see: *Leninskaya Smena* (Lenin's Successors). Alma-Ata, 27 February 1991.
8. *Znamya* (Banner). 1991, No. 1.
9. *Soviet Steppes.* 8 June 1930.

Chapter XIII

1. *Soviet Steppes.* 7 July 1930.
2. Ibid., 23 August 1930.
3. Ibid., 19 November 1930.
4. Ibid., 24–29 November 1930.
5. Ibid., 24 December 1930.
6. Sixth Plenary Session of the Kazakhstan Area Committee of the All-Union Communist Party (Bolsheviks), 1933. (Stenographic Report). Alma-Ata, 1936, p. 145.
7. *Kazakhstanskaya Pravda.* 5 January 1991.
8. *Soviet Steppes.* 3 October 1931.
9. Ibid., 1 September 1931.
10. Ibid., 30 September 1931.
11. Ibid., 27 November 1931.

Chapter XIV

1. Archive of the Central Committee of the Communist Party of Kazakhstan, Collection 141, Subdivision 1, File 5233, Sheets 8–9.
2. Ibid., F. 141, Inventory 1, File 5233, Sheet 40.
3. Ibid., F. 141, Inventory 1, File 5233, Sheets 7–7 verso.
4. *Znamya* (Banner). 1989, No. 2, p. 176.
5. *Nezavisimaya Gazeta* (Independent Newspaper). 16 April 1992.
6. *Zarya* (Dawn). 1988, No. 10.
7. *Nash Sovremennik* (Our Contemporary). 1989, No. 11, p. 119.
8. *Znamya* (Banner). 1989, No. 6, p. 47.
9. Ibid., p. 75.

Chapter XV

1. *Caucasian Kazakh.* Belgrade, 1933, No. 3, p. 6.

2. V.V. Shulgin, *Days.* 1920. Moscow, 1989, p. 71.

3. *Kazakhstanskaya Pravda.* 14–17 January 1989.

4. *Industrialnaya Karaganda* (Industrial Karaganda), 8 May 1988.

5. *Aktyubinskii Vestnik* (Aktyubinsk Gazette). 30 May 1992.

6. *Rodina* (Homeland). 1989, No. 8, p. 35.

7. *Zeitin Akishev,* Zaual (The Ordeal). Alma-Ata, 1991, p. 93.

Chapter XVI

1. Archive of the Central Committee of the Communist Party of Kazakhstan. F. 141, Inventory 1, File 5233, Sheets 79–92.

2. Quotation from: *Hunger in the Kazakh Steppes.* Alma-Ata, 1991, p. 140.

3. Archive of the Central Committee of the Communist Party of Kazakhstan. Collection 141, Subdivision 17, File 607, Sheets 1–14.

4. Quotation from: *Rodina* (Homeland). 1989, No. 9, p. 50.

5. See: Sixth Plenary Session of the Kazakhstan Area Committee of the All-Union Communist Party (Bolsheviks). (Stenographic Report). Alma-Ata, 1936.

6. *Znamya* (Banner). 1989, No.1, p. 205.

7. *Questions of the History of the CPSU.* 1964, No. 1.

8. *Leninskaya Smena* (Lenin's Successors). 19 October 1988.